# INNOVATING STRATEGY PROCESS

T0305328

## Strategic Management Society Book Series

The Strategic Management Society Book Series is a cooperative effort between the Strategic Management Society and Blackwell Publishing. The purpose of the series is to present information on cutting-edge concepts and topics in strategic management theory and practice. The books emphasize building and maintaining bridges between strategic management theory and practice. The work published in these books generates and tests new theories of strategic management. Additionally, work published in this series demonstrates how to learn, understand, and apply these theories in practice. The content of the series represents the newest critical thinking in the field of strategic management. As a result, these books provide valuable knowledge for strategic management scholars, consultants, and executives.

### Published

*Strategic Entrepreneurship: Creating a New Mindset*
Edited by Michael A. Hitt, R. Duane Ireland, S. Michael Camp, and Donald L. Sexton

*Creating Value: Winners in the New Business Environment*
Edited by Michael A. Hitt, Raphael Amit, Charles E. Lucier, and Robert D. Nixon

*Strategy Process: Shaping the Contours of the Field*
Edited by Bala Chakravarthy, Peter Lorange, Günter Müller-Stewens, and Christoph Lechner

*The SMS Blackwell Handbook of Organizational Capabilities: Emergence, Development and Change*
Edited by Constance E. Helfat

*Mergers and Acquisitions: Creating Integrative Knowledge*
Edited by Amy Pablo and Mansour Javidan

*Strategy in Transition*
Richard A. Bettis

*Restructuring Strategy: New Networks and Industry Challenges*
Edited by Karel O. Cool, James E. Henderson, and René Abate

*Innovating Strategy Process*
Edited by Steven W. Floyd, Johan Roos, Claus D. Jacobs, and Franz W. Kellermanns

# Innovating Strategy Process

Edited by

Steven W. Floyd, Johan Roos, Claus D. Jacobs, and
Franz W. Kellermanns

**Blackwell**
Publishing

BLACKWELL PUBLISHING
350 Main Street, Malden, MA 02148–5020, USA
108 Cowley Road, Oxford OX4 1JF, UK
550 Swanston Street, Carlton, Victoria 3053, Australia

First published 2005 by Blackwell Publishing Ltd

*Library of Congress Cataloging-in-Publication Data*

Innovating strategy process / edited by Steven W. Floyd ... [et al.].—1st ed.
   p. cm.—(Strategic Management Society book series)
  Includes bibliographical references and index.
  ISBN 1-4051-2939-5 (hbk : alk. paper)
  1. Strategic planning. 2. Management. I. Floyd, Steven W., 1950–II. Series.
HD30.28.I538 2005
658.4'012—dc22

                        2004019637

A catalogue record for this title is available from the British Library.

ISBN 13: 978-1-4051-2939-8

For further information on
Blackwell Publishing, visit our website:
www.blackwellpublishing.com

# Contents

# Contributors

**Bhardwaj, Gaurab**
Babson College, Babson Park, MA, USA
e-mail: *gbhardwaj@babson.edu*

**Camillus, John C.**
University of Pittsburgh, PA, USA
e-mail: *camillus@katz.pitt.edu*

**Canales, J. Ignacio**
IESE Business School, University of Navarra, Barcelona, Spain
e-mail: *DOCCanales@iese.edu*

**Chakravarthy, Bala**
Institute for Management Development, Lausanne, Switzerland
e-mail: *chakravarthy@imd.ch*

**Corbett, Andrew C.**
Rensselaer Polytechnic Institute, Pittsburgh, PA, USA
e-mail: *corbea@rpi.edu*

**Cuervo-Cazurra, Alvaro**
University of Minnesota, MN, USA
e-mail: *acuervo@csom.umn.edu*

**Dess, Gregory**
University of Texas at Dallas, TX, USA
e-mail: *gdess@utdallas.edu*

**Dhanaraj, Charles**
University of Indiana, IN, USA
e-mail: *dhanaraj@iupui.edu*

**Fabian, Frances**
Belk College of Business Administration, University of North Carolina, Charlotte, USA
e-mail: *ffabian@email.uncc.edu*

**Flaherty, Karen E.**
Oklahoma State University, OK, USA
e-mail: *pappask@okstate.edu*

**Floyd, Steven W.**
University of Connecticut, CT, USA
e-mail: *steven.floyd@business.uconn.edu*

**Garud, Raghu**
New York University, NY, USA
e-mail: *rgarud@stern.nyu.edu*

**Gedajlovic, Eric**
University of Connecticut, CT, USA
e-mail: *eric.gedajlovic@business.uconn.edu*

**Germans, Fedde**
Erasmus University Rotterdam, The Netherlands
e-mail: *f.germans@fbk.eur.nl*

**Hafsi, Taieb**
H.E.C. Montreal, Canada
e-mail: *taieb.hafsi@hec.ca*

**Hounshell, David A.**
Carnegie Mellon University, Pittsburgh, PA, USA
e-mail: *hounshel+@andrew.cmu.edu*

**Huff, Anne Sigismund**
London Business School, UK and University of Colorado, USA
e-mail: *ahuff@london.edu*

**Jacobs, Claus D.**
Imagination Lab Foundation, Lausanne, Switzerland
e-mail: *claus@imagilab.org*

**Johnson, Gerry**
University of Strathclyde, Glasgow, UK
e-mail: *gerry@gsb.strath.ac.uk*

**Karnøe, Peter**
Copenhagen Business School, Denmark
e-mail: *pka.ioa@cbs.dk*

**Kellermans, Franz W.**
Mississippi State University, MS, USA
e-mail: *fkellermanns@cobilan.msstate.edu*

**Koppius, Otto**
Erasmus University Rotterdam, The Netherlands
e-mail: *o.koppius@fbk.eur.nl*

**Kriger, Mark**
Norwegian School of Management BI, Norway
e-mail: *mark.kriger@bi.no*

**Lane, Peter J.**
University of New Hampshire, NH, USA
e-mail: *peter.lane@unh.edu*

**Lechner, Christoph**
University of St. Gallen, Switzerland
e-mail: *christoph.lechner@unisg.ch*

**Lumpkin, G.T.**
University of Illinois at Chicago, IL, USA
e-mail: *tlumpkin@uic.edu*

**Lyles, Marjorie A.**
University of Indiana, IN, USA
e-mail: *mlyles@iupui.edu*

**Marx, Karolin**
University of St. Gallen, Switzerland
e-mail: *karolin.marx@unisg.ch*

**Melin, Leif**
Jönköping International Business School, Sweden
e-mail: *leif.meli@jibs.hj.se*

**ogilvie, dt**
The State University of New Jersey, NJ, USA
e-mail: *dt@business.rutgers.edu*

**Pappas, James M.**
Oklahoma State University, OK, USA
e-mail: *pappas@okstate.edu*

**Paroutis, Sotirios**
University of Bath, UK
e-mail: *s.paroutis@bath.ac.uk*

**Pettigrew, Andrew**
University of Bath, UK
e-mail: *a.m.pettigrew@bath.ac.uk*

**Ramos, Miguel**
University of Minnesota, MN, USA
e-mail: *mramos@csom.umn.edu*

**Regnér, Patrick**
Stockholm School of Economics, Sweden
e-mail: *patrick.regner@hhs.se*

**Roos, Johan**
Imagination Lab Foundation, Lausanne, Switzerland
e-mail: *johan@imagilab.org*

**Statler, Matt**
Imagination Lab Foundation, Lausanne, Switzerland
e-mail: *matt@imagilab.org*

**Steensma, H. Kevin**
University of Washington, WA, USA
e-mail: *steensma@u.washington.edu*

**Thomas, Howard**
University of Warwick, UK
e-mail: *howard.thomas@wbs.ac.uk*

**Victor, Bart**
Vanderbilt University, Nashville, TN, USA
e-mail: *bart.victor@owen.vanderbilt.edu*

**Vilà, Joaquim**
IESE Business School, University of Navarra, Barcelona, Spain
e-mail: *jvila@iese.edu*

**Volberda, Henk W.**
Erasmus University Rotterdam, The Netherlands
e-mail: *h.volberda@fac.fbk.eur.nl*

**Vos, Rogier**
Erasmus University Rotterdam, The Netherlands
e-mail: *r.vos@fbk.eur.nl*

**Whittington, Richard**
University of Oxford, UK
e-mail: *richard.whittington@sbs.ox.ac.uk*

**Zahra, Shaker A.**
Babson College, Babson Park, MA, USA
e-mail: *szahra@babson.edu*

# Innovating Strategy Process: An Overview of the Book

## The Starting Point

In early August 2002 the board of the Strategic Management Society (SMS) approved Johan Roos and Steve Floyd's proposal to stage an SMS "mini-conference." Nine months later in May of 2003, the Strategy Process Interest Group of the SMS organized a mini-conference entitled Innovating Strategy Processes. Published some one-and-half years after the conference, this book is the outcome of our aspiration to bring some of the learning from that mini-conference to a wider audience.

The mini-conference was co-sponsored by the Strategic Management Society, the Swiss-based Imagination Lab Foundation,[1] and the US-based University of Connecticut. It was held at the university's campus in Stores, Connecticut. As co-chairs, Steve and Johan chose the intentionally ambiguous phrase "innovating strategy processes" to encourage submissions on three closely related themes:

1. connecting strategy development processes to innovative outcomes;
2. creating new and innovative ways to develop strategy; and
3. exploring innovative research approaches to study strategy process.

The idea was to bring together scholars, consultants, and executives at the leading edge of strategy process research and practice. Our goals were:

- To identify new conceptual frameworks and models to help strategy processes nurture innovation within firms.
- To reflect on practical experience with strategy processes as they relate to innovation.
- To experiment with innovative strategy process techniques.

More specifically, the conference was aimed at identifying and revisiting new and existing theories about the relationship between strategy processes and innovation within organizations. Prospective contributors had the opportunity to submit a conventional academic paper, a case presentation, or a proposal for a facilitated workshop (see Table I.1).

**Table I.1**   Formats of participants' contributions

| Conference stream | Participant contribution | Format |
|---|---|---|
| New concepts and models | Research on strategy processes for nurturing innovation | Academic papers presentations |
| Reflections on experience | Single- or multi-firm experience with innovating strategy processes | Case presentations |
| Experimenting with new techniques | Facilitation of innovative strategy process technique or experiential exercise | Facilitated workshops |

Scholars, consultants, and managers based in Europe, the United States, Australia, and South East Asia submitted over 80 proposals. Eighteen senior scholars[2] served as members of the program review panel, selecting the 35 contributions and the 43 people who presented at the conference. Selection criteria were:

- the extent to which submissions went beyond what has been previously addressed in the strategy process literature;
- the extent to which they went beyond the logics of research and practice that dominate our field; and
- the extent to which they promote interaction.

The format of the conference was designed to encourage involvement and participation of all three of the SMS core constituencies: scholars, consultants, and managers. Academic paper presentations were intertwined with case presentations and facilitated workshops. During a single day participants could, for instance, engage in a small group dialogue, listen to a formal presentation by a scholar or a manager, as well as experience hands-on and facilitated strategy tools.

As co-editors we have sought to transfer some of the enthusiasm we experienced during the conference to this book. We selected only a few of the most innovative conference contributions and invited the authors to refine their ideas into book chapters. We also invited several more senior scholars in the field who were associated with the mini-conference to contribute personal and reflective essays. Breaking with tradition, we have abstained from synthesizing these chapters into a coherent whole. Instead, we allow the chapters to speak for themselves. We do offer, however, an outline of the book and a table summarizing the research papers that appear in the book (see Appendix to this Introduction).

## Outline of the Book

As another guide, we have grouped the contributions into four parts. Three of these represent distinctions that we made inductively based on the selection of papers from the conference. The fourth was conceived after the fact; it serves as a kind of capstone for what comes before.

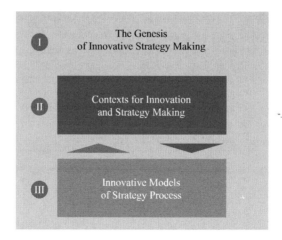

Figure I.1

The first three sections of the book are (see Figure I.1):

- Part I: The Genesis of Innovative Strategy Making
- Part II: Contexts for Innovation and Strategy Making
- Part III: Innovative Models of Strategy Process

Naturally, grouping the papers and essays is an imperfect process, but the categories are logically appealing and fairly accurate as a way of differentiating the work.

In other volumes of this kind, editors often write an integrative chapter that synthesizes earlier chapters and points out directions for future research. Instead of this, however, we solicited independent work from three of the most accomplished and reflective people in the field. We felt this would make better use of precious pages and offer the reader more value. In addition, the book closes with an essay by Johan Roos that we all feel makes an important statement about why we do the work we do and what it means. We hope readers will appreciate this very personal approach to closing the book. In the next several paragraphs we briefly describe the content of each section of the book.

## Part I: The Genesis of Innovative Strategy Making

Has any scholar ever seen an innovation as it emerged? Normally, innovations are only identified in retrospect – when they lead to a notorious success story. In this section of the book, however, three essays and four papers examine where innovative strategies come from and the initial conditions of strategy making. Gregory Dess and G.T. Lumpkin discuss the links between the entrepreneurial orientation of an organization and the exploration and exploitation activities within in it. They show how environmental factors can inhibit or enhance these influences. Continuing entrepreneurship, but this time in established companies, Eric Gedajlovic and Shaker Zahra argue that one source of strategy lies in the governance systems of organizations. According to these authors, governance systems determine the distribution of authority and influence and thereby affect the firms' entrepreneurial activities and how established companies learn. Peter Lane's essay suggests that managers in companies of all sizes would do well to examine science as a source of innovative strategy. He argues that firms must better understand the underlying topography of the knowledge frontier and the role that science plays in shaping its fertility.

In the first of the papers in this part, Patrick Regnér explores how diverse factors and mechanisms contribute to the development of capabilities, strategy, and competitive advantage. Juan Ignacio Canales and Joaquim Vilà examine the interaction between top and middle management in terms of legitimation and show how strategy making helps to translate strategy into action. Claus Jacobs and Matt Statler discuss the challenge of strategy creation as the paradox of "intending emergence" and demonstrate how the concept of serious play can inform the development of a theory of strategy creation. Similarly concerned with an alternative view on strategy, Frances Fabian and dt ogilvie explore how a fine arts metaphor relates to strategy making as a process involving creative, action-based skills.

## Part II: Context for Innovation and Strategy Making

The strategy process literature has explored the actors and settings of strategic decision making. However, multiple levels and sites still need to be identified and contingencies in these settings need to be made explicit. In the first of three essays, Marjorie Lyles, Charles Dhanaraj, and Kevin Steensma reflect on these complexities and argue that researchers should challenge themselves to address such issues directly. Similarly, Henk Volberda argues that single-theme explanations for strategy processes have reached their limit and that strategy process scholars should adopt research strategies that consider joint outcomes of managerial adaptation and environmental selection. His essay offers a conceptual framework for doing so. Raghu Garud and Peter Karnøe also take up the question of context–process interaction. Using three fascinating cases, they show how a multiplicity of actors, material artifacts, rules, and routines combine to shape decision making.

Sotirios Paroutis and Andrew Pettigrew look at context as an organization-level variable. They describe strategy process in multi-business firms and examine the execution of strategy over time, and show how such firms experiment over time with different ways of making strategy. Alvaro Cuervo-Cazurra and Miguel Ramos offer an explanation of strategy process in an international context. They integrate seemingly competing models of internationalization and show that there are underlying complementarities among them. James Pappas and Karen Flaherty look at context from the inside out by examining the role of boundary-spanning employees in the firm's strategy. Their empirical study investigates informal controls as levers of strategic renewal under conditions of uncertainty.

Karolin Marx and Christoph Lechner focus on the intra-organizational network as a context for strategy making. They argue that the relationship between the extent to which an initiative is embedded within the network and the success of the initiative is curvilinear. Continuing with the network as context, Franz Kellermanns and Steven

Floyd integrate insights from the resource-based view, conflict theory, and the strategic consensus literature. They argue that constructive confrontation among central actors in the network is necessary for successful resource accumulation and show how the structure of the network affects this process.

## Part III: Innovative Models of Strategic Process

The third part of the book begins with two essays. Mark Kriger's essay asks: "What really is strategic process?" Sweeping in its scope, he lays bare the diversity of responses to this rather basic question. Then, he offers a framework that integrates a broad range of theories on strategic process. Within this extensive body of research, one very basic issue – what strategists actually *do* – may have been largely ignored. Gerry Johnson, Richard Whittington, and Leif Melin begin their essay with this observation and go on to argue that research should begin to focus on the detailed practices which constitute the day-to-day activities of organizational life and which relate to strategic outcomes. Their essay offers a critique of strategy process research and suggests benefits of the activity- or practice-based view.

In the first of three research papers in this part of the book, Andrew Corbett continues with a rather micro-orientation toward innovative strategy processes. He argues that strategy is a form of entrepreneurial practice and that variations in individual cognitive and learning processes affect the development of strategic renewal. Extending the purely cognitive view, Otto Koppius, Fedde Germans, and Rogier Vos investigate the affective dimension in strategic decision making. In an interpretative case study, they explore the role of emotional attachment in a Dutch start-up company. Gaurab Bhardwaj, John Camillus, and David Hounshell also offer a detailed case study. Their paper provides an interesting account of how strategy making can be seen as a process of a moving, anchored search in the pursuit of long-term growth.

## Part IV: Integrating Theory and Practice

The final part of the book is devoted to reflective essays focused on the "big issues" facing innovative strategy process research. In the first of these, Anne Huff worries about structural factors in university environments that appear to limit the amount of strategy process research being done, and suggests some actions that might increase our impact on innovation and other important topics. She suggests in particular more multilevel analysis and further collective work on topics addressed in this volume, including entrepreneurship, motivating action, politics, role conflict, and values.

Bart Victor discusses how we justify the difficult process we call strategy making. He argues that the principal justification is not cost/benefit in an economic sense. Instead, the effort that leadership devotes to strategy making is morally required. That is, leadership has a moral obligation to form strategic intent with care. Failure to do so would be tantamount to negligence. His conclusion is that strategy making is unavoidably moral.

"The field of strategy has no future except close to reality," argue Taieb Hafsi and Howard Thomas in their essay. The strategy researcher's problem is similar to that of the practitioner. While practitioners do not have to justify their decisions intellectually, they must be able to survive the consequences. Also, like the practitioner, the strategy researcher muddles in the dark. Hafsi and Thomas conclude that strategy, as a field of study, should be devoted to the development of conceptual frameworks that bring research and practice together.

Bala Chakravarthy also focuses his remarks on the issue of making strategy research more relevant to practice. Based on several examples, he observes that organizations need research that addresses the problems inherent in sustaining performance while simultaneously searching for future opportunity. How can academia help firms that are engaged in continuous self-renewal? Chakravarthy argues that researchers need to confront the real dilemmas faced by practitioners, but avoid converting these into what he calls "phoney debates".

Finally, in his essay Johan Roos argues that because our field is about humans, and humans interacting, strategy researchers should remain in the first person, rather than escaping into the convention of "third person anonymity". Two anecdotes illustrate Johan's own struggle to remain outside his work. To support his wish to remain the narrator, he draws on the Aristotelian ideal of *phronesis*. For the practice of strategy research, phronesis: (i) enhances our self-awareness as scholars; (ii) helps us understand more about what is going on; (iii) forces us to take a moral stance; (iv) calls for additional experiments with methodologies; and (v) changes the discourse in our field. Roos also suggests that *phronesis* may be significant to how managers approach the practice of strategy.

### Overview of paper contributions

This book has something to offer each of the major constituencies of the Strategic Management Society. For the reflective executive, there are new ideas and rich case descriptions that are likely to trigger creative thinking about how to design a more innovative strategy process. For consultants, there are many new conceptual frameworks for analyzing and designing strategy process – some that integrate and others that dis-integrate what has come before. Academic readers especially will relish the diversity and creativity behind the 12 research papers found in this volume. Each is innovative in the question it addresses, and many are also innovative in their approach or research methodology. Collectively they signal the future direction of the field. Finally, the book offers a series of reflective essays by senior scholars who have thought long and hard about strategy process over most, if not all, of their productive careers. These insights are likely to prove beneficial to all three SMS constituencies and to anyone with an interest in the field of strategic management.

## Acknowledgements

With respect to the mini-conference, we would like to extend our heartfelt thanks to all of the participants and program review committee members. We would also like to thank Dan Schendel and John McGee for supporting the conference from the beginning, and especially Bala Chakravarthy for his wise counsel and committed leadership to the process. The Strategy Process Interest Group and V.K. Narayanan were also instrumental in co-sponsoring the conference.

Melissa Foreman from the Management Department at the University of Connecticut, Lauren Habegger from Imagination Lab, and Franz Kellermanns provided superb conference support, coordination, and logistics. Without them, none of what you read here would have been possible. Our thanks to the whole team for their professional manner and enthusiastic collaboration.

With respect to this volume, a special thanks to our authors, not only for their wonderful ideas and contributions but also for their willingness to work within very tight deadlines. We are also grateful to Michael Hitt, Series Editor, for having encouraged and supported the book. We also express our thanks to Rosemary Nixon, Joanna Pyke, and Tessa Hanford of Blackwell Publishing for their support and superb collaboration. Last but by no means least, Carla Svehlik and Antoinette Price were immensely helpful in the editorial process.

## Notes

1. Imagination Lab Foundation in Lausanne, Switzerland, is a research organization devoted to fostering innovative thinking and practices in strategic management (www.imagilab.org).
2. These were: Mary Crossan, Greg Dess, James Frederickson, Raghu Garud, Gerry Johnson, Mark Kriger, Peter Lane, Christoph Lechner, Michael Lubatkin, Marjorie Lyles, Andrew Pettigrew, Richard Priem, Patrick Regnér, Nicolaj Siggelkow, Gabriel Szulanski, Henk Volberda, Richard Whittington, and Shaker Zahra.

# Appendix: An outline of the book

| | Regnér | Canales and Vilà | Jacobs and Statler | Fabian and ogilvie | Paroutis and Pettigrew | Cuervo-Cazurra and Ramos | Pappas and Flaherty | Marx and Lechner | Kellermanns and Floyd | Corbett | Koppius, Germans, and Vos | Bhardwaj, Camillus, and Hounshell |
|---|---|---|---|---|---|---|---|---|---|---|---|---|
| **Definition of strategy process** | Development phase for new competitive positions; influenced by managerial actions, context, and chance | The result of multilevel organizational interplay to reach a strategy | Creative practice of meaning generation involving cognitive, social, and affective aspects | The steps taken from the idea of a strategy to analyzing and implementing it | Actions of individuals, groups, and teams inside and outside of the organization, engaged in the making of strategy | Sequence of decisions and events related to a firm's international expansion | Evolution of decisions and actions over time that explain how key capabilities are developed | Development of strategic initiatives (from idea to capability) | Exchange of strategy related information across organizational hierarchies | Intentions, actions, and behaviors of individuals and groups that lead to and support strategy | A series of decisions and activities by actors that need to be coordinated to reach a strategic goal | Sequence of considerations, choices, and outcomes over time |
| **Practical issue addressed** | How diverse factors and mechanisms contribute and develop capabilities, strategy, and competitive advantage | How the interaction between top and middle management helps translate strategy into action | How contextual design elements enable actual processes of strategy generation | How fine arts metaphors can inform strategy making | The realities around what, who, and how of strategy making in multibusiness firms | Clarification of insights from fragmented and competing research streams on the firm's internationalization process | Do boundary-spanning employees take on strategic roles that contribute to firm strategy? | How to manage the social interfaces between an initiative and the parent organization | The importance and the management of resource accumulation decisions | The role and importance of individual effects in the firm's strategic renewal process | The existence of emotional attachment in strategic decision making and its possible consequences | How decisions are actually made in the pursuit of long-term growth |
| **Research question** | Where do capabilities, competitive advantage, and strategy come from and how do inter-firm differences develop? | How is the top and middle management interplay resolved to originate a strategy that translates into managerial action? | How can we conceptualize the paradox of strategy creation as intending emergence? | How can the strategy formulation process be more effective? | How is strategy made in multibusiness firms? What are the capabilities required to make strategy and how do such companies develop them? | How does a firm internationalize? | Can informal controls be used to leverage strategic renewal under conditions of uncertainty? | What is the relationship between embeddedness and the success of strategic initiatives? | How can conflict and consensus be beneficially managed in the resource accumulation process? | How do variations in individual cognitive and learning processes affect the development of ideas and opportunities for a firm's strategic renewal? | How does emotional attachment impact the strategic decision-making process? | What is the nature of the search process of decision makers in their pursuit of their firm's long-term growth? |

| | Regnér | Canales and Vilà | Jacobs and Statler | Fabian and ogilvie | Paroutis and Pettigrew | Cuervo-Cazurra and Ramos | Pappas and Flaherty | Marx and Lechner | Kellermanns and Floyd | Corbett | Koppius, Germans, and Vos | Bhardwaj, Camillus, and Hounshell |
|---|---|---|---|---|---|---|---|---|---|---|---|---|
| **Theoretical lens** | A strategy process perspective combined with an application of resource and dynamic capabilities views to strategy pre-history development | Autonomous versus induced behavior as well as bottom-up and top-down sources of influence | A practice-based view of strategy complemented with psychological, philosophical source theories of play | Creative action-based lens that looks at strategy as art | Established strategy literature, micro-strategy, and theories of multibusiness firms | Organizational theory | Transaction cost economics and social exchange theory | Strategic initiatives and social embeddedness | Resource-based view, network analysis, strategic consensus and conflict theory | Psychology and entrepreneurship | Strategic decision making, emotion theory, conflict theory | Decision-making and search processes |
| **Research methodology** | Descriptive and conceptual | Case study | Descriptive and conceptual | Descriptive and conceptual | Exploratory study using semi-structured interviews with strategy directors from eight FTSE-100 companies and archival data | Descriptive and conceptual | Question-naire of matched dyads using moderated hierarchical regression analysis | Descriptive and conceptual | Descriptive and conceptual | Both qualitative and quantitative: long interviews and a survey with a quasi-experiment | Inductive, qualitative case study | Field-based case research based on historical data. We are looking at an extensive collection of internal documents from the DuPont Company during the period 1902–21 |
| **Key findings/propositions** | Chance, initial conditions, necessity, serendipity, and inductive strategy making have the potential to produce competitive advantage | Legitimating strategic initiatives is the mechanism that resolves top and middle managers' interplay into a guide for managerial action | The concept of serious play sensitizes researchers to understanding of the inherent paradox of strategy creation – intending emergence | Art should be included in researching, crafting, and teaching strategy formulation | Multibusiness firms are experimenting over time and in context with different ways of making strategy and developing capabilities to make strategy | Diverse and seemingly competing models of internationalization are in reality complementary; the limitations of one model are solved by another | Informal controls are positively related to strategic activities – that linkage was moderated by market turbulence | There is a curvilinear relationship between structural, positional, relational, and cognitive embeddedness and the success of strategic initiatives | Constructive confrontation is necessary for successful resource accumulation and organizational performance. Structural network characteristics need to be managed to facilitate constructive confrontation | Individual cognitive abilities have a significant effect on a firm's ability to develop entrepreneurial strategies for strategic renewal | Affective conflict increases when emotional attachment is present | In their pursuit of their firm's long-term growth, decision makers follow a "moving, anchored search" process due to the high uncertainty and ambiguity, and the long time horizon involved |

| Intended contribution (as suggested by the authors) | | | | | | | | | | | |
|---|---|---|---|---|---|---|---|---|---|---|---|
| Adds to the discussion of origins of strategy and new value creation from a strategy process perspective | Contributes to the literature describing actors in the strategy process with a discussion of the mechanisms resolving relationships between managerial levels in the creation of strategy in use | Contributes to a theory of strategy creation in terms of understanding the conditions for the possibility of strategy to emerge, and introduces serious play as an analytical lens to do this | Offers a model for strategy formulation that focuses on creating new strategies, and provides a theoretical basis for the reported effectiveness of a range of associated process skills | Develops a set of preliminary categories for the making of strategy in multi-business firms | Contributes to the literature of international business, integrating competing explanations on the internationalization process | Shows how control systems can also be used to get employees to go above and beyond traditional job roles and effect strategic renewal | Focuses explicitly on the factors associated with the social context of strategic initiatives | A socially complex and longitudinal model of resource accumulation decisions; importance of structural antecedents is argued for conflict research | Contributes to both the strategic renewal literature and the entrepreneurship literature | Broadens the view of strategic decision making beyond the purely cognitive and/or political perspectives | Contributes to the literature on strategic decision-making processes, and long-term growth based on corporate strategy and innovation |

# The Genesis of Innovative Strategy Making

# CHAPTER ONE

# Entrepreneurial Orientation as a Source of Innovative Strategy

Gregory Dess, G.T. Lumpkin

Innovation is a central activity for firms that want to launch new ventures and renew their firm's strategic efforts (Covin and Miles, 1999; Guth and Ginsberg, 1990). Successful innovation is often complex and requires that firms exhibit multiple talents and competencies. The concept of exploration and exploitation (March, 1991) captures the breadth of activities that firms must be capable of to successfully innovate. That is, firms must be capable of effectively exploring innovation options through activities such as scanning, experimentation, R&D, and new product development as well as successfully exploiting new-found possibilities by efficiently deploying resources and organizing work activities. All this must be done in a context that takes into consideration technology, competitors, and the business environment surrounding the innovation process.

Firms that exhibit a strong entrepreneurial orientation (EO) may have an advantage when it comes to undertaking innovation via exploration and exploitation activities. EO refers to the strategy-making practices and processes that managers engage in to identify and create venture opportunities. EO has five dimensions – autonomy, innovativeness, proactiveness, competitive aggressiveness, and risk taking – which permeate the decision-making styles of the firm members (Covin and Slevin, 1991; Lumpkin and Dess, 1996). Many firms that are successful innovators attribute much of their success to an entrepreneurial orientation (McGrath and MacMillan, 2000).

In this chapter, we will address two issues that help explain how an entrepreneurial orientation may enhance the innovation process. First, we will discuss the links between each of the five dimensions of EO and exploration and exploitation activities. Second, we will address how environmental munificence, complexity, and dynamism can inhibit or enhance EO as well as exploitation/exploration initiatives.

## The Links between EO, Exploration, and Exploitation

In general, we believe that firms with a strong entrepreneurial orientation will pursue innovation goals more effectively. Prior research has suggested that firms are often strong in some aspects of EO but exhibit only moderate or low levels of other EO dimensions (Lumpkin and Dess, 2001). In a similar way, different strengths are needed to pursue the different aims of exploration and exploitation. First, we address the extent to which different aspects of EO contribute to the exploration and exploitation process. As a caveat, we recognize that all five dimensions of EO could be strongly related to both exploration and exploitation. For example, innovativeness could involve both the development and introduction of major new products and services for an organization, as well as relatively minor activities that improve one of the activities in a firm's value chain (Porter, 1985). Clearly, the former would focus on exploration while the latter would represent exploitation. However, we will endeavor to develop arguments to support each dimension's primary relationship to exploitation or exploration.

The dimensions of innovativeness and autonomy are well matched to the task of exploration. Innovativeness refers to a willingness to introduce newness and novelty through experimentation and creative processes aimed at developing new products and services, as well as new processes (Miller and Friesen, 1984). Such activities are necessary for firms that are exploring opportunities for entrepreneurial development. Autonomy refers to independent action by an individual or team aimed at bringing forth a business concept or vision and carrying it through to completion. Firms that wish to explore venture opportunities often must create environments where innovation team members are free to explore possibilities without the influence of strategic norms or organizational traditions that may impede the discovery process (Burgelman, 1983). Proactiveness, which involves a forward-looking, opportunity-seeking perspective (Miller, 1983), may also contribute to a firm's exploration efforts. Therefore:

> **Proposition 1:**   Firms that are high in innovativeness, autonomy, and proactiveness will more effectively pursue exploration in the innovation process.

Two other dimensions of entrepreneurial orientation – risk taking and competitive aggressiveness – are well suited to the task of exploiting innovation opportunities. Firms that effectively pursue new ventures must have a bias for action. That is, they must make decisions and take steps even in the face of uncertainty and/or competitive threats. Risk taking involves making decisions and taking action without certain knowledge of probable outcomes; some undertakings may also involve making substantial resource commitments in the process of venturing forward (Baird and Thomas, 1985). Firms that exploit opportunities must be willing to assume financial and business risks in order to be effective. Such activities must be pursued energetically. Competitive aggressiveness requires intense action that is aimed at outperforming industry rivals and is characterized by a combative posture and/or an assertive response to threats from competitors who seek to capitalize on similar innovations (Venkatraman, 1989). Proactiveness, which involves acting ahead of competitors in anticipation of changes in demand (Miller, 1983), may also strengthen a firm's ability to exploit innovation opportunities. Thus:

> **Proposition 2:**   Firms that are high in risk taking, competitive aggressiveness, and proactiveness will more effectively pursue exploitation in the innovation process.

## The Role of Environment in the Innovation Process

The success of any innovation effort will be affected to some extent by the business environment that surrounds it. When scholars investigate variation in organizational processes and performance outcomes among firms, it becomes important to consider both the resources available within organizational environments as well as the information uncertainties facing managers who are trying to navigate within such environments (Castrogiovanni, 2002). Such a perspective incorporates the two approaches that Aldrich and Mindlin (1978) and others have used to conceptualize organizational environments: (i) as a source of information; and (ii) as a stock of resources. Accordingly, dynamism and complexity indicate the extent of environmental uncertainty. Munificence, on the other hand, reflects the degree of resource abundance in the environment. Dess and Beard (1984) have provided theoretical and empirical support for these dimensions which are also consistent with Child's (1972) "three conditions . . . singled out as of particular importance" – environmental illiberality, variability, and complexity. In the sections below, we will discuss the impact of environment on the effectiveness of innovation efforts.

### Environmental dynamism

Environmental dynamism reflects the rate of unpredictable change in a firm's environment (Duncan, 1972; Thompson, 1967) with regard to changes in "customer tastes, production or service technologies, and the modes of competition in the firm's principal industries" (Miller and Friesen, 1984: 277). Dynamism impairs managers' ability to both predict future events as well as their impact on organizations.

Highly dynamic environments require a strong emphasis on exploration for new opportunities for firms to be innovative, take a proactive stance, and assume risk. Such contexts pose numerous challenges for incumbent firms (Miller and Friesen, 1984; Zahra, 1993) and passive behaviors tend to lead to deteriorating performance. This is because the bases for competitive advantages, industry structure, and product performance standards are short lived or in a constant state of flux (Karagozoglu and Brown, 1988).

Alternatively, at low levels of dynamism (i.e. stable environments), firms do not need to form and maintain many network linkages nor are they required to develop more complex and exploratory competitive strategies (Aldrich, 1979). In stable environments, organizations that develop internal routines and procedures that become standardized through process management activities are likely to do well because the need for innovative and proactive behavior as well as learning requirements are minimal (Eisenhardt, 1989). Therefore:

> Proposition 3: The extent of exploration and exploitation will be affected by environmental dynamism:
> (A) Firms competing in dynamic environments will have a greater level of exploration than firms competing in stable environments; and
> (B) Firms competing in dynamic environments will have a lower level of exploitation than firms competing in stable environments.

## Environmental complexity

Child's (1972) conceptualization of environmental complexity as "the heterogeneity of and range of an organization's activities" is consistent with others (e.g. Duncan, 1972). Thompson (1967) has contended that managers facing more complex (i.e. heterogeneous) environments will perceive greater uncertainty and have greater information-processing requirements than managers facing simple environments.

Firms competing in complex environments must engage in proactive behavior and monitor many sectors of the environment. Such information-gathering processes inevitably lead to greater differences within management teams with regard to formality of structure, interpersonal orientation, and time orientation (Lawrence and Lorsch, 1967). Such divergence in perspectives makes consensus in strategy making more difficult (Dess and Origer, 1987). Similarly, Khandwalla (1976) found that managers in such environments were more likely to implement multifaceted and comprehensive strategies. Formulating complex strategies requires enhanced innovative and proactive behavior in order to penetrate new product markets and develop new technologies. Firms which have networks characterized by diversity and weak ties will benefit from requisite variety, non-redundancy, and overall greater access to information – helping to ensure successful and novel strategies.

Although increasing levels of environmental complexity would necessitate greater exploration of new product-market opportunities as opposed to exploitation of existing opportunities, we suggest that a point of diminishing returns eventually comes into play. We would argue that as environments become increasingly complex, human cognitive limits to rationality become a salient factor (Simon, 1957), despite an organization's capacity for assimilating new knowledge (Cohen and Levinthal, 1990). That is, satisfying behavior wherein the selection of "acceptable" as opposed to "optimal" alternatives take place, thus suppressing innovative initiatives. Organizations decentralize structures, monitor many segments of the environment, and must partition the environment within which they choose to compete. Thus, with greater complexity, an orientation toward innovation and exploration activity decreases and there is greater emphasis placed on exploitation of select product markets and technologies as opposed to further search behavior in newer domains. As opposed to novel, innovative strategies, firms will tend to engage in more intense competitive aggressiveness to protect existing domains. Thus:

> Proposition 4:   The extent of exploration and exploitation will be affected by environmental complexity:
> (A) Firms competing in complex environments will have an inverted U-shaped relationship with exploration. Moderate levels, but not low or high levels, of complexity will be positively associated with exploration.
> (B) Firms competing in complex environments will have a U-shaped relationship with exploitation. Low or high levels, but not moderate levels, of complexity will be positively associated with exploration.

### Environmental munificence

Starbuck (1976) and Aldrich (1979) both suggest that environmental munificence reflects the degree to which the environment can support sustained growth; organizations engage in proactive and innovative endeavors to seek out environments that support growth and stability. Firms competing in munificent environments have opportunities to generate slack resources (Cyert and March, 1963), which enable them to explore new product-market domains and alternate strategies. Slack can also serve as a means of conflict resolution and provide additional incentives for experimentation as well as "buffer" organizations during periods of scarcity.

In less munificent (or hostile) environments, however, the intensity of competition exerts strong pressures on a firm to become competitively aggressive in order to exploit present markets in order to defend existing positions. Fewer resources are available for engaging in innovative and proactive behavior. Here, there is a greater need for interlocking organizational arrangements (Pfeffer and Leblebeci, 1973), a greater need for "strategic discipline" (Porter, 1980), and firms are more oriented toward conserving limited resources (Chakravarthy, 1982). Further, strong network ties and dense networks become critical in building trust as well as facilitating the efficient transfer of information to implement rather stable, unchanging strategies as firms engage in more intense competitive behavior. As noted by Miller and Friesen: "Extensive risk taking, forceful proactiveness, and a strong emphasis on novelty can be very hazardous when competitive conditions are more taxing" (1983: 223). Therefore:

> Proposition 5:   The extent of exploration and exploitation will be affected by environmental munificence.
> (A) Firms competing in munificent environments will have a greater level of exploration than firms competing in hostile environments; and
> (B) Firms competing in munificent environments will have a lower level of exploitation than firms competing in hostile environments.

## Conclusion

In this chapter we have briefly addressed two issues: the relationship between the five dimensions of EO and exploitation/exploration activities and the impact of environmental munificence, complexity and dynamism on exploration and exploitation initiatives. Clearly, given space constraints, further theoretical work is called for. In addition to strengthening the theoretical arguments that are advanced, research could explore, for example, the joint effects of the dimensions of EO on exploration and exploitation initiatives as well as how multiple dimensions of the environment would jointly impact exploration and exploitation. Further, hypotheses could address which elements of an industry's structure have the strongest impact on the efficacy of EO dimensions and exploitation/exploration activities. Such research would provide new insights on how firms effectively create new ventures and revitalize their capacity for innovative endeavors.

## References

Aldrich, H.E. 1979. *Organizations and Environments*. Englewood Cliffs, NJ: Prentice-Hall.

Aldrich, H.E. and Mindlin, S. 1978. Uncertainty and dependence: Two perspectives on environment. In L. Karpik (ed.), *Organization and Environment*, pp. 149–70. Beverly Hills, CA: Sage.

Baird, I.S. and Thomas, H. 1985. Toward a contingency model of strategic risk taking. *Academy of Management Review*, 10(2): 230–43.

Burgelman, R.A. 1983. A process model of internal corporate venturing in the diversified major firm. *Administrative Science Quarterly*, 28: 223–44.

Castrogiovanni, G.J. 2002. Organizational task environments: Have they changed fundamentally over time? *Journal of Management*, 28: 129–50.

Chakravarthy, B. 1982. Adaptation: A promising metaphor for strategic management. *Academy of Management Review*, 7: 35–44.

Child, J. 1972. Organizational structure, environment, and performance: The role of strategic choice. *Sociology*, 6: 1–22.

Cohen, W. and Levinthal, D. 1990. Absorptive capacity: A new perspective on learning and innovation. *Administrative Science Quarterly*, 35: 128–52.

Covin, J.G. and Miles, M.P. 1999. Corporate entrepreneurship and the pursuit of competitive advantage. *Entrepreneurship Theory and Practice*, 23(3): 47–63.

Covin, J.G. and Slevin, D.P. 1991. A conceptual model of entrepreneurship as firm behavior. *Entrepreneurship Theory and Practice*, 16(1): 7–24.

Cyert, R.M. and March, J. 1963. *A Behavioral Theory of the Firm*. Englewood Cliffs, NJ: Prentice-Hall.

Dess, G.G. and Beard, D.W. 1984. Dimensions of organizational task environments. *Administrative Science Quarterly*, 29: 52–73.

Dess, G.G. and Origer, N.K. 1987. Environment, structure, and consensus in strategy formulation: A conceptual integration. *Academy of Management Review*, 12: 313–30.

Duncan, R.B. 1972. Characteristics of organizational environments and perceived environmental uncertainty. *Administrative Science Quarterly*, 17: 313–27.

Eisenhardt, K.M. 1989. Making fast strategic decisions in high velocity environments. *Academy of Management Journal*, 32: 543–76.

Guth, W.D. and Ginsberg, A. 1990. Guest Editor's introduction: Corporate entrepreneurship. *Strategic Management Journal*, 11: 5–15.

Karagozoglu, N. and Brown, W.B. 1988. Adaptive responses by conservative and entrepreneurial firms. *Journal of Product and Innovation Management*, 5: 269–81.

Khandwalla, P. 1976. The techno-economic ecology of corporate strategy. *Journal of Management Studies*, 2: 263–78.

Lawrence, P. and Lorsch, J. 1967. *Organization and Environment*. Boston, MA: Harvard University Press.

Lumpkin, G.T. and Dess, G.G. 1996. Clarifying the entrepreneurial orientation construct and linking it to performance. *Academy of Management Review*, 21(1): 135–72.

Lumpkin, G.T. and Dess, G.G. 2001. Linking two dimensions of entrepreneurial orientation to firm performance: The moderating role of environment and life cycle. *Journal of Business Venturing*, 16: 429–51.

March, J.G. 1991. Exploration and exploitation in organizational learning. *Organization Science*, 2: 71–87.

McGrath, R.G. and MacMillan, I. 2000. *The Entrepreneurial Mindset*. Cambridge, MA: Harvard Business School Press.

Miller, D. 1983. Entrepreneurship correlates in three types of firms. *Management Science*, **29**: 770–91.

Miller, D. and Friesen, P.H. 1983. Strategy-making and environment: The third link. *Strategic Management Journal*, **4**: 221–35.

Miller, D. and Friesen, P.H. 1984. *Organizations: A Quantum View*. Englewood Cliffs, NJ: Prentice-Hall.

Pfeffer, J. and Leblebeci, H. 1973. The effect of competition on some dimensions of organization structure. *Social Forces*, **52**: 268–79.

Porter, M.E. 1980. *Competitive Strategy*. New York: The Free Press.

Porter, M.E. 1985. *Competitive Advantage*. New York: The Free Press.

Simon, H.A. 1957. *Administrative Behavior*. New York: The Free Press.

Starbuck, W.H. 1976. Organizations and their environments. In M.D. Dunnette (ed.), *Handbook of Organizational Psychology*, pp. 1069–123. Chicago, IL: Rand McNally.

Thompson, J.D. 1967. *Organizations in Action*. New York: McGraw-Hill.

Venkatraman, N. 1989. Strategic orientation of business enterprises: The construct, dimensionality, and measurement. *Management Science*, **35**(8): 942–62.

Zahra, S.A. 1993. Environment, corporate entrepreneurship, and financial performance: A taxonomic approach. *Journal of Business Venturing*, **8**: 319–40.

# CHAPTER TWO

# Entrepreneurship, Organizational Learning, and Capability Building: A Governance Perspective

Eric Gedajlovic, Shaker A. Zahra

Entrepreneurial activities in established companies have two objectives: nurturing and upgrading existing organizational capabilities while building new ones that promote growth (Zahra, 1996). Managing these two seemingly complementary goals can lead to serious conflicts in managing the firm. Efficiency-enhancing routines can enrich the variety of a firm's existing capabilities, allowing it to combine different skills and then apply them in pursuing growth and profitability. These routines can also reduce creeping inertia and allow the firm to safeguard against core rigidities that might develop over time.

In this chapter, we argue that building routines for radically new capabilities or upgrading existing ones is a major challenge for established companies. One source of difficulty lies in the governance systems that determine the distribution of authority, power, and expertise within established companies and influence their willingness and ability to venture beyond their existing skills and competencies. Governance systems also determine the types of entrepreneurial activities that firms undertake and, as result, influence the learning processes associated with developing and acquiring new knowledge.

Our focus on governance systems goes well beyond established companies' formal boards. Rather, we pay special attention to the subtle but pervasive influence of formal and informal power among senior managers and their subordinates on the initiation and pursuit of entrepreneurial activities. Our analysis recognizes the importance of entrepreneurial activities in countering the inertial forces that exist in established companies, thereby setting the stage for the exploration of new ideas that can lead to building new capabilities.

## Competence Traps and Organizational Learning

Path dependencies and narrow organizational search in the vicinity of existing knowledge oftens constrain established companies' ability to develop radically innovative ideas for new products, processes, and systems (March, 1991). New ideas or business models have to fight for their survival and acceptance within existing bureaucracies and against managers' preoccupation with ongoing operations. Though building new capabilities is essential for long-term success, it is also a process that is fraught with dangers as existing units may sabotage new initiatives and fight ideas coming from outside their operations. Building new capabilities is a costly, time-consuming process that entails serious risks for senior managers. Experiments in innovation and strategic change sometimes fail and those that succeed may take a longer period of time to reach profitability. These forces increase companies' reliance on well-proven skills and lead to competence traps; situations where a firm's skills fail to keep up to date with the changing competitive landscape (Ahuja and Lampert, 2001).

Some companies excel in developing organizational systems that simultaneously harvest existing capabilities while incubating new ones. These organizations accept the idea that tension between the old and new is a normal part of the process of entrepreneurship and that these tensions should be cultivated. These firms often create separate units and structures that accommodate the unique challenges of different businesses. They also adopt different performance appraisal, compensation, and reward systems (Sathe, 2003). These organizations view the costs associated with different systems as the price to be paid to stimulate entrepreneurship and achieve strategic flexibility. Strategic flexibility rests on the firm's ability to develop and exploit a varied set of capabilities *and* retain the capacity to quickly change the mix of these capabilities (Volberda, 1996). Flexibility enables the company to change its product offerings and respond to market and technological shifts rapidly (Eisenhardt and Martin, 2000; Teece, Pisano, and Shuen, 1997).

The need to achieve strategic flexibility by promoting entrepreneurship to create varied capabilities that could be revised quickly raises major challenges for governance systems (Chesbrough, 2000). In younger start-ups, governance usually reflects property rights. However, in established companies where ownership and control are often separated, governance systems tend to be crafted in a way that harmonizes the objectives of owners and executives. The resulting control systems and compensation schemes have varying and conflicting implications for different types of organizational capabilities. Understanding these differential effects requires attention to the link between governance, decision rules, and organizational learning (Zahra and Flatotchev, 2004) – an issue that we discuss next.

## Decision Rules and Organizational Learning

Understanding the importance of governance for capability development requires an appreciation for decision rules. These decision rules are fundamental to how organizations learn, manage knowledge, and interact with their external environments. They take the form of standard operating procedures regarding task parameters, record keeping, and information processing as well as criteria for resource allocation decisions. Cyert and March (1963) view these procedures as the operationalization of the firm's knowledge stock and its method for interacting with the environment. Such decision rules institutionalize satisfying solutions to recurring problems, but are also the source of organizational inertia that constrain organizational learning and condition subsequent patterns of interactions between the firm and its external environment.

Nelson and Winter (1982) suggest that organizational routines encompass both formal and tacit decision rules pertaining to operational and strategic matters. These routines develop over time as the result of firm–environment interactions; they embody the organization's stored knowledge or memory. Further, routines are decision rules that are prone to substantial path dependence and are regarded as persistent, self-sustaining, and heritable. These repetitive routines become strongly imprinted on an organization in the form of reliable and predictable, but also relatively inert, systems and processes. Organizational routines affect not only contemporaneous processes, but they also strongly condition a firm's evolutionary trajectory; the skills it learns and the capabilities it accumulates over time.

Decision rules ensure that organizations and stakeholders do not spin out of control or lose sight of basic organizational objectives. They also reduce uncertainty by codifying standard responses to recurring environmental events. Decision rules also help to overcome problems related to the cognitive biases of decision makers and the retention of tacit knowledge (Foss, 2003). These rules may facilitate complex and coherent organizational responses to complex environmental stimuli. They may also synthesize and communicate collective knowledge that promotes the creation of the social capital necessary to build and sustain a competitive advantage. Paradoxically, these decision rules might inhibit organizational learning (March, 1991) by imposing highly restrictive constraints that can take on an importance unto themselves.

In addition to being either more tacit or more formal, decision rules also range along a continuum from simpler to quite complex. Complex rules have the capacity to store more organizational knowledge, but are also more inert. Brown and Eisenhardt (1997) characterize simple decision rules as "semistructures" that provide general guiding principles, but also support a broad range of action and afford decision makers significant autonomy in interpreting and implementing within those parameters. Because complex rules have an inertial effect on organizations, relatively simple rules can be propitious in highly dynamic environments (Eisenhardt and Martin, 2000). Simple rules are integral to the development of dynamic capabilities (Teece, Pisano, and Shuen, 1997).

While simple decision rules support change-oriented organizational capabilities, their development may come at the expense of learning and knowledge retention. Since organizations store much of their stock of knowledge in decision rules (March, 1991), their potential storage capacity is important for knowledge management. The capacity of organizational routines and procedures to store knowledge is a function of their complexity. Since more knowledge can be stored in complex routines than simpler ones, the costs associated with learning and the absence of the capacity to store new knowledge can become a significant barrier to organizational learning. The absence of complex processes may also adversely influence absorptive capacity, limiting the firm's ability to recognize, value, assimilate, and exploit new sources of information (Zahra and George, 2002).

Complex routines and procedures engender compliance and optimization within existing means-ends relationships. Simple routines and procedures create greater variance and often identify new means-end relationships. Such differences in the effect of complex and simple rules map nicely onto March's (1991) distinction between "the exploration of new possibilities" versus the "exploitation of old certainties." By favoring simple decision rules, companies may sacrifice exploration for exploitation, causing existing capabilities to deteriorate.

To summarize, while a large body of research emanating from Cyert and March (1963) and Nelson and Winter (1982) describes how organizational routines and procedures influence the type and pace of capability development, this literature is silent on the antecedents of these decision rules. We believe that a corporate governance perspective can help to overcome this important gap in the organizational learning and knowledge literatures (Zahra and Flatotchev, 2004). In the remainder of this article, we develop a governance perspective that identifies governance as an antecedent of the type of decision rules organizations use to learn as they pursue entrepreneurial initiatives.

## Governance System, Entrepreneurship, and Capability Building

In contrast to agency and transaction-cost conceptualizations of governance, our concept of governance considers not only incentives but also the character of authority relationships and norms of legitimacy that prevail in a firm (Gedajlovic, Lubatkin, and Schulze, 2004). Thus, governance refers to the structured and reinforcing system of authority relations, norms of legitimacy, and incentives that exist in a firm. A governance system imposes fundamental decision rules about the character and purpose of the firm, the basis for and division of prerogatives and responsibilities among key participants, and the means by which relations between these participants are structured. Such decision rules directly impact three fundamental questions: Who should control the organization? For whose benefit? And in what manner?

The literature suggests that decision rules, routines, and procedures in organizations are hierarchical such that higher order routines strongly influence lower order ones (Teece, Pisano, and Shuen, 1997). Thus, an organization's system of governance embodies seminal decision rules that cascade throughout the firm and condition lower level processes and how it learns, manages its stock of knowledge, and interacts with its external environment. To illustrate the links among governance, decision rules, entrepreneurship, and capability building, we examine two archetypal forms of governance, the owner-managed firm and the professional-managed firm.

### The owner-managed firm (OMF)

The defining governance characteristic of the OMF is that the rights and responsibilities of ownership and management are coupled in the hands of a single individual. This governance system provides high-powered incentives in the form of large upside/ downside risk for the owner-manager and consequently toward efficiency in operations and profit-maximizing behavior. The coupling of ownership and control also grants founders the classic property rights of *usus* (the right to use one's property as one sees fit), *abusus* (the right to alter, modify, or destroy one's property), and *usus fructus* (the right to the profits generated by an asset). The coupling of property rights with managerial control provides owner-managers with the authority to put the firm's resources to their desired use, and the legitimacy and incentive to exercise that authority. The nature of authority and norms of legitimacy in OMFs also mean that they strongly reflect the expertise and personality of their founders, reflecting a multitude of factors such as their upbringing, education, social contacts, cultural heritage, and work experience. Thus, even in large OMFs, organizational goals and performance targets manifest the owner-manager's idiosyncratic goals. Further, the firm's culture is defined by personal norms and is a "tool" operated by and for the benefit of owner-managers.

Owner-managers, who have largely unfettered discretion, define their firms' decision rules. This may occur through a combination of formal and informal processes, resulting in a set of idiosyncratic but relatively simple decision rules regarding the personal goals of owner-managers. Compared to firms with more diffused and complex patterns of authority, these simple decision rules give OMFs significant advantages in pursuing ephemeral business opportunities in dynamic markets. The centralized authority structures and the simple decision rules of OMFs also enable them to excel at opaque transactions and informal contracting, which other types of management may find difficult. The authority and legitimacy afforded owner-managers causes considerable variance in OMFs' strategies and performance outcomes. This often results in less reliable organizations that are prone to failure, but are also more likely to be successful at exploration activities or the discovery of new opportunities and the quick development of capabilities necessary to exploit them. These firms are apt to foster a willingness to engage in radical entrepreneurial activities that generate new knowledge. This knowledge serves as the foundation of new organizational capabilities.

Still, the concentration of authority in the hands of owner-managers may work against the development of complex decision rules. Owner-managers tend to be highly possessive of their property and decision rights and may perceive complex and formal systems as a potential threat to their authority. This concentration of power may stifle employees' pursuit of entrepreneurial opportunities and reduce experimentation with new activities that build new capabilities. Further, some OMFs face serious resource constraints that can stifle broad organizational learning. Some OMFs have difficulty in accessing labor and other factor markets or have difficulty hiring and retaining high quality employees and managers. These variables can inhibit the development of the complex systems necessary to partake in exploitative learning, negatively impacting the firm's absorptive capacity and subsequent capacity to build new capabilities.

**The professionally managed firm (PMF)**

A key characteristic of the PMF is the separation of ownership and control. The literature has focused on the incentive features of the governance arrangements in PMFs, concluding that the incentives of professional managers are low-powered because they are paid a straight salary or a mix of salary and market-based incentives. Also, because professional managers don't possess the same rights to profits as owner-managers, their interests are better served by pursuing growth and diversification strategies rather than in maximizing profit. Managers may also advance their own interests at the expense of their shareholders, unless effectively constrained or provided with a strong incentive to do otherwise.

In their role as agents, professional managers hold fiduciary powers "in trust" and need to justify their decisions in terms of their impact upon others (e.g., shareholders) rather than in terms of their own preferences or goals. The legitimacy of their actions is determined by laws and customs and is vetted by the legal system and financial markets. Authority is of the legal-rational variety, diffused within the hierarchy and across highly trained specialists and is vested in the position, not the individual. Decision rules are developed through formal processes (e.g., strategic planning, capital budgeting) and evaluated based on their impact on stakeholders. Thus, the governance of the PMF engenders complex routines, which are developed and operated by highly trained specialists. These routines can promote organizational learning, have positive knowledge management implications, and are also difficult to imitate because of their social complexity and causal ambiguity. Thus, they can form the basis of sustainable competitive advantages. At the same time, the complexity of these routines also makes them relatively inert and impedes organizational responses to disruptive changes in the environment. Consequently, PMFs are suited for exploitation or optimization activities within known parameters (March, 1991). This is useful in upgrading existing capabilities, but may not foster the development of radically new ones.

The norms of legitimacy and authority structures of PMFs also foster a managerial ethos that values rational discourse and quantification more than intuition and qualitative considerations. Such an ethos makes PMFs less likely to pursue exploration activities or make truly *de novo* entrepreneurial discoveries. Exploration activities are oriented towards producing variance rather than optimizing means-ends; they are more risky and have a lower expected payoff than exploitative activities (McGrath, 2001). Norms of legitimacy in PMFs enable managers to commit resources to more certain exploitative activities than less legitimate exploration. Over time, such decision rules may become strongly imprinted on and routinized in the organization, limiting the sorts of capabilities that can be effectively developed and exploited.

## Implications and Conclusion

Our analysis suggests the need for greater attention to the role of governance in shaping the organizational context in which new capabilities are developed and effectively utilized in pursuing entrepreneurial opportunities. Governance systems' pervasive influence goes well beyond providing the incentives for entrepreneurial risk-taking that leads to exploration, learning, and new capability to development. This influence shapes the selection of the various entrepreneurial initiatives and thus the knowledge necessary to build those capabilities. Like March (1991), we see serious trade-offs in exploration and exploitation activities. We have argued that a governance perspective offers rich insights into the behavioral foundations of organizational learning that is integral to successful entrepreneurship. In doing so, a governance perspective suggests the sorts of levers that may be used in managing and selecting a position in relation to the exploration/exploitation trade-off.

## References

Ahuja, G. and Lampert, C.M. 2001. Entrepreneurship in the large corporation: A longitudinal study of how established firms create breakthrough inventions. *Strategic Management Journal*, **22**: 521–43.

Brown, S.L. and Eisenhardt, K.M. 1997. The art of continuous change: Linking complexity theory and time-paced evolution in relentlessly shifting organizations. *Administrative Science Quarterly*, **42**: 1–34.

Chesbrough, H. 2000. Designing corporate ventures in the shadow of private venture capital. *California Management Review*, **42**(3): 31–49.

Cyert, R.M. and March, J.C. 1963. *A Behavioral Theory of the Firm*. Englewood Cliffs, NJ: Prentice-Hall.

Eisenhardt, K.M. and Martin, J.A. 2000. Dynamic capabilities: What are they? *Strategic Management Journal*, **21**: 1105–21.

Foss, N.J. 2003. Bounded rationality and tacit knowledge in the organizational capabilities approach: An assessment and re-evaluation. *Industrial and Corporate Change*, **12**(2): 185–201.

Gedajlovic, E., Lubatkin, M., and Schulze, W. 2004. Crossing the threshold from founder management to professional management: A governance perspective. *Journal of Management Studies*, forthcoming.

March, J. 1991. Exploration and exploitation in organizational learning. *Organization Science*, **2**: 71–87.

McGrath, R.G. 2001. Exploratory learning, innovative capacity, and managerial oversight. *Academy of Management Journal*, **44**(1): 118–31.

Nelson, R. and Winter, S. 1982. *An Evolutionary Theory of Economic Change*. Cambridge, MA: Harvard University Press.

Sathe, V. 2003. *Corporate Entrepreneurship*: Tom *Managers and New Business Creation*. Cambridge, UK: Cambridge University Press.

Teece, D.J., Pisano, G., and Shuen, A. 1997. Dynamic capabilities and strategic management. *Strategic Management Journal*, **18**: 509–33.

Volberda, H.W. 1996. Toward the flexible form: How to remain vital in hypercompetitive environments. *Organization Science*, **7**(4): 359–74.

Zahra, S.A. 1996. Governance, ownership, and corporate entrepreneurship: The moderating impact of industry technological opportunities. *Academy of Management Journal*, **39**(6): 1713–35.

Zahra, S.A. and Flatotchev, I. 2004. Governing the entrepreneurial firm: A knowledge-based view. *Journal of Management Studies*, forthcoming.

Zahra, S.A. and George, G. 2002. Absorptive capacity: A review, reconceptualization, and extension. *Academy of Management Review*, **27**(2): 185–203.

Zahra, S.A. and Nielsen, A.P. 2002. Sources of capabilities, integration, and technology commercialization. *Strategic Management Journal*, **23**(5): 377–98.

# CHAPTER THREE

# Homesteading on the Endless Frontier: Mapping Science to Cultivate Innovation

Peter J. Lane

Over the past 20 years emerging fields of scientific research, such as biotechnology, genomics, and nanotechnology, as well as advances in other materials sciences, analytical chemistry, and optics have spawned innovations in health care, electronics, and a number of other industries. The business press and the managers of many companies have focused on the secondary outcomes of the science, the patentable technologies that grow out of them, and paid considerably less attention to understanding the scientific trends themselves. This myopic view arises from two tendencies. First, the commercial and economic potential of new discoveries is much harder to assess for science than for technology. Second, existing strategic management theories and techniques overlook science or treat it as a synonym for technology. These tendencies have left many managers unprepared to strategically manage the science behind new technologies, especially those managers outside traditionally science-based industries like pharmaceuticals or chemicals. Managers need new perspectives on the role of science in innovation to help their firms survive and thrive in this challenging environment. This chapter develops a new perspective by weaving together insights from two landmark events in U.S. history.

Toward the end of World War II, President Roosevelt asked Vannevar Bush, director of the Office of Scientific Research and Development (OSRD), for his thoughts on how the potential benefits of science should be used during peacetime to improve health care, create new enterprises and jobs, and raise the national standard of living. Bush's response was the landmark report *Science: The Endless Frontier* (1945), which laid much of the groundwork for government funding of non-defense research, the modern research university, and the role of industry in commercially applying the insights of basic science. Almost a century earlier, the United States sought to capitalize on a different kind of potential, and farmers and ranchers moved west to carve out homesteads along the geographic frontier. Bush himself draws a parallel between these two frontiers: "Although these [geographic] frontiers have more or less disappeared, the frontier of science remains." Following Bush's lead, in this chapter, I offer an examination of the strategies that homesteaders used along America's geographic frontier and suggest the lessons for today's managers as they attempt to stake their claims on the frontiers of scientific knowledge.

## Homesteading on the U.S. Western Frontier

The Homestead Act of 1862 played a critical role in the westward expansion of the United States. Signed into law by Abraham Lincoln, this act permitted any head of a household at least 21 years of age to claim a 160-acre parcel (a quarter square mile) of undeveloped government land. The "homesteader" had to provide proof of improving the lot by building a home, living on it, and farming it for five years to be eligible for a land patent from the U.S. government. The opportunity to gain legal title to land for hard work, ingenuity, and minimal fees ($18) convinced thousands of families to undertake the risks of moving west. By the time that homesteading opportunities vanished in the 1930s, more than 270 millions acres (about 10 percent of the area of the United States) had been claimed and settled under this act.

The Homestead Act's generous terms also proved the undoing of many settlers. No prior farming experience was required. The "quarter sections" of land were adequate for farming in the eastern frontier near the Mississippi River, where there was rich soil, adequate rainfall, and timber for building. But their size was too small to support settlers in the relatively arid and treeless western plains. Some families with more than one member aged 21 or older would claim several adjacent plots and work together to try to make them viable. Many family groups succeeded in adapting to the less fertile western lands. Many others did not and after years of hard work were left with claims to worthless land.

## Science and Technology along the Endless Frontier

Just as the Homestead Act encouraged the settlement of the American West with grants of free land, Vannevar Bush argued that laws encouraging patenting ". . . stimulate new invention and . . . make it possible for new industries to be built around new devices or new processes. These industries generate new jobs and new products, all of which contribute to the welfare and the strength of the country." Bush's report summarized in memorable quotes the prevailing views of science and technology: "Basic research is performed without thought of practical ends" in universities that are "relatively free from the adverse pressure of commercial necessity." Applied science (technology development) is closely linked to "commercial necessity" and is therefore better conducted by industry. Despite these differences, Bush saw links between basic research and commerce, with science serving as "the pacemaker of technological progress." Industry's challenge lies in anticipating the future directions of this pacemaker.

In recent years Bush's views of science and technology have been criticized as being too linear: science leads to technology which leads to products (CSPO, 1995). Bush's critics would argue that the impetus to explore new areas of science sometimes comes from technological advances, such as new or significantly improved analytical instruments. The net result is a series of reciprocal flows where advances in one type of knowledge trigger advances in the other. In the words of one author, science and technology have become "dancing partners" (Rip, 1992).

A careful reading of Bush's report, however, reveals a more nuanced view than suggested in his famous quotes: "A science such as physics, or chemistry, or mathematics is not the sum of two discreet parts – one pure, and the other applied. It is an organic whole, with complete interrelationships throughout. There should be no divorcing of applied science from its parent systems . . ." The inexorable intertwining of science and technology is also evident in Bush's own experience as an MIT professor and entrepreneur. In short, while Bush termed science "the frontier" in the title of his report, the report's core message was that the interactions of scientific research and technological development create an endless frontier of knowledge.

The idea that science is the partner leading the dance has gained recent empirical support. One study found that patents which cite scientific papers as part of their prior art are themselves more frequently cited by other patents and thus, by inference, more valuable (Fleming and Sorensen, 2004). Another study found that the more a firm's portfolio of patents cites science, the greater its market-to-book ratio (Deng, Lev, and Narin, 2001). A study of German firms concluded: "the science base of technological activities . . . determines competitiveness" (Grupp, 1997: 19). Taken together, these findings suggest that while the competitive implications of science are more difficult to discern, doing so is essential for firms competing on the endless frontier.

## Homesteading Challenges on the Geographic and Knowledge Frontiers

Corporations in the late twentieth and early twenty-first centuries are much larger and more sophisticated entities than the homesteading families of the late nineteenth century. But there are similarities between how corporations explore and make claims on the knowledge frontier through innovation and how families responding to the Homestead Act explored and made claims on the geographic frontier (see Table 3.1). Exploring those similarities can shed light on some of the challenges that firms now face.

In both contexts, the "homesteaders" seek to acquire legal control over a potentially valuable location by demonstrating that they have developed new and productive uses for it. On the physical frontier the location was 160 acres of terrain, and the legal claim was a land patent. On the knowledge frontier the location is a defined space in technological terrain and the legal claim is a utility patent. In both cases, realizing the potential economic value of the claim means using it to produce a stream of marketable outputs (crops and livestock, products and services). The success of either type of homesteader is a function of their effort, their ingenuity, and, most especially, the fertility of the location that they have claimed. Fertility in both cases means the long-term ability to produce marketable goods or services. The fertility that in large

**Table 3.1**  Homesteading as a strategy: Cultivating profit on the geographic and knowledge frontiers

|  | U.S. geographic frontier (mid-19th to mid-20th century) | Endless frontier of knowledge (mid-20th century to ?) |
|---|---|---|
| Type of homesteader | Family | Corporation |
| Potentially valuable asset | Land | Knowledge |
| Legal claim on the asset | Land patent | Utility patent |
| Basis of legal claim | New productive use of land | New productive use of knowledge |
| Economic value creation process | Use land to grow marketable crops and livestock | Use patent to develop marketable products and services |
| Factors influencing creation of economic value | Geographic location, effort, ingenuity and legal claim | Knowledge location, effort, ingenuity, and legal claim |
| Critical feature of location | Fertility: long-term ability to grow marketable crops | Fertility: long-term ability to develop marketable inventions |
| Determinants of fertility | Rich soil combined with favorable climate | Rich science base supported by ongoing research |
| Traditional homesteading strategy | Identify most fertile location acquire rights, and develop it | Identify most fertile location, acquire rights, and develop it |
| Typical methods of assessing fertility | Judge fertility yourself / Ask the local guides / Follow the wagons | Judge fertility yourself / Seek expert opinions / Follow industry bandwagons |
| Common problems of typical assessment methods | Inexperience and bias / Inexperience, bias, and motives / Late mover and group think | Inexperience and bias / Inexperience, bias, and motives / Late mover and group think |
| Costs for homesteaders with infertile locations | Escalating commitment / Abandon land and move on / Be a merchant, not a farmer | Escalating commitment / Abandon knowledge and move on / Exploit others' discoveries |
| New strategy for more effective homesteading | Map physical topography, underlying structure and climate trends / Identify the most fertile areas and most easily improved areas / Exploit those areas using the most appropriate techniques | Map the technology topography, underlying science, and research trends / Identify the most fertile areas and most easily improved areas / Exploit those areas using the most appropriate techniques |

part determined the fates of geographic homesteaders was a function of the richness of the soil and favorability of the climate. The fertility that determines the success of knowledge homesteaders arises from another set of factors – the richness of the underlying science base and the likelihood that current research trends will continue to add valuable new insights to that area of science. In short, assessing the fertility of a space – whether physical or technological – is the cornerstone of successful homesteading strategy.

Assessing the fertility of potential homesteads was a major challenge for nineteenth-century settlers. Many relied on their own judgment – even though they had no experience with the new territories and were biased by what they had experienced in other regions. In some cases, they had no experience in farming whatsoever. Others relied on the advice of local experts, often self-proclaimed, who not only suffered from the same cognitive limitations as the settlers, but often had self-serving motives (e.g., land speculation, acquisitions for railroads).

One strategy was to band together with a group of other settlers to share the risks of travel in a wagon train, and then hopefully to collaborate on selecting and developing the new plots of land. A wagon train, however, is susceptible to the same limitations as individual settlers. Even if it avoids those problems, collective decision-making processes may result in selecting land which optimizes for the wagon train members as a whole but does not meet the needs of individual settlers. Furthermore, while a wagon train may be needed for the journey, traveling companions may quickly become rivals at the end of the trail.

Companies face many of the same challenges when trying to assess the fertility of areas along the knowledge frontier. Their own prior R&D experiences facilitate accurate assessments in related areas but can cause them to discount or misinterpret the evidence from other areas (Lane and Lubatkin, 1998). Companies often try to address these limitations by seeking guidance from recognized experts. Yet experts are subject to similar cognitive limitations and may engage in self-interested promoting of a particular scientific perspective. Assembling panels of multiple experts cannot fully offset these dangers. The greater the breadth of perspectives on the panel, the more difficult it will be for them to find the common language and shared assumptions needed to reach consensus. In some cases, companies may feel pressure to follow an industry trend to invest in certain types of R&D. While there is a sense of safety in jumping on an industry bandwagon, tagging along with the crowd is rarely an effective strategy.

Overestimating the fertility of a location creates serious problems for both types of homesteaders. Having publicly committed to developing a location, they are likely to continue to invest in its development despite evidence that it is a lost cause. This is due not only to the loss of face, but also to the high costs of abandoning a claim and starting the homesteading process over again. Some failed homesteaders try to reposition themselves as middlemen. In this scenario, farmers become merchants, and companies focus on adapting and commercializing the patents of others.

## A New Approach to Homesteading on the Endless Frontier

Advances in agriculture have made assessing the potential fertility of land easier and more accurate. Today U.S. farmers use pictures and data from satellites to create accurate maps of topography, soil types, geological structures, and climatic trends. This detailed information allows farmers to match the best crops and cultivation methods with the characteristics of each distinctive microclimate on their farm. This has led to today's high level of farm productivity.

Managers need to follow this example and develop more accurate and objective methods of mapping locations along the knowledge frontier. Unfortunately, the tools for mapping this frontier have not developed as quickly as those for mapping geographic frontiers. There has been some work on mapping the topography of science, starting with Eugene Garfield in the 1970s, but there has been relatively little work on mapping the fertility of different areas of science. The one exception is SciTech Strategies, a consulting group that has validated measures of science fertility using a large sample of the most highly cited scientific papers. Several groups of academics, consultants, and data providers are working on mapping patents, and a number of measures of patent value have been developed. To date, however, the mapping and assessment of science fertility has been neither comprehensive nor fully linked to the mapping and assessment of technology.

Simply put, managers still lack the types of tools and techniques for modern homesteading that U.S. farmers routinely use. Several companies are trying to develop new tools that meet these requirements. SciTech Strategies, for example, has developed a method of science mapping that includes all the papers published by reputable peer-reviewed scientific and technological journals, rather than just a sample of them. (See www.mapofscience.com for more details.)

In preparation for the next generation of mapping tools, managers need to begin to rethink their methods of evaluating and investing in opportunities along the endless frontiers. As Bush noted in his letter to President Roosevelt which accompanies the report:

> Science offers a largely unexplored hinterland for the pioneer who has the tools for his task. The rewards of such exploration both for the Nation and the individual are great. Scientific progress is one essential key to our security as a nation, to our better health, to more jobs, to a higher standard of living, and to our cultural progress.

## References

Bush, V. 1945. *Science: The Endless Frontier*, U.S. Office of Scientific Research and Development, Report to the President on a Program for Postwar Scientific Research. Washington, DC: Government Printing Office.

Center for Science, Policy, and Outcomes (CSPO). 1995. *Science: The Endless Frontier: Learning from the Past, Designing for the Future*. Tempe, AZ: CSPO.

Deng, Z., Lev, B. and Narin, F. 2001. Science and technology as predictors of stock performance. *Financial Analysts Journal*, **55**: 20–32.

Fleming, L. and Sorenson, O. 2004. Science as map in technological search. *Strategic Management Journal*, forthcoming.

Grupp, H. 1997. The links between competitiveness, firms' innovative activities and public R&D support in Germany: An empirical analysis. *Technology Analysis and Strategic Management*, **9**(1): 19–33.

Lane, P.J. and Lubatkin, M. 1998. Relative absorptive capacity and interorganizational learning. *Strategic Management Journal*, **19**: 461–77.

Rip, A. 1992. Science and technology as dancing partners. In P. Kroes and M. Bakker (eds.), *Technological Development and Science in the Industrial Age*, pp. 231–70. Amsterdam: Kluwer.

# CHAPTER FOUR

# The Pre-history of Strategy Processes

Patrick Regnér

## Introduction

The notion of competitive advantage is a core aspect of strategic management research and originates from firms implementing strategies that other current or potential firms ignore or are unable to exploit (Barney, 1991). Established strategic management theories explain these competitive advantages once recognized, but it is not entirely clear what the characteristics are of the processes and factors leading up to them. The characteristics that accompany competitive advantage have been examined at length, but their origins have been less discussed (Cockburn, Henderson, and Stern, 2000; Henderson, 2000). This chapter focuses on the sources of strategy and, in particular, the pre-history of strategy processes.

The two most influential strategic management research directions of the last two decades, the industrial organization (IO) based strategy perspective (e.g. Porter, 1980, 1981) and the resource-based view (RBV) (e.g. Barney, 1986, 1991; Wernerfelt, 1984) have compellingly established that strategy grows out of exploitation of industry and resource structures. However, how new value and competitive advantage are created in the first place is less well understood. It is indeterminate how market imperfections in terms of entry barriers (Porter, 1980, 1981) and isolating mechanisms (Rumelt, 1984) in reality are created or discovered (Cockburn, Henderson, and Stern, 2000; Henderson, 2000).

When it comes to the question from where and whom new strategies originate the two directions seem to have a similar position. Most often the question is simply ignored altogether, but at times the implicit assumption appears to be that the two respective frameworks could be used in prospective ways (Henderson, 2000). Even though not explicitly spelled out, the spirit in at least some portions appears to suggest that senior managers would be central in the development of competitive advantage and strategy, making insightful strategic choices that build entry barriers and isolating mechanisms (e.g. Porter, 1980: xiv; Barney, 1991: 104).

In contrast to these strategy-content perspectives, strategy process research (e.g. Johnson, 1987; Mintzberg, 1978; Mintzberg and McHugh, 1985; Pettigrew, 1985; Quinn, 1980) has provided rich and systematic descriptions showing that strategy making involves a variety of actors and various contextual influences. However, there still seem to be few clear theoretical structures concerning where new strategies and competitive advantage in fact come from. In brief, the questions of the origins of competitive advantage and strategy have received limited attention since most current strategy research starts with the assumption that a strategy in some form already exists, neglecting the very early stages of strategy development. It appears as if there is a fallacy of aggregative thinking where macro structures regarding competitive advantage and macro strategy processes have been carefully analyzed while micro aspects and the pre-history of strategy, how strategies come to be strategies in the first place, have been overlooked.

There has, however, been some recent interest in the origins of strategy (Cockburn, Henderson, and Stern, 2000), methods of wealth creation (Moran and Ghoshal, 1999), the dynamic capabilities behind new strategic positions (Eisenhardt and Martin, 2000; Helfat, 2003; Teece, Pisano, and Shuen, 1997), and the role of initial conditions (Cockburn, Henderson, and Stern, 2000; Holbrook *et al.*, 2000). In addition, a new micro perspective on strategy processes and strategy making is emerging (Johnson, Melin, and Whittington, 2003; Regnér, 2003). This chapter builds on this research and tries to start to fill the gap regarding the origins and pre-history of strategy process. It begins with a discussion about the conditions and factors out of which new competitive advantage and strategy may come from and it differentiates between diverse strategy candidates and their possible interactions early on in strategy processes. Essentially it focuses on a simple, but fundamental question in strategic management: Where does strategy come from? The emphasis is on the pre-historic conditions and characteristics that provide the initial context and foundation for strategy processes and, in the end, competitive advantage.

The point of departure in this chapter is the analogy that in the same way as resources and capabilities *per se* need to be idiosyncratic, rare, and inimitable, in order to create value it seems as if the strategy process leading up to new competitive advantages and new strategies may need to encompass similar properties. With this as a backdrop the objective is to describe and analyze the origins and process antecedents of new strategies. It examines the phase before a strategy has been identified or defined as a strategy, thus, a stage prior to what usually has been examined in strategy process studies. It attempts to conceptually describe strategy process characteristics in this very early development of new competitive advantages and strategies. An important thesis is that while there is a contradiction between more deterministic processes and factors and more voluntaristic ones in early strategy development there is also an important complement between them. Next the possible strategy candidates in the pre-history of strategy are discussed and the following two sections focus on their specifics and interactions.

## Strategy Pre-history: Possible Strategy Candidates

New competitive advantage and strategy cannot easily be created. Strong competitive pressures quickly threaten any new value or strategy and erode any possible profits

(Schoemaker, 1990). In fact, contemporary strategic management theories suggest that luck and superior information might be the only ways to competitive advantage or abnormal profits (Barney, 1986). A process theory concerning the origins of strategy needs to build on and take into consideration these observations in contemporary strategy content research. It seems as if strategy processes need to encompass similar characteristics regarding idiosyncrasy, rarity, and inimitability in line with the resource-based and dynamic capabilities views. Hence, strategy processes generating competitive advantage are likely to involve idiosyncratic properties in developing and discovering new market opportunities and capabilities. They most probably involve hidden resources and opportunities that can only be seen and detected through unconventional means. This implies that embryonic strategy processes are likely to be quite complex and distant from any widespread and common ones. They will probably not be as close as one might expect to those that can be read about in strategic management textbooks, those about which management consultancy firms preach, or those that corporate executives often officially describe. An analysis of the pre-history of strategy processes needs to take these aspects and arguments into consideration, which implies moving beyond descriptions of managerial choice, design, and action, and instead investigating alternative strategy process characteristics.

It is possible to identify some likely and partly overlapping strategy candidates in the pre-history of strategy that potentially can provide for competitive advantage. First, and perhaps most obviously, luck and chance might play an important role (Barney, 1986; Porter, 1991; Stinchcombe, 2000). Another potential ingredient is the initial conditions of firms and strategies at their founding (Cockburn, Henderson, and Stern, 2000; Helfat and Lieberman, 2002; Holbrook *et al.*, 2000; Levinthal, 1997; Stinchcombe, 1965). There might also be initial disadvantages that force firms into a certain direction that later turns out to create value. Hence, necessity might be another candidate in the process of strategy and competitive advantage development (Porter, 1991; Wernerfelt, 1984). Closely related to chance is serendipity, the lucky, but not effortless, discovery of strategic opportunities (Denrell, Fang, and Winter, 2003), which possibly could be yet another strategic candidate. Finally, another possible factor involved is managerial choice, design, and action. This is, of course, the most recognized and celebrated candidate, reflecting strategic management's undeniably normative character. On the one hand it might involve careful deductive thinking and action (Andrews, 1980; Lorange and Vancil, 1977), which still seems to be a principal explanation among many theorists and practitioners. On the other hand, greater unsystematic and inductive managerial strategy making prevails in many descriptive accounts (Johnson, 1987; Mintzberg and McHugh, 1985; Pettigrew, 1985; Quinn, 1980).

While these diverse strategy candidates have been observed earlier and their specific role in any pursuit is extremely difficult to determine, their details and interactions in the embryonic stages of strategy making have been less discussed. There seems to be little cumulative knowledge when it comes to the sources of and interactions between these candidates in the pre-history of strategy process. Although the role of factors outside top management's control is sometimes discussed generally (e.g. Barney, 1986; Porter, 1991), or in terms of general contextual influences (Johnson, 1987; Mintzberg, 1978; Pettigrew, 1985, Quinn, 1980), or in terms of autonomous strategy making (Bower, 1970; Burgelman, 1983a, 1983b), the analysis here attempts to identify specific strategy candidates in the pre-history that might provide for competitive advantage.

## Chance, Initial Conditions, and Necessity

Pure *chance* and luck may clearly play a role in strategy development (Barney, 1986; Porter, 1991; Stinchcombe, 2000). The emphasis on path dependency and "sticky" assets in the resource-based view implies that incidental historical circumstances may play an important role. Firm resources that are most likely to provide competitive advantage are simply not amenable to managerial influence (Barney, 2001; Priem and Butler, 2001). Similarly, strategy process research has shown that accidents and haphazard events may play a significant role in strategy development (Mintzberg, 1978; Pascale, 1984; Pettigrew, 1985; Regnér, 1999). However, it might seem less useful to analyze chance as such, instead examining chance events and conditions as antecedent strategy-making ingredients and interacting factors with managerial action and design can provide important knowledge about strategy origins and development. Related to chance is the role of *initial conditions*. The importance of initial conditions for technological development and firm performance has been established both within examinations of technological change (e.g. Dosi, 1982; Nelson and Winter, 1982; Levinthal, 1998) and strategic management (Cockburn, Henderson, and Stern, 2000). It has been demonstrated that prior experience within a certain area might be a valuable asset and may provide the basis for subsequent competitive advantages (Carroll *et al.*, 1996; Holbrook *et al.*, 2000; Klepper and Simmons, 2000). Pre-adaptation – the biological term for characteristics developed for one application that by chance prove to be useful for alternative, yet unanticipated, applications (Cattani, 2003) – and asymmetries – inimitable differences between firms that in their initial states could in no way be considered valuable (Miller, 2003) – have been shown to be decisive for selective and competitive advantage.

*Necessity* is another strategic candidate related to chance at the origins of strategy. Essentially this constitutes the opposite of having initial conditions; instead the firm is short of certain resources and capabilities. Lack of experience and resources could force firms into certain directions that subsequently might produce competitive advantage (Porter, 1991) or they may adopt such a strategy path by mistake. In other words, initial disadvantages and necessity (Porter, 1991; Wernerfelt, 1984) may be sources of new competitive advantages as well. In brief, the circumstances leading up to the creation of certain capabilities and competitive advantages might have been forced upon the firm and were inescapable due to environmental pressures from competitors and customers or due to lack of resources.

Even if chance and haphazard, initial, and necessity conditions play an important role in the origins of strategy these deterministic forces do not exclude more voluntaristic ones. Initial conditions might result from historical managerial manipulations and may provide a raw material that managers can discover and later creatively apply, change, and complement. Managers may develop valuable assets without being aware of the later potential for competitive advantage and/or they may discover valuable assets accidentally without actually seeking them. Similarly, this also goes for necessity. Firms might be forced into a certain strategic direction due to certain environmental conditions or lack of resources, but managers might have contributed to this process as well. They may implement other strategic goals that force the firm in a certain direction and/or they may build certain capabilities that undermine others. Moreover, they have a role in discovering and compensating for these shortcomings, even if it is defensive. It might seem meaningless to give managers any credit at all for building capabilities that initially might only provide extra costs, but which later turn out to be essential initial conditions or to give them credit for undermining the existence of some capabilities that later by necessity forces the firm into a certain direction and provide for competitive advantage. However, it needs to be recognized that in strategic complexity (Regnér, 2001; Schoemaker, 1990) the borderline, between on the one hand proactively (but without complete understanding) or reactively (due to necessity) building capabilities that later happen to provide for competitive advantage and, on the other hand, insightfully and intentionally building such capabilities, often is indistinct.

This relates to the role of serendipitous events in strategy development. Capabilities might be serendipitously created or discovered and inadvertently provide for competitive advantage. *Serendipity,* the phenomenon of discovering or developing valuable things not initially sought for, may play an important role in the origins of new value creation and strategy. Recently it has been argued that the process of discovering a strategic opportunity is likely to be serendipitous since it is only discovered after some time – the low-hanging fruits have already been picked – and involves complex combinations of many commodities (Denrell, Fang, and Winter, 2003). In order for any firm to spot a hard to recognize opportunity, however, it needs to already be in possession of quite a few of the required components.

Chance events, initial and necessity conditions, and serendipity could provide a basis for idiosyncratic and inimitable processes generating new competitive advantage. Even though determinism plays an important role in this pre-history to strategy process, it is important to observe that some possibilities of managerial influence and intentionality might interact with these forces. This indicates a less deterministic function of these pre-history characteristics of strategy and some role for managers in the very early embryonic stages of strategy development. Chance has to be captured, initial conditions need to be created and discovered, and necessity involves action and change. The serendipity involved in this process is distinct from pure chance by its necessary condition of alertness and flexibility (Denrell, Fang, and Winter, 2003). It requires will, effort, attentiveness, and experimentation from managers even though the lucky external flow of environmental changes is essential for this to materialize. This indicates that more voluntaristic forces including managerial manipulation might interact with more deterministic ones in the creation of new strategy and competitive advantage.

## Serendipity and Inductive Strategy Making

Serendipitous development and discovery of vital resources and opportunities requires appropriate management activities and cognitive abilities. It seems reasonable to expect that serendipity is more likely to happen to those following deviant activities and processes rather than those following textbook and management consultancy step-by-step processes and activities. In order to be valuable and detect undiscovered resources and opportunities and create entirely new resources and capabilities the activities generating new value need not be widespread and easily imitable. On the contrary, they are likely to involve idiosyncratic properties and most probably deviate considerably from any prescriptive planning processes. Empirical investigations verify that under more complex circumstances, such as the creation of new competitive advantages, strategy processes diverge from a traditional rational planning ideal. The differences are most evident in uncertain strategic decisions (Mintzberg, Raisinghani, and Théoret, 1976), in unstable (Mintzberg, 1973; Fredrickson and Mitchell, 1984), or fast-changing environments (Eisenhardt and Martin, 2000), and in strategy creation (Regnér, 2003). In brief, it seems as if new strategies that provide for competitive advantage might originate in managerial activities that are unconventional and idiosyncratic. They are likely to involve exploratory strategy activities like trial and error, informal noticing, and experiments. In addition, they can be expected to involve more peripheral actors and middle managers, which has been demonstrated in strategy development and renewal (Burgelman, 1983a; Fulop, 1991; Kanter, 1982; Regnér, 2003) and in strategic management more generally (Floyd and Wooldridge, 1997). In sum, creative and exploratory strategy activities may be important for new strategy development, but they might not always be intentionally so – they are likely to promote serendipitous developments and discoveries.

Strategy activities are intimately linked to managerial beliefs and frameworks (Weick, 1979, 1995). Actions are based on and involve a certain view of the world or a knowledge structure (Walsh, 1995), but they also generate feedback that might make managers and firms adjust these. In order to detect initial conditions and find new directions due to necessity and in general creatively combine and transform resources and capabilities in strategy development, it seems as if cognition and knowledge structures need to differ compared to common and established ones. It is reasonable to expect that sensemaking (Weick, 1995) and attached knowledge structures that follow the prevailing way of doing things in an industry, an industry recipe (Grinyer and Spender, 1979), or any general and predictable beliefs and knowledge would not be expected to generate new value. Rather, sensemaking and knowledge structures that deviate from the conventional and involve new views of the world are more likely to create value and competitive advantage. Managers and organizational units with alternative knowledge structures have the potential to sense and understand signals and environmental developments in a way that deviates from those that are attached to core and established knowledge structures and therefore they are more likely to discover new value and strategies. The strategy activities and sensemaking described above does not belong to the traditional category of strategy making, but might still play a crucial role in the initial strategy development stages. It can be described as *inductive strategy making* (Regnér, 2003) including externally oriented and explorative activities involving experiments, trial and error, ad hoc problem solving, and informal noticing.

Once discovered and created, new resources and capabilities need to be appropriately and fully exploited. This may provide a role for more traditional *deductive strategy-making* including an industry and exploitation focus involving analysis, planning, routines, and formal intelligence (Regnér, 2003) when the pre-history strategy phase is over. It is worth noticing that it appears as if both dynamic (Eisenhardt and

Martin, 2000; Teece, Pisano, and Shuen, 1997) and ordinary capabilities (Winter, 2003) belong to this second category of strategy making and, thus, enter later in strategy processes that produce entirely new value and competitive advantage. However, as the diverse strategy candidates in the pre-history of strategy development overlap so does inductive and deductive strategy making.

## Conclusions

This chapter adds to the discussion of the origins of strategy and new value creation (Cockburn, Henderson, and Stern, 2000; Henderson, 2000; Moran and Ghoshal, 1999), but from a strategy process perspective. It proposes and examines possible strategy candidates involved in the very early phases of strategy development, such as chance, initial conditions, necessity, serendipity, and inductive strategy making. These strategy process factors are rare, inimitable, and obscure and therefore have the potential to produce competitive and sustainable advantage. Paradoxically it seems as if strategy making needs to involve factors partly outside management control and also strategy activities distant from discrete and controlled strategic choices based on prescriptive frameworks, analyses, and plans in order to provide for competitive advantage. However, clearly these pre-history strategy candidates are uncertain and inexact and the inductive strategy making involved undoubtedly includes many weaknesses and biases. On the other hand, apart from providing idiosyncratic and potentially valuable characteristics for capability development and discovery, biased decision making could be beneficial when strategic issues are characterized by complexity (Busenitz and Barney, 1997). Similarly, March and Cohen (1974) have emphasized that "sensible foolishness" is an important ingredient in decision making under ambiguity (and, thus, in strategic complexity) since it allows for the development of preferences, values, and aspirations.

The chapter addresses a central tenet in strategic management, namely, whether more profitable and successful firms differ systematically from others or if it is primarily a result of chance (Henderson, 2000; Stinchcombe, 2000). A compromise is suggested: strategy processes that generate new value and competitive advantage involve chance and serendipity as well as intentional managerial activity and design.

The managerial implications indicate that the pre-history of strategy is likely to involve relatively more luck, serendipity, and inductive strategy making compared to what has traditionally been associated with strategy making. However, even in serendipity intentionality enters at some point of time and once opportunities, initial conditions, and necessities are discovered intentionality enters more clearly and inductive strategy making takes over and later traditional deductive strategy making dominates. In other words, the analysis presented here provides encouraging as well as depressing news for strategy makers. If chance, hidden initial conditions, and necessity together with deviating strategy activities and knowledge structures are important ingredients in the development of competitive advantage, there might not be much insight to be gained from an examination of successful strategy processes and the role of managerial influence might diminish. In addition, the inclusion of serendipity, deviant perceptions of the world, and a great deal of exploration, etc. are all mechanisms that are likely to be extremely costly. On the other hand, the analysis shows that although initial and necessity conditions might play an important role in the creation of competitive advantage they do so in conjunction with managers possessing insights into them. Managers also discover, develop, and actively complement them with other resources and capabilities through inductive strategy making. In addition, the analysis indicates that economists might not be completely right in expecting competitive advantage to dissipate easily through the market. The cumbersome processes of serendipity and inductivity show that competitors are likely to be slow in detecting and copying them. The big question of strategy for managers in this analysis becomes one of knowing when to apply which type of strategy activity. One needs to know when general efforts in terms of alertness and flexibility are due, when inductive strategy making is appropriate, and when to apply more traditional deductive procedures.

This chapter represents a first incomplete cut on the pre-history of strategy processes and clearly has many limitations. It simply brings up some possible strategy candidates and characteristics that might be important in the initial stages of strategy development and starts a discussion about what might be significant in the early formation of competitive advantage. More research on the processes of strategy origins is clearly warranted. One of the most challenging aspects of the examination of strategy pre-history is methodological. Managers and other observers quickly retrospectively rationalize strategies and it is almost an insurmountable task to recreate the complexity and ambiguity of the circumstances at the origins of strategy and the various conditions, chance events, and experiments involved. However, this is necessary if we are to capture and analyze the pre-history of strategy and the real sources of competitive advantage.

## References

Andrews, K.R. 1980. *The Concept of Corporate Strategy*. Homewood, IL: Irwin.

Barney, J.B. 1986. Strategic factor markets: Expectations, luck, and business strategy. *Management Science*, **32**: 1231–41.

Barney, J.B. 1991. Firm resources and sustained competitive advantage, *Journal of Management*, **17**: 99–120.

Barney, J.B. 2001. Is the resource-based "view" a useful perspective for strategic management research? Yes. *Academy of Management Review*, **26**: 41–56.

Bower, J.L. 1970. *Managing the Resource Allocation Process: A Study of Corporate Planning and Investment*. Boston, MA: Harvard Business School Press.

Burgelman, R.A. 1983a. A model of the interaction of strategic behavior, corporate context, and the concept of strategy. *Academy of Management Review*, **8**: 61–70.

Burgelman, R.A. 1983b. A process model of internal corporate venturing in the diversified major firm. *Administrative Science Quarterly*, **28**: 223–44.

Busenitz, L.W. and Barney, J.B. 1997. Differences between entrepreneurs and managers in large organizations: Biases and heuristics in strategic decision-making. *Journal of Business Venturing*, **12**: 9–30.

Carroll, G.R., Bigelow, M.D., Seidel, M.D., and Tsai, L. 1996. The fates of de novo and de alio producers in the American automobile industry, 1885–1981. *Strategic Management Journal*, **17**: 117–38.

Cattani, G. 2003. Preadaptation, firm heterogeneity and technological performance: A study of the evolution of optical communications, 1970–1995. Working paper, The Wharton School University of Pennsylvania.

Cockburn, I.M., Henderson, R.M., and Stern, S. 2000. Untangling the origins of competitive advantage. *Strategic Management Journal*, **21**: 1123–45.

Denrell, J., Fang, C., and Winter, S.G. 2003. The economics of strategic opportunity. *Strategic Management Journal*, **24**: 1123–45.

Dosi, G. 1982. Technological paradigms and technological trajectories. *Research Policy*, **11**: 147–62.

Eisenhardt, K.M. and Martin, J.A. 2000. Dynamic capabilities: What are they? *Strategic Management Journal*, **21**: 1105–21.

Floyd, S.W. and Wooldridge, B. 1997. Middle management's strategic influence and organizational performance. *Journal of Management Studies*, **34**(3): 465–86.

Fredrickson, J.W. and Mitchell, T.R. 1984. Strategic decision processes: Comprehensiveness and performance in an industry with an unstable environment. *Academy of Management Journal*, **27**: 399–423.

Fulop, L. 1991. Middle managers: Victims or vanguards of the entrepreneurial movement. *Journal of Management Studies*, **28**: 25–44.

Grinyer, P. and Spender, J.C. 1979. *Turnabout: Managerial Recipes for Strategic Success*. New York: Associated Business Press.

Helfat, C.E. 2003. *The SMS Blackwell Handbook of Organizational Capabilities – Emergence, Development and Change*. Malden, MA: Blackwell Publishing.

Helfat, C.E. and Lieberman, M.B. 2002. The birth of capabilities: market entry and the importance of pre-history. *Industrial and Corporate Change*, **11**(4): 725–60.

Henderson, R.L. 2000. Luck, leadership, and strategy. In J. Baum and F. Dobbin (eds.) *Economics Meets Sociology in Strategic Management: Advances in Strategic Management*, p. 17. Greenwich, CT: JAI Press.

Holbrook, D., Cohen, W.M., Hounshell, D.A., and Klepper, S. 2000. The nature, sources, and consequences of firm differences in the early history of the semiconductor industry. *Strategic Management Journal*, **21**: 1017–41.

Johnson, G. 1987. *Strategic Change and the Management Process*. Oxford, UK: Blackwell.

Johnson, G., Melin, L., and Whittington, R. 2003. Micro strategy and strategizing: Towards an activity-based view. *Journal of Management Studies*, **40**: 3–22.

Kanter, R.M. 1982. The middle manager as innovator. *Harvard Business Review*, **60**(4): 95–105.

Klepper, S. and Simons, K.L. 2000. Dominance by birthright: Entry of radio producers and competitive ramifications in the US television receiver industry. *Strategic Management Journal*, **21**: 997–1016.

Levinthal, D.A. 1997. Adaptation on rugged landscapes. *Management Science*, **43**: 934–50.

Levinthal, D.A. 1998. The slow pace of rapid technological change: Gradualism and punctuation in technological change. *Industrial and Corporate Change*, **7**: 217–47.

Lorange, P. and Vancil, R.F. 1977. *Strategic Planning Systems*. Englewood Cliffs, NJ: Prentice-Hall.

March, J.G. and Cohen, M.D. 1974. *Leadership and Ambiguity*. Boston, MA: Harvard Business School Press.

Miller, D. 2003. An asymmetry-based view of advantage – Overcoming the sustainability–attainability dilemma. *Strategic Management Journal*, **24**: 961–75.

Mintzberg, H. 1973. Strategy-making in three modes. *California Management Review*, **16**: 44–53.

Mintzberg, H. 1978. Patterns in strategy formation. *Management Science*, **24**: 934–48.

Mintzberg, H. and McHugh, A. 1985. Strategy formation in an adhocracy. *Administrative Science Quarterly*, **30**: 160–97.

Mintzberg, H., Raisinghani, D., and Théoret, A. 1976. The structure of "unstructured" decision processes. *Administrative Science Quarterly*, **21**(6): 246–75.

Moran, P. and Ghoshal, S. 1999. Markets, firms and the process of economic development. *Academy of Management Review*, **24**(3): 390–412.

Nelson, R. and Winter, S. 1982. *An Evolutionary Theory of Economic Change*. Boston, MA: Harvard University Press.

Pascale, R. 1984. Perspectives on strategy: The real story behind Honda's success. *California Management Review*, **26**: 47–72.

Pettigrew, A.M. 1985. *The Awakening Giant – Continuity and Change in Imperial Chemical Industries*. Oxford, UK: Blackwell.

Porter, M.E. 1980. *Competitive Strategy*. New York: The Free Press.

Porter, M.E. 1981. The contributions of industrial organization to strategic management. *Academy of Management Review*, **6**: 609–20.

Porter, M.E. 1991. Towards a dynamic theory of strategy. *Strategic Management Journal*, **12**: 95–117.

Priem, R.L. and Butler, J.E. 2001. Is the resource-based "view" a useful perspective for strategic management research? *Academy of Management Review*, **26**: 22–40.

Quinn, J.B. 1980. *Strategies for Change – Logical Incrementalism*. Homewood, IL: Irwin.

Regnér, P. 1999. *Strategy Creation and Change in Complexity – Adaptive and Creative Learning Dynamics in the Firm*. Published doctoral dissertation. Stockholm: Institute of International Business, Stockholm School of Economics.

Regnér, P. 2001. Complexity and multiple rationalities in strategy processes. In H.W. Volberda and T. Elfring (eds.), *Rethinking Strategy*. London: Sage.

Regnér, P. 2003. Strategy creation in the periphery: Inductive versus deductive strategy making. *Journal of Management Studies*, **40**: 57–82.

Rumelt, R.P. 1984. Towards a strategic theory of the firm. In R.B. Lamb (ed.), *Competitive Strategic Management*. Englewood Cliffs, NJ: Prentice-Hall.

Schoemaker, P.J. 1990. Strategy, complexity, and economic rent. *Management Science*, **36**: 1178–92.

Stinchcombe, A.L. 1965. Social structure and organizations. In J.G. March (ed.), *Handbook of Organization*. Chicago, IL: Rand-McNally.

Stinchcombe, A.L. 2000. On equilibrium, organizational form, and competitive strategy. In J. Baum and F. Dobbin (eds.), *Economics Meets Sociology in Strategic management: Advances in Strategic Management*, p. 17. Greenwich, CT: JAI Press.

Teece, D.J., Pisano, G., and Shuen, A. 1997. Dynamic capabilities and strategic management. *Strategic Management Journal*, **18**: 509–33.

Walsh, J. 1995. Managerial and organizational cognition: Notes from a trip down memory lane. *Organizational Science*, **6**(3): 280–321.

Weick, K.E. 1979. *The Social Psychology of Organizing*. New York: Random House.

Weick, K.E. 1995. *Sensemaking in Organizations*. Thousand Oaks, CA: Sage.

Wernerfelt, B. 1984. A resource-based view of the firm. *Strategic Management Journal*, **5**: 171–80.

Winter, S.G. 2003. Understanding dynamic capabilities. *Strategic Management Journal*, **24**: 991–5.

# CHAPTER FIVE

# Strategy Formation Effects on Managerial Action

## J. Ignacio Canales, Joaquim Vilà

The way an organization conceives and generates strategy has a major impact on the outcome of its strategy process. This chapter focuses on the interaction between top and middle management and their sources of influence as a property of strategy making. Theory and research have set forth that top managers shape strategy making (Hambrick, 1998; Iaquinto and Fredrickson, 1997; Lovas and Ghoshal, 2000). In contrast, another large body of research has studied how middle managers act as agents of strategy making (Dutton *et al.*, 2001; Floyd and Wooldridge, 2000). Similarly, the influence on strategy making has been expressed as either top-down or bottom-up, each source developing rather independently (Burgelman, 1991). The main top-down source of influence is the strategic intent (Hamel and Prahalad, 1989). The "issue-selling" activities (Dutton and Ashford, 1993) and the type of involvement in the strategy process of middle managers (Floyd and Wooldridge, 1992) are the bottom-up sources. If each level affects strategy making separately, how is the top and middle management interplay resolved to originate a strategy that translates into managerial action?

Managerial action, observed in concrete strategic initiatives, is used as a focal concept from where we aim at developing theory on how strategy is generated from the middle and top management interplay. Our answer to the previous question suggests that *legitimation* of strategic initiatives is what resolves top and middle managers' interplay into a guide for managerial action. This legitimizing mechanism, as it emerged from a longitudinal case study of the RACC automobile club, agrees with the notion that "legitimation justifies the institutional order by giving a normative dignity to its practical imperatives" (Berger and Luckman, 1967: 93). From the present study, we argue that achieving legitimacy of strategic initiatives is a mutually conferred status, held by both top and middle managers. The interplay between top and middle managers is central to strategy making (Hart, 1992). It enables managers to grasp strategy, addressing Guth and MacMillan's (1986) concern on getting commitment from organizational members. As such, strategy turns into the guiding element that is then reflected in subsequent concrete actions. While the difficulties leaders encounter in aligning organizational action with the strategic intent have been emphasized (Mintzberg, Ahlstrand, and Lampel, 1998), the present study aims at shedding light on how an organization that purposively manages legitimation overcomes these difficulties.

In the first section, we present the theoretical underpinnings of this study. Second, we justify the use of a case study design and offer a brief description of the case study company. Third, we dig into the evolution of 14 strategic initiatives and the methods used to obtain, reduce, and analyze these data. Finally, we present the discussion and the conclusion of this study.

## On Top-Down and Bottom-Up Perspectives

Strategy making can be viewed as the result of multilevel organization interplay (Bower, 1970; Hart, 1992). Building on Hart's (1992) modes of strategy making, we have specified possible roles for top and middle management levels. The roles played by top and middle management can range from the former dispatching strategy and the latter receiving it for implementation, to top management sponsoring lower level managers' initiatives emerging from below as well as the entrepreneurial initiatives developed by middle managers. In between these two extreme combinations, in general, top management will provide direction, while middle managers will participate to some degree in strategy making (Hart, 1992).

Along this multilevel interplay, the strategy-making processes comprise induced and autonomous behaviors (Burgelman, 1983, 1991, 1996). Induced behavior represents the guiding character of strategy. By building on initiatives within the scope of the organization's current strategy, induced behavior is viewed as a major inertial force (Burgelman, 1991). However, we expand this notion by allowing for induced behavior to be also a source of renewal (Floyd and Wooldridge, 2000). Top management may in advance set the path for change, by conveying the strategic intent as the objective function, thus providing a guiding character (Lovas and Ghoshal, 2000). Setting and conveying the strategic intent is understood in the present study as the opening stage of the interaction between middle and top managers.

Conversely, Burgelman (1991) reserves autonomous behavior for initiatives that emerge outside the current strategy. Middle managers can conceptualize new strategies by combining autonomous initiatives with firms' strengths (Burgelman, 1983). In this study, we broaden the possible effect of autonomous behavior, allowing for renewal to be also favored by bottom-up initiatives, which are aligned with the strategic purpose put forward. We permit the ability of conscious adaptation (Floyd and Wooldridge, 2000; Lovas and Ghoshal, 2000).

We regard renewal as a possible outcome of both conscious adaptation and autonomous behavior. Strategic renewal is used as the change in an organization's core competencies and/or change in its product market domains (Floyd and Lane, 2000). In sum, we recognize that managers at all levels of the organization may play a role in strategic renewal, and that their behavior may be both purposeful and inadvertent (Mintzberg, 1978). We regard strategy making as intervening between the strategy concept and managerial action. Accordingly, strategy making is not restricted to planning and analysis, but viewed as the ample organizational phenomena through which strategy is formed (Burgelman, 1983).

## "The RACC" and a Case Study Approach

The purpose of this study suits the use of the case study method. First, the nature of the managerial interplay in strategy making, as a multilevel and organization-wide phenomenon, lends itself to fine-grained inquiry rather than a quantitative measurement (Chakravarthy and Doz, 1992). Second, the relationship between managerial interplay and managerial action calls for the understanding the dynamics present within a single setting. Third, the use of exploratory case research enables consideration of new ideas and propositions to be applied in further research (Yin, 1994).

We have anchored our inquiry in three subprocesses: the objective function setting (primarily induced behavior); the idea-generation/issue-selling process (primarily autonomous); and the interplay between top management and middle managerial levels. As indicated by Eisenhardt (1989) and Yin (1994), we relied on these ex-ante constructs leaning on existing theory. These allow for iterative contrasting of theory against evidence, and prevent ongoing research diverging from the original intention.

The company chosen, the RACC Automobile Club, was an exceptionally revealing case. First, this company is a multi-business organization that had grown by 30 percent annually in turnover over the last five years. One key reason for this growth was the recently implemented approach to strategy making, which diverged from the traditional practice of strategic planning and promoted participation. Second, the company used well-defined strategic initiatives to promote change. Third, the CEO guided strategy formation by means of an objective function. Fourth, the nature of the institution as a multi-service provider, forces the company to operate in different markets, providing diversity of contexts and different levels of analysis. This type of data richness will tend to be found in large organizations, yet unattainable to study in depth due to their size. In this case, the data richness of a large scale is replicated, yet the relative size of the company makes it traceable.

RACC, the case study company, is a centenary institution, which offers member affiliation, road assistance, insurance brokering, traveling, sports, and other associated services to the household customer. In addition, they had no equal in their organizing of the three motor sports world championships: Formula 1; Moto Grand Prix; and World Rally Car. Its competitors arise from other automobile clubs and from specialized companies competing with each individual business unit. With 32 executives in key management positions, and a total of 1500 employees, RACC had achieved impressive growth over the last years, i.e. 30 percent in turnover, 16 percent in affiliated members, and 18 percent in cash flow until 2003.

## Collecting Data and Assembling the Story

We collected data on RACC's strategy-making process from May 2001 until June 2003, though the period studied covered from 1996 to 2003. Various sources of

**Table 5.1**   Indicative list of interviews at the RACC Automobile Club

| Level | Job title | Number of interviews in stage 1 | Number of interviews in stage 2 |
|---|---|---|---|
| 1 | Chief executive officer | 1 | 1 |
| 2 | Planning and supervision director | 1 | 1 |
| 2 | Operations and after-sales director | — | 1 |
| 2 | Marketing and corporate communication | — | 1 |
| 2 | Commercial director | — | 1 |
| 2 | Director of products and services | — | 1 |
| 3 | Strategic planning director | 2 | 4 |
| 4 | Planning staff | 1 | 1 |
| 4 | Planning staff | — | 1 |
|   | Total | 5 | 12 |

evidence were obtained, including interviews and public and private company documents as well as archival data. We conducted 17 interviews, ranging from 2 to 3 hours long, with a median of 140 minutes. A list of interviews and participants' levels appears in Table 5.1. All interviews were recorded and transcribed, totaling 230 pages. The 573 pages of company documents consisted of strategic planning files, as well as specific records and files on the definition and advance of 14 strategic initiatives. Archival data and company documents were filed into a database for trouble-free retrieval. Multiple sources of data gave us grounds to determine the internal and external contexts in which strategy making was developed at RACC. Additionally, having different types of evidence allowed for triangulation in data analysis (Miles and Huberman, 1994).

For data collection we followed a two-stage approach. The first stage's intention was to comprehend the entire strategy-making process. For this purpose we used company documents and in-depth interviews. Our aim was to describe the effect the objective function setting had on strategy development. This objective function became the starting point for the interplay between top and middle managers.

From the first stage's inquiry, it emerged that the CEO brought forth the objective function and then, a call for participation shaped strategy into specific initiatives. His appointment as the new CEO in October of 1995, stood as a turning point in the company's history. With his arrival the primary objective was to create order within the organization. Next, in 1996 he promoted the generation of initiatives and participation from all levels of the organization. In an exploration effort, managers were invited to develop projects, become their owners, and carry them out. This exploration period instilled a skill in developing team projects with clear and measurable goals. As time elapsed and projects succeeded, the CEO awareness of the aspiration of the organization became the strategic intent as an objective function. As such, the CEO announced an aggressive national expansion. Clearly set and grounded in the organization, the objective function became the guiding factor from where new initiatives could be generated. Thus, a new strategic exercise became necessary to translate the objective function into concrete strategic initiatives. This exercise was carried out by mid-2000. With the participation of 100 persons going down six levels in the organization, projects were formulated and developed by different multidisciplinary teams under the light of a clear and grounded objective function. In the 2002 annual report the CEO, referring to the development of the strategic plan, indicates that:

> The significant level to which those people who work in this organization identify with the club is a key to the Strategic Plan which is both ambitious and totally feasible.

We assembled RACC's case focusing on the interplay between top and middle managers. More specifically, we inductively extracted episodes of top and middle managers' interaction from the conveyance of the strategic intent as well as from managerial participation, as it was briefly narrated above.

## Examination of the Strategic Initiatives

### Data collection

In the second stage, we dug deeper into the evolution of specific strategic initiatives. Our aim was to learn about the interplay between the objective function setting and the generation of such initiatives. In order to gain insight into the subtle nature of these interactions, we selected the tactic of embedded units of analysis (Yin, 1994), i.e. strategic initiative and managerial action. Hence, managerial action was embedded from inception, the point at which the idea had appeared, to the conclusion of strategic initiatives. We inquired about managers' use of strategy as well as how the strategic intent was deployed along the life of strategic initiatives. A fundamental reason for centering on strategic initiatives was to provide the interviewee with a context of where managerial action takes place, avoiding anecdotal talk and centering on facts rather than opinions (Silverman, 2001).

We followed 14 strategic initiatives of different types. They covered a period of time ranging from two to seven years; the median was two and a half years. The initiatives were selected following snowball or chain sampling (Miles and Huberman, 1994).We incrementally identified examples in which the evolution pattern of initiatives varied, adding initiatives until no new pattern emerged. The 14 initiatives chosen accounted for 72 percent of the company's portfolio. Then, we collected the documents in which each initiative's evolution had been recorded. These were internal files that described the evaluation, description, and important events of each initiative. Next, we performed in-depth interviews with key managers, i.e. the unit's chief, responsible for each strategic initiative, and executives from the planning and supervision department (Table 5.1). An interview protocol ensured that the same themes were covered in each interview, aiming at reliability (Yin, 1994).

### Data analysis

Validity of the constructs was extracted from the interview data by considering the interviewee's causal explanations as testable, and contrasting it with other respondents and internal documents. In addition, looking for alternative explanations between the two researchers and directing attention to internal processes was self-imposed. We used three sources of evidence to analyze the evolution of each strategic initiative (Yin, 1994).

In order to analyze and interpret the evolution of strategic initiatives we have leaned on the Bower–Burgelman process model (Bower, 1970; Burgelman, 1983). This model portrays three organizational levels (top, middle, and bottom) and three process stages (definition, impetus, and commitment). For each initiative, along the guidelines of Miles and Huberman (1994), we codified interviews and archival data according to the three process stages and extracted which organizational level had been most influential in each stage.

The three distinct phases this process model recognizes are: (i) definition, which clarifies economic and technical considerations of a new investment; (ii) impetus, where proposals go through a process of evaluation; and (iii) commitment where resources are deployed around the new project. The three generic levels of managers are senior level, middle level, and bottom level. For our specific case we have deemed the CEO and board of directors as top level, the second and third descending levels of managers as middle level, and the bottom as the operating level managers. The second-level managers, who were the core informants of our interviews, played a pivotal role connecting the CEO and organizational members. On the one hand, they formed part of the "executive committee" with the CEO, and on the other hand they were local heads of their respective units. Consequently, we have deemed them as middle level in line with Floyd and Lane's (2000) description.

From the coding done for each initiative, we deduced a sequence to draw a critical path for each initiative. In this fashion, we portrayed which activities had driven the initiative across the three stages (definition, impetus, commitment), and which organizational levels had driven its development. Our intention was to untangle how the objective function interacted with the initiatives generated.

We used the Bower–Burgelman model because it displays a critical path documenting the strategy-making process. Thus, comparison of initiatives is made possible since they can be plotted together in the same matrix. Besides, this model allows the presentation of bottom-up and top-down forces simultaneously, offering a graphical representation for these two sources of influences.

**Patterns in strategic initiatives**

From the 14 strategic initiatives followed, 11 were carried out with different degrees of success. Of the others, one was kept at the resource allocation phase, and two had not succeeded. After drawing the critical paths for each initiative, we placed them in three groups, based on common patterns and characteristics. We named the first group "Flow", the second "Cascade", and the third "Spring", to illustrate the nature of their different features. We left out the two non-successful initiatives to be analyzed separately. A brief description of each strategic initiative studied, including its classification group is presented in Table 5.2.

The Flow group presents strategic initiatives originated and formulated at middle level, in this case at the unit's head level. The Flow initiatives were originated and evaluated at middle level. Once feasibility was assessed, they were presented to the top level. This presentation was not strategy blind, since typically initiatives had been

**Table 5.2**  Description of the 14 strategic initiatives studied

| | Initiatives | Type | Brief description |
|---|---|---|---|
| 1 | Geographic expansion | Cascade[2] | Main initiative, it embodies the core of the strategic intent. It sets exponential expansion as target |
| 2 | RACC Master Card expansion | Flow[2] | Expand the use of affiliated credit card to new territories |
| 3 | Driving academy product | Flow[2] | Customize and extend driving academy service |
| 4 | Paper work lobby | Flow[2] | Customize and expand paper work lobby |
| 5 | Increase travel service | Cascade[2] | Expand production of travel service |
| 6 | Expansion positioning | Flow[2] | Expand brand image in new territories |
| 7 | Mechanic shop car | Cascade[3] | Expand service to new territories |
| 8 | Renting vehicles | Failure[2] | Offer rental cars as a new integrative product |
| 9 | Travel services in new domain | Spring[3] | Sell travel services to small companies |
| 10 | Active channel development | Spring[1] | Develop alternative selling channels |
| 11 | Central operations service (COS) | Spring[1] | Centralize back office |
| 12 | Insurance | Flow[3] | Redefine intermediary relationship |
| 13 | Marco Polo | Cascade[2] | Offer customized travel products |
| 14 | Life insurance | Failure[3] | Create a life insurance company |

Note: [1] developed prior to the strategic plan; [2] developed alongside the strategic plan; [3] developed after the strategic plan.

raised within the spirit of the objective function. The second group, Cascade, portrays initiatives originated at top management level and developed by middle and bottom level. Cascade initiatives would appear to match the typical top-down approach. Yet, these were not set out by command, but rather as an extension of the agreed-upon objective function. The Spring group represents initiatives to some extent from bottom levels. Spring initiatives were developed through autonomous behavior but at the same time they embodied the objective function. Initiatives of this type were closely related to improving the bottom-level's daily work. This last group includes one initiative developed fully autonomously and two developed partially autonomously. The three groups include five, four, and three initiatives respectively. A diagram presenting the representative sequence for each group is shown in Figure 5.1, with an example of the analysis carried out for all 14 initiatives.

*Legitimation.*    When both top and middle management judged strategic initiatives to be valid and sound, they were carried out smoothly. After this common feature appeared, middle and top management interplay was resolved and mutual acceptance of aspirations and postures was reached. We have named this feature *legitimation*, as this term illustrates that strategic initiatives were officially allowed and intimately accepted by both middle and top management. Legitimation can be described as the property through which a proposed strategic initiative was made official and subsequently encouraged to be carried out. This feature showed that each other's

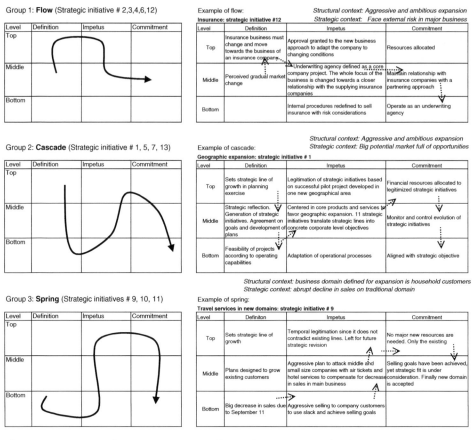

**Group 1: Flow** (Strategic initiative # 2,3,4,6,12)

| Level | Definition | Impetus | Commitment |
|---|---|---|---|
| Top | | | |
| Middle | | | |
| Bottom | | | |

Example of flow: — Structural context: Aggressive and ambitious expansion
Insurance: strategic initiative #12 — Strategic context: Face external risk in major business

| Level | Definition | Impetus | Commitment |
|---|---|---|---|
| Top | Insurance business must change and move towards the business of an insurance company. | Approval granted to the new business approach to adapt the company to changing conditions | Resources allocated |
| Middle | Perceived gradual market change | Underwriting agency defined as a core company project. The whole focus of the business is changed towards a closer relationship with the supplying insurance companies | Maintain relationship with insurance companies with a partnering approach |
| Bottom | | Internal procedures redefined to sell insurance with risk considerations | Operate as an underwriting agency |

**Group 2: Cascade** (Strategic initiative # 1, 5, 7, 13)

| Level | Definition | Impetus | Commitment |
|---|---|---|---|
| Top | | | |
| Middle | | | |
| Bottom | | | |

Structural context: Aggressive and ambitious expansion
Example of cascade: — Strategic context: Big potential market full of opportunities
Geographic expansion: strategic initiative # 1

| Level | Definition | Impetus | Commitment |
|---|---|---|---|
| Top | Sets strategic line of growth in planning exercise | Legitimation of strategic initiatives based on successful pilot project developed in one new geographic area | Financial resources allocated to legitimized strategic initiatives |
| Middle | Strategic reflection. Generation of strategic initiatives. Agreement on goals and development of plans | Centered in core products and services favor geographic expansion. 11 strategic initiatives translate strategic lines into concrete corporate level objectives | Monitor and control evolution of strategic initiatives |
| Bottom | Feasibility of projects according to operating capabilities | Adaptation of operational processes | Aligned with strategic objective |

**Group 3: Spring** (Strategic initiatives # 9, 10, 11)

| Level | Definition | Impetus | Commitment |
|---|---|---|---|
| Top | | | |
| Middle | | | |
| Bottom | | | |

Structural context: business domain defined for expansion is household customers
Example of spring: — Strategic context: abrupt decline in sales on traditional domain
Travel services in new domains: strategic initiative # 9

| Level | Definiton | Impetus | Commitment |
|---|---|---|---|
| Top | Sets strategic line of growth | Temporal legitimation since it does not contradict existing lines. Left for future strategic revision | No major new resources are needed. Only the existing |
| Middle | Plans designed to grow existing customers | Aggressive plan to attack middle and small size companies with air tickets and hotel services to compensate for decrease in sales in main business | Selling goals have been achieved, yet strategic fit is under consideration. Finally new domain is accepted |
| Bottom | Big decrease in sales due to September 11 | Aggressive selling to company customers to use slack and achieve selling goals | |

**Figure 5.1**   Groups of strategic initiatives (drawn from common development patterns)

impressions had been validated, regarding desirable goals and courses of action. The 11 successful initiatives were legitimized, regardless of our classification group

Four procedural conditions stood out as necessary for legitimation to occur. First, through strategy making, each other's roles had to be clearly set. Second, at no point could one actor proceed as judge and jury at the same time. In the executive committee, as a collegiate body, its members either presented a project or judged it, but not both. Third, objectivity had to prevail over any other considerations. Analysis of possible options as opposed to an advocate posture, as well as reflection and discussion, relegated political activity and rendered legitimation. Finally, evaluation and analysis as the basic means to produce strategic conversation had to be done thoroughly.

These four conditions illustrate how legitimation was a result of both top and middle levels' sources of influence. However, three initiatives did not succeed in getting support. These were the two non-successful initiatives and one in the Spring group (i.e. 7, 13, and 9, respectively). The main reason they did not achieve full success was that they were not deemed as valid either by the top or the middle level. This fact shows the importance of legitimation as a property that validates strategic initiatives through mutual compromise.

*Scratching.*    Top management did not grant legitimation alone. It also required unit-level management to positively assess the initiative. This assessment was developed through what informants called "scratching on the project". Scratching was described as the thorough assessment for feasibility, which resulted in unit-level managers either believing in the initiative or discarding it. The concept of scratching was used in the sense of digging beyond the surface, as deep as possible, to evaluate potential value and viability of an initiative, particularly if new capabilities were needed. Once an initiative had been scratched on, unit-level managers would typically set goals, timing, an action plan, and pertinent indicators for the initiative in order to further propose it. If new capabilities were considered necessary the proposal had to offer a way to achieve them. Scratching was aimed at rendering sufficient arguments for the initiative to be brought for legitimation. Top management appraisal, on the other hand, was done based on the quality of the arguments derived from scratching, as well as fit for the initiative with the objective function. The CEO, the rest of the unit managers, and at times even the board, acted as judges in a committee, while the unit manager in charge of the initiative would have to defend it with his/her team. This stage was where the four conditions for legitimation were crucial for the process. Although the four conditions were met in all three groups to achieve legitimation, the sequence of events differed for each group.

## Legitimation and scratching in each group

In the Flow group, scratching was performed regardless of top management direction, yet the objective function was kept as the guiding element. Once the scratching phase was developed, initiatives were presented to the executive committee. The strategic initiative number 12 is illustrative. This initiative was a reaction to changes from the external environment, which demanded a major restructuring of the insurance intermediary business. After the strategic plan had been set, it emerged that the future of the main business was threatened. Since adaptation of the business model was mandatory, legitimation was achieved upfront. Middle-level scratching was carried out and top management gave way for them to generate and carry out a new business model. The legitimation mechanism made official a new way to head towards the objective function, since the former plan was not a stiff and rigid program. The evolution of initiative 12 suggests that, although needed change came from an external event, the second-level and top management interplay unraveled the predicament. Top management was judicious enough to let second-level management figure out the specific characteristics the project would take, trusting that the outcome would be the best possible.

In the Cascade group, top management, namely the board of directors and the CEO, delivered initiatives. Next, one unit manager was given the assignment. Then he had to scratch for its feasibility and potential value with the unit's team. Once assessed, the initiatives were presented to the executive committee. In the Cascade group, unless the initiative was widely considered as crucial, it was hard for it to reach legitimation. Support in the organization depended on how grounded the initiative was in the organizational members' aspirations. In one of the non-successful initiatives, namely initiative number 8, the definition was ambiguously devised by top management, not seized by middle level, and thus lay dormant. Though it was deemed to fit the existing strategy by top level, it was not grounded in the organization. This issue prevented the interplay between top and lower level managers. Without this interplay, no legitimation took place. While the initiative was kept in their portfolio, it was never further developed.

However, not all Cascade group initiatives failed. Although initiative number 1 was also developed in Cascade, it was deeply grounded in the organization as the logical path for the company's growth, and it was the core of the objective function. In addition, it embodied a strong aspiration for RACC's employees. The subsequent scratching activity at unit level was intense enough to provide ideas and generate the capabilities to make this initiative a reality. The initiative, though induced, was not imposed. It was able to fall into the logic of organizational members, and it was proven in a pilot project before it was definitely launched. The evolution of this initiative suggests that change can be achieved through induced strategic initiatives. Successful renewal, exemplified by this new market–product orientation, was done top-down, yet grounded in the organization. The directing role of top management was crucial in the Cascade group. It was not a heroic CEO that was essential, but his ability to perceive the demands of the social context and enact them.

The initiatives from the Spring group were delivered by line managers, mostly with urgency and as response to market stimuli. For this reason, scratching was done either immediately or once the new initiative was already operating. Although scratching could provide the rigorous and objective analysis needed for legitimation, it generally lacked the strategic fit with the objective function. This is the case of initiative number 9. Due to external events, the installed capacity to sell travel services to household customers was used for small enterprise customers. This autonomous initiative was allowed, but not legitimized. It was seen as useful to face a temporary crisis and achieve sales objectives, but doubts remained on its fit with the objective function. Although it increased revenue, it was not located in the market desired by the company. In terms of Burgelman (1983), initiatives such as this one were not allowed to determine the strategic context. The "strategic context" reflects attempts of managers "to link autonomous strategic behavior at the product market level into the corporation's concept of strategy" (Burgelman, 1983: 66). In the present study, the corporate concept of strategy contained in the objective function, guided and fostered the springing of strategic initiatives.

Evidence from the development of strategic initiatives found at RACC guided us through the theory development process. The diagram in Figure 5.2 describes the essential elements of the evolution of strategic initiatives. The key issue in the figure is that the interplay between top and middle management brings into being strategic initiatives. This interplay is the common ground by which the initiatives of both top and middle level managers can reach legitimation. Idea generation and issue selling originate from all levels of the organization (i.e., top management (TM), middle management (MM), and organizational members (bottom level)), yet stem from a

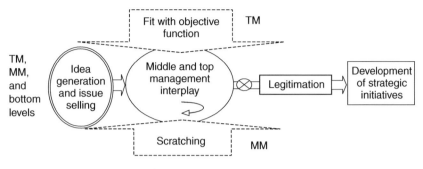

**Figure 5.2**    Strategic initiatives within strategy-making

previously accepted objective function. Then, initiatives are brought into middle and top management interplay. If this interplay produces legitimation, strategic initiatives are carried out. If the initiative is not granted legitimation it would tend to get stuck. The process conditions for legitimation to happen are the four conditions mentioned before: distinctive roles; not to play judge and jury; objective discussion; and rigorous analysis. The content conditions of each initiative were to fit the objective function and to pass the scratching scrutiny.

## Conclusions: Strategy Originated in a Social Process

In the present chapter we have tackled some aspects of the origin of strategy from the interplay between managerial levels. If top-down sources of influences were the sole foundation of strategy making, it would be analogous to Burgelman (1991), where these influences are seen as only maintaining the status quo. Conversely, under a strictly bottom-up influence, scarce strategic renewal, which could be originated as projects are brought up without a guiding purpose. From our case study data, we have suggested that the junction of these sources is what generates strategy in use. Particularly, we have described how the objective function can inspire the development of initiatives that transform an aspiration into concrete managerial actions. In this line we have put forth the concept of legitimation as the mechanism that consolidates cooperation between managerial levels.

   Legitimation is different from previously used concepts as agreement (Iaquinto and Fredrickson, 1997; Jehn, 1995; Wooldridge and Floyd, 1989) or consensus (Dess and Priem, 1995; Homburg, Krohmer, and Workman, 1998; Iaquinto and Fredrickson, 1997). While consensus, generally operationalized as agreement, is a necessary condition for coordinated action (Barr and Huff, 1997), legitimation integrates agreement but adds a connection to the social context of the organization. "Actors do not behave or decide as atoms outside the social context, nor do they adhere slavishly to a script written for them . . . Their attempts at purposive action are instead embedded in concrete, ongoing systems of social relationships" (Granovetter, 1985: 485). Legitimation is not only agreement on certain premises, but also a compromise to act that stems from the social interaction of the managerial interplay.

Legitimation is also the process that shapes values and beliefs in translating strategy into managerial initiatives.

The evidence from this study confirms the findings of others, which have found that a guiding character of strategy and its internalization from organizational members is desirable among companies. To Ghoshal and Bartlett (1994), shared norms and values that shape the way individual managers think and act, seek to maintain organizational coherence in the face of increasing complexity and uncertainty. In addition, to Lovas and Ghoshal (2000), the guiding character of strategy is suggested as a key way to achieve coherence. Similarly, to Masifern and Vilà (1998), strategy guides daily action if coherence is achieved through a shared framework in the minds of managers. Evidence at RACC indicates that the participative practices enhance strategy-making value. When a major part of the managerial levels interact to germinate strategy and further deploy it into specific projects, the effort to focus the objective function provides guidelines for managerial action.

The objective function was not mere abstraction. As evidenced in the present study it drove conscious adaptation. It took root and inspired managers to generate initiatives because it was perceived as feasible and ambitious, but at the same time nurtured from the aspirations of the organization. Under these conditions, the induced strategy-making process enables the objective function to bind the organization. The analysis of this case study offers a view on how strategy is built by managers' interplay, and in turn used to guide managers. Strategy formation seems to be more efficiently made if nurtured by a broad-based managerial participation, and ambitiously triggered by top management.

This chapter complements the literature on actors of strategy. The "issue-selling" framework essentially posits that middle managers learn how to pack and sell initiatives to top management (Dutton *et al.*, 2001). We add the concept of legitimation, within the managerial interplay, as a manifestation of "sold issues", and describe a process through which issues are negotiated. In addition, we supplement the middle management involvement literature (Floyd and Wooldridge, 1992, 2000) by exploring the concept of scratching, through which initiatives are proposed. Finally, we explore top and middle management interplay as a generator of strategy, further exploring the notion proposed by Hart (1992).

The results of this study encourage further research in a larger number of organizations, yet this illustrative case signals a future path. This path calls for the analysis of the interplay between middle and top management in different contexts. Describing the particulars of legitimation under different settings would extend the reach of understanding on the origins of strategy.

We are able to state three concluding remarks. *First*, the legitimation mechanism, through which strategic initiatives are brought into being, is a promising construct through which the interplay between top management and organizational members is reflected. *Second*, generating strategy with active participation and mutual deliberation, but without abdication from the directing role of top management, nurtures strategy internalization. *Finally*, renewal can take place not only through autonomous behavior, but also via conscious adaptation, provided that both aspirations and contributions of managers at different levels are legitimized. Overall, the results of the study emphasize the importance of generating strategy with guided and active participation to obtain subsequently conscious action.

## Acknowledgments

We thank Africa Ariño, Gregory Dess, Steven Floyd, James Fredrickson, Anne Huff, Michael Lubatkin, and Lori Rockett for their helpful comments on earlier drafts of this chapter. Together with them, the editors of this volume, particularly Claus Jacobs, and one anonymous reviewer increased the quality of our work. Despite our appreciation to these scholars, mistakes remain our own.

## References

Barr, P.S. and Huff, A.S. 1997. Seeing isn't believing: Understanding diversity in the timing of strategic response. *Journal of Management Studies*, **34**: 337–70.

Berger, P.L. and Luckman, T. 1967. *The Social Construction of Reality*. New York: Doubleday Anchor.

Bower, J.L. 1970. *Managing the Resource Allocation Process: A Study of Corporate Planning and Investment*. Boston, MA: Division of Research, Graduate School of Business Administration, Harvard University.

Burgelman, R.A. 1983. A process model of internal corporate venturing in the diversified major firm. *Administrative Science Quarterly*, **28**: 223–44.

Burgelman, R.A. 1991. Intraorganizational ecology of strategy making and organizational adaptation: Theory and field research. *Organization Science*, **2**: 239–62.

Burgelman, R.A. 1996. A process model of strategic business exit: Implications for an evolutionary perspective on strategy. *Strategic Management Journal*, **17**: 193–214.

Chakravarthy, B. and Doz, Y. 1992. Strategy process research: Focusing on corporate self-renewal. *Strategic Management Journal*, **13**: 5–14.

Dess, G.G. and Priem, R. 1995. Consensus-performance research: Theoretical and empirical extensions, *Journal of Management Studies*, **32**: 401–17.

Dutton, J.E. and Ashford, S.J. 1993. Selling issues to top management. *Academy of Management Review*, **18**: 397–428.

Dutton, J.E., Ashford, S.J., O'Neill, R.M., and Lawrence, K.A. 2001. Moves that matter: Issue selling and organizational change. *Academy of Management Journal*, **44**: 716–36.

Eisenhardt, K.M. 1989. Building theories form case study research. *Academy of Management Review*, **14**: 532–50.

Floyd, S.W. and Wooldridge, B. 1992. Middle management involvement in strategy and its association with strategic type. *Strategic Management Journal*, **13**: 153–67.

Floyd, S.W. and Wooldridge, B. 2000. *Building Strategy from the Middle: Reconceptualizing Strategy Process*. London: Sage.

Floyd, S.W. and Lane, P.J. 2000. Strategizing throughout the organization: Managing role conflict in strategic renewal. *Academy of Management Review*, **25**: 154–78.

Ghoshal, S. and Bartlett, C. 1994. Linking organizational context and managerial action: The dimensions of quality of management. *Strategic Management Journal*, **15**: 91–112.

Granovetter, M. 1985. Economic action and social structure: The problem of embeddedness, *American Journal of Sociology*, **91**: 481–510.

Guth, W.D. and MacMillan, I.C. 1986. Strategy implementation versus middle management self-interest. *Strategic Management Journal*, **7**: 313–27.

Hambrick, D.C. 1998. Corporate coherence and top management team. In D.A. Nadler, D.C. Hambrick, and M. Tushman (eds.), *Navigating Change: How CEOs, Top Teams and Boards Steer Transformation*, pp. 123–40. Boston, MA: Harvard University Press.

Hamel, G. and Prahalad, C.K. 1989. Strategic intent. *Harvard Business Review*, May/June: 63–77.

Hart, S.L. 1992. An integrative framework for strategy-making process. *Academy of Management Review*, 17: 327–51.

Homburg, C., Krohmer, H., and Workman, Jr., J.P. 1998. Strategic consensus and performance: The role of strategy type and market-related dynamism. *Strategic Management Journal*, 20: 339–57.

Iaquinto, A.L. and Fredrickson, J.W. 1997. Top management team agreement about the strategic decision process: A test of some of its determinants and consequences. *Strategic Management Journal*, 18: 63–75.

Jehn, K. 1995. A multimethod examination of the benefits and detriments of intragroup conflict. *Administrative Science Quarterly*, 40: 256–82.

Lovas, B. and Ghoshal, S. 2000. Strategy as guided evolution. *Strategic Management Journal*, 21: 875–96.

Masifern, E. and Vilà, J. 1998. Interconnected mindsets: Strategic thinking and the strategy concept. In M.A. Hitt, J.E. Ricart i Costa, and R.D. Nixon (eds.), *New Managerial Mindsets: Organizational Transformation and Strategy Implementation*, pp. 15–34. Chichester, UK: Wiley.

Miles, M.B. and Huberman, A.M. 1994. *Qualitative Data Analysis: An Expanded Sourcebook* (second ed.). Thousand Oaks, CA: Sage.

Mintzberg, H. 1978. Patterns in strategy formation. *Management Science*, 24: 934–48.

Mintzberg, H., Ahlstrand, B., and Lampel, J. 1998. *Strategy Safari*. New York: The Free Press.

Silverman, D. 2001. *Interpreting Qualitative Data: Methods for Analysing Talk, Text and Interaction* (second ed.). London: Sage.

Wooldridge, B. and Floyd, S.W. 1989. Strategic process effects on consensus. *Strategic Management Journal*, 10: 295–302.

Yin, R.K. 1994. *Case Study Research: Design and Methods* (second ed.). London: Sage.

# CHAPTER SIX

# Strategy Creation as Serious Play

## Claus Jacobs, Matt Statler

## Introduction

Strategy researchers seem to have struggled to develop a theory of strategy creation. We believe this difficulty might be eased somewhat if the field had a notion of intentionality that allowed us to acknowledge emergent change. We here present *serious play* as a descriptive framework for activities through which the conditions of the possibility of emergence may be intentionally created. In this sense, the purpose of this chapter is *to consider strategy creation as a kind of serious play*.

## Intending Emergence

Recently, Regnér (2003) observed that there are relatively few answers to the question of how managers actually create strategy in practice. Whittington (2003) similarly calls for a more enhanced, detailed understanding of the where and how of strategy creation. Cockburn and Henderson (2000) have taken an important step in this direction and investigated the initial conditions of the origins of competitive advantage in strategy creation. In response to these observations and preliminary efforts, we approach the task of developing a theory of strategy creation with two assumptions: first, that strategy is intentional; and second, that it is emergent. Guided by these assumptions, we consider how and to what extent the emergence of strategy can be intended.

We assume that strategy is intentional. The standard notion of intentionality that is presupposed in strategy research refers to actions that are *deliberately directed* towards the achievement of some *purpose*. For example, Chandler (1962: 15) referred to strategy's generic purpose as the "determination of the basic long-term goals and objectives of an enterprise and the adoption of courses of action and the allocation of resources necessary for carrying out these goals". In a distinct, but similar formulation strategy has been characterized as a rational, top-down process through which goals are identified and achieved by the firm (e.g. Ansoff, Declerck, and Hayes, 1976).

More recently, the purpose of strategy has been defined as the attempt to provide the organization with a direction (Rumelt, Schendel, and Teece, 1994) and as a means for achieving sustainable competitive advantage (Hoskisson *et al.*, 1999).

More specifically, within *strategy content* research, the industrial organization approach defines the purpose of strategy as the matching of external market opportunities with internal firm competencies (e.g. Porter, 1980, 1985). In contrast, the resource-based view argues that the purpose of strategy involves the identification and development of internal, hard-to-imitate firm characteristics that generate above-market returns (e.g. Barney, 1991, 1997; Wernerfelt, 1984, 1995). The *strategy process* research stream focuses its efforts on the systematic examination and description of the role of specific actors in strategy as well as the importance of a variety of context factors (e.g. Floyd, 2000; Floyd and Wooldridge, 1997; Mintzberg and McHugh, 1985; Pettigrew, 1985). And yet, this research stream remains content to analyze the different roles and context factors that constrain or enable the achievement of goals and objectives, without calling into question the intentionality that guides the analysis.

While we acknowledge the many points of distinction between the different views cited here, it seems that they all presuppose a notion of intentionality that involves clearly defined purposes and actions that are deliberately directed to achieve those purposes. In each case, a linear, causal relationship between intentional actions and performance outcomes for the firm is presupposed.[1] The problem with this notion of intentionality is that it cannot adequately accommodate or explain strategy's inherently emergent character.

Indeed, we also assume that strategy is emergent. Mintzberg and Waters (1985) were the first to differentiate between deliberate and emergent strategies. They applied this distinction in such a way as to call attention to the fact that strategies proceed not just from the directives that are issued by the leadership team, but also from ideas that were never implemented, and from what emerged during the journey. In that respect, Mintzberg argued that the only way we can comprehend a strategy is in retrospect, as a pattern in a stream of actions. In an unrelated but parallel development, emergence has been theorized extensively within the field of complex adaptive systems theory (Holland, 1995). Here, the idea is that complex systems, defined as systems of agents, experience nonlinear interaction among themselves and tend to exhibit sudden and often surprising behavior at another level of scale. Just as the pattern of the ground appears to change as you take off in an airplane and gain height, complex adaptive systems exhibit the same kind of shift of patterns. This "emergent" effect is seen in natural as well as social systems. Thus, in accordance with this metaphorical concept borrowed from the natural sciences and systems theory (and as a further specification of Mintzberg's colloquial use of the term), strategy can be considered an emergent phenomenon because it involves a series of complex interactions between individual agents.

For example, Stacey (1996: 287) portrays emergence as the unintended, unpredictable outcomes ("global patterns") of intentional behavior of actors in social systems "that cannot be produced from the local rules of behaviour that produce them." Similarly applying complexity and systems theory in the context of strategy research, MacIntosh and Maclean (1999: 301) refer to emergence as a property of a system characterized by nonequilibrium conditions as well as nonlinear, random developments that "create new system configurations in a way which is largely indeterminate." As descriptively compelling as these theories of emergent strategy making might be, it seems that they – in our view unnecessarily – struggle to leave room for intentionality. Indeed, the emergent pattern of action cannot be chosen or predicted in advance, and thus it cannot provide a purpose to which actions may be deliberately directed.

Thus while we are willing to grant that strategy creation might well involve a deliberate, conscious act, or even a series of such acts, we do not presuppose that there is or must be a direct, causal relationship between these intentional actions and the outcomes or results for the firm. Indeed, we assume that an irreducible multiplicity of other factors bear systemically upon the moment as well, contributing to its dynamics in a way as to make the outcomes of any particular action unpredictable. In this sense, the notion of "strategy creation" implies a certain paradox: is it possible to intend emergence? How can one engage in the paradoxical task of intentionally creating an inherently emergent phenomenon?

In search for a better understanding of this apparent paradox, we here consider the similarly paradoxical concept of serious play. In the following section, we will explore how serious play might provide us with a more subtle way to reflect on intentionality, emergence, and the relationship between them.

## The Adjacent Possible: Playing Seriously

Psychologists have long recognized that play serves the primary development of cognitive skills such as the capacity to conduct logical operations (especially following Piaget and Inhelder, 1958) as well as the capacity to understand meaning in specific contexts (Vygotsky and Cole, 1978). At another level of analysis, play has been shown to enhance the emotional sense of competence or fulfillment that may serve as a precondition for effective cognitive functioning (Erikson, 1963). In turn, sociologists and anthropologists have identified the crucial importance of play for the development of the skills generally required to function in social communities (Mead, 2001), as well as for the development of particular social institutions (with regard to law, religion, government, cf. Huizinga, 1950) and forms of cultural identity (Geertz, 1973).

Organizational theory has explored the possibility that *play* might provide people who *work* with an adjacent possible mode of activity, one that has significant benefits even though it functions at the boundaries of instrumental rationality (March, 1979).[2] Following this line of thinking, we should not presuppose an unnecessarily fixed and static notion of the "goal," "purpose," or "objective". In this context, the "technology of foolishness" requires strategy makers to acknowledge that goals change with time, as do the values on the basis of which the decisions were made to pursue those goals. This ambiguity functions as one of the limits of intentional action within behavioral theories of decision making. In such circumstances, playfulness appears to provide:

> . . . a natural outgrowth of our standard view of reason. A strict insistence on purpose, consistency and rationality limits our ability to find new purposes. Play relaxes that insistence to allow us to act "unintelligently" or "irrationally", or "foolishly" to explore

alternative ideas of possible purposes and alternative concepts of behavioural consistency" (March, 1979: 77)

As we have seen above, a theory of strategy creation similarly requires a notion of intentionality that can accommodate emergent change. What March provides us with, is the suggestion that such a notion can be modeled on the characteristics of *play*.

In the interest of identifying such characteristics more precisely, we turn to consider how *play* has been understood in adjacent streams of literature. Most broadly speaking, play has been characterized as a "a mode of being" characterized by "to-and-fro movements" that take place "in-between" participants (Gadamer, 2002: 101ff). This philosophical definition directs our attention to the "modal" (i.e., processual) characteristics of human action. It furthermore provides an ontological frame for the following two descriptive characteristics of the playful mode of human activity: the first, pertaining to human adaptive variability (Sutton-Smith, 1997), and the second, pertaining to the imaginative creation of meaning (Winnicott, 1971). Our working definition will be: *Play is a mode of human activity that increases adaptive variability through the imaginative creation of meaning.*

A prominent line of argument from the field of educational psychology has characterized play as a mode of activity that enhances human adaptive potential (Sutton-Smith, 1997). It is thus precisely the diversity of play activities (not to mention the diversity of concepts of play) which recommends them most for our consideration in the context of strategy creation. Because play "contains so much nonsense, so much replication, and is so flexible . . . it is a prime domain for the actualization of whatever the brain contains. And for that matter, speaking in behavioral rather than neurological terms, [it] is typically a primary place for the expression of anything that is humanly imaginable" (1997: 226). Phrased descriptively with respect to different modes of human action, play thus appears as an "exemplar of cultural variability" that provides an arena within which new alternatives may legitimately be explored (1997: 230). This series of claims extends March's account by conceptualizing play not simply as the boundary condition of productive work, but as the primary frame within which human adaptive variation occurs.

Furthermore, it suggests that such variability pertains not only to our motor reflexes, but also additionally to our capacity to make sense of the world that surrounds us. A distinct stream of psychological research describes playas the process through which meaning is created as such (Winnicott, 1971). Following this influential line of thinking, the infant first attaches meaning to a "transitional object" that marks an ambiguous area of experience within which the self is not fully differentiated from the environment. This transitional object involves more than merely the material object as such (e.g., a source of food). Additionally, the transitional play involves a *primary process of object relations* through which differentiations of inside and outside, self and other, and real and unreal are actually in the process of being accomplished. In turn, this primary experience gives rise to a series of increasingly complex patterns of relationships (i.e., meaning). These patterns are not lost with the passage of childhood, but instead retained throughout life "in the intense experiencing that belongs to the arts and to religion and to imaginative living, and to creative scientific work" (Winnicott, 1971: 14). In this context, play refers precisely to those processes through which people imaginatively create meaning in ambiguous circumstances. Synthesizing these two lines of argument, we suggest that the adaptive variability of play can be associated with the human imaginative capacity to create and discover meaning. Phrased descriptively, through imaginative play, humans cultivate adaptive potential. The question is then: *To what extent can people play with the deliberate intent to adapt?*

From a certain perspective, we can say that people are intrinsically, not extrinsically, motivated to play. The term "autotelic", referring to something that serves as an end in itself rather than a means to some other end, has been used to distinguish play and other flow-like experiences from work (e.g. Csikszentmihalyi, 1990). Following this strict terminological distinction, as soon as someone tries to accomplish something else (e.g., making money) through play, then the activity becomes "telic" or goal-oriented. If someone engages in play with the intent to produce some determinate goal or outcome, then the playful mode of activity shifts to become work.[3] This distinction has significant consequences for our consideration of the adaptive potential of play – can such potential be cultivated deliberately, or if we play with the intent to adapt, then have we strictly speaking ceased to play and begun to work? At issue is the extent to which people can be intrinsically motivated by the play activity itself, and nevertheless still play with the intent to allow as-yet indeterminate benefits to emerge.

In this regard, the concept of *serious play* appears to preserve the intrinsic motivation of play activities (as well as the nonlinear causality of emergent change) while focusing intentionality not on the emergent, adaptive outcomes themselves, but rather *on the conditions for their possibility*. Because Gadamer (2002: 102) accepts the apparent conceptual paradox of the phrase "serious play", and affirms it as a crucial aspect of what he refers to as the playful mode of being, it is worthwhile to cite him at length:

> Play has a special relation to what is serious . . . More important, play itself contains its own, even sacred, seriousness. Yet, in playing, all those purposive relations that determine active and caring existence have not simply disappeared, but are curiously suspended. The player himself knows that play is only play and that it exists in a world determined by the seriousness of purposes. But he does not know this in such a way that, as a player, he actually *intends* this relation to seriousness.

Following this line of thinking, one may play in full knowledge that the activity might have potentially important benefits. And yet, one does not presume to be able to know in advance what those benefits might be, so in this sense the goal remains indeterminate. Similarly, one does not presume to be able to know in advance what the relationship might be between the intentional action and its outcome. In spite of these limitations, one can nevertheless play seriously, that is, with the intent to increase adaptive variability through the imaginative creation of meaning. Our descriptive claim is thus that when we engage in serious play, we create the conditions for the possibility of the emergence of new forms of meaning and new patterns of action.

## Reflecting on Strategy Creation as Serious Play

We began by assuming that strategy involves both intentionality and emergence, and that based on these assumptions, strategy creation would somewhat paradoxically involve *intending emergence*. We found that the theoretical difficulties presented by this apparent paradox arise in part due to a need within strategy research for a more subtle understanding of both intentionality and emergence. In an effort to develop this understanding by reference to an adjacent possible activity, we considered play as a distinct mode of human activity characterized by the enhancement of adaptive variability through the imaginative creation of meaning. Extending March's claim that we should "accept playfulness in organizations" (1979: 80), our suggestion is that we should consider *strategy creation as a form of serious play*. We now consider the theoretical and methodological implications of this claim.

First and foremost, a better theoretical understanding of *intending emergence* is required if the field is to develop a theory of strategy creation. We have taken an initial step in this direction and problematized the mode of intentionality by identifying two variables that merit further consideration: the indeterminacy of the objective, and the indeterminacy of the relationship between intentional action and outcome. Traditional business logic begins with the definition of strategic objectives. But as we have seen, the playful *creation* of such strategic objectives might involve an ongoing, transitional process characterized by fundamental ambiguity and indeterminacy. Similarly, strategy research traditionally seems to presuppose a linear, causal relationship between intentional action and outcome. But as we have seen, we must acknowledge the limits of the capacity of any single actor to bring about change in a complex world. Given these limitations, the most we can hope for is to create the conditions for the possibility of emergence.

It is interesting to note that the play theories introduced above were built empirically on descriptive, narrative and participatory accounts of play activities and experiences. We noted at the outset how, by contrast, the field of strategy research lacks descriptive accounts of strategy creation. In this light, we can only begin to speculate about what the most relevant conditions for its emergence might be. And yet, if we allow our speculation to be guided by the concept of serious play, then we must acknowledge that cognitive, social, and emotional factors are all potentially relevant for consideration.

As a single example of how such research might proceed, we find a promising avenue in the work of philosopher Mark Johnson (1987), who discusses different modes of intentionality as he explores the embodied, perceptual aspects of the human imagination. On his analysis, even the most basic modes of logic (i.e., must, may, can) have their roots in embodied experience. In light of such a claim, it seems likely that future strategy research could address a wider range of variables, including embodied, perceptual, and affective dimensions of experience, in such a way as to enable a more precise differentiation of the distinct modes of intentionality that pertain to strategy creation.

Secondly, with respect to the methodological implications relevant to studying such phenomena, one systematic challenge consists in the fact that researchers are rarely present during the process of its creation. As Regnér (2003) and Cockburn and Henderson (2003) indicate, future research should thus focus on the "initial conditions" of strategy creation. But how exactly does one study these conditions? Clearly, a detached observer can hardly understand what is going on in the context she studies. In line with Chakravarthy and Doz (1992), we agree that more exploratory, participatory research is needed if we are to understand the origins of strategy. What is considered intentional or emergent depends on the local, contextual practices through which meaning is intersubjectively negotiated and reified. In this regard, we are inspired by the recent call to explore and understand "the detailed processes and practices which constitute the day-to-day activities of organizational life and which relate to strategic outcomes" (Johnson, Melin, and Whittington, 2003: 3). This stream of research conceives of practice as an ontology rather than as a phenomenon (Orlikowski, 2000, 2002), and thereby directs our attention to contextual, local activities that previously went unnoticed (e.g. Balogun, Huff, and Johnson, 2003; Heracleous, 2003; Jarzabkowski, 2003; Whittington, 1996, 2003).

It should be acknowledged that a great deal of strategy research takes place when the researchers engage with firms in a consultative role. Rather than presenting a risk to objectivity and generalizability, we believe that such situations might provide researchers with an opportunity to experiment with the contextual conditions (as well as the mode) of strategy development practices such as management retreats or strategy workshops.

One illustrative example of this kind of research has dealt with the relationship between strategy process and strategy content (Roos, Victor, and Statler, forthcoming). In a series of consulting and executive education assignments, the authors engaged with three top management teams from different organizations in strategy development processes. With the explicit consent of the participants, they experimented with alternative modes and media of strategy creation. In particular, the mode was characterized by different levels of experience (i.e., cognitive, social, and emotional), and a more playful, open attitude toward emergence. The medium, in turn, consisted of small, three-dimensional construction toy materials, which the participants used to make and express meaning about phenomena relevant to their strategy. Throughout this series of action research experiments, attention was paid to the relationship between the change in the mode and medium process variables to see if there was a corresponding change at the level of the strategy content. The authors suggest in conclusion that new strategy content can emerge when the mode and medium constraints on a strategy process are changed.

We believe that additional experimentation of this sort might shed light on different modes of intentionality, the variability of the conditions for emergence, and ultimately, on strategy creation as such. If we pursued such an approach, might not the field of strategy research itself become more *seriously playful*?

## Acknowledgments

We are grateful to Bala Chakravarthy, Steven Floyd, and Patrick Regnér as well as our colleagues at the Imagination Lab Foundation for their valuable feedback and suggestions on earlier versions of the manuscript.

## Notes

1. We acknowledge the related notion of "strategic intent" (Hamel and Prahalad, 1989). However, rather than a normative suggestion, we aim at an analytical perspective on intentionality.

2. We have chosen March as a starting point for our argument in this section because, although a number of organizational theorists have considered play (e.g., with regard to identity and career choice (Ibarra, 2003), behavior motivation (Glynn, 1994), creativity (Amabile, 1996), and product development (Schrage, 2000)), he has considered play not only normatively or as an object of study, but additionally as part of a descriptive theoretical framework.

3. Play theorist Roger Caillois (1961) considers what is perhaps the most difficult borderline activity, gambling, and claims that even though money may change hand between participants, because there is no wealth produced through the game of chance itself (excepting of course the wealth that may be created by a casino that makes a business of providing gamblers with games of chance), it cannot be considered productive. Relatively easier to distinguish are professional and amateur sporting activities, where on one hand people compete for profit and on the other hand people compete "for the love of the game".

## References

Amabile, T. 1996. *Creativity in Context*. Boulder, CO: Westview Press.

Ansoff, H.I., Declerck, R.P., and Hayes, R.L. 1976. *From Strategic Planning to Strategic Management*. New York: Wiley.

Balogun, J., Huff, A.S., and Johnson, P. 2003. Three responses to the methodological challenges of studying strategizing. *Journal of Management Studies*, **40**(1): 197–224.

Barney, J.B. 1991. Firm resources and sustained competitive advantage. *Journal of Management*, **17**: 99–120.

Barney, J.B. 1997. *Gaining and Sustaining Competitive Advantage*. Reading, MA: Addison-Wesley.

Caillois, R. 1961. *Man, Play, and Games*. Chicago, IL: University of Illinois University Press.

Chakravarthy, B.S. and Doz, Y. 1992. Strategy process research: Focusing on corporate self-renewal, *Strategic Management Journal*, **13**: 5–13.

Chandler, A.D. 1962. *Strategy and Structure*. Boston, MA: MIT Press.

Cockburn, I.M. and Henderson, R.M. 2000. Untangling the origins of competitive advantage. *Strategic Management Journal*, **21**: 1123–45.

Csikszentmihalyi, M. 1990. *Flow: The Psychology of Optimal Experience*. New York: Harper and Row.

Erikson, E.H. 1963. *Youth: Change and Challenge*. New York: Basic Books.

Floyd, S.W. 2000. Strategizing throughout the organization: Managing role conflict in strategic renewal. *Academy of Management Review*, **25**: 154–77.

Floyd, S.W. and Wooldridge, B. 1997. Middle management's strategic influence and organizational performance. *Journal of Management Studies*, **34**: 465–87.

Gadamer, H.G. 2002. *Truth and Method*. New York: Continuum.

Geertz, C. 1973. *The Interpretation of Cultures: Selected Essays*. New York: Basic Books.

Glynn, M. 1994. Effects of work, task cues, and play task cues on information processing, judgment, and motivation. *Journal of Applied Psychology*, **79**(1): 34–45.

Hamel, G., and Prahalad, C.K. 1989. Strategic intent. *Harvard Business Review*, **67**: 63–76.

Heracleous, L. 2003. *Strategy and Organization: Realizing Strategic Management*. Cambridge, UK: Cambridge University Press.

Holland, J. 1995. *Hidden Order*. Reading, MA: Perseus Books.

Hoskisson, R.E., Hitt, M.A., Wan, W.P., and Yiu, D. 1999. Theory and research in strategic management: Swings of a pendulum. *Journal of Management*, **25**(3): 417–56.

Huizinga, J. 1950. *Homo ludens: A Study of the Play Element in Culture*. London: Routledge, Kegan Paul.

Ibarra, H. 2003. *Working Identity: Unconventional Strategies for Reinventing Your Career.* Boston, MA: Harvard Business School Press.

Jarzabkowski, P. 2003. Strategic practices: An activity theory perspective on continuity and change. *Journal of Management Studies*, **40**(1): 23–55.

Johnson, G., Melin, L., and Whittington, R. 2003. Micro strategy and strategizing: Towards an activity based view. *Journal of Management Studies*, **40**(1): 3–22.

Johnson, M. 1987. *The Body in the Mind.* Chicago, IL: University of Chicago Press.

MacIntosh, R. and Maclean, D. 1999. Conditioned emergence: A dissipative structures approach to transformation. *Strategic Management Journal*, **20**(4): 297–316.

March, J.G. 1979. The technology of foolishness. In J. March and J.P. Olsen (eds.), *Ambiguity and Choice in Organizations* (2nd edn.), pp. 69–81. Bergen: Universitetsforlaget.

Mead, M. 2001. *Coming of Age in Samoa: A Psychological Study of Primitive Youth for Western Civilization.* New York: Perennial Classics.

Mintzberg, H. and McHugh, A. 1985. Strategy formation in an adhocracy. *Administrative Science Quarterly*, **30**: 160–97.

Mintzberg, H. and Waters, J.A. 1985. Of strategies, deliberate and emergent. *Strategic Management Journal*, **6**: 257–72.

Orlikowski, W.J. 2000. Using technology and constituting structure: A practice lens for studying technology in organizations. *Organization Science*, **11**(4): 404–28.

Orlikowski, W.J. 2002. Knowing in practice: Enacting a collective capability in distributed organizing. *Organization Science*, **13**(3): 249–73.

Pettigrew, A.M. 1985. *The Awakening Giant: Continuity and Change in Imperial Chemical Industries.* Oxford, UK: Blackwell.

Piaget, J. and Inhelder, B. 1958. *The Growth of Logical Thinking from Childhood to Adolescence: An Essay on the Construction of Formal Operational Structures.* New York: Basic Books.

Porter, M.E. 1980. *Competitive Strategy. Techniques for Analyzing Industries and Competitors.* New York: The Free Press.

Porter, M.E. 1985. *Competitive Advantage. Creating and Sustaining Superior Performance.* New York: The Free Press.

Regnér, P. 2003. Strategy creation in the periphery: Inductive versus deductive strategy making. *Journal of Management Studies*, **40**(1): 57–82.

Roos, J., Victor, B., and Statler, M. forthcoming. Playing seriously with strategy. *Long Range Planning.*

Rumelt, R.P., Schendel, D., and Teece, D.J. 1994. Fundamental issues in strategy. In R.P. Rumelt, D. Schendel, and D.J. Teece (eds.), *Fundamental Issues in Strategy – A Research Agenda*, pp. 9–47. Boston, MA: Harvard Business School Press.

Schrage, M. 2000. *Serious Play: How the World's Best Companies Simulate to Innovate.* Boston, MA: Harvard Business School Press.

Stacey, R.D. 1996. *Complexity and Creativity in Organizations.* San Francisco: Berrett-Koehler.

Sutton-Smith, B. 1997. *The Ambiguity of Play.* Cambridge, MA: Harvard University Press.

Vygotsky, L.S. and Cole, M. 1978. *Mind in Society: The Development of Higher Psychological Processes.* Cambridge, MA: Harvard University Press.

Wernerfelt, B. 1984. A resource-based view of the firm. *Strategic Management Journal*, **5**: 171–80.

Wernerfelt, B. 1995. The resource-based view of the firm: Ten years after. *Strategic Management Journal*, **16**: 171–4.

Whittington, R. 1996. Strategy as practice. *Long Range Planning*, **29**(5): 731–5.

Whittington, R. 2003. The work of strategizing and organizing: For a practice perspective. *Strategic Organization*, **1**(1): 117–25.

Winnicott, D.W. 1971. *Playing and Reality.* London: Tavistock.

# CHAPTER SEVEN

# Strategy as Art: Using a Creative Action-Based Model for Strategy Formulation

Frances Fabian, dt ogilvie

*With an apple I will astonish Paris.*

**Paul Cezanne**

## Introduction

Strategic decision making is both an art and a science. Historically, however, the emphasis of strategy research has been on the *science* of strategic decision making (Bettis, 1991) rather than on the *art* of strategic decision making. Recent discussions in strategy research argue that firms need to be better at the innovation side of strategy, pointing out the need and benefits of exploration over exploitation (March, 1991; Sutton, 2001), rule breaking over game playing (Markides, 1997; Sutton, 2001). In this chapter, we suggest an approach to strategy formulation that may help researchers and managers gain insights into the issue of *creating new strategy*, creating something that did not exist before: new business models or new ways of doing business.

While a growing literature addresses procedures and practices that aid in bringing about innovation (e.g. Hargadon, 2003; Kelley, 1995), it is not easily integrated into our formalized views of strategy processes. A failing has been that we have not explicitly acknowledged a set of necessary tasks associated with the "art" of strategic innovation, perhaps because these tasks tend to be associated with seemingly more ineffable skills such as creativity, intuition, tacit knowledge, action-based knowledge, and the process of socially constructing reality.

By placing artistic tasks into a more explicit model, composed of the three tasks of *motivation*, *expression*, and *construction of acceptance*, we believe process research can be made more cumulative and inclusive. For instance, studying how culture instills passion and enhances creativity is part of the motivational task of strategy formulation;

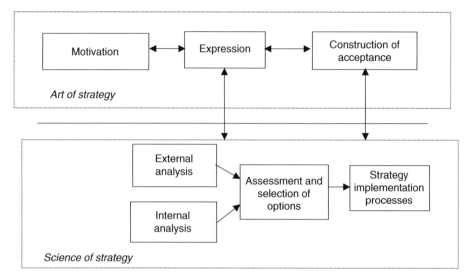

**Figure 7.1**   Toward a More Complete Model of Strategy Formulation

learning how to craft strategy through an ever-changing evolution toward a profitable "realized" strategy entails the skills associated with the expression of an idea; and the use of symbolism to communicate and persuade others to accept innovation as part of a new socially constructed reality is part of the construction of acceptance. We view this artistic model of strategy process as one that energizes and works in tandem with the more widely researched tasks of formulation, i.e., environmental and internal analysis, the assessment of options, and the implementation of strategy through organizational design (see Figure 7.1).

Most important, a key point is that this model draws on an entirely different set of skills than currently emphasized in prevalent models (evidenced by the kinds of skills taught in most business school curricula). Specifically, strategy formulation frameworks stress the analysis of existing information, along with quantitative assumptions about future variables, to pursue optimal alternative courses of action. These models, which reach their hallmark in disciplines like finance and economics, are key to strategy process tasks and indicative of the "science" of strategy. We believe that a model that incorporates an alternative set of skills associated with the more artistic tasks of strategy, while not able to be "formula-ized" can be "formalized" enough to advance our carrying out of strategy innovation processes. To best generate such a model, we make a metaphorical leap to an "artistic paradigm," alluding to a fine arts way of thinking and viewing the world generously throughout the text. We use fine art to represent an approach to innovation we believe is heavily underdeveloped in research, teaching, and practice.

## Drawing from the Fine Arts

While there is a menu of choices to define "art," we will allude to specific stories from the fine arts, such as famous painters, because they are especially easy to conceptualize in regard to the parallels we want to make in strategy formulation. Indeed, as we will draw on later, Joas has noted that the aesthetic arts have provided a basis for expositing a theory of creative action at least as far back as the work of the German philosopher Herder in the late 1700s (1997: 80–2).

## The artistic process

We use artists' observations and stories to explain a three-stage model of "motivation–expression–construction of acceptance" that illuminates different aspects of formulating innovation. To our knowledge, these ideas have not been linked together as part of a more complete model of strategy formulation processes associated with creating innovative strategies. Moreover, they depart from perspectives that emphasize the accumulation, processing, and analysis of existing environmental and organizational information (e.g., Huber, 1991), arguably the premise of the great bulk of strategy process research and the conventional strategy formulation process.

*Motivation.*   The motivation stage refers to the internal, personal stage that encapsulates all of the aspects that provide the foundation for inspiration. The term "motivation" emphasizes the volitional aspect of the mental and emotional preparation for innovative inspiration. For artists, it is often evidenced through the depiction of the unsaid, or that which is usually left unseen (intentionally or not). The motivation stage is strongly associated with the generation of creativity, defined as "the ability to produce or bring into existence something that was not there before, something new, an extension of our base of knowledge" (Dennard, 2000). Thus Caravaggio in the 1500s (who was followed by a movement known as Caravaggists) changed perspective, light, and size to bring the sacred to a(n) (unseemly) human level – protesting against the beauty of classicism by irreverently painting the deceased Virgin Mary with uncovered feet (thus leading to the refusal of his work).

When such innovators do speak for themselves, there is generally a highly passionate and connected energy associated with their efforts, a passion that reflects tenacity in the face of resistance and persistence in the face of failure. Goya, one of the more independent artists at the turn of nineteenth-century Spain, was deeply committed to revealing the brutality and banality of man, inscribing a preliminary drawing with the words: "The author dreaming. His one intention is to banish harmful beliefs commonly held and with this work of Caprichos to perpetuate the solid testimony of truth."

The central insight from the motivation stage of our model is the necessity for a passion that energizes action at the emotional level that may very well be necessary to spark creative insight. We believe research overly focuses on the epiphenomenon when it emphasizes the intellectual conditions in formulating strategy while ignoring the central role of motivation in sparking insight.

*Expression.*   The expression stage in our model conveys the uneasy reconciliation that inspired motivation must make with the boundaries of real objects and tools that constrain and change how thought is brought into the external world. The painter learns what he paints and sees in the process of painting. Leonardo da Vinci encapsulated this duality over 500 years ago: "Movement is said to have two natures because it is made of different powers; in fact, it falls into two parts, of which one is spiritual and one is material. What is spiritual in us is made of the power of the imagination; what is material is made of the material bodies" (Madrid Manuscript I).

This requirement to bring the idea into our material world leads to the insight that the process entailed must become part of the idea itself. As da Vinci explained, "A good painter has two chief objects to paint – man and the intention of his soul. The former is easy, the latter hard, for it must be expressed by gestures and the movement of the limbs" (de la Croix and Tansey, 1980: 787). In this sense, the motivation that formulates a new idea is a small, albeit key, part of formulation that due to its mysterious and wonderful origins often overshadows the messiness of implementation. But new ideas are not hatched so much as they are co-evolved in a micro-environment; one in which there are iterative loops in which thought inspires action, but action produces un-thought of results, which further inspire and refine the direction of initial thought. Thus, as Schwartz explains, "Creating art is about building a relationship with the materials, the process, yourself . . . It is a visual conversation" (2001: 58).

*Construction of acceptance.* Our view of art as a metaphor for issues in strategic innovation recognizes the uneven trials that artists have long undergone to introduce new work into their existing culture. The "construction of acceptance" stage describes the process that they undergo to legitimate their innovation against the resistance of the extant culture. Construction of acceptance reflects the necessity to recognize the highly interpersonal nature of innovation that requires acknowledging resistance and, moreover, persuading and compelling others to accept the innovation.

An artist underrated in his role of constructing acceptance for his work is Vincent Van Gogh. Van Gogh came from a family of Dutch art dealers and spent his early career in this occupation, immersed in the art paradigm of his age (including a stint of a few years in England where he became an admirer of British engravers). While his grave mental health is often highlighted in his biography, his time living with Gauguin, and his connections with his brother, Theo, a prominent art dealer in Paris, entailed a considerable conduit for communicating his vision of his art. There are over 700 letters to Theo detailing his concern that his work be understood for its intentional innovation. Consider Van Gogh's observation, "And I should not be surprised if the Impressionists soon find fault with my way of working, for it has been fertilized by the ideas of Delacroix rather than by theirs" (de la Croix and Tansey, 1980: 787).

Here we see both the resistance and the inspiration for the innovation made explicit. Other letters chronicle critical insights into what Van Gogh sought in his works, including efforts to engage the paradigm with many pieces directly inspired by previous works (for instance, specifically citing his studies after Delacroix, Daumier, Dore, and Millet). Without the conduit of Theo Van Gogh, it is highly unlikely that the motivated, and clearly "expressive," Vincent Van Gogh would have left us any legacy at all.

When we consider this stage of our model, we address the need to acknowledge and recognize the role of the audience in the innovation process.

## Parallels and Extensions for Innovative Strategy Formulation

> Artists who seek perfection in everything are those who cannot attain it in anything.
> (Eugene Delacroix (1798–1863))

We believe strategy research, in its appropriate emphasis in previous decades to inject increased rigor (e.g., Camerer, 1985) from its roots as an ad hoc, case study, curriculum capstone "course," has veered too far from recognizing the art associated with formulating strategy. Clearly, the emphasis on research that seeks to find relationships among strategy variables to predict performance is central to improving the "exploitation" (March, 1991) aspect of strategy, which works in tandem with the explorative elements of formulating new strategy to drive constant organizational renewal (Crossan, Lane, and White, 1999). An example of such an approach is Porter's (1980) popular "SWOT" analysis of strategy formulation that emphasizes information processing through analysis of the firm and its task environment to develop the firm's strategy. Its "scientific" focus arises from its disciplinary roots in industrial organization economics, but moreover, it reflects a systematic, analytical approach to formulating strategy with underlying assumptions consistent with the scientific method. By relying on the assumption that superior rents (i.e. monopoly rents) reflect superior positioning in the market, strategy formulation is an exercise in classifying the elements of the environment and the firm in an effort to position a business in a given industry structure (Prahalad and Hamel, 1994). Failure, then, is indicative of poor analysis, incomplete knowledge, or poor execution toward the correct answer.

This science side of strategy is based on several assumptions. First, it holds that there are stable causal laws that underlie a firm's performance in the market. Second, it assumes that the collection and analysis of data will reveal what those laws are, thus offering contingent sets of relationships among the environment, its competencies, and firm performance. Further, it assumes an objective, analyzable, quantifiable, environment, and that the same laws that determine outcomes today will govern events in the future.

Extending this perspective on formulation has led to a considerable research stream: e.g., analysis of environmental dimensions (Staw and Szwajkowski, 1975; Dess and Beard, 1984); deficits in managerial cognition (e.g., Ireland *et al.*, 1987; Sutcliffe, 1994); prescriptive tools such as the five forces framework and SWOT analysis (Porter, 1980); as well as numerous algorithms to calculate and select strategic alternatives, like the Ansoff growth model, BCG, and SPACE matrices (Thompson, 2001), to name a very few.

However, this perspective falls short on some important tasks in strategy formulation. Peters and Waterman (1982) early believed that the bias toward rational models was partly responsible for the poor performance of companies in meeting the new environment of foreign competition. Mintzberg (1994) argued that the prevalent planning approach suffered from the "fallacies" of prediction, detachment, and formalization. Others have noted that the model has not integrated new theoretical imperatives such as pursuing strategic intent and competing on capabilities (Liedtka and Rosenblum, 1996).

In contrast, strategy formulation aimed at innovation requires a more context-sensitive, iterative process that aims at shaping an unknown future. Thus, any formulation approach that emphasizes the ability to generalize across contexts, and to formulate a long-term plan that reflects historical, empirically valid variable relationships, is particularly unsuited for this aspect of strategy formulation. Furthermore, skills associated with the artful tasks of strategy (useful in creating a malleable future) – i.e., motivation, expression, and construction of acceptance – are not well addressed by the "science" side of strategy.

We believe the emphasis on assessing the environment using models like the above is a crucial exercise in the strategy process. It provides a compelling framework for managers to grasp the choices and difficulties with implementation of a strategy in the near term. It also highlights the drawbacks of a current strategy. As strategy formulation is useless without informed implementation, the model is integral to strategic success. We are interested, however, in reconsidering its adequacy for serving as the predominant foundation for strategy formulation.

The essential point is that scientific pursuit and artful expression, while mutually exclusive in their realization, are still complementary in their contribution. As explained by Weisskopf (1979), "We cannot at the same time experience the artistic content of a Beethoven sonata and also worry about the neurophysiological processes in our brains" (1979: 478). He makes other equally compelling allusions – the ability to enjoy a starry sky or study its celestial movements, the ability to contemplate the poetic metaphor of a sunset or consider the light refraction of particulate matter in the atmosphere. The one does not preclude the significance of the other, but rather serves a different and equally necessary purpose.

## The goal of strategy and its mirror to art

Consistent with much of the above, we will premise our view of strategy formulation, specifically in regard to the pursuit of innovation, along the following: "The goal of strategy is to create the future such that the firm gains a competitive advantage through breaking or changing the rules of the game, thus enabling it to earn abnormal profits. These creative strategies are realized predominantly through action, over analysis." The product of such a view of strategy formulation, i.e., the successful new "painting" that comes out of a strategy process, is likely to highlight the following characteristics.

> There are painters who transform the sun to a yellow spot, but there are others who, with the help of their art and their intelligence, transform a yellow spot into the sun. (Pablo Picasso)

*Creating a nonexistent future.* The fine artist transforms a blank canvas into a compelling piece of art, one in which the multitude of possibilities in colors, styles, textures, and subjects makes foreknowledge of the work by others impossible. The goal of strategy to create the unknowable future is similar (Prahalad and Hamel, 1994). An implicit assumption of the scientific approach to formulation is that we estimate and assess various future scenarios predicted from past experience. In contrast, innovative strategy is actually about the *creation of a future* that does not presently exist and is not presently predictable. This is an important ontological break – there are more variables and media than the scientific method can accommodate, and strategists have some discretion in shaping or changing the industry they face.

> Each painting has its own way of evolving . . . When the painting is finished, the subject reveals itself. (William Baziotes)

*To act, not to analyze.*    Artists must express their ideas through constant iterative actions and reactions in order to produce their piece. Each brushstroke affects the aesthetic of the picture, while bounding and driving the next brushstroke; the picture unfolds at the same time that it is created, and moreover it becomes a very physical act in which the artist's ideas bump against hard objects in reality. Like the creation of a fine painting, strategy is not a replica of a mental picture, but rather the pursuit of that picture.

Management research has now long been acquainted with Weick's views of enactment, selection, and retention, and his emphasis on action for generating knowledge, i.e., "the failure to act is the cause of most organizational ineffectiveness" (Weick, 1979: 267). We believe that when Mintzberg (1987: 72) emphasizes the critical role of the manager who "manages a process in which strategies (and visions) can emerge as well as be deliberately conceived," the parallel to artistic expression becomes clear. Just as you cannot create an artist by teaching art history, you cannot create a strategist by simply analyzing the firm and its task environment; the strategist needs creative action-based skills (ogilvie, 1998).

> There is only one difference between a madman and me. I am not mad. (Salvador Dali)

*Abnormal profits.*    Many artists succeed because they represent beauty or ideas in new ways previously unthinkable. Correspondingly, the Austrian school asserts, "the goal of strategy formulation centers not on limiting competitive forces but rather on entrepreneurial discovery" (Jacobson, 1992: 785). Abnormal profits accrue to firms whose innovations create disequilibrium conditions in the market that persist for some time, giving them an advantage over competitors. The goal of managers, then, is to create conditions to earn those abnormal profits. Clearly, logically deducible strategies, i.e., ones that can be generated by systematic scientific approaches, are less likely to lead to abnormal profits for any appreciable time period, since they are easily imitable (Grant, 1991; Lippman and Rumelt, 1982) by logical analysis.

> Art is either plagiarism or revolution. (Paul Gauguin)

*To gain a competitive advantage, create the rules of the game.*    Just as artists have consistently broken the rules of their contemporaries with new approaches (e.g. pointillism, chiaroscuro, mannerism) or new subjects (the holy, the peasant, the sexual) that fundamentally change what acceptable art is, so do successful firms. Firms gain competitive advantage by creating new rules for the game (Markides, 1997). Markides studied more than 30 companies that successfully attacked industry leaders, finding that these firms were successful because they either broke or changed the rules of the game in their industries by developing new and creative ways to compete in their marketplaces. This reinvention of the game is central to the tenets of the Austrian school of strategy (see Jacobson, 1992, for a discussion of this school). Additionally, it is at the heart of modern conceptualizations of hypercompetition (D'Aveni, 1994), and disruptive innovation (Christensen, 1997).

## Toward a New Model of Strategy and its Formulation

Above we offered theoretical arguments that the artistic model is consistent with imperatives for innovative strategy formulation, as we have defined it. By extending the identified tasks of motivation–expression–construction of acceptance to strategy formulation, we believe we move toward a theoretical framework that integrates a substantial number of strategy research streams and helps identify the role of their theoretical contributions.

### Foundational skills and tasks

> Only when he no longer knows what he is doing does the painter do good things.
> (Edgar Degas)

A major problem with delineating the artistic model for strategy formulation is that there are not clear, "scientifically valid," causal relations between particular skills and successful outputs. Ontologically, we recommend the work of Joas (1997) in regard to the philosophical foundation for a more explicit use of action theory (dating at least as far back as the work of Parsons, 1937) along with a more holistic understanding of the role of human creativity that extends far beyond the strictures of "rational" action. Here, though, we believe that it is sufficient to refer to the central skills in this perspective as stemming from the use of techniques reflecting creative action-based approaches to decision making (ogilvie, 1998; ogilvie and Fabian, 1999). Below we briefly examine streams of strategy processes that we believe are especially indicative of the skills and concepts necessary to further formalize the role of motivation, expression, and the construction of acceptance in strategy formulation processes.

> True art is characterized by an irresistible urge in the creative artist. (Albert Einstein)

*Motivation.* This task in strategy formulation encompasses the conditions and processes necessary for individuals to gain a new creative insight. Clearly, there has long been an informal groundswell of support for encouraging creativity in firms, revealed in numerous articles (e.g., *California Management Review*, special issue, Fall 1997; Sutton, 2001; Kelley, 1995). High motivation and intensity (Marakas and Elam, 1997) are critical first steps in the creative process. Creativity usually arises out of involvement with the issue, either on an emotional or intuitional level (Simon, 1987), or because of strong intrinsic motivation (Amabile, 1997). Motivation is central to concepts such as "flow," which encompasses the timeless feeling of immersion in a project

(Csikszentmihalyi, 1997). Additionally, related theory such as how to tap into "self-transcending knowledge" (Scharmer, 2001) is consistent with the skills necessary to enhance motivation for innovative strategy formulation.

In translating this to organizational implications, we argue that activities associated with generating creativity require a mental "buy-in" by the participants. Unlike its scientific counterpart, it cannot be performed objectively and formulaically; thus, observable proficiency in quantitative methods, for instance, is not informative for this task. If organizations must get creative to survive (Markides, 1997; Staw, 1997; Sutton, 2001), then they must hire creative top managers, convince their existing top managers that creativity can be learned (Marakas and Elam, 1997), or create a "culture of creativity" (Kelley, 1997; ogilvie and McDaniel, 2004) to foster conditions for innovative insights to arise.

> Painting is an attempt to come to terms with life. There are as many solutions as there are human beings. (George Tooker)

*Expression.*    Expression is the ability to bring ideas into a workable form through taking action and responding to ongoing action. This is the most elusive aspect of strategy formulation, and perhaps one of the most underdeveloped areas of strategy research. On the other hand, there is a rich legacy of interest in the connection between doing and knowing (Polanyi, 1964). The action taken to express an idea requires a highly contextualized awareness and self-awareness. Strategy as art might rely on using tacit knowledge from past actions – i.e., recognizing the role of "intuition" (Poincare, 1952; Simon, 1987; Khatri and Ng, 2000) in guiding action. Intuition is not irrational, though to some extent it is unscientific, as it represents years of experience that are tacitly and unconsciously tapped (Khatri and Ng, 2000; Scharmer, 2001). Importantly, Hutchins' (1995) detailed study on cognition implies that intuitive skills are tightly interwoven with long-term iterations between thinker and context, "Humans create their cognitive powers by creating the environments in which they exercise those powers" (1995: xvii). Skills in expression must thus also emphasize learning from present action – such as using small experiments and accepting and embracing ongoing (small) failures (Sitkin, 1992).

Organizationally, this demands learning more on the value of experience, but becoming savvier about appropriate experiences for different conditions (Bergh, 2001). Improving present action calls for processes that promote experimenting with a variety of actions in real time, aimed to introduce variation into the context and gain knowledge about the workability of ideas, and advantages over competitors (Miles, Snow, and Sharfman, 1993). Additionally, decision makers must be taught to rely on real-time operational indicators rather than forecasted information to build intuition, speed, and performance (Eisenhardt, 1989). Moreover, through encouraging skills in accommodating inevitable "failures," the strategist avoids multiple organizational dysfunctions associated with a culture that avoids failure at all cost (Sitkin, 1992).

> An artist is somebody who produces things that people don't need to have but that he – for some reason – thinks it would be a good idea to give them. (Andy Warhol)

*Construction of acceptance.* This final task is perhaps the most overlooked area for skills necessary for successful strategy innovation and refers to the (usually interpersonal) work involved in communicating innovation so that it will be received in context. Weick's (1979) views of enactment are a key research stream focusing on the importance of building shared views of reality to allow for cooperation. Creative action-based techniques include gaining contextual cues to understand influential others, as well as shaping contextual cues to persuade those others. Individual skills associated with this task include abilities such as sympathetic insight into others, evidenced in recent support for the role of "emotional intelligence" (Goleman, 1997). Additionally, the skill of reframing information to promote an innovation's benefits may justify a prominent role for symbolic processes (see Feldman and March, 1981; Pfeffer, 1981). Dutton (1986) likewise emphasized how effective managers set the issue agenda by changing perceived issue characteristics, gaining sponsorship, and determining the agenda's structure.

Organizationally, the reception of innovation may be improved through designing structures aimed at promoting such reception. Bower's (1970) work on the role of product champions, for instance, implies the need to promote the internal networks of relationships that can foster innovation. Ackoff's (1998) arguments on the nature of transformational leadership stress the importance of being able to construct acceptance across an organization. Indeed, his logic is completely consistent with a strategy as art view, as he premises his arguments with the idea that leadership is actually an aesthetic function.

> Every great work of art has two faces, one toward its own time and one toward the future, toward eternity. (Daniel Barenboim)

## Implications for Strategy Research

Reconceptualizing the central task of strategy formulation has two important implications for strategy research. First, the scientific contributions to strategy formulation need to be reassessed in regard to how usefully they have performed to date in creating new and innovative strategies. Some of this research has proven great fodder for researchers – e.g., "how much, if any, diversification is appropriate for performance?" Yet, it is highly unlikely that this stream of research has helped corporate strategy formulation to much of a measurable degree (Bettis, 1991). It is unlikely managers can "properly" identify the extent or even category of their diversification (are GE and Newell unrelated diversifiers?). Moreover, given the constantly changing empirical findings over performance, most strategists are unlikely to believe that empirical findings for last year are more relevant than their own calculations. While large sample empirical research is informative, its direct findings are not as useful. This implies that research needs to better address the question of "what might this research do to help strategists improve their decision making?" if it is to provide guidance for practicing managers.

Second, more research is called for on the identity, the implementation, and the performance characteristics of creative action-based skills. This approach to decision making seems to exist in its own vicious circle outside of the paradigm: it lacks concrete support to become established, which it lacks because without establishment in the more mainstream paradigm, little empirical rigor is devoted to it. Surmounting this problem is the task of a few inspired researchers who can find resources to begin establishing such a line of research. As noted by Robinson (2002) for instance, "Creativity has had a bad press. People see it as opposed to academic standards – something you do on retreats during an hour's brainstorming. But creativity is a function of the intelligence that everyone has. We underestimate it because we underestimate our intelligence. We need to reassess the way we think about ability, intelligence and creativity." A first step is to begin the "construction of acceptance" of such an approach through sponsorship from societies, conferences, journals, and business school courses.

## Implications for Practice

The model we have presented has important implications for praxis. Although many businesses say they wish to be creative, most organizations "are structured so that creativity is the exception, rather than the rule" (ogilvie and McDaniel, 2004: 1; Nemeth, 1997), despite the evidence that creative organizations are successful (e.g., Markides, 1997). Recognizing that the strategy formulation process can be broken into two basic approaches; i.e., using artful skills to create new strategies, and "science" skills to plan and implement those strategies, may be helpful for managers to reconceptualize their practices. Necessarily, creating new strategies comes before planning and implementing them. While motivation is sequentially first in this process, expression and construction of acceptance may have an interactive relationship with the elements of the science of strategy (see Figure 7.1).

*Motivation.*  The hallmark of many successful organizations is the existence of unusually committed and motivated employees (e.g., Starbucks, Wal-Mart, Southwest Airlines). Such businesses prove that commitment and excitement are not a function of career glamour, but an organizational attribute. Moreover, they stand in stark contrast to research that emphasizes mainly monetary and punitive incentives of command and control systems to keep employees within the parameters of their pre-designed job duties. As one district manager explained, "What makes Starbucks different is our passion for what we do. We're trying to provide a great experience for people, with a great product. That's what we all care about" (Starbucks website). Collins (2001) also found that passion characterized his great companies. If an organization seeks to renew itself continuously in the marketplace, a strategy as art perspective puts the motivation of firm members as a priority issue.

*Expression.*   Of course, such motivation is only useful if organizations make space for employees to express and act on their commitment. Expression cannot be aimless, the goal is to allow employees to use their judgment and experience in creating strategy in context. Consider that the idea of providing coffee sit/to go shops is not especially innovative, but the idea that customers should view the transaction as beyond mundane is novel. Starbucks allows employees to use contextual, on-the-spot judgment (i.e., intuition) to decide minor yet critical issues for their innovation (e.g., what music is appropriate for this crowd?). After facing numerous requests for music titles and even CDs, the firm recognized that customers appreciate the "music editing" services consistent with Starbucks' cultural appeal, leading to the launch of Hear Music, which by 2003 released 14 albums including single holiday albums that sold around 100,000 units (*International Herald Tribune*, 2004). Organizations that want to innovate need conduits for testing context, as well as to prepare to adjust action given contextual feedback.

*Construction of acceptance.*   Organizations also have to view themselves as in the job of building a community, one in which they have to construct shared meanings, by listening to, making sense of, and shaping their context. This "sense making cannot be achieved by the manager alone. Rather the creation of new meanings and landscapes are not imposed but developed jointly" (Gold and Holman, 2001: 387). The rising interest in storytelling (Bennis, 1995) for leaders suggest that this may be an effective way to build support for both new ideas and joint action among organizational members.

Finally, organizations need to create cultures that are supportive of the messy business of being creative and accept that being truly creative means allowing for failure. The advice to build a culture of creativity (ogilvie and McDaniel, 2004) and a philosophy that promotes action (Pfeffer and Sutton, 1999) recognizes that driving out fear and promoting courage are concomitant with a creative action-based approach to formulating new strategies, new products, and new processes. Just think: If Edison had worked for the typical modern organization, we might all be sitting around today with torches and candles, without electric lights, TVs, computers, etc. It is through failure that managers and organizations learn. The idea, perhaps counterintuitive, is to "Fail early and fail often!" as David Kelley, CEO of IDEO admonishes, rather than take the stance, as the CEO of a major multimedia conglomerate told the second author, "We don't tolerate failure!"

While most firms are proficient at the analytical tasks required for planning and implementation, many are deficient at the tasks required for creation of novel strategies. It is this aspect of strategy formulation that requires an artful approach. Managers must pay attention to the development of skills in generating creativity, motivation, expression, and construction of acceptance. The personal creativity of a few managers is not enough, firms must develop a culture of creativity that allows for action, experimentation, failure, diversity, dissent, and all of the ferment evidenced in creating art.

## Implications for Teaching Strategy

Similarly, business schools should reassess how they teach strategy in light of the need for managers to develop innovative strategies.

*Motivation.*   Pedagogically, this is perhaps the greatest obstacle in the conventional MBA and business programs. Much of the curriculum is based on solving for the right answer, and the questionable success of the MBA program once its graduates enter the real world is well documented (Pfeffer and Fong, 2002). It is time we stop deriding professors because they "make good dog and pony shows," and try instead to recognize that "motivational" speakers are demanded internationally because they provide an essential element of good decision making. The implications are that there is a big difference between teaching students how to get the right answer and motivating students to want to provide answers at all. Currently, the unspeakable truth is that professors try to dumb down material to meet the disappointingly low energy of students to learn the material – a low motivation currently buttressed by fear of gaining a low grade point average (GPA) for the job market. Once students arrive in the job market, they do not know how to direct motivation for solving the right (easy), prefabricated answer into a motivation that is actually useful to their employer – such as how to creatively and aggressively jump into uncertain environments and (fearlessly!) learn from one's actions.

*Expression.*   Certainly, the curriculum of business schools is not known for rewarding subjective, wayward attempts at formulating a plan of action, and students are not clamoring for such a change. Nevertheless, the ability to take risks and learn need not be limited by the current system of grading. In the fine arts, students build a portfolio of projects that allow future consignees to evaluate the artist's progress and potential. Similarly, many of the entrepreneurial/consulting/financial programs are beginning to allow for "extra-curricular" projects in which students tackle real-world problems. The "personal" diary of such experiences could be much more valuable to an employer than a course grade, and is easily validated through interactions in the interviews. Students might also be encouraged to build portfolios of special business interests on the web, where they record their forecasts, assess their failures, and improve their understanding – perhaps interacting with outside audiences. The idea is that the "expression" of business thinking moves to the forefront and becomes accessible to the future "employer" rather than the current system of course grades, which usually reflect very short-term mastery of limited content, or more pessimistically, grade inflation.

*Construction of acceptance.*   Current business curricula are close to bereft of programs to instill these skills. The closest they come to tapping this dimension is in peer evaluations of group projects and, for those few courageous schools that have it, "professional conduct" grades. It is not clear what options exist to build these skills, but curriculum planners should look for "projects" where students cannot get the answer without persuading others to contribute to it. For example, a popular entertainment venue has become the interactive mystery play in which the audience must collaborate with the actors and other audience members to solve a mystery. Real-life (and in some cases, computer) simulations that use these types of interactions to build the information "solution" might provide some of the best practice arenas for these kinds of skills.

Or, if conceptual insight were to be key, business schools could transform their "feedback" system (professor evaluations and "meetings with the Dean") to a "storytelling" system that would show both students and faculties the complexities of organization (see Boje, 1995). Unfortunately, a justifiable incentive system in relation to "grading" may be the most difficult part of implementing these kinds of programs.

## Conclusion

To gain superior performance, we argue that managers must draw on the ability to use a creative action-based approach to strategy formulation to augment the conventional scientific approach. We premised these arguments by thinking about how artists have described their venture in hope that such observations offered insightful parallels to the task of strategy formulation. Clearly, strategy formulation has progressed admirably from plumbing the methods of science. But, to the extent that it has downplayed the art of formulation, strategic management has lost something integral along the way. We believe promoting this natural component of the strategy formulation process through a firmer theoretical foundation will enhance the quality of strategic thinking, the usefulness of strategy research, and the success of a business school experience.

## References

Ackoff, R.L. 1998. A systemic view of transformational leadership. *Systemic Practice and Action Research*, **11**: 23–36.

Amabile, T.M. 1997. Motivating creativity in organizations: On doing what you love and loving what you do. *California Management Review*, **40**: 39–59.

Bennis, W. 1996. The leader as storyteller. *Harvard Business Review*, **74**: 154–9.

Bergh, D.D. 2001. Executive retention and acquisition outcomes: A test of opposing views on the influence of organizational tenure. *Journal of Management*, **27**: 603–22.

Bettis, R.A. 1991. Strategic management and the straightjacket: An editorial essay. *Organization Science*, **2**: 315–19.

Boje, D.M. 1995. Stories of the storytelling organization: A postmodern analysis of Disney as "TamaraLand". *Academy of Management Journal*, **38**: 997–1035.

Bower, J.L. 1970. *Managing the Resource Allocation Process*. Cambridge, MA: Harvard University Press.

Camerer, C. 1985. Redirecting research in business policy and strategy. *Strategic Management Journal*, **6**: 1–15.

Christensen, C. 1997. *The Innovator's Dilemma*. Cambridge, MA: Harvard Business Press.

Collins, J. 2001. *Good to Great: Why Some Companies Make the Leap . . . and Others Don't*. New York: Harper Business.

Crossan, M., Lane, H.W., and White, R.E. 1998. An organizational learning framework: From intuition to institution. *Academy of Management Review*, **24**(3): 522–37.

Csikszentmihalyi, M. 1997. *Creativity: Flow and the Psychology of Discovery and Invention*. New York: HarperPerennial.

D'Aveni, R. 1994. *Hypercompetition*. New York: The Free Press.

de la Croix, H. and Tansey, R. 1980. *Gardner's Art through the Ages*, 7th edition. New York: Harcourt Brace Jovanovich.

Dennard, R.H. 2000. Creativity in the 2000s and beyond. *Research Technology Management*, **43**(6): 23–5.

Dess, G. and Beard, D. 1984. Dimensions of organizational task environments. *Administrative Science Quarterly*, **29**: 52–73.

Dutton, J.E. 1986. Understanding strategic agenda building and its implication for managing change. *Scandinavian Journal of Management Studies*, **3**. Reprinted in Louis Pondy, R.J. Boland, and H. Thomas (eds.), (1988), *Managing Ambiguity and Change*, pp. 3–24. New York: Wiley.

Eisenhardt, K.M. 1989. Making fast strategic decisions in high-velocity environments. *Academy of Management Journal*, **32**: 543–76.

Feldman, M.S. and March, J.G. 1981. Information in organizations as signal and symbol. *Administrative Science Quarterly*, **26**: 171–6.

Gold, J. and Holman, D. 2001. Let me tell you a story: An evaluation of the use of storytelling and argument analysis in management education. *Career Development International*, **6**: 384–95.

Goleman, D. 1997. *Emotional Intelligence*, New York: Bantam Books.

Grant, R.M. 1991. The resource-based theory of competitive advantage: Implications for strategy formulation. *California Management Review*, **33**(3): 114–34.

Hargadon, A. 2003. *How Breakthroughs Happen: The Surprising Truth About How Companies Innovate*. Cambridge, MA: Harvard Business School Press.

Huber, G.P. 1991. Organizational learning: The contributing processes and the literatures. *Organization Science*, **2**: 88–115.

Hutchins, E. 1995. *Cognition in the Wild*. Cambridge, MA: MIT Press.

*International Herald Tribune*, February 29, 2004. http://www.iht.com/articles/118806.html.

Ireland, D., Hitt, M.A., Bettis, R.D., and Auld de Porras, D. 1987. Strategy formulation process: Differences in perceptions of strength and weakness indicators and environmental uncertainty by managerial level. *Strategic Management Journal*, **8**: 469–85.

Jacobson, R. 1992. The "Austrian" school of strategy. *The Academy of Management Review*, **17**: 782–808.

Joas, H. 1996. *The Creativity of Action* (translated by J. Gaines and P. Keast). Chicago, IL: University of Chicago Press.

Kelley, T. 1995. *The Art of Innovation: Lessons in Creativity from IDEO, America's Leading Design Firm*. New York: Doubleday.

Khatri, N. and Ng, H.A. 2000. The role of intuition in strategic decision making. *Human Relations*, **53**(1): 57–86.

Liedtka, J.M. and Rosenblum, J.W. 1996. Shaping conversations: Making strategy, managing change. *California Management Review*, **39**: 141–58.

Lippman, S.A. and Rumelt, R.P. 1982. Uncertain imitability: An analysis of inter-firm differences in efficiency under competition. *Bell Journal of Economics*, **23**: 418–38.

Marakas, G.L. and Elam, J.J. 1997. Creative enhancement in problem solving: Through software or process? *Management Science*, **43**: 1136–46.

March, J.G. 1991. Exploration and exploitation in organization learning. *Organization Science*, **2**: 71–87.

Markides, C. 1997. Strategic innovation *Sloan Management Review*, **38**: 9–24.

Miles, G., Snow, C.C., and Sharfman, M.P. 1993. Industry variety and performance. *Strategic Management Journal*, **14**: 163–77.

Mintzberg, H. 1987. Crafting strategy *Harvard Business Review*, **65**(4): 66–75.

Mintzberg, H. 1994. *The Rise and Fall of Strategic Planning*. New York: The Free Press.

Nemeth, C.J. 1997. Managing innovation: When less is more. *California Management Review*, **40**: 59–75.

ogilvie, d. 1998. Creative action as a dynamic strategy: Using imagination to improve strategic solutions in unstable environments. *Journal of Business Research*, **41**: 49–56.

ogilvie, d. and Fabian, F.H. 1999. Decision-making requirements for future organizational leaders: A creative action-based approach. In J. Hunt (ed.), *Leadership Challenges of the Twenty-First Century Army*. New York: JAI Press.

ogilvie, d. and McDaniel, R.R. Jr. 2004. Organizational creativity and complexity: Balancing on the edge of chaos. Presented at the 2004 Strategic Management Society Conference, San Juan, Puerto Rico.

Peters, T. and Waterman, R. 1982. *In Search of Excellence*. New York: Harper and Row.

Pfeffer, J. 1981. *Power in Organizations*. Marshfield, MA: Pitman.

Pfeffer, J. and Fong, C.T. 2002. The end of business schools? Less success than meets the eye. *Academy of Management Learning and Education Journal*, 1(1): 78–96.

Pfeffer, J. and Sutton, R.I. 1999. Knowing "what" to do is not enough: Turning knowledge into action. *California Management Review*, 42(1): 83–102.

Poincare, H. 1952. *Science and Method*. New York: Dover (originally published as *Science et Methode*, 1908).

Polanyi, M. 1964. *Personal Knowledge Towards a Post Critical Philosophy*. New York: Harper and Row.

Porter, M.E. 1980. *Competitive Strategy*. New York: The Free Press.

Prahalad, C.K. and Hamel, G. 1994. Strategy as a field of study: Why search for a new paradigm? *Strategic Management Journal*, 15: 5–16.

Robinson, K. 2002. Hands across the ocean. *Business Voice*, May.

Scharmer, C.O. 2001. Self-transcending knowledge: Sensing and organizing around emerging opportunities. *Journal of Knowledge Management*, 5(2): 137–50.

Schwarz, D. 2001. Making art of work. *Association for Quality and Participation*, Spring: 54–8.

Simon, H.A. 1987. Making management decisions: The role of intuition and emotion. *Academy of Management Executive*, February: 57–64.

Sitkin, S.B. 1992. Learning through failure: The strategy of small losses. In B.L. Staw and L.L. Cummings (eds.), *Research in Organizational Behavior*, 14: 231–66.

Starbuck's website, February 29, 2004. http://www.starbucks.com/aboutus/jobcenter.asp.

Staw, B.M. 1997. From the guest editor. *California Management Review*, 40: 2.

Staw, B.M. and Szwajkowski, E. 1975. The scarcity–munificence component of organizational environments and the commission of illegal acts. *Administrative Science Quarterly*, 20: 345–54.

Sutcliffe, K.M. 1994. What executives notice: Accurate perceptions in top management teams. *Academy of Management Journal*, 37(5): 1360–78.

Sutton, R.I. 2001. The weird rules of creativity. *Harvard Business Review*, 79: 94–108.

Thompson, J. 2001. *Strategic Management*, 4th edition. London, UK: Thomson.

Weick, K.E. 1979. *The Social Psychology of Organizing*, second edition. New York: Random House.

Weisskopf, V.F. 1979. Art and science. *The American Scholar*, 48: 473–5.

# Contexts for Innovation and Strategy Making

# CHAPTER EIGHT

# Critical Issues in Learning Processes

## Marjorie A. Lyles, Charles Dhanaraj, H. Kevin Steensma

As researchers who have been studying organizational learning processes for what seems like a long time, we recognize the difficulties involved in separating learning activities from other organizational processes. Learning processes are not easily observed nor is the linkage between learning and performance readily apparent. Yet, there is the belief by many scholars, including ourselves, that learning and knowledge development are critical capabilities for a firm. This chapter attempts to identify issues that we see in researching learning processes in firms. We identify these issues individually as a means of clarifying their impact on learning as a knowledge-creating process (Vera and Crossan, 2003).

## Know-How Processes

Know-how is embedded in the organizational members and processes. Theorists have identified that firms utilize their experience and the vicarious learning from others to build routines, adaptations, and standardizations that can be transferred (Argote, 1999; Baum, Li, and Usher, 2000). Based on organization learning theory of routines, we would expect that the more experience an organization has at a particular activity, such as acquisitions, the more likely that it would be to repeat the action in a similar fashion and that it would be more successful over time (Winter, 1987).

Yet, many organizational know-how approaches emphasize flexibility and embrace novelty in attempting to build on the firm's experience base. Frequently this is caused by the changing environmental conditions and because of the uniqueness of each experience that does not wholly lend itself to repetition (Argote, 1982; Argote, Beckman, and Epple, 1990; Miner, Bassoff, and Moorman, 2001; Dyer and Singh, 1998). Given this uniqueness of many organizational experiences, knowledge transfer is often difficult, and it is unlikely that standardized routines for managing unique situations exist (Doz and Hamel, 1998; Szulanski, 1996). In this sense, management of know-how under conditions of uncertainty is a dynamic capability of the firm. Extending this further, several authors have addressed the importance of learning from surprises, novelty, and rapidly changing conditions (Crossan, Lane, and White, 1999; Eisenhardt and Martin, 2001; Reuer, Park, and Zollo, 2002).

March (1991) suggests two types of learning: exploitation in which the processes and outcomes are more certain and the time horizon shorter; and exploration in which the outcomes are unpredictable and there are longer time horizons. Know-how of managing under conditions of novelty seems to follow more closely explorative learning. For example, Reuer, Park, and Zollo (2002) suggest that the relationship between alliance know-how and performance may be different from knowledge gained in studies of manufacturing or administrative contexts because of the novelty of the situations. Thus, the usefulness of exploitive know-how is for a shorter time period than other know-how that is based on more of an explorative nature because of the uncertainty and changing conditions of the learning environment (Simonin, 1999). Research that addresses the importance of learning under dynamic and changing conditions is greatly needed. We should not be seduced by studying know-how processes under conditions that are repetitive and relatively certain.

## Knowledge Characteristics

As one would expect, learning is also influenced by the knowledge characteristics such as its *tacitness, complexity,* and/or *ambiguity* (Simonin, 1999; Anand and Khanna, 2000). There is some agreement that organizations can create new knowledge by combinative capabilities, by combining different pieces of existing knowledge (Kogut and Zander, 1992, 1996; Zander and Kogut, 1995). Thus, one of the most important characteristics of knowledge is the inherent nature of tacit and explicit knowledge that makes them inseparable and creates "chunking" of knowledge (Simon, 1978). Tacit knowledge is an integral component of explicit knowledge, and it is a wrong assumption that explicit knowledge that involves repetitive tasks contains no tacit component.

At the same time, most research has treated tacit knowledge as separate from explicit knowledge without recognition of the interplay between them. Uzzi (1997) is an exception and states that it "appeared that the transfer of fine-grained information between embedded ties is consistent with Herbert Simon's notions of chunking and expert rationality, in that ... it is ... more fully understood because it is processed as composite chunks". Indeed, Polanyi (1966: 322) notes that tacit knowledge clarifies how the sum of the parts works together. In essence, tacit knowledge lends meaning to many explicit routines in an organization. Few researchers have directly addressed the differences and linkages between tacit and explicit knowledge or have explored the learning processes that create chunking.

## Absorptive Capacity

Knowledge generation and transfer require both diversity and absorptive capacity (Lyles, 1988; Lyles and Salk, 1996; Makhija and Ganesh, 1998; Dussauge, Garrette, and Mitchell, 2000). While diversity suggests unrelated knowledge bases, absorptive capacity would point to related knowledge bases across the units exchanging knowledge (Cohen and Levinthal, 1990).

There is also additional thinking that extends the original concept of absorptive capacity. Zahra and George (2002) identify that there are two types of capacity: potential capacity and realized capacity, the latter addressing knowledge transformation and exploitation. Van Den Bosch, Volberda, and De Boer (2001) suggest that socialization capabilities, which refer to the ability of the firm to produce a shared ideology, may influence learning by specifying broad, tacitly understood rules for appropriate action under unspecified contingencies. There is also prior evidence that absorptive capacity impacts R&D performance (Cockburn and Henderson, 1998; Cohen and Levinthal, 1990). Lane, Salk, and Lyles (2000) measure the components of absorptive capacity and show strong support that understanding and assimilating knowledge impacts knowledge acquisition and that utilization impacts performance. Thus the concept of absorptive capacity identifies the importance of the accumulation of knowledge depth because as a concept it assumes that new knowledge builds upon a related knowledge structure that already exists.

At the same time, there are some arguments that absorptive capacity can limit creativity and innovation because absorptive capacity is putting boundaries on the learning that is recognized and that is considered valuable. Creativity and innovation may involve moving away from the current knowledge structure by incorporating tangential ideas or concepts. Researchers need to be careful in refining absorptive capacity such that they do not eliminate channels for innovation.

## Social Embeddedness

A more recent development in learning research focuses on the role of social capital in learning. In a similar vein, Nonaka (1994) emphasizes the role of "socialization" in the diffusion of knowledge within organizations. Kale, Singh, and Perlmutter (2000) suggest that relational capital between partners enhances learning capability, simultaneously mitigating the transactional concerns. Makhija and Ganesh (1997) argue that through social networking processes, the highest order learning and the most tacit knowledge become shared. They identify the central role of the social or community orientation of knowledge, an aspect that Cohen and Levinthal's (1990) conceptualization of absorptive capacity does not explicitly mention. Recent work on social capital (Cohen and Prusak, 2001: 4) provides a comprehensive conceptual framework:

> Social capital consists of the stock of active connections among people, the trust, mutual understanding, and shared values and behaviors that bind the members of human networks and communities and make cooperative action possible.

They suggest trust, loyalty, and membership as three dimensions of social capital. This provides a parsimonious and efficient operationalization of the social aspects of learning. However, the cognitive aspects such as absorptive capacity and its relationship to social capital and the learning processes need to be explored further.

## Corporate Commitment to Organizational Learning and Knowledge Activities

Most research has approached learning processes almost as closed systems, ignoring the impact of the organizational agenda. Kogut and Zander (1996) suggest that firm boundaries in essence provide a context for knowledge to be developed and exploited, and emphasize the role of coordination, identity, and learning as key activities of the firm. Furthermore, a firm's competitiveness and performance is determined, in part, by the resources that it has at its disposal (Wernerfelt, 1984). Some resources are more valuable and difficult to imitate. These enable the firm to distinguish itself from its competitors (Barney, 1991). Yet, one of the lessons learned from Bower's work (1970 ) is the importance of the resource allocation process within firms. Similarly the organizational agendas that influence resource allocation also impact what learning and knowledge is valued and supported within the firm.

Managing learning and knowledge transfer have been topics in the organizational literature for a while (Doz and Hamel, 1998; Dyer and Singh, 1998; Reuer, Park, and Zollo, 2002). Firms have chosen various structures to manage these activities: some are ad hoc in their approach, some are more structured, and some are computerized. For example, Alavi and Tiwana (2003) suggest that firms that create a dedicated approach to knowledge management are on the cutting edge of capitalizing on the benefits of that knowledge. We may not agree totally, but we do recognize that the commitment of a firm to knowledge, its development, its transfer, and its utilization is important. We also expect that the degree of management resource commitment assists in creating rent-generating resources that increase the firm's knowledge generation and utilization capabilities.

## Self-Awareness as a Critical Element

In studying organizational learning we cannot separate the people from the process: without the people in the organization, there would be no process. However, in our research, we find that many managers are not self-conscious of their management behavior and are totally unaware of learning processes. Roos (chapter 25, this volume) draws our attention to the importance of "I" in doing research and likewise, it is important for us to help managers recognize the importance of "I" in their own work. Without managers who are reflective and aware of organizational processes, it is difficult for us to truly understand organizational learning processes.

In summary, we react to research on learning processes that borders on treating learning creation, transfer, and utilization, as simple processes. While the issues we have raised deserve to be taken seriously and addressed individually, we hope that others recognize that we should not treat them as totally distinct factors of learning processes. They, along with many other frames for analyzing learning processes, are convenient categories that we use for enhancing our discussions and typologies. We must remember that they are not truly separate. As researchers and teachers, we should be challenging ourselves to extend our field by addressing the full complexities of the organizational learning processes we study.

# References

Alavi, M. and Tiwana, A. 2003. Knowledge management: The information technology dimension. In M. Easterby-Smith and M. Lyles (eds.), *The Blackwell Handbook of Organizational Learning and Knowledge Management*, pp. 104–121. Oxford, UK: Blackwell.

Anand, B.N. and Khanna, T. 2000. Do firms learn to create value? The case of alliances. *Strategic Management Journal*, **21** (Special Issue): 295–315.

Argote, L. 1982. Input uncertainty and organizational coordination in hospital emergency units. *Administrative Science Quarterly*, **27**: 420–34.

Argote, L. 1999. *Organizational Learning: Creating, Retaining, and Transferring Knowledge*. Boston, MA: Kluwer Academic.

Argote, L., Beckman, S.L., and Epple, D. 1990. The persistence and transfer of learning in industrial settings. *Management Science*, **36**: 140–54.

Barney, J. 1991. Firm resources and sustained competitive advantage. *Journal of Management*, **17**(1): 99–120.

Baum, J.A., Li, S.X., and Usher, J.M. 2000. Making the next move: How experiential and vicarious learning shape the locations of chains' acquisitions. *Administrative Science Quarterly*, **45**(4): 766–801.

Bower, J. 1970. *Managing the Resource Allocation Process*. Boston, MA: Harvard Business School Press.

Cockburn, I. and Henderson, R. 1998. Absorptive capacity, co-authoring behavior, and the organization of research in drug discovery. *Journal of Industrial Economics*, **46**: 157–83.

Cohen, D. and Prusak, L. 2001. *In Good Company: How Social Capital Makes Organizations Work*. Boston, MA: HBS Press.

Cohen, W.M. and Levinthal, D.A. 1990. Absorptive capacity: A new perspective on learning and innovation. *Administrative Science Quarterly*, **35**: 128–52.

Crossan, M., Lane, H., and White, R. 1999. An organizational learning framework: From intuition to institution. *Academy of Management Review*, **24**: 522–38.

Dussauge, P., Garrette, B., and Mitchell, W. 2000. Learning from competing partners: Outcomes and durations of scale and link alliances in Europe, North America, and Asia. *Strategic Management Journal*, **21**(2): 99–126.

Doz, Y. and Hamel, G. 1998. *Alliance Advantage: The Art of Creating Value through Partnering*. Boston, MA: Harvard Business School Press.

Dyer, J. and Singh, H. 1998. The relational view: Cooperative strategy and sources of interorganizational competitive advantage. *Academy of Management Review*, **23**(4): 660–79.

Eisenhardt, K.M. and Martin, J.A. 2001. Dynamic capabilities: What are they? *Strategic Management Journal*, **21**: 1105–21.

Kale, P., Singh, H. and Perlmutter, H. 2000. Learning and protection of proprietary assets in strategic alliances: Building relational capital. *Strategic Management Journal*, **21**(3): 217–37.

Kogut, B. and Zander, U. 1992. Knowledge of the firm, integration capabilities, and the replication of technology. *Organization Science*, **3**: 383–97.

Kogut, B. and Zander, U. 1996. What firms do? Coordination, identity, and learning. *Organization Science*, **7**(5): 502–18.

Lane, P., Salk, J., and Lyles, M.A. 2001. Knowledge acquisition and performance in transitional economy international joint ventures. *Strategic Management Journal*, **22**(12): 1139–62.

Lyles, M.A. 1988. Learning among joint-ventures sophisticated firms. *Management International Review*, **28**(4): 85–98.

Lyles, M.A. and Salk, J.E. 1996. Knowledge acquisition from foreign parents in international joint ventures: An empirical examination in the Hungarian context. *Journal of International Business Studies*, **29**(2): 154–74.

March, J.G. 1991. Exploration and exploitation in organization learning. *Organization Science*, **2**: 71–87.

Makhija, M.V. and Ganesh, U. 1997. The relationship between control and partner learning in learning-related joint ventures. *Organization Science*, **8**: 508–27.

Miner, A.S., Bassoff, P., and Moorman, C. 2001. Contours of organizational improvisation and learning. *Administrative Science Quarterly*, **46**: 304–37.

Nonaka, I. 1994. A dynamic theory of organizational knowledge creation. *Organization Science*, **5**(1): 14–37.

Polanyi, M. 1966. *The Tacit Dimension*. Garden City, NY: Doubleday.

Reuer, J., Park, K. and Zollo, M. 2002. Experiential learning in international joint ventures: The roles of experience heterogeneity and venture novelty. In F. Contractor and P. Lorange (eds.), *Cooperative Strategies and Alliances*. Amsterdam: Elsevier.

Simon, H. 1978. Rationality as process and as product of thought. *American Economic Review*, **68**: 1–16.

Simonin, B.L. 1999. Ambiguity and the process of knowledge transfer in strategic alliances. *Strategic Management Journal*, **20**(7): 595–623.

Szulanski, G. 1996. Exploring internal stickiness: Impediments to the transfer of best practice within the firm. *Strategic Managment Journal*, **17** (Winter Special Issue): 27–43.

Uzzi, B. 1997. Social structure and competition in interfirm networks: The paradox of embeddedness. *Administrative Science Quarterly*, **42**: 35–67.

Van den Bosch, F., Volberda, H.W., and de Boer, M. 2001. Coevolution of firm absorptive capacity and knowledge environment: Organizational forms and combinative capabilities. *Organization Science*, **10**: 551–68.

Vera, D. and Crossan, M. 2003. Organizational learning and knowledge management: Toward an integrative framework. In M. Easterby-Smith and M. Lyles (eds.), *Blackwell Handbook of Organizational Learning and Knowledge Management*, pp. 122–41. Oxford, UK: Blackwell.

Wernerfelt, B. 1984. A resourced-based view of the firm. *Strategic Management Journal*, **5**(2): 171–80.

Winter, S.G. 1987. Knowledge and competence as strategic assets. In D.J. Teece (ed.), *The Competitive Challenge: Strategies for Industrial Innovation and Renewal*. Cambridge, MA: Ballinger.

Zander, U. and Kogut, B. 1995. Knowledge and the speed of the transfer and imitation of organizational capabilities: An empirical test. *Organization Science*, **6**(1): 76–92.

Zahra, S.A. and George, G. 2002. Absorptive capacity: A review, reconceptualization, and extension. *Academy of Management Review*, **27**(2): 185–203.

# CHAPTER NINE

# Rethinking the Strategy Process: A Co-evolutionary Approach

## Henk W. Volberda

## Introduction

It is becoming increasingly obvious that single-theme explanations for strategy processes have reached their limit and that strategy process scholars should adopt research strategies that consider joint outcomes of managerial adaptation and environmental selection (cf. Dooley and Van de Ven, 1999; Van de Ven and Grazman, 1999: 186; Van de Ven and Poole, 1995). *Selection* perspectives view strategy processes as highly restricted by resource scarcity, convergence to industry norms, and structural inertia. In other words, the strategic activities of successful firms are very similar and limited to strengthening and exploiting their existing core competencies. By contrast, *adaptation* perspectives suggest that firms can and do change, overcoming their rigidities. That is, successful firms learn to behave differently and explore new competencies.

In this chapter, I investigate the strategy processes of multi-unit firms by considering environmental selection *jointly* with managerial adaptation (Volberda and Lewin, 2003; Lewin and Volberda, 1999). I look at three levels of analysis in the strategy process – the *environment*, the headquarters or *top management* of the multi-unit firm, and the *front-line* or business unit managers – and how these levels co-evolve over time. The result is a managerial framework of *four idealized strategy processes* – emergent, directed, facilitated, and transformational (see Figure 9.1). This framework suggests a coherent set of answers to the following questions (Volberda and Baden-Fuller, 2003; Volberda, Baden-Fuller, and Van den Bosch, 2001):

- What roles do managers at the corporate and unit level play in these strategy processes (top versus frontline, middle line)?
- How do they share knowledge with each other across organizational boundaries (intra-organizational learning)?
- What are the outcomes of these strategy processes (industry rules)?

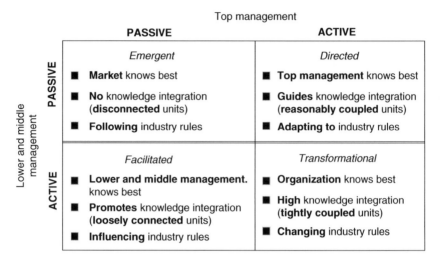

**Figure 9.1**   Strategy process configurations. Source: Volberda *et al.*, 2001

## The Emergent Strategy Process: Follow the Market

The emergent strategy process is rooted in the assumption that some managers believe that they should be essentially outwardly oriented or passive, their role being to amplify market forces and market signals for the benefit of the unit managers. For example, top managers set their business units targets based on profits, rather than internal processes such as speed of new product development, and then typically reward their middle and unit managers with bonuses closely linked to these targets.

The emergent strategy process has low administrative costs, and is common among many high-performing conglomerates in stable mature environments. Units often perform very well in the short term, selecting carefully among their capabilities to achieve maximal returns. Failure has clear sanctions: when a division or unit is "selected out", it is closed, sold, or finds its resources withdrawn. The emergent strategy process is usually defended in terms of its suitability to dealing with mature slow-moving environments, with little evidence of synergies between units that cannot be done through the market. The benefit of the emergent approach is in avoiding the myopia of being wedded to particular ideas or notions; a trap that mature firms can fall into even in mature environments. Historically many firms have adopted this approach when the industry was stable. It is doubtful that this strategy process is suited to volatile environments where there is a need to build synergies.

## The Directed Strategy Process: Top Management should be in Control

In directed strategy processes, top managers believe they have some power over their environment. In this perspective, strategy processes are driven by *a priori* managerial intentions with cascade-down development. A key role for top management is to provide the purpose or strategic intent in guiding strategy processes. As a result of top-down strategy making, multi-unit firms make their strategy changes deliberately, adapting to changes in their competitive environment, with top management explicitly managing the balance of exploration and exploitation by bringing in new competencies to some units while utilizing well-developed competencies in others.

Directed strategy processes typically result in interference in the way units are structured, and the way they allocate resources internally. Top management may have a preferred organization design (such as the matrix) and a capital allocation rule ($x$ percent to new products, $y$ percent to improving processes). Top management typically argues that highly integrated firms need direction and hierarchy for regulation of internal change and that careful coordination is vital to avoiding the possibility that different units go off in different directions. The risk of "paralysis by analysis" is always present, making this strategy process difficult in dynamic, rapidly changing environments. The directed strategy process appears to be particularly suited to firms experiencing steady growth or decline, where the benefits of hierarchy in terms of formal planning and control can be fully realized.

But what to do in situations when following the market is not enough or top management is not in control? The other two strategy processes, facilitated and transformational, represent more clearly possible patterns for the multi-unit firms of tomorrow. These processes are much less common in mature environments and represent significant challenges to traditional management thinking. They require front-line and middle management to take a more active stand. They are more complex and co-evolutionary and require more subtle approaches to management.

## The Facilitated Strategy Process: Increase Variety of Strategic Initiatives

In the facilitated strategy process, lower levels of management are active in the choices for and mechanics of renewal. Top management's role is to create a strategic context for nurturing and selecting promising strategic initiatives by ensuring maximum incentives for front-line initiative. The logic of this process is that front-line managers have the most current knowledge and expertise and are closer to the routines and sources of information that are critical to innovative outcomes. Top management can act as the retrospective legitimizer (Burgelman, 1983) or judge and arbiter (Angle and Van de Ven, 1989) in support of lower level initiatives. In the facilitated strategy process, top management moves away from having profit targets and market share as the sole objectives for measurement, and takes a more balanced internal-external perspective, adding actions such as the frequency of new product and service introduction, and the operation of goals such as the share of revenues from new ideas. In addition, top management may intervene in guiding the structure of units, suggesting or directing forms of organizing.

By comparison with the emergent strategy process, multi-unit firms in this configuration are likely to show a more balanced portfolio of exploitation units and exploration units and allow much more potential for learning across the firm's units. Yet the thinness of the top management group and the lack of significant resources devoted to moving knowledge can make intra-corporate learning more limited than in other strategy processes. While the facilitated process is far more difficult for top management to handle, it has the potential to yield far greater results when the environment is turbulent and there is a need for coordination between units. However, top management's lack of direct control over the organization makes it difficult for the multi-unit firm to engage in any large-scale developments that require central coordination or synergy across units. The facilitated strategy process is therefore appropriate in highly complex and dynamic markets where deliberate strategy of any kind becomes difficult.

## The Transformational Strategy Process: Mobilize a Company-wide Change Process

In the transformational strategy process, top management still believes that it can influence the environment, but also believes in working closely with the lower levels. Involvement of front-line managers is seen as essential to the strategy process, and, in this sense, the process can be described as holistic, with a close link between collective cognitions and the process of strategic change (Barr, Stimpert, and Huff, 1992). Transformational strategy processes are associated with significant unlearning, new ways of thinking and new mindsets, different paths of technology, and particular kinds of corporate entrepreneurship.

The corporate entrepreneurship literature suggests this journey is a holistic exercise that eventually involves the whole business, requiring systemic rather than piecemeal changes in the multi-unit firm. This change may cascade through the organization, and it is quite clear that organizations can move in cycles between one extreme (exploitation) and the other (exploration), with periods of systemic exploration when the organization is renewing and changing its skills and competencies (Volberda, 1996). This strategy process therefore is likely to be characterized by an imbalance between exploration and exploitation.

In transformational strategy processes, the top management team is led by a chief executive who is much more than an administrator; he or she is a transformational leader who drives the process from the front but involves others and brings them along too. Transformational strategy processes demand that the whole organization must be involved if radical change encompassing new technologies and new processes is to be accomplished. For the multi-unit firm this process is quite different from directed strategy processes. Besides transformational leadership, it emphasizes the importance of the middle managers as entrepreneurs who connect the differing levels of the organization. This is not the case of one level driving another, but of team working among levels and functions (Wooldridge and Floyd, 1990).

Transformational strategy processes are often associated with narrowly defined technological trajectories, but wide dispersion in other dimensions, for example, large multinational firms, where all the divisions are in a closely related business and the environment is evolutionary but punctuated by occasional radical shifts. In such cases the importance of intra-organization learning (Birkinshaw and Hood, 1998) is often high (transmitting best practice from one country to another). When occasional radical shifts are necessary, the firm can rise to the challenge.

## Future Strategy Process Research

Organizations are not static, and often resist attempts at simple categorization. As McKelvey (1997) points out, we must be careful in our modeling of human systems not to forget the possibility of choice. While strategy processes are highly idiosyncratic, I used (following McKelvey, 1997) idealized models in terms of pure strategy processes as one of the approaches to the problem of idiosyncrasy. Of course, the proof of the pudding is in the eating. What is the evidence in this chapter that our four strategy process configurations facilitate and stimulate accumulation of knowledge? The paucity of good empirical work gives us pause for thought. Cross-sectional survey-based studies and economic time series modeling (firm is treated as a black box) by far dominate the empirical research landscape (Volberda and Lewin, 2003). We need more long-term studies of how strategy processes evolve and emerge over very long periods of time where several of the strategy process configurations can be compared, not just two at a time. Unfortunately the number of such studies is very small (cf. Barr, Stimpert, and Huff, 1992; Huygens *et al.*, 2001; Jenkins and Floyd, 2001; Van de Ven and Grazman, 1999).

### Implications for performance

The performance implications of our strategy process configurations have not been explored in detail. For instance, is one of these idealized strategy processes more successful than the others? The emergent strategy process represents an extreme, where top management amplifies market pressures, often enforcing more rigorous standards than would otherwise be imposed. There is no doubt that for substantial periods of time, firms have done very well by adopting such emergent processes. Directed strategy processes appear to be particularly suited to firms experiencing steady growth or decline, where the benefits of hierarchy in terms of formal planning and control can be fully realized. However, in these emergent and directed processes firms can at best follow or adapt to industry rules.

In contrast, in *transformational strategy processes* where the front-line managers are working closely with top managers, learning is intense and diversity among levels and groups leads to exploration and rejuvenation. Here, top management sees its role as overcoming the market forces of selection, forcing fast-track adaptive and learning behavior. The firm may even change the rules of the industry. As a developmental model, it sounds ideal, but the resulting path appears to have drawbacks. It may be poor at dealing with technological discontinuities, and the journey may not be sustainable over time because of the supreme effort required to keep all of the parties involved. The firm may lurch from states of high exploration to high exploitation, placing severe demands on managerial capacity.

On the other hand, scholars specialized in complexity theory provide valuable evidence that *facilitated strategy processes* may be very effective (Brown and Eisenhardt, 1998; Anderson, 1999; Volberda, 1998). Here, the strategy process proceeds rapidly. Top management effects small probes in a characteristic rhythm, recombining the portfolio of units, so that novelty is deliberately generated without destroying the best elements of past experience. Top management operates on unit managers indirectly, taking advantage of the tendency for myriad local interactions to self-organize into a coherent pattern. Rather than shaping the pattern that constitutes strategic renewal (directed process), managers shape the context within which it emerges, speeding up co-evolutionary processes.

### Strategy process configurations as sources of competitive advantage

Our strategy processes point to important lessons for practicing managers. By setting up the benchmark as "selection", where managers are seen as passive, I am suggesting that there are real choices for managers to make, explicitly or implicitly. These choices include four different strategy processes (see Figure 9.1). Each of these is distinctive in its benefits and costs. Each differs in efficacy according to environmental stimuli, and each implies differences in roles for top and front-line management. This chapter offers potential insights into some of the consequences of these choices. In doing so, I hope to help managers in mastering strategy, mobilizing change, and creating competitive advantage.

## References

Anderson, P. 1999. Complexity theory and organization science. *Organization Science*, **10**(5): 216–32.

Angle, H.L. and Van de Ven, A.H. 1989. Suggestions for managing the innovation journey. In A.H. Van de Ven, H.L. Angle, and M.S. Poole (eds.), *Research on the Management of Innovation*, pp. 663–97. New York: Harper and Row.

Barr, P.S., Stimpert, J.L., and Huff, A.S. 1992. Cognitive change, strategic action, and organizational renewal. *Strategic Management Journal*, **13**: 15–36.

Birkinshaw J. and Hood, N. 1998. Multinational subsidiary evolution: Capability and charter change in foreign-owned subsidiary companies. *Academy of Management Review*, **23**(4): 773–95.

Brown, S.L. and Eisenhardt, K.M. 1998. *Competing on the Edge: Strategy as Structured Chaos.* Boston, MA: Harvard Business School Press.

Burgelman, R.A. 1983. A model of the interaction of strategic behavior, corporate context, and the concept of strategy. *Academy of Management Review*, **8**(1): 61–70.

Dooley, K.J. and Van de Ven, A.H. 1999. Explaining complex organizational dynamics. *Organization Science*, **10**(3): 358–72.

Huygens, M., Baden-Fuller, C., Van den Bosch, F.A.J., and Volberda, H.W. 2001. Coevolution of firm capabilities and industry competition: Investigating the music industry, 1877–1997. *Organization Studies*, **22**(6): 971–1011.

Jenkins, M. and Floyd, S. 2001. Trajectories in the evolution of technology: A multi-level study of competition in Formula I racing. *Organization Studies*, **22**(6): 945–71.

Lewin, A.Y. and Volberda, H.W. 1999. Prolegomena on coevolution: A framework for research on strategy and new organizational forms. *Organization Science*, **10**(5): 519–34.

McKelvey, B. 1997. Quasi-natural organization science. *Organization Science*, **8**(4): 352–80.

Van de Ven, A.H. and Grazman, D.N. 1999. Evolution in a nested hierarchy: A genealogy of twin cities' health care organizations, 1853–1995. In J.A.C. Baum and B. McKelvey (eds.), *Variations in Organization Science: In Honor of Donald T. Campbell.* London: Sage.

Van de Ven, A.H. and Poole, M.S. 1995. Explaining development and change in organizations. *Academy of Management Review*, **20**(3): 510–40.

Volberda, H.W. 1996. Toward the flexible form: How to remain vital in hypercompetitive environments. *Organization Science*, 7(4): 359–87.

Volberda, H.W. 1998. *Building the Flexible Firm: How to Remain Competitive*. Oxford, UK: Oxford University Press.

Volberda, H.W. and Baden-Fuller, Ch. 2003. Strategic renewal processes in multi-unit firms: Generic journeys of change. In B. Chakravarthy, G. Mueller-Stewens, P. Lorange, and C. Lechner (eds.), *Strategy Process: Shaping the Contours of the Field*, pp. 208–32. Oxford, UK: Blackwell.

Volberda, H.W., Baden-Fuller, Ch., and Van den Bosch, F.A.J. 2001. Mastering strategic renewal: Mobilizing renewal journeys in multi-unit firms. *Long Range Planning*, Special Theme: Mastering Strategic Renewal: Lessons from Financial Services, **34**(2): 159–78.

Volberda, H.W. and Lewin, A.Y. 2003. Co-evolutionary dynamics within and between firms: From evolution to co-evolution. *Journal of Management Studies*, **40**(8): 2111–36.

Wooldridge, B. and Floyd, S.W. 1990. The strategy process, middle management involvement and organizational performance. *Strategic Management Journal*, **11**: 231–41.

# CHAPTER TEN

# Distributed Agency and Interactive Emergence

## Raghu Garud, Peter Karnøe

There is now an emerging perspective that considers agency to be distributed across actors, artifacts, rules, and routines (Hutchins, 1995; Callon and Law, 1997). Such a perspective on agency implies that it would be difficult to attribute the outcomes of strategic actions to any single person. Rather, dynamic interactions between actors, artifacts, rules, and routines generate an "action net" within which strategic processes unfold (Czarniawska, 1997). It is to flesh out this process of interactive emergence that we write this chapter.

Our argument is as follows. A multiplicity of actors are involved in the process of interactive emergence (Garud and Karnøe, 2003; Van de Ven and Hargrave, 2003). These actors have different frames and their levels of involvement can vary over time (Bijker, Hughes, and Pinch, 1987; Weick, 1995, Callon, 1998). Material artifacts, rules, and routines that emerge provide some degree of durability to social interactions (Latour, 1991; March, 1994; Law, 1999). Yet, there is fragility in this apparent stability. As complex processes unfold, the locus of agency can easily shift from one part of the network to another part.

Interactive emergence stands in stark contrast to traditional views on strategy (see also Pettigrew, 1992). The "design school" (Mintzberg, Ahlstrand, and Lampel, 1998), for instance, celebrates the ability of a small group of people to analyze the strategic situation, chart out contingencies, and evaluate alternatives to generate a full-blown strategic plan. It is the task of organizational "foot soldiers" to implement these plans.

To develop our perspective on interactive emergence, we first provide an overview of the literature on distributed agency. We then develop a grounded feel for interactive emergence by offering accounts of processes that emerged as: (i) a group of plane crash victims struggled to survive; (ii) employees at 3M engaged in a process that led to the development and commercialization of Post-it Notes; and (iii) a multiplicity of organizational types became involved to jointly create a cochlear implant technological field.

## Distributed Agency

We build upon a "connectionist hypothesis" in cognition to introduce the notion of distributed agency (Granovetter, 1973; Sandelands and Stablein, 1987; Weick and Roberts, 1993; Garud and Kotha, 1994). To explain this position, we use the human brain as an analogy (Churchland, 1986; Arbib, 1989). Using layman's terms, bundles of neurons comprise several modules within the brain. Modules, richly connected with one another are "specialized" in certain functions, yet have a redundancy of functions built into them (Morgan, 1986). The specific connections that are activated and the strength of ties play an important role in determining the overall response pattern of the system.

Such distributed agency can be seen in the working of social groups. Hutchins (1995) described the navigation of ships into harbors, a task that one would normally ascribe to a small group of people including the ship's captain. Hutchins' description convincingly dispels this myth (see also Tsoukas, 1996). Agency is clearly distributed across people and artifacts and across time and space. Actors such as helmsmen, quartermasters, and "men on the cranks" all perform critical tasks in navigating the ship into harbor. Indeed, material artifacts, rules, and routines hold disturbed actors in time, place, and sequence to generate a successful outcome.

## Interactive Emergence in Three Settings

We explore the implications of such a distributed perspective for strategic action by providing three analytical cases. These cases were chosen to illustrate the applicability of interactive emergence across a wide variety of phenomena. As we describe these cases, we not only reinforce the themes that we have introduced, but also develop additional insights.

### Escaping disaster

The first case builds upon a detailed account of the trials and tribulations of a handful of plane crash survivors as they navigated their way through cold mountainous terrain to eventual safety (Read, 1974). Immediately after their plane crashed, survivors looked to two medical students for their expertise to treat the wounded. These medical students' influence over the group began to wane, however, as medicines ran out and as the critically wounded passed away. Acting as a mediator between different members of the group, the captain of the plane then emerged as a leader. The captain suggested that rescue would be soon forthcoming and that, therefore, the group should not leave the crash site. The availability of parts of the plane as shelter from the cold certainly must have factored into survivors' decision to heed the captain's advice.

Over time, as rescue did not materialize and as food supplies began to dwindle, the captain began loosing his legitimacy. A critical turning point in the dynamics of the group occurred when a person came to the conclusion that they would have to cannibalize the dead in order to survive. The articulation and justification of this concept was a watershed moment. Indeed, the locus of action shifted from the captain to those who were ready to cannibalize.

Even these details are sufficient to illustrate several points about distributed agency and interactive emergence. For instance, the locus of action can shift from one part of a network to another over time as actors with different frames and levels of involvement interact with one another. As the ordeal unfolded, the influence of even the person who proposed the consumption of human flesh receded as emerging social dynamics brought other members to the fore. Survivors began coddling three individuals who were identified to attempt an escape. At the same time, a group of cousins took over the maintenance of the social dynamics that emerged.

The description also illustrates the importance of material artifacts and social rules in determining distributed agency. It was the availability of medicines that afforded the students powers to influence others in the first place. These powers disappeared, however, as the medicines were depleted. Similarly, the presence of aircraft parts that offered shelter from the cold factored in survivors' decisions to await rescue rather than risk death trying to escape. It was only with the depletion of food that decisions were made to first cannibalize and then to attempt an escape.

It appears that the emergent decision context determined who would lead and the role that they would play. Analyzing this story, Smith (1977) had this provocative proposition to offer:

> When changes are taking place in response to extreme pressures, it often is most unclear what should happen to produce a new form of stability in which both directionality and internal coherence are present. What an individual might do personally to provide leadership is unclear and speculative. Instead, each new set of stresses causes changes in group memberships or behaviors, which, in turn, moves the system toward some new equilibrium. As this happens power, authority, critical resources, and ability to influence events become distributed differently than before.

Eventually, two members escaped from the treacherous mountains and the survivors were rescued. One would have thought that the group's ordeal was over, but it was not. Once back in civilization, the group had to explain their decision to cannibalize. And, it is at this point that a person who had so far played a minor role emerged as the person who could offer a compelling explanation as to why they had cannibalized. In other words, once again the locus of action shifted. Reflecting on this point, Smith (1977) concluded,

> Acts of leadership, then, are merely responses to the forces that emerge from the exchanges among groups within the system, and it would not be valid to construe them as reflecting a conscious intent to lead. If, in hindsight, an act appears to have been one of effective leadership, it may have been virtually accidental at the time it happened and identifiable as leadership only in retrospect.

What does this case tell us about distributed agency and interactive emergence? It suggests that strategy as a process builds upon the actions and interactions of many actors, each actor with a different set of competencies and with different frames. As the strategic landscape shifts through a transformational process, so does the locus of action. In other words, resources, legitimacy, and power shift through a process of interactions (Stacey, 2003).

## Emergence of Post-it Notes

These themes are to be found in the development of new products as well. Consider the development of Post-it Notes at 3M Corporation. It was sometime in the 1970s that a corporate scientist by the name of Silver first stumbled upon a glue that did not glue. Given that Silver was attempting to create a material that glued, most people would have rejected his experiment as a failure, but not Silver. Marveling at the structure of the material under the microscope, Silver became convinced that this strange but interesting substance could be of some value. It was with a quest to look around for a "problem" for his "solution" that Silver set about trying to entice his colleagues at 3M to take a look (Lindhal, 1988).

At 3M, innovation is truly a distributed process. When people think of an idea, they walk around and try to mobilize attention and resources to pursue their pet projects. In any other place, "bootlegging" would be considered as an unauthorized use of company-wide resources, but not at 3M. Indeed, in a place where "technology belongs to the corporation", employees are expected to "bootleg." Articulating the distributed processes that unfold during innovation at 3M, Fry explained:

> At 3M we've got so many different types of technology operating and so many experts and so much equipment scattered here and there, that we can piece things together when we're starting off. We can go to this place and do "Step A" on a product, and we can make the adhesive and some of the raw materials here, and do one part over here, and another part over there, and convert a space there and make a few things that aren't available (from Nayak and Ketteringham, 1986: 66–7).

Despite a culture that fosters such a collective process of bricolage, Silver first encountered indifference and resistance from his colleagues. Most 3M people said, "What can you do with a glue that does not glue?" Yet, Silver persisted. In looking for a problem for the "solution" that he had stumbled upon, Silver showed his weak glue to a number of his colleagues and, in the process, succeeded in seeding their minds with thoughts about his strange glue.

Generating such top-of-the-mind awareness for this weak glue paid off. At first, the glue was put on boards onto which paper could be stuck. But, the critical breakthrough occurred when another scientist, Art Fry, suddenly got an inspiration. One day, at a church, Fry suddenly remembered the weak glue that his friend Silver had created as he struggled to mark the pages in his book of songs. What if the glue could be applied to pieces of paper, Fry thought, and, at that moment, the concept of Post-it Notes emerged.

These events provide us with a way to think about individuals' roles within an emerging collective as being purposive even if outcomes are not predictable (Garud and Karnøe, 2001). Prototypes play an important role in shaping such processes. Actors' mental models are externalized as prototypes that begin serving as boundary objects (Star and Griesemer, 1989) around which actors with different frames grapple (Schrage, 2000). It is only through the circulation of these prototypes among actors whose own identities emerge in the process that a product concept emerges (Latour, 1991).

It is easy to attribute the success of such initiatives to a few individuals – Fry or Silver in the Post-it Notes case. However, such attribution would be misplaced. Fry noted:

> There are so many hoops that a product idea has to jump through. It really takes a bunch of individuals to carry it through the process. It's not just a Spence Silver or an Art Fry. It's a whole host of people. It's a classic 3M tale. I couldn't have done what I did without Silver. And without me, his adhesive might have come to nothing (from Lindhal, 1988: 17).

Indeed, Post-it Notes could not have come about without the critical involvement of people such as 3M's Nicholson and Ramey from marketing. To generate momentum for the idea, Nicholson and Ramey hit upon the idea of offering free samples to others to play with. Eventually, because of Nicholson and Ramey's efforts, Lehr, the CEO of the company, became involved. Lehr and his colleagues designed and implemented a plan to mobilize the interests of fellow Fortune 500 Company CEOs by sending them samples of Post-it Notes. The idea was to "hook" these CEOs onto Post-it Notes, and, in this objective, Lehr and his colleagues were successful.

What can we learn about interactive emergence from the Post-it Notes story? As with other in-depth accounts of product development, the locus of action shifts from one person to another as a product goes back and forth getting transformed in the process and, in turn, transforming the process. Searching for an apt metaphor to represent such a messy but progressive process, Nonaka and Takeuchi (1995) suggested that the development of a new product is not unlike the movement of a ball in a rugby game as team members take turns to take the ball forward, occasionally conferring with one another about how they should proceed.

### Cochlear implant industry emergence

Distributed and parallel processes that constitute interactive emergence can be found in the emergence of technological fields as well (Garud and Karnøe, 2003). To illustrate, we provide a brief description of the emergence of cochlear implants, a biomedical device that offers the profoundly deaf a sensation of sound (Garud and Van de Ven, 1989). As with other technological fields, a number of organizations were involved in the emergence of the cochlear implant field. Among others were commercial firms such as 3M and Nucleus. Also involved were academic and research institutions such as the University of Melbourne and the House Ear Institute (HEI). Organizations including the National Institutes of Health (NIH) and the Food and Drug Administration (FDA) also became involved with the process in their role as sponsor and regulator.

Actors in each of these organizations operated with different frames and were differentially engaged with emergent processes at different points in time. For instance, scientists at the HEI and the University of Melbourne made critical contributions to the development of the field much before others. It was the decision by the 3M Corporation to commercially develop cochlear implants that jumpstarted commercial activities. Actors at the FDA played a critical role in shaping commercial development, whereas actors at the NIH played a pivotal role much later in the development of the technology.

A "cross-elasticity" of emergent ties between 3M and other organizations is illustrative of interactive emergence. At a very early stage, 3M explored a collaborative relationship with researchers at the University of Melbourne. When this effort did not materialize, researchers at the University of Melbourne entered into a collaborative relationship with Nucleus, a firm that eventually turned out to become one of 3M's biggest rivals. In this case, an aborted effort at collaboration led to the creation of a competitor.

3M emerged as a broker between several parties when it entered into a collaborative relationship with the HEI and the Hochmairs of Vienna. Eventually, 3M's brokering role extended to include the FDA as well. Again, a cross-elasticity of ties became evident when the FDA granted 3M approvals to market its device based on the HEI technology. Soon thereafter, 3M announced that it would begin developing Hochmairs' extra-cochlear technology. In the process, a competitive relationship emerged, not only between HEI and Hochmairs, but also between HEI and 3M.

Both the HEI and the Hochmairs had been pursuing a single-channel technology; an approach that 3M believed would offer patients opportunities to benefit from a simple yet safe device while preserving the cochlea for future upgrades. Nucleus, in contrast, chose to pursue multi-channel technology, believing that such an approach offered them and their patients maximum flexibility to migrate to future devices. The two technologies offered different "affordances" (Gibson, 1979; Norman, 1988) to each firm and had an important bearing on the dynamics that unfolded over time.

It is not possible for us to go into all the details of these differential affordances, but we will highlight one critical episode to illustrate our point. The FDA, soon after granting its approval for the commercial release of the 3M–HEI single-channel devices, announced that products based on multi-channel technology would soon become available. The FDA's announcement was a pivotal moment that had the effect of shifting the center of action from 3M's "value net" (Brandenburger and Nalebuff, 1996) that revolved around the single-channel technology to Nucleus' value net that revolved around the multi-channel technology.

The shift from 3M's value net to Nucleus' value net was completed when an actor that had so far played a low-key role organized an event that had a lasting impact on the emergence of the field. Coming to a conclusion that there still existed a deep controversy about which technology would yield the best results, the NIH organized a consensus development program at Bethesda, Maryland, in 1988. Within a matter of days, a group of around 400 researchers who congregated at the conference came to a conclusion that multi-channel technology offered superior options over single-channel technology. Nucleus' position as the leader was solidified.

How does the cochlear implant case confirm and extend our understanding of interactive emergence? It does so in several ways. First, it confirms that the strategic landscape shifts in the process of interactive emergence. When these fundamental shifts occur, actors find themselves in new positions and relationships. The description appears to confirm the notion of structural holes that brokers such as 3M fill, but a closer examination suggests that these structural holes are "enacted spaces" (Weick, 1995) that can shift from one place in the network to another. Such dynamics should not be surprising given the compulsive nature of technological change (Rosenberg, 1982), where bottlenecks and opportunities are bouncing around networks because of technological changes, knowledge flows, and strategic interactions.

## Implications and Conclusion

As may be apparent from our description, interactive emergence is a perspective that can be productively applied to gain insights on a range of phenomena. Indeed, we see several consistent patterns that we have already alluded to so far. These processes are driven by the involvement of a multiplicity of actors with different frames and levels of involvement. As they interact, actors create material artifacts and organizational routines that afford certain opportunities and constraints. A socio-technical ensemble (Bijker, 1995) emerges through action, and, in the process, the locus of action may shift from one set of actors to another. In sum, interactive emergence represents "ecologies of interconnecting activities within which simple ideas of linear casual order and power are hard to sustain" (March and Simon, 1993).

The three cases also illuminate specific extensions to our understanding of distributed agency and interactive emergence. For instance, the group survival case highlights self-organizing transformative processes wherein the presence or absence of material artifacts affords different actors emergent opportunities to play influential roles. The Post-it Notes case highlights the importance of material artifacts as boundary objects that facilitate the interactions of actors with different frames. The cochlear implants case highlights cross-elasticity of ties that constitute a network and illuminates how collaborative relationships can become competitive over time.

What is the meaning of individual agency in such a conceptualization? Distributed agency and interactive emergence suggest that it would not be appropriate to attribute the outcomes of strategic processes to any one actor. Yet, distributed agency and interactive emergence hold important implications for individual agency within an emerging action net. We know that everyday managerial life consists of "sorting and ordering" (Bowker and Star, 1999) disconnected fragments of things, tools, events, and actors that are all incorporated into strategic frames. At key moments, though, these ordinary actors are called upon to perform extraordinary tasks as pockets of leadership opportunities emerge. Individual agency, then, is defined by the intersection of opportunities and constraints that individuals confront as they engage with an emerging network of actors, material artifacts, rules, and routines.

## Acknowledgments

We thank Paul Duguid, Roger Dunbar, Kristian Kreiner, and Kamal Munir for holding ongoing conversations with us on this topic. We thank Nandita Garud for her editorial help.

# References

Arbib, M.A. 1989. *The Metaphorical Brain: Neural Networks and Beyond*. New York: Wiley.

Bijker, W. 1995. *Of Bicycles, Bakelites, and Bulbs: Toward a Theory of Sociotechnical Change*. Cambridge, MA: MIT Press.

Bijker, W., Hughes, T., and Pinch, T. 1987. *The Social Construction of Technological Systems: New Directions in the Sociology and History of Technology*. Cambridge, MA: MIT Press.

Bowker, G.S. and Star, S.L. 1999. *Sorting Things Out: Classification and its Consequences*. Cambridge, MA: MIT Press.

Brandenburger, A. and Nalebuff, B.J. 1996. *Co-opetition*. New York: Doubleday.

Callon, M. 1998. The embeddedness of economic markets in economics. In M. Callon (ed.), *The Laws of the Market*, pp. 1–57. Oxford, UK: Blackwell.

Callon, M. and Law, J. 1997. After the individual in society: Lessons on collectivity from science, technology and society. *Canadian Journal of Sociology*, 22: 165–82.

Churchland, P.S. 1986. *Neurophilosophy*. Cambridge, MA: MIT Press.

Czarniawska, B. 1997. *Narrating the Organization: Dramas of Institutional Identity*. Chicago, IL: Chicago University Press.

Garud, R. and Karnøe, P. 2001. Path creation as a process of mindful deviation. In R. Garud and P. Karnøe (eds.), *Path Dependence and Creation*, pp. 1–38. New York: Lawrence Erlbaum.

Garud, R. and Karnøe, P. 2003. Bricolage vs. breakthrough: Distributed and embedded agency in technology entrepreneurship. *Research Policy*, 32: 277–300.

Garud, R. and Kotha, S. 1994. Using the brain as a metaphor to model flexible productive units. *The Academy of Management Review*, 19(4): 671–98.

Garud, R. and Van de Ven, A.H. 1989. Technological innovation and industry emergence: The case of cochlear implants. In A.H. Van de Ven, H.L. Angle, and M.S. Poole (eds.), *Research on the Management of Innovation: The Minnesota Studies*, pp. 489–535. New York: Harper and Row.

Gibson, J.J. 1979. *The Ecological Approach to Visual Perception*, Boston, MA: Houghton Mifflin.

Granovetter, M. 1973. The strength of weak ties. *American Journal of Sociology*, 78: 1360–80.

Hutchins, E. 1995. *Cognition in the Wild*. Cambridge, MA: MIT Press.

Latour, B. 1991. Technology is society made durable. In J. Law (ed.), *A Sociology of Monsters: Essays on Power, Technology and Domination*, pp. 103–31. London: Routledge.

Law, J. 1999. After ANT: Complexity, naming, and topology. In J. Law and J. Hassard (eds.), *Actor Network Theory and after*. Oxford, UK: Blackwell.

Lindhal, L. 1988. Spence Silver: A scholar and a gentleman. *3M Today*, 15(1): 12–17.

March, J.G. 1994. *A Primer on Decision Making*. New York: The Free Press.

March J.G. and Simon, H.A. 1993. *Organizations*. New York: Wiley.

Morgan, G. 1986. *Images of Organization*. Beverly Hills, CA: Sage.

Mintzberg, H., Ahlstrand, B., and Lampel, J. 1998. *Strategy Safari: A Guided Tour Through the Wilds of Strategic Management*. New York: The Free Press.

Nayak, P.R. and Ketteringham, J.M. 1986. *Breakthroughs!* New York: Rawson Associates.

Nonaka, I. and Takeuchi, H. 1995. *The Knowledge-Creating Company*. New York: Oxford University Press.

Norman, D.A. 1988. *The Psychology of Everyday Things*. New York: Basic Books.

Pettigrew, A.M. 1992. Character and significance of strategic process research. *Strategic Management Journal*, 13: 5–16.

Read, P. 1974. *Alive: The Story of the Andes Survivors.* New York: J.B. Lippincott.

Rosenberg, N. 1982. *Inside the Black Box: Technology and Economics.* New York: Cambridge University Press.

Sandelands, L.E. and Stablein, R.E. 1987. The concept of organization mind. In S. Bacharac and N. DiTomaso (eds.), *Research in the Sociology of Organizations,* pp. 135–61. Greenwich, CT: JAI Press.

Schrage, M. 2000. *Serious Play: How The World's Best Companies Simulate to Innovate.* Boston, MA: Harvard Business School Press.

Smith, K. 1977. An intergroup perspective on individual behavior. In J.R. Hackman, E.E. Lawler III, and L.W. Porter (eds.), *Perspectives on Behavior in Organizations.* New York: McGraw-Hill.

Stacey, R. 2003. *Strategic Management and Organizational Dynamics.* New York: Pitman.

Star, S. and Griesemer, J. 1989. Institutional ecology, "translations" and boundary objects. Amateurs and professionals in Berkeley's Museum of Vertebrate Zoology, 1907–39. *Social Studies of Science,* **19**: 387–430.

Tsoukas, H. 1996. The firm as a distributed knowledge system: A constructionist approach. *Strategic Management Journal,* **17**: 11–25.

Van de Ven, A. and Hargrave, T. 2003. "Converging Perspectives on Institutional Change in Technology and Social Movements," paper presented at Academy of Management Meetings in Seattle, WA, August 5, 2003.

Weick, K. 1995. *Sensemaking in Organizations.* Beverly Hills, CA: Sage.

Weick, K. and Roberts, K. 1993. Collective mind in organizations: Heedful interrelating on flight decks. *Administrative Science Quarterly,* **38**(3): 357–81.

# CHAPTER ELEVEN

# Making Strategy in the Multi-business Firm

Sotirios Paroutis, Andrew Pettigrew

## Introduction

Over the past decades, process scholars have been trying to capture how strategy is formulated and implemented in contemporary organizational settings (Chakravarthy and Doz, 1992; Pettigrew, 1992; Van de Ven, 1992). The result has been a number of rich studies exploring the actors and settings of the strategy process. Recent research has pointed out the importance of strategy practices (e.g. *Journal of Management Studies*, **40**(1), January 2003). Building on these studies we are interested in two broad questions: How is strategy made in multi-business firms? What are the capabilities required to make strategy? The purpose of this chapter is to present some preliminary empirical findings around these two questions. Eight interviews with strategy directors from the UK banking, energy, utility, and pharmaceutical sectors serve as the primary source of these findings. The interviews were conducted in March and April 2002 as pilots for a bigger research project that examines the realities of making and executing strategy in multi-business firms over time. Evidence from these pilot interviews suggest that there is no clear way to make strategy. Instead firms experiment with different ways of making strategy and developing the capabilities to make strategy.

Why are these multi-business firms experimenting with how they make strategy? Following a contextualist approach (Pettigrew, 1985, 1987) we believe that the strategy-making process cannot be properly understood unless one examines the context within which this process has emerged and this context cannot be properly understood unless one studies it over time. More in-depth research could focus on the contextual conditions of multi-business firms as well as the actions and interactions of managers and their teams at both the corporate center and the business unit levels. Overall, our goal is to provide some empirical insights into the what, who, and how of strategy making in multi-business firms. As a result, a large proportion of this chapter is dedicated to the evidence derived from our pilot study. For a more detailed theoretical background of this project please refer to Paroutis and Pettigrew (2001). This chapter is organized as follows: the first section outlines the background and method of the pilot; the second offers the main empirical findings; and the third and final section presents the conclusions and implications for future research.

## Background and Research

### Background

Three areas provide the background for this research: the established literature on strategy making and strategy processes; newer research on micro-strategy and strategizing; and research about multi-business firms. Previous studies on strategy-making processes have often concentrated on a specific, often limited, set of themes or actors. As a result, the process typologies tend to depict strategy in terms of static states (Webb and Pettigrew, 1999). Studies of managerial decision making (Fredrickson, 1986; Miller and Friesen, 1978) emphasize the behavioral aspects of strategists but the resulting cognitive studies are poorly linked with the strategy process. This demonstrates the need to approach how strategists influence the strategy-making process not only by taking decisions, but also by shaping the conduct and context of that process. Strategy-process research (e.g. Chakravarthy and Doz, 1992; Mintzberg, 1978; Pettigrew, 1992; Van de Ven, 1992) examines how strategies are shaped within companies, implemented and validated. For the study of multi-business firms learning can be taken from process studies which analyze sequences of actions and the context in which these actions are situated (Pettigrew, 1985). Examining action in context allows a much richer appreciation of the multiple factors influencing the strategy process.

The second group of literature involves recent research on micro-strategy and strategizing. This is an area where contributions are growing (e.g. *Journal of Management Studies* Special Issue on "Micro-Strategy and Strategizing", **40**(1), January 2003). Strategizing refers to the micro-level, day-to-day processes and practices through which organizational members construct and enact strategies (Whittington, 1996). Using these insights we approach in this chapter the making of strategy as an ongoing process in context (Webb and Pettigrew, 1999). We develop this approach from two aspects where previous empirical research is limited: the practices of strategists and their teams; and the capabilities to make strategy. The first aspect concerns the actions of managers involved in making strategy across different organizational levels. The focus here is not only on the upper echelon (Finkelstein and Hambrick, 1996), but also the wider set of strategy staff, advisors, and their teams. The second aspect refers to the capabilities to make strategy. Questions on capabilities have been raised in much strategic management writing (Grant, 1991; Teece, Gary, and Shuen, 1997). However, there is scarce empirical evidence about the capabilities required by managers to make strategy.

This study is concerned with multi-business firms. The main characteristic of these firms is their organizational structure that consists of a corporate center and business units (Goold and Campbell, 1987; Williamson, 1975). These units often have particular objectives, structures, leadership styles, and systems. As a result, there are multiple ways of spotting issues, setting priorities, and developing strategic initiatives within the same firm. This creates complex political dynamics between the center and the periphery during the strategy process. These characteristics present multi-business firms with unique challenges during their strategy-making process. Next, we present the methodology for this pilot study.

## Pilot site selection, data collection, and analysis

The selection of companies to conduct the pilot study followed a two-phase approach. In the first phase four UK industries were identified (utilities, banking, energy, and pharmaceuticals) and in the second phase eight multi-business firms within these industries were chosen. These industries have undergone significant changes over the past decade. For example, in the UK utility market deregulation has broken up the electricity value chain and the traditional model of vertically integrated utilities has been abandoned. New generation technologies have also reduced the minimum thresholds of entry in the market. The dual contextual effects of deregulation and new technologies have indeed changed the utility sector. In the second phase a list of UK-based companies from these four industries was generated. To ensure that the firms were large multi-business firms the list was compared with the FTSE-100 (December 2001) and Forbes International-500 (2001). The new list was then filtered according to the geographic proximity of their headquarters. Finally, eight firms (which we refer to as: UtilCoA, UtilCoB, BankCoA, BankCoB, BankCoC, EnergyCoA, EnergyCoB, PharmaCo) were selected as potential sites for the pilots and letters were sent to their strategy directors. All directors responded positively to our request. The interviews were semi-structured and a carefully designed interview pro forma was used. The choice of questions was guided by the content, process, and context analytical framework for research on strategic change (Pettigrew, 1985, 1987). The intention of using this framework was to capture holistically the strategy-making process. Each interview lasted approximately 100 minutes. Seven interviews were tape-recorded and fully transcribed. Company reports and strategy presentations were also used to complement the interviews.

This pilot study has a number of limitations. First, a single, senior strategy manager from the corporate center of each company was interviewed. As a result, we portray their personal understanding of a complex phenomenon. More significantly, we approach the making of strategy using evidence only from the corporate center. However, the bigger research project does incorporate evidence from the business units. Second, these interviews offer limited room for pattern recognition and detailed comparison of evidence across the firms. It has to be noted that we are not using these interviews in the place of in-depth case studies but as means towards an initial appreciation of strategy making in multi-business firms. The content, context, and process framework alongside relevant propositions informed our initial research strategy (Paroutis and Pettigrew, 2001). The transcripts were systematically studied using an inductive and deductive approach. This developmental research strategy resulted in categories that are anchored both in the literature and our empirical evidence. In what follows, we present two broad categories of findings about making strategy and the capabilities to make strategy (refer to Table 11.1).

**Table 11.1** The set of preliminary categories after the pilot interviews

**Making strategy**

| The meaning of strategy | Explicit | |
|---|---|---|
| | Implicit | |
| Participants in the strategy process | Participants by position | CEO<br>Board of directors<br>Top management team<br>Middle management<br>Operating management |
| | Participants by influence | Internal advisors<br>External advisors<br>Strategy teams at the center<br>Strategy teams at the periphery |
| Practices around the strategy process | Deductive | Routine projects<br>Planning process |
| | Inductive | Strategic initiatives<br>Negotiation and dialogue process |

**Strategizing capabilities**

| Strategizing capabilities in contemporary business | Technical abilities | |
|---|---|---|
| | Social, political, and communication skills | |
| | Meta-level abilities | Conceptual skills<br>Creativity |
| Developing strategizing capabilities | Internally | Career development<br>Internal advisors<br>Internal training process |
| | Externally | Hiring<br>External advisors<br>External training process |

## Some Findings from the Pilot Study

### Making strategy

The first category of analysis explores the characteristics around the creation of strategy in multi-business firms. In the following sections three subcategories under "making strategy" are presented: "the meaning of strategy" about the content of strategy; "participants in the strategy process" about those involved in strategy; and "practices around the strategy process" about the activities of those strategists.

*The meaning of strategy.*   One of the initial questions posed to the directors of strategy during the pilot interviews was about the meaning of strategy. The goal here was to record the constituting elements of strategy in multi-business firms. By extending Burgelman's model (2002) we suggest that the concept of strategy in multi-business firms has (a) explicit and (b) implicit elements. The explicit elements have the following attributes: they are formal (written down in company documents); readily identifiable by the organizational members; and relatively enduring over time. The implicit elements are more informal, open to debate and dialogue between the organizational members, and tend to change frequently over time. Operationally, the explicit and implicit elements refer to the vision, principles, values, and goals associated with the concept of strategy. The main criterion here is whether these elements are perceived as implicit or explicit by the organizational members. Hence, in some companies the strategy standards could be perceived as implicit, thus they are formed through debate, while in other organizations strategy standards might be implicit and thus they are relatively enduring. These initial findings also indicate that over time multi-business firms are experimenting with different explicit and implicit elements in their strategy.

First, our evidence suggests that the explicit elements of strategy reflect the particular contextual conditions of each multi-business firm. In EnergyCoA, for example, a set of aspirations communicated by the corporate center defines the content of strategy: "it is an aspiration . . . and [our] strategy describes the route . . . [to] get there" (Director, EnergyCoA). In EnergyCoB strategy is directly linked with a set of explicit rules which provide an ongoing bias to the decision-making processes: "all entities have strategies but their real operating strategies are a mix of implicit and explicit rules by which decisions get taken" (Director, EnergyCoB). These principles are often linked with the top management "when he [the CEO] talks strategy he means some really very high level principles" (Director, EnergyCoB), "clearly it's the meta-principles which the Board are principally approving" (Director, EnergyCoB). The meaning of strategy is also associated with different sets of values in different firms reflecting their particular contextual characteristics. In UtilCoA, for instance, the historical legacy of the first CEO is influencing the current way of making strategy: "[strategy] has meant different things over time . . . in the early days it was the high level direction of the business which was very much owned by the then chief executive . . . his personal belief sets almost drove that" (Director, UtilCoA).

Alongside these explicit rules and priorities, multi-business firms use implicit elements. Here, the distinction between operations and strategy becomes blurred: "people, down to operating staff, they have rules which I would actually recognize as strategies although they are much more pragmatic and much more short term" (Director, EnergyCoB). Evidence from the pilots suggests that these implicit aspects of strategy are often the result of dialogue and conflict processes between the center and the periphery. For the director in EnergyCoB, the dialogue between the center and the units is vital in determining corporate strategy, "that process of dialogue where you get comfortable that the operating management are sharing the same mental model . . . is very important".

Overall, these preliminary findings suggest that the notion of strategy in multi-business firms has both implicit and explicit elements. More specifically, managers in these firms use different combinations of explicit and implicit notions to define their strategy. In EnergyCoB, the implicit elements of strategy are central ingredients in their strategy. Here, the organizational members know that they can influence these elements through the dialogue process. Over time, some elements can move from being explicit to become more implicit. But why does this movement occur? Guided by the context, process, and content framework (Pettigrew, 1987) we believe this movement is related to the context of these firms. The changing technological and economic environment requires equally responsive and flexible strategy processes. For some multi-business firms this means increasing the explicit elements while others adopt more implicit elements. From the inner context, changes in the political setting can cause a movement from explicit to implicit elements.

*Participants in the strategy process.*   Here we expose those involved in the strategy-making process of multi-business firms. The strategy process is often associated with managers at upper hierarchical levels (Finkelstein and Hambrick, 1996). In this pilot study, however, we extend our scope to the wider set of actors involved in strategy (Floyd and Wooldridge, 2000). For that reason, we use two broad categories: participants by position, and participants by influence. Participants by position enter the strategy process because of their hierarchical position. They can be identified by their management level (refer to Table 11.1). Participants by influence enter the strategy process using their influence base. This base refers to their perceived credibility, their expertise, their political skills, and social networks. Alongside individuals, strategy teams with a strong influence base also enter the strategy-making process. Managers often belong to both categories of participants. For the purposes of the present chapter we portray four groups of practitioners by influence: internal advisors (managers acting as consultants across the firm); external advisors (consultants); strategy teams at the center (group level managers); and strategy teams at the periphery (business unit managers).

Strategy teams at the center we found to be mainly responsible for formulating the strategic principles and for ensuring that business unit teams participate effectively in the strategy process: "we are altogether around 15 people. And our role is to see that . . . there are no contradictions within the different parts of the organization" (Director, PharmaCo). The role of the strategy teams at the periphery is then to develop and execute local strategic goals. However, units within the same multi-business firm often have varied markets and resources. Therefore, they may also have different views on what issues are strategic or not. This often creates tensions and conflicts with the center. The resolution of these tensions differs significantly across the firms we examined often depending on the style of leadership that each firm follows. For instance, in UtilCoB most issues are resolved through an ongoing process of dialogue between the center and the units. In contrast, in BankCoA each unit has less room to negotiate, "we tell the businesses pretty much what we would expect to see in a strategy for their business . . . I don't care frankly who the businesses want to get in to help them develop their strategy as long as it meets the standards" (Director, BankCoA).

Another team of strategists are the internal advisors. This group includes a number of experienced managers whose role is to counsel on a variety of strategic issues. These advisors establish critical communication links between the center and the periphery and challenge the strategic outcome of business units: "part of our role [as internal advisors] . . . has been . . . challenging a lot more their [business unit] strategy and setting high standards for strategy development" (Director, BankCoA). External advisors are also important in strategy making: "we use [consultancy firm], when it comes to looking into the industry, the market and how we are perceived by the analysts" (Director, PharmaCo). For the director in BankCoA these advisors also serve political objectives, "they have credibility . . . the chairman might be more prepared to believe something he hears from [consulting firm] than he might be towards me". Other firms use external advisors less: "strategy really had to come out of our management team . . . the mindset should be to understand the way consultants work and . . . define precisely what you want from them" (Director, UtilCoA).

Overall, these pilot study findings provide some insights into the managers and teams involved in making strategy in multi-business firms. Different firms use these actors in different ways to make strategy. For example, in PharmaCo external advisors were used by both the center and the units, while in UtilCoB only the center was allowed to hire consultants. But why do some managers/teams gain entry to the strategy process while others don't? To answer this question we need to examine what constitutes a strong base of influence for managers and their teams. In UtilCoA, for example, the managing director of one of the businesses has a strong influence base across the firm because of his extensive social networks and his long experience in the utility sector. It is also noteworthy that participants by influence often access the strategy process by using political activities such as lobbying, coalition formulation, conflict, and bargaining (Narayanan and Fahey, 1982).

*Practices around the strategy process.*    This analytical category concerns the actions of those involved in making strategy in multi-business firms. The focus here is on the practices of strategic actors and their teams (Grant, 2003). Our initial findings reveal two broad complementary sets of practices: inductive and deductive. This suggests a two-side character of strategic practices. The inductive side is creative and experimental, while the deductive includes formal actions and routines (Feldman, 2000). Most of the inductive practices take place during new activities such as strategic initiatives, while the deductive practices evolve around standard processes, like the annual planning cycle. This finding corresponds to the induced/autonomous actions of the Burgelman model (2002) and the evidence reported by Regnér regarding strategy creation in multinational firms (2003). We extend these findings, by presenting some empirical evidence around the inductive and deductive practices.

Evidence from the interviews suggests that inductive practices can be traced back to strategic initiatives. In UtilCoB, for instance, a set of strategic initiatives is linked with the group-level business plan: "we have got a plan that says if this is where you want to be . . . [these are] the particular initiatives that are going to deliver that' " (Director, UtilCoB). At the same time, initiatives act as the setting where business unit and corporate center managers negotiate about strategic issues. Strategic initiatives are also regarded as an answer to the environmental challenges that multi-business firms are increasingly facing. As one manager notes, "I think the big opportunities are not there anymore. We need . . . [a] different frame of mind" (Director, EnergyCoA).

Alongside the inductive activities around strategic initiatives, deductive activities can be found around the strategic-planning process. Our evidence suggests that the importance of the planning or budgetary processes in the overall strategy-making process varies across the eight multi-business firms. For some companies planning is considered as a routine used to communicate the strategic objectives. For others, planning is perceived as the principal way of translating the strategic aspirations into specific facts and projects. For the director in BankCoA planning helps implement the group's corporate strategy, "the plans would be very heavily based on the agreed strategies . . . it's more like the implementation I suppose of strategy." However, for other firms strategy making is not only about developing and delivering a plan; as another of our interviewees explains: "there is a lot more than purely delivering the plan, and that is where strategy starts to come in, strategy starts to show the strategic choices that you intend to make in the future or at least, the information you will take into account to start making these choices" (Director, EnergyCoA).

Our evidence suggests that multi-business firms use combinations of inductive and deductive practices to make strategy. In this section we focused our attention on the planning mechanisms and strategic initiatives as the settings where these practices occur. But why do multi-business firms experiment with alternative practices? Again, by examining the inner and outer context of these firms we can get some insights to this question. For example, UtilCoA experienced pressures for increasing economic returns from outer contextual factors (bankers, the stock exchange, and analysts). In order to deal with these conditions UtilCoA managers started experimenting with innovative (for the utility sector) ways of making strategy. Inner contextual conditions can also lead to the adoption of particular practices. In BankCoC, the current CEO supports more deductive practices during the strategy process compared to his predecessor. This experimentation with alternative combinations of deductive and inductive practices can be perceived as an innovation contest with firms that manage the combination successfully and others who fail to do so and face the consequences.

## Strategizing capabilities

The purpose of this analytical category is first to illustrate the capabilities required by managers during strategy making, and second to expose the ways these capabilities are developed in multi-business firms. For example, when UK utilities expanded their operations in the United States, managers were expected to deal with the new requirements of the American business environment. Managers in general are under pressure to deliver year-to-year increases in results. But what kind of capabilities do managers need? Here we were guided by the management development literature in developing initial categories of analysis. These were then refined using our empirical evidence. The broad category "strategizing capabilities" entails two sets of findings "strategizing capabilities in contemporary business" and "developing strategizing capabilities". These two analytical themes we examine below.

*Strategizing capabilities in contemporary business.*   Here we examine the specific capabilities required by strategists during the strategy-making process. Following the management development literature (Burgoyne, 1989; Winterton and Winterton, 1999) and our evidence we identified three broad categories of capabilities: technical abilities; social, political, and communication abilities; and meta-level abilities. Technical abilities enable managers to analyze strategic issues, while the social, political, and communication skills allow them to interact with other managers and work in strategy teams. Our evidence also suggests that managers require a third complementary set of abilities termed meta-level (Meldrum and Atkinson, 1998). These enable managers to utilize their knowledge in novel ways and provide new insights during the strategy process. Two sets of meta-level abilities are presented below: conceptual skills and creativity. Some of these categories correspond to findings from the management development literature (Amabile, 1997). However, these examinations fail to present how the process of developing capabilities unfolds over time or how it is linked with the strategy-making process. Further, many of these studies use questionnaires (Dulewicz, 1992) to gauge general managerial abilities. In contrast this study focuses on the capabilities required to conduct strategy.

Regarding technical abilities, our evidence suggests that companies increasingly hire individuals who demonstrate analytic skills: "that was fine for the past but I think what you need now is more people who can say 'well there is a complete different model over here'" (Director, BankCoA). Accordingly, the director of BankCoA believes that future CEOs will need to think more strategically, "they will inevitably be people who are much more adept at thinking about totally different strategic positioning . . . rather than thinking about incremental change". The social, political, and communication skills are the second set of capabilities we identified during these pilot interviews. Most directors noted that managers need to master the political process and communicate effectively: "a strategist needs to be extremely well positioned in the organizational politics. A strategist is not a provider of solutions he is a partner in the development of solutions . . . an independent thinker and a challenger" (Director, EnergyCoA). The third set of capabilities required during the strategy-making process is described as meta-level. We identified two sets of meta-level abilities: conceptual skills and creativity. Regarding conceptual skills, the director of EnergyCoA notes that a strategist should be able to demonstrate not only analytical thinking but also conceptual thinking. The management development system of his company, however, favors analytical thinking: "a strategist needs . . . to translate that [analysis] into a concept of ideas . . . so that's what I mean by conceptual versus analytical thinking . . . we do reward analytical thinking but we don't reward conceptual thinking". But why is conceptual thinking so important? This kind of thinking allows managers to synthesize alternatives in complex situations. These alternatives, according to the directors, are central during the strategy process: "the core skill is to be able to take a very varied degree of circumstance . . . and conceptualize that to arrive at a hypothesis" (Director, EnergyCoB). The second meta-level ability identified during the pilots is creativity. As the director of BankCoA pointed out, "the ones who will succeed in . . . the future will be the ones who are creative thinkers rather than instrumentalists".

Summarizing, the growing changes in the context of the firms we examined have led them to focus their attention on the capabilities required to make strategy. These changes refer to their inner and outer context. Accordingly, the practices of strategists are changing. We contend that in order to engage in these new practices managers need three broad sets of capabilities: technical abilities; social, political, and communication skills; and meta-level abilities. Next we examine how these capabilities are developed.

*Developing strategizing capabilities.* Here we explore how multi-business firms develop the capabilities to make strategy. The pilot interviews demonstrate that there are two areas where this development can be located: internally, when firms use localized resources and externally, when firms use external resources. Regarding the development of capabilities internally, there is evidence that the corporate center often plays a leading role in shaping the capabilities of business unit managers. This role is clear in BankCoA: "I don't think competency level is high enough in the business units and part of our role . . . has been to raise their competency level" (Director, BankCoA). Another way of developing the capabilities internally is through initiatives in the area of knowledge management. Both UtilCoA and UtilCoB use these kinds of initiatives to locate, store, and utilize insights from managers during strategy projects.

Firms also develop their capabilities externally to fill any capability gaps: "we've got some boxes where we didn't have any people with the right capabilities so we're recruiting externally" (Director, UtilCoB). According to almost all interviewees, recruiting external experts is a way to enrich their capabilities, "because he [external expert] comes from a totally different background he questions everything . . . and that has been fascinating" (Director, BankCoA). An alternative way to bring the outsider's point of view in the strategy process is by hiring strategy consultants. These consultants bring into the process, not only their tools and models but also the communication and political skills to deliver specific strategic outcomes. The engagement with consultants also acts as a learning experience for those involved in strategy. UtilCoA, for example, has transferred and customized some skills from their past consulting relationships to their current practices: "the acquisition of [company X] was very heavily supported by [consulting firm], so there was a lot of skills transfer from [consulting firm] to [UtilCoA] . . . so when we acquired the [company Y] we were able to run that value delivery process without consultant support" (Director, UtilCoA). Concluding, the findings exposed in this section provide some initial insights into the realities of making strategy in multi-business firms. Table 11.1 summarizes these findings.

## Conclusions

This chapter makes a dual contribution to the strategy process literature. First, it presents a set of analytical categories anchored in both the literature and our empirical evidence. Second, it offers some preliminary insights into the making of strategy in multi-business firms that could guide future research in this area. Our evidence (from eight pilot interviews) suggests that there is no widely accepted approach on how to make strategy. Instead, over time multi-business firms are experimenting with different ways of making strategy and developing the capabilities to make strategy. More specifically, they experiment with different combinations of: explicit and implicit elements around the meaning of strategy; participants by influence and participants by position during their strategy process; and inductive and deductive strategy practices. These firms also realize in different ways the capabilities required by their managers to make strategy and then develop these capabilities using different combinations of internal and external methods. It is the particular way that each company deals (or does not deal) with this set of challenges that defines the unique character of their strategy-making process. For example, BankCoB employs mainly explicit notions on what strategy means, participants by position during the strategy process, and deductive practices. Also technical abilities are required by BankCoB managers, and their capabilities are developed internally. Regarding the making of strategy, explicit routine rules and meta-level principles are blended with implicit creative notions of what exactly strategy is or should be. As a result, firms develop customized views around the meaning of strategy.

There was also evidence that strategy teams at the center are responsible for developing and communicating the main guidelines and rules across the group, while the strategy teams at the periphery are aiming to operationalize and deliver specific strategic objectives. Also, external advisors act as providers of strategy models and decision-making tools not available internally. They also get involved in the political and power arena. In almost all the firms we examined internal advisors were used alongside external consultants.

But what are the factors behind these various ways of making strategy? The main argument here is that the contextual changes identified by the INNFORM survey (Pettigrew *et al.*, 2003), driving companies to adopt innovative forms of organizing are also driving them towards adopting complementary ways of making strategy. The activities around strategy and organization should not be perceived as two discrete practices but as closely linked together. The focus here is not so much on organizational strategies and forms in themselves, but on the continuous processes involved in moving towards and moving along such strategies and forms (Whittington and Melin, 2003). As Lord John Browne, the CEO of BP notes, "our strategy is our organization" (Day, 2001). The INNFORM research identified that a convergence of economic, technological, informational, and political factors is behind the emergence of innovative forms of organizing. Following a contextualist approach (Pettigrew, 1985, 1987), we suggest that changes in these factors influence the strategy-making process in multi-business firms. For example, in order to explain the current way strategy is made in UK utilities one needs to examine the dual contextual effects of deregulation and technology innovations over the past decade. New strategizing capabilities and practices are now required in a sector previously sheltered from competition. Hence, some utilities have embraced more implicit elements in their strategy and encouraged more inductive practices from their managers. Alongside the outer context, changes in the inner context of firms are also shaping strategy making. For instance, decentralizing, downscoping, delayering, outsourcing, and other changes in the forms of organizing (Pettigrew, Massini, and Numagami, 2000), we believe change the boundaries and settings where strategy managers and their teams act and interact during the strategy process. Accordingly, changes in the forms of organizing have a knock-on effect on the way strategy is made. As the director of UtilCoB notes, "what was very clear to us was that simply changing our structure wasn't going to do it . . . you've got to take the human, the process and the structural piece all together otherwise the process doesn't work".

The findings we exposed in this chapter have the potential to offer a number of interesting insights if we approach them in a holistic fashion. This is true since the meaning of strategy, the participants, their practices, and capabilities are all interrelated and complementary elements of the strategy process. More empirical evidence is required to achieve such holistic treatment. We can, however, use the theoretical links across these categories to gain some early holistic insights. For example, the adoption of implicit elements around the meaning of strategy could be associated with inductive strategy practices. In this case, informal strategic objectives and standards are used to support and signal the creative actions of strategists across the firm. Another noteworthy link is between practices and capabilities. More specifically, inductive practices are expected to require meta-level abilities while deductive practices should utilize more technical abilities. This realization can have important implications for management education (Whittington, 1996).

Future research in this area could be based on three broad themes: strategy making and execution in and between multi-business firms; strategizing capabilities; and organizing and strategizing. Regarding the first theme, process scholars could focus on questions like: How is strategy made and executed across different business units within the same firm? How do strategy teams at the corporate center interact with strategy teams at the business units? How and why does the relationship between the central and peripheral strategy teams impact on the strategy process? The research agenda here need not be guided just by trends of survey results but by micro-pattern recognition in the practices and processes of making and executing strategy within and across different multi-business firms.

Within the second theme of strategizing capabilities, empirical attempts would entail the following lines of questioning. How do multi-business companies realize the capabilities required to make strategy? How are strategizing capabilities defined, created, and dissolved in different eras of organizational development? How are strategy teams with appropriate capabilities built at various levels in the firm to deliver high quality strategy outcomes?

Another arena for future research is that of organizing and strategizing. Our pilot interviews suggest that in the modern multi-business firm the verbs of organizing and strategizing "capture the realities of continuous innovation" (Pettigrew, Massini, and Numagami, 2000) better than the nouns: organization and strategy. For process research, of major interest here are the actual ways managers and their teams realize and manage the duality of strategizing and organizing. What are the pathways and progress of new organizational forms and what are the consequences for the making and execution of strategy? How are issues of organizing and strategizing managed in and around the strategy process? How are these issues managed in different eras of organizational development?

In this chapter we have signaled some realities around the making of strategy in eight multi-business firms. What is clear is that there are big challenges in understanding and managing the complexities and challenges of making strategy in these firms. For the process scholar, we have suggested some broad areas and questions for future research. Attention to these empirical questions, informed by theoretical advances in strategizing, organizing and strategizing capabilities in and between firms, will advance our knowledge of the strategy process in multi-business firms.

# References

Amabile, T. 1997. Motivating creativity in organizations: On doing what you love and loving what you do. *California Management Review*, **40**(1): 39–58.

Burgoyne, J. 1989. *Management Development: Context and Strategies*. Aldershot, UK: Gower.

Burgelman, R.A. 2002. *Strategy is Destiny: How Strategy-Making Shapes a Company's Future*. New York: The Free Press.

Chakravarthy, B.S. and Doz, Y. 1992. Strategy process research: focusing on corporate self-renewal. *Strategic Management Journal*, **13**: 5–14.

Day, J. 2001. Organizing for growth. *The McKinsey Quarterly*, **2**: 4–5.

Dulewicz, V. 1992. Assessment of management competencies by personality questionnaires. *Selection and Development Review*, **8**(1): 1–4.

Feldman, M.S. 2000. Organizational routines as a source of continuous change. *Organization Science*, **11**(6): 611–29.

Finkelstein, S. and Hambrick, D. 1996. *Strategic Leadership: Top Executives and Their Effects on Organizations*. Minneapolis: West Publishing.

Floyd, S.W. and Wooldridge, B. 2000. *Building Strategy from the Middle: Reconceptualizing Strategy Process*. Thousand Oaks, CA: Sage.

Fredrickson, J.W. 1986. The strategic decision process and organizational structure. *Management Review*, **11**(2): 280–97.

Goold, M. and Campbell, A. 1987. *Strategies and Styles: The Role of the Centre in Managing Diversified Corporations*. Oxford, UK: Blackwell.

Grant, R.M. 1991. The resource-based theory of competitive advantage: Implications for strategy formulation. *California Management Review*, **33**: 114–35.

Grant, R.M. 2003. Strategic planning in a turbulent environment: Evidence from the oil majors. *Strategic Management Journal*, **24**: 491–517.

Meldrum, M. and Atkinson, S. 1998. Meta-abilities and the implementation of strategy: Knowing what to do is simply not enough. *Journal of Management Development*, **17**(8): 564–75.

Mintzberg, H. 1978. Patterns in strategy formation. *Management Science*, **24**(9): 934–48.

Miller, D. and Friesen, P. 1978. Archetypes of strategy formulation. *Management Science*, **24**: 921–33.

Narayanan, V.K. and Fahey, L. 1982. The micro-politics of strategy formulation. *Academy of Management Review*, **7**: 25–34.

Paroutis, S. and Pettigrew, A.M. 2001. Practicing strategy and developing strategizing capabilities: A research prospect. Paper presented at the 17th EGOS Colloquium, Lyon, France.

Pettigrew, A.M. 1985. *The Awakening Giant: Continuity and Change in Imperial Chemical Industries*. Oxford: Blackwell.

Pettigrew, A.M. 1987. Context and action in the transformation of the firm. *Journal of Management Studies*, **24**(6): 649–70.

Pettigrew, A.M. 1992. The character and significance of strategy process research. *Strategic Management Journal*, **13**(Special Issue): 5–16.

Pettigrew, A.M., Massini, S., and Numagami, T. 2000. Innovative forms of organising in Europe and Japan. *European Management Journal*, **18**(3): 259–73.

Pettigrew, A.M., Whittington, R., Melin, L., Sanchez-Runde, C., Van Den Bosch, F., Ruigrok, W., and Numagami, T. (eds.), 2003. *Innovative Forms of Organizing: International Perspectives*. London: Sage.

Regnér, P. 2003. Strategy creation in the periphery: Inductive versus deductive strategy making. *Journal of Management Studies*, **40**(1): 57–82.

Teece, D., Gary, P., and Shuen, A. 1997. Dynamic capabilities and strategic management. *Strategic Management Journal*, **18**(7): 509–33.

Van de Ven, A.H. 1992. Suggestions for studying strategy process: A research note. *Strategic Management Journal*, **13**: 169–88.

Webb, D. and Pettigrew, A.M. 1999. The temporal development of strategy: Patterns in the UK insurance industry. *Organization Science*, **10**(5): 601–21.

Whittington, R. 1996. Strategy as practice. *Long Range Planning*, **29**(5): 731–5.

Whittington, R. and Melin, L. 2003. The challenge of organizing/strategizing. In A.M. Pettigrew, R. Whittington, L. Melin, C. Sanchez-Runde, F. Van Den Bosch, W. Ruigrok, and T. Numagami (eds.), *Innovative Forms of Organizing: International Perspectives*. London: Sage.

Williamson, O.E. 1975. *Markets and Hierarchies: Analysis and Anti-trust Implications*. New York: The Free Press.

Winterton, J. and Winterton, R. 1999. *Developing Managerial Competence*. London: Routledge.

# CHAPTER TWELVE

# Explaining the Process of Internationalization by Building Bridges among Existing Models

Alvaro Cuervo-Cazurra, Miguel Ramos

How does a firm internationalize? Several models of the process of internationalization, or the sequence of events that occurs when a firm expands into other countries have been generated to answer this question. The models have been presented as competing explanations of the internationalization process. The result of this diversity of explanations is not only a fragmentation of knowledge, but also an obscuring of current knowledge regarding the process of internationalization. Researchers working on one model tend to dismiss the insights of other models. This is unfortunate not only for the advancement of theory, but also for the guidance that academics and consultants informed by theory can provide to managers.

In this chapter we contribute to a better understanding of the internationalization process by clarifying the boundaries of existing models in terms of their level of analysis, the period of time studied, and the underlying organizational theory of change adopted by each model. We also draw connections among them, indicating how the insights of one model can help solve the limitations of another. Such an analysis shows that, as a research community, we have a fairly extensive understanding of the topic. The analysis also helps identify areas that would require further attention in future research, particularly the connection with innovation and performance.

## Existing Models of the Internationalization Process

Reviews of the literature (Andersen, 1993; Melin, 1992) have traditionally discussed three internationalization process models: the product cycle model (Vernon, 1966); the innovation-related model (Bilkey and Tesar, 1977; Cavusgil, 1980; Czinkota, 1982; Reid, 1981); and the incremental or Uppsala model (Johanson and Vahlne,

Table 12.1  Summary of existing models of the internationalization process

| Model | Traditional internationalization process models | | | Other internationalization process models | | |
|---|---|---|---|---|---|---|
| | Life cycle | Incremental | Innovation-related | Structural | Internalization | FDI-expansion |
| Key references | Vernon, 1966 | Johanson and Wiedersheim-Paul, 1975; Johanson and Vahlne, 1977, 1990 | Bilkey and Tesar, 1977; Cavusgil, 1980; Czinkota, 1982; Reid, 1981 | Stopford and Wells, 1972; Bartlett and Ghoshal, 1989; Prahalad and Doz, 1987 | Buckley and Casson, 1976; Fina and Rugman, 1996 | Kogut, 1983; Chang, 1995 |
| Theoretical basis | Life-cycle concept and international economics | Behavioral economics | Behavioral economics | Contingency theory | Transaction costs economics | Options theory and resource-based thinking |
| View of the internationalization process | Changes in the location of activities in industry | Changes in activities within the country and changes in presence across countries | Changes in managerial attitudes | Changes in structure used to operate across countries | Change in mode of entry into the country | Changes in scope within the country |
| Driver of change in sequences | Life cycle of product | Development of knowledge | Change in attitudes | The need to integrate foreign operations | Transaction costs | Creation of options |
| Level of analysis | Industry (product) | Management New foreign operation Overall foreign expansion | Management Overall foreign expansion | Overall foreign expansion | New foreign operation | New foreign operation |
| Period of operation | From domestic firm to complex MNE | From domestic firm to MNE | From domestic firm to active exporter | From exporter to complex MNE | From exporter to MNE | From simple to complex MNE |
| Organizational theory of change | Life cycle | Life cycle | Dialectical | Evolutionary | Teleological | Teleological |
| Limitations of the model discussed in the literature (areas that can be improved by other models) | It is an explanation of industry-level movements rather than firm behavior | It is limited to the initial stages of internationalization It is overly deterministic | It is a refinement of the incremental model It is limited to the initial exporting effort | It is not a model of internationalization but of the changes in the organization that accompany internationalization | It is does not discuss relationships among operations in different countries | It does not discuss trade as means of internationalization It is does not discuss relationships among operation in different countries |

Note: For a discussion of some of the writings see for example Andersen (1993) and Melin (1992).

1977; Johanson and Wiedersheim-Paul, 1975). However, we identify other models that tackle additional aspects of the expansion across borders: the internalization model (Buckley and Casson, 1976; Fina and Rugman, 1996); the structural model (Bartlett and Ghoshal, 1989; Prahalad and Doz, 1987; Stopford and Wells, 1972); and the foreign direct investment (FDI)-expansion model (Chang, 1995; Kogut, 1983). These are summarized in Table 12.1. We briefly review the explanations of the internationalization process provided by each model.

The product cycle model uses the micro-economic concept of the product life cycle, taken from the marketing literature, to explain the macro-economic phenomenon of foreign trade and investment. Sales and production move across countries based on the four stages in a product's life cycle: introduction, growth, maturity, and decline. In the introduction stage, sales and production occur in the home country. As demand grows and the product matures, sales and later production move to developed countries and then to developing countries. In the decline stage, production in the home country stops and the product is imported from developing countries.

The incremental model is based on the behavioral theory of the firm and assumes that managers' lack of knowledge about foreign markets is an obstacle for international expansion. As a result, the firm internationalizes incrementally in order to develop the necessary knowledge to operate abroad. The model proposes two separate sequences for the internationalization process. One is for the overall foreign expansion of the firm, where the "psychic distance" between the home and foreign country limits transfer of information; as a result, the firm's expansion to more distant countries is gradual. The other sequence concerns the development of a new foreign operation, where the firm increases its commitment to a given country in stages: no export activities, exports via independent representatives, sales subsidiary, and production subsidiary. These two sequences are based on an implicit sequence of stages at the management level that reflects the transformation of their knowledge, which is initially limited to the home country, and later expands to encompass multiple foreign markets.

The innovation-related model builds on behavioral economics, arguing that internationalization is the outcome of an information-processing approach that changes the attention and beliefs of managers about foreign markets. This results in two proposed sequences, one at the management level, where managers move their attention from the home country to foreign countries, and another at the level of the firm's overall foreign expansion, where the firm transforms itself from a domestic player into an active exporter.

The structural model deals primarily with the organizational structure implications of the internationalization process. It proposes a sequence of structures to coordinate the increase in scale and scope that results from the overall foreign expansion. The firm begins with no special structure for international operations, then develops an international division within the existing structure, then a divisional structure by product or geographic area, and finally it may establish a matrix structure. These structures reflect alternative ways of managing operations.

The internalization model explains the growth of the firm relative to markets. It focuses primarily on the initial mode of entry into the country and discusses the selection of the most efficient mode given specific firm and market conditions at a certain time; this model accounts best for changes in entry modes as conditions change.

The FDI-expansion model analyzes the sequence of FDI activities in a country. It combines ideas from options theory with concepts from resource-based thinking, discussing the new options available with each additional FDI activity undertaken by the firm in the host country. Previous activities serve as platforms for later developments.

## Clarifying the Relationships among Models

The preceding literature review reveals the richness and diversity of the various models of the internationalization process. However, such a wide variety of explanations often encourages compartmentalization of perspectives, producing isolated branches of research (Van de Ven and Poole, 1995: 510). As specific theories are refined through testing, there is pressure to adopt a single theory as the primary one and subordinate the others. As a result, the researcher develops a "trained incapacity" to appreciate aspects not mentioned in his or her theory (Poole and Van de Ven, 1989: 563).

We depart from this tradition and instead appreciate the contribution of each model. We do this by clarifying the boundaries of each model in terms of three aspects: the time period considered; the level of analysis; and the organizational theory of change that is adopted. This clarification helps build connections among the models, so that the insights offered by one model can help solve the limitations of another (Poole and Van de Ven, 1989). The analysis of the time period considered in each model reveals that the temporal limitations imposed by a given model can be resolved by others. The study of level of analysis indicates that different levels are addressed by each model; the models can thus complement one another, allowing a better understanding of the internationalization process. The analysis of the organizational theory of change helps us understand the drivers of transformation over time, and appreciate the different modes of change. All this assists us in generating predictions and suggestions for managerial action.

### Clarifying the relationship among models by period of time

We present the models in an order that explains how they complement each other to provide a full explanation of the transformation of international operations over time; from the time the firm is a domestic company to the time it is an international firm, that is, a company with foreign sales, until it is a complex multinational enterprise (MNE), that is, a firm with foreign direct investment (FDI) activities across many countries. Thus, the models are subject to "temporal" separation (Poole and Van de Ven, 1989).

The innovation-related model explains the initial stages of internationalization. It begins with a firm that is purely domestic, and whose managers are focused on the domestic operations. It then explains changes in managerial attitudes as the firm becomes an international firm and exports proactively. However, it does not discuss the expansion of the firm via FDI nor its later transformations.

The incremental internationalization model focuses on the firm's international expansion from the point at which it starts exporting until it produces abroad. It also accounts for the initial selection of the countries into which the company will expand, moving from those that are psychically closer to the country of origin to those that are more distant. However, it does not analyze the firm once it becomes a complex MNE and broadens its operations within foreign countries, developing connections among them.

The internalization model explains the firm's initial entry into a country once it has taken the decision to expand abroad, where the firm chooses to serve the country via exports, licenses, or by using alternative FDI modes. Although the model addresses changes in entry mode, it does not discuss the transformation of the operations of the firm later in time as the firm broadens its activities abroad.

The FDI-expansion model focuses on the expansion of the firm once it has become an MNE and is broadening its FDI operations in a given country. It accounts for expansion within the country once the firm has established its initial value-added activity, analyzing the broadening of operations and diversification beyond the initial area of activity. As such, the model does not analyze the initial internationalization of the firm through exports, focusing instead on its expansion using FDI.

The structural model examines the firm's transformation from the time that it is simply an exporter up until the point at which it becomes a complex MNE. It begins with a firm that is already exporting, and then examines the firm's need to transform its structure as it increases its foreign operations. These transformations must occur not only as a result of the increase in foreign sales, but also because of the increase in complexity of selling and operating in multiple countries with diverse operations.

Finally, the product cycle model applies throughout the entire internationalization process, from the time the firm is a domestic company until it finally engages in reverse imports. The company develops innovations for the local market, exports to other countries to satisfy the demand for its products, and later establishes foreign production facilities in order to take advantage of the lower production costs and standardization of technology. Production eventually moves out of the country where the innovation originated.

## Clarifying the relationship among models by level of analysis

The models of the internationalization process focus on different levels of analysis. We discuss three levels of analysis: the management level; the level of a foreign operation in a given country; and the level of the firm's overall foreign expansion. Thus, the models are subject to "spatial" separation (Poole and Van de Ven, 1989).

The innovation-related model operates primarily at the level of management, explaining the transformation of managerial attitudes towards foreign markets, although it also examines the overall foreign expansion. The conflict between domestic and external pressures is solved with the transformation of managers' attitudes towards internationalization. As such, the active internationalization of the firm through exports is enabled by the transformation of the management team's attitudes regarding the importance of foreign markets.

The incremental internationalization model has two principal levels of application: the level of the foreign operation, and the level of the firm's overall foreign expansion across various countries. The first application examines the changes in operations within a given country as the firm increases its commitment to the country, from exports to sales representatives to production. The second application centers on the selection of countries to enter. The firm first expands towards countries that are psychically closer, only later selecting more distant countries, increasing its overall international presence. The model has implications at the management level, where the firm internationalizes incrementally as managers develop tacit knowledge of how to operate abroad.

The FDI-expansion model applies at the level of the foreign operation, where the firm increases its value-added activities in the host country. The firm initially invests in the same line of business in which it is currently operating in its home country; it later diversifies into related business lines in the foreign country.

The internalization model focuses on the foreign operation. The theory's principal strength lies in the analysis of the individual transaction as the firm enters the new foreign country. Recent developments have addressed the change in the entry mode as conditions in the country vary.

The structural model applies primarily at the level of the firm's overall foreign expansion. The increase in scale and diversity of international operations creates the need to coordinate them differently, inducing the transformation of the firm's overall structure to promote links among operations in different countries and facilitate the transfer of resources among them.

Finally, the product cycle model applies at the level of the industry to which the firm's product belongs. The movement of production into foreign markets applies not only to a given firm, but also to the other firms whose products belong to the same industry because competitors follow each other.

## Clarifying the relationship among models by organizational theory of change

A third way to identify the boundaries and the potential connections among models is the analysis of the organizational theories of change adopted by each. Studies of process must make explicit the theory of organizational change used (Van de Ven, 1992): life cycle, evolutionary, dialectical, or teleological. This classification clarifies the driver of change of the internationalization process models and reveals their assumptions and boundaries.

The product cycle model provides a life-cycle explanation of the internationalization process. Life-cycle theories present a sequence of linear and irreversible stages that enable the entity to grow as a function either of its development or of characteristics present since its inception (Van de Ven and Poole, 1995: 513–15). Change is governed by rules of logic that prescribe the unfolding of change in a unitary sequence of stages or phases. In the product cycle model, sales and production move across countries based on the stages of the product: introduction, growth, maturity, and decline.

The incremental internationalization model also follows a life-cycle process theory of organizational change (Forsgren, 2002: 267). The model has a strong life-cycle view of the internationalization process, because it "expects that the internationalization process, once it has started, will tend to proceed regardless of whether strategic decisions in that direction are made or not" (Johanson and Vahlne, 1990: 12). More specifically, "regarding the first establishment of sales subsidiaries, they do not seem to have been a step in a conscious and goal directed internationalization" (Johanson and Vahlne, 1977: 25).

The innovation-related model primarily reflects a dialectical process of organizational change. Dialectical theories begin with the assumption that organizational entities exist in a pluralistic world of conflicting forces that compete with one another (Van de Ven and Poole, 1995: 517). The transformation of the entity results from the confrontation of a thesis and an antithesis, which compete for domination and control. These oppositions imply a conflict that can alter the status quo and lead to change, either through the development of a synthesis or through the replacement of the thesis by the antithesis. In the innovation-related model, the conflict between the existing thesis of managers focused on the domestic market and the antithesis of the demands of external markets results in a change in managerial attitudes and the replacement of exclusive domestic orientation with a synthesis of domestic and international orientation. This dialectical transformation of managerial attitudes is reflected in the firm's internationalization, where the company moves from being uninterested in foreign markets to being highly involved in exporting.

The structural model follows an evolutionary theory of organizational change with some dialectical notions of transformation. Evolutionary theories argue for selection among competitors within a population according to the prescribed sequence of variation, selection, and retention events (Van de Ven and Poole, 1995: 518). Variation is the creation of new routines, competencies, or organizational forms, which is our focus. Selection is the differential elimination of certain types of variations as the environment selects the units that best fit the resource base of an environmental niche through competition for scarce resources. Retention is the preservation, duplication or reproduction of selected variations, involving forces that perpetuate and maintain certain selected entities. While the structural model may not present an explicit evolutionary motor, it can be interpreted under this theory of organizational change (Westney and Zaheer, 2001) with some dialectical notions. Change is precipitated by dialectical conflicts between the current organization of activities and emerging pressures. Internal selection pressures arise from increasing scale, growing complexity, and internal diversity, as well as increasing coordination requirements derived from international expansion. External selection pressures arise from multiple-country, industry, or supranational institutional environments. Such pressures strain the firm to the point where key features must change if it is to grow or survive.

The FDI-expansion model reflects a teleological theory of organizational change. Teleological theories argue for the purposeful transformation of the entity to achieve a predetermined objective through the establishment of a goal, implementation, and the adaptation of means in order to achieve the goal (Van de Ven and Poole, 1995: 518–19). The entity constructs an end state, takes action to reach it, and monitors progress. There is no prescribed rule, direction, or sequence of stages as development occurs; equifinality is possible. In the FDI-expansion model, the firm evaluates the motivations and modes of internationalization, assessing their ability to achieve value based on the resource set of the firm. The company develops, transfers, and utilizes resources both within and across countries. This emphasis on the final purpose driving the behavior of the firm implies a teleological theory of organizational change.

**Table 12.2** Integrating the insights of existing models of the internationalization process

| Level of Analysis | | None | Low (some exports) | Medium (exports, some FDI) | High (exports and FDI) | Very high (exports, FDI, internal trade) | Organizational Theory of Change |
|---|---|---|---|---|---|---|---|
| **Management** | Attention and attitude | Focused on domestic market | Start to shift towards foreign countries because of orders from abroad | Focus on foreign markets, active decision to serve foreign markets | Focus on foreign markets to coordinate operation abroad | Focus on foreign markets to develop resources and operations abroad | Dialectical |
| | Knowledge | Limited to the domestic market | Learning-by-doing, fulfilling requests from foreign markets helps develop knowledge | Deliberate learning, decision making to select country of expansion and obtain knowledge in order to operate abroad | Grafting, use external methods of learning, develop knowledge to coordinate operations | Active development and transfer of knowledge across subsidiaries | Dialectical |
| | Caveats in sequence | Prior experience of managers and use of external methods of knowledge development facilitate a quicker and deeper internationalization (skip steps) | | | | | Teleological |
| **Foreign operation** | Commitment | No foreign activity in foreign country | Downstream activities abroad (market knowledge, sales) | Additional downstream activities abroad (distribution) | Additional upstream activities abroad (production, supply) | Diversification of activities abroad (related industries) | Teleological with life-cycle notions |
| | Value creation | No foreign activities in foreign country, domestic value creation | Serve foreign country via exports, create value from higher use of existing resources in additional markets | FDI in foreign country to serve foreign clients better, learn about their needs, add value to products | Additional FDI to create value abroad rather than simply transferring value-creation resources from home operations | Additional FDI to create value by using resources in existing foreign operation in other lines of business abroad | Teleological with life-cycle notions |
| | Caveats in sequence | The objective of international expansion (resource acquisition), difficulty in transferring products across borders (service firms), and prior experience in other countries (being an MNE) facilitate a quicker and deeper internationalization (skip steps) | | | | | Teleological |
| **Overall foreign expansion** | Number and relationships among countries | Home country | Few countries with clients similar to home country to make use of resources developed in home country | More countries with clients similar to home country or where products can be adapted easily | More countries with clients similar to existing operations, not only home country | Many diverse operations in many countries, creating relationships among operations | Teleological |
| | Organization and coordination of operations | Manage operations in home country | Alter structure to facilitate increase in scale of operations | Alter structure to facilitate increase in scope of operations | Alter structure to facilitate increase in complexity of operations | Alter structure to facilitate the development and transfer of resources across countries | Evolutionary with dialectical notions |
| | Caveats in sequence | Diversity of operations in home country facilitates a quicker and deeper internationalization (skip steps) | | | | | Teleological |

*Degree of internationalization* spans columns None through Very high.

The internalization model also explains internationalization in a teleological manner. It accounts for the selection of the most efficient mode, given particular firm and market conditions at a certain time. Changes in the environmental conditions lead to the rethinking of the mode of operation abroad.

## Building Bridges among Existing Models

The preceding discussion highlights the differences between models and their separation across time periods, levels of analysis, and organizational change theories. Table 12.2 summarizes and integrates the insights of these models to distill what we know of the internationalization process, thus building bridges across models. Whereas in Table 12.1 we highlighted the differences across models, in Table 12.2 we try to establish connections among them. To do so, we present the firm's internationalization process over time and across levels of analysis. We begin at the point at which the company is a purely domestic firm, and move forward to the point at which it is a complex MNE. We discuss the resulting internationalization process at three levels: management; operations in one country; and overall foreign expansion. As we analyze the internationalization process, we indicate how organizational theories of change are more applicable for certain variables at the different levels of analysis. Although we describe the resulting model in a sequence, this is not intended to imply that firms will necessarily follow these stages in this exact sequence; that is, we do not claim that this is a life cycle. We indicate conditions under which firms may jump stages.

At the management level, the internationalization process is reflected in a change in managers' attention, attitude, and knowledge. They progress from focusing solely on the domestic market to focusing on both domestic and foreign markets. When the firm is first established, managers tend to focus on serving the needs of existing clients. Their attention is thus directed towards the domestic market, and the firm tends to develop products that address the needs of clients in the domestic market and enable the firm to create value. However, the firm may start receiving requests from clients located in foreign countries. These requests create new demands on managers' attention, since they are potential avenues for growth and value creation. The firm will serve these requests by exporting the product, but managers will still be primarily focused on the domestic market, since it is the main source of value creation. As the number and size of requests increase, managers may start considering foreign markets as potential profitable outlets, switching their attention from the domestic market to foreign markets. Managers develop knowledge about foreign markets, at the same time they alter their attention to the needs of clients abroad. The change in the managerial level is thus accomplished primarily through a dialectical process.

The internationalization process at the level of a foreign operation is reflected in the firm's increasing commitment to the foreign country, from low levels such as sales or distribution to higher levels such as diverse production facilities. This enables the firm to create value. The initial expansion of the firm is likely to be through exports. Exports facilitate additional value creation with limited additional investments. The firm is able to sell more products based on innovations it has already developed, thus achieving additional returns on previous investments. Additionally, by exporting, the firm reduces the need to incur investments in the foreign country, limiting the need for scarce financial and managerial resources. Later, the firm engages in FDI to increase value-creation abilities and better serve clients. Additionally, the development of new resources in the country during the firm's operation there facilitates further expansion. This includes not only a change in the entry mode to better create value, but also the expansion of operations into new activities. A teleological model with some life-cycle notions primarily drives this change in the foreign operation, as the firm uses alternative methods and means to create value.

At the level of overall foreign expansion, the internationalization process is reflected in the change from serving one foreign country to running a disparate set of operations across multiple countries. These changes require the firm to select which countries to serve and how to organize the foreign operations. The selection of the initial country of expansion is determined by the combination of the desire to create value and the need to avoid problems. The firm can create value by serving clients that are willing to pay for the products it is already producing. These clients are likely to be those that are similar to clients the firm is already serving in the domestic market; in this case they will have similar needs, which the firm's innovations and products can satisfy. However, the firm must take into account the potential problems it could encounter as a result of operating in different competitive and institutional environments. This is particularly important during the initial expansion, at which point the firm has no experience in operating in other countries. Therefore, the firm will select countries that are similar to countries where it is already operating to ease the expansion. As the firm enters different countries, this creates variation in the operations that may result in the selection of more appropriate modes of entry, operation, and coordination of activities, resulting in a change in organizational structure. As such, a combination of a teleological and evolutionary model of change drives the overall foreign expansion.

## Conclusions

In this chapter we have reviewed the internationalization process literature in order to clarify existing explanations and build bridges among them. We have argued that it is useful to specify the time period, level of analysis, and theory of organizational change underlying each internationalization process model, in order to clarify their boundaries. We later take advantage of this specification in order to integrate existing knowledge of the internationalization process into a model that distills what we know about the expansion of the firm across borders.

This exercise has some limitations that can be addressed in future research. First, we have typified the models and provided a general overview of each to facilitate comparison. This helped us provide a connection among them. Future work could build on this and generate not only a connection but also a deeper integration of the models. Second, we identified the differences among models in terms of level of analysis, time period, and theory of organizational change, as these are key dimensions for the comparison of alternative models. Other researchers can take other variables and establish additional comparisons, aiding the appreciation of the diversity and richness of insight; however, they should also try to establish links to assist in building an integrated body of knowledge.

There are two additional areas of interest that internationalization process research must better address in the future: the relationship with innovation, and the connections to superior performance. First, the analysis of the internationalization process can be understood as the way in which a firm that has developed innovations in its home country can benefit from these by transferring them abroad (Vernon, 1966). However, the internationalization process not only helps the firm benefit from existing innovations, but also allows it to develop new innovations. The firm may enter new countries to benefit from the knowledge that is there; moreover, as it adapts and operates in new countries, it develops new knowledge that can lead to further innovations both in the foreign country and in the home country. In this way, the internationalization process becomes both a means for furthering the use of existing innovations and a mechanism for developing new ones (Bartlett and Ghoshal, 1989; Birkinshaw and Nobel, 1998).

Second, the analysis of the internationalization process must better connect to the performance of the firm, examining how different processes can enable it to achieve superior performance. This line of research has already begun; see, for example, the work of Vermeulen and Barkema (2002), who analyze the pace, rhythm, and scope of the internationalization process and how these are related to overall firm performance, or discussions of the accelerated internationalization of small entrepreneurial firms (Oviatt and McDougall, 1994). A related line of analysis is the study of performance at the level of the foreign operation; this could examine not only the most appropriate mode of entry into the foreign country under a given set of circumstances, but also the internationalization process that enables the achievement of superior performance.

In sum, the internationalization process has generated a large body of knowledge that can help both researchers and managers better understand how to move across countries. To achieve this, however, we must appreciate the value of alternative points of view, examine how as a community we have advanced our understanding, and identify the areas that require additional attention.


## Acknowledgments

The comments of the acting editor Franz Kellermanns, an anonymous reviewer for the book, Kent Eriksson, Mats Forsgren, Tom Murtha, Myles Shaver, Andy Van de Ven, and anonymous reviewers and participants at the Strategic Management and Organization Seminar at the University of Minnesota, the European International Business Academy Annual Meeting in Paris, the Strategic Management Society mini-conference on Strategy Process at the University of Connecticut, and the Academy of International Business Annual Meeting in Monterey helped clarify the arguments in earlier versions of the paper. The financial support of the University of Minnesota is gratefully acknowledged. All errors remain ours.

122   Alvaro Cuervo-Cazurra, Miguel Ramos

## References

Andersen, O. 1993. On the internationalization process of firms: A critical analysis. *Journal of International Business Studies*, **24**: 209–31.

Bartlett, C.A. and Ghoshal, S. 1989. *Managing Across Borders*. Boston, MA: Harvard Business School.

Bilkey, W.J. and Tesar, G. 1977. The export behavior of smaller Wisconsin manufacturing firms. *Journal of International Business Studies*, **9**: 93–8.

Birkinshaw, J. and Nobel, R. 1998. Innovation in multinational corporations: control and communication patterns in international R&D. *Strategic Management Journal*, **19**: 479–97.

Buckley, P. and Casson, M. 1976. *The Future of the Multinational Corporation*. London: Macmillan.

Cavusgil, T.S. 1980. On the internationalization process of firms. *European Research*, **8**: 273–81.

Chang, S.J. 1995. International expansion strategy of Japanese firms: Capability building through sequential entry. *Academy of Management Journal*, **38**: 383–5.

Czinkota, M.R. 1982. *Export Development Strategies: US Promotion Policies*. New York: Praeger.

Forsgren, M. 2002. The concept of learning in the Uppsala internationalization process model: A critical review. *International Business Review*, **11**: 257–78.

Fina, E. and Rugman, A.M. 1996. A test of internalization theory and internationalization theory: The Upjohn Company. *Management International Review*, **36**: 199–213.

Johanson, J. and Vahlne, J.E. 1977. The internationalization process of the firm: A model of knowledge development and increasing foreign market commitments. *Journal of International Business Studies*, **8**: 23–32.

Johanson, J. and Vahlne, J.E. 1990. The mechanism of internationalization. *International Marketing Review*, **7**: 11–24.

Johanson, J. and Wiedersheim-Paul, F. 1975. The internationalization of the firm: Four Swedish case studies. *Journal of Management Studies*, **12**: 305–22.

Kogut, B. 1983. Foreign direct investment as a sequential process. In C. Kindleberger and D. Audretsch (eds.), *The Multinational Corporation in the 1980s*. Cambridge, MA: MIT Press.

Melin, L. 1992. Internationalization as a strategy process. *Strategic Management Journal*, **13** (Winter Special Issue): 99–118.

Oviatt, B.M. and McDougall, P.P. 1994. Toward a theory of international new ventures. *Journal of International Business Studies*, **25**: 45–64.

Poole, M.S. and Van de Ven, A.H. 1989. Using paradox to build management and organization theories. *Academy of Management Review*, **14**: 562–78.

Prahalad, C.K. and Doz, Y. 1987. *The Multinational Mission*. New York: The Free Press.

Reid, S.D. 1981. The decision-maker and export entry and expansion. *Journal of International Business Studies*, **12**: 101–12.

Stopford, J.M. and Wells, L.T. 1972. *Managing the Multinational Enterprise*. New York: Basic Books.

Van de Ven, A.H. 1992. Suggestions for studying strategy process: A research note. *Strategic Management Journal*, **13** (Summer Special Issue): 169–88.

Van de Ven, A.H. and Poole, M.S. 1995. Explaining development and change in organizations. *Academy of Management Review*, **29**: 510–40.

Vermeulen, F. and Barkema, H. 2002. Pace, rhythm, and scope: Process dependence in building a profitable multinational corporation. *Strategic Management Journal*, **23**: 637–50.

Vernon, R. 1966. International investment and international trade in the product cycle. *Quarterly Journal of Economics*, **80**: 190–207.

Westney, E.D. and Zaheer, S. 2001. The multinational enterprise as an organization. In A.M. Rugman and T.L. Brewer (eds.), *The Oxford Handbook of International Business*. New York: Oxford University Press.

# CHAPTER THIRTEEN

# Informal Controls at Work: Affecting Behavior Amidst Uncertainty

James M. Pappas, Karen E. Flaherty

In recent years, the term "strategic renewal" has garnered a great deal of interest in the management literature (cf. Floyd and Lane, 2000). Typically depicted as an evolutionary process (Burgelman, 1991), renewal has been associated with changes in a firm's product–market strategy, strategic position, or the development of innovative behaviors that can alter a firm's core capabilities (Floyd and Wooldridge, 2000). However, while renewal offers significant benefits, firms are still confronted with the problems associated with uncertainty (Floyd and Lane, 2000; Thompson, 1967). At the individual level, for example, employees are often given mixed messages about the roles that they should undertake in order to enhance firm profitability. Employees are often expected to be able to successfully deploy existing competencies and simultaneously seek innovations that could redirect the prevailing strategic focus of the firm.

To understand the effects of uncertainty (e.g. role conflict, environmental dynamism) within the context of strategic renewal, we first examine how organizations adopt and utilize specific management control systems (Marginson, 2002). We argue that such controls can simultaneously lessen the inherent problems associated with uncertainty while instilling the employee with a stronger sense of direction that drives the development of new and innovative capabilities. Thus, control system management is viewed as a vital strategic mechanism that can foster the renewal of key organizational capabilities (Chakravarthy *et al.*, 2003).

The primary purpose of this chapter is to extend the existing body of renewal literature by empirically examining the impact of informal control on employees' behaviors while simultaneously exploring the impact of uncertain conditions. Drawing on the vast and often inconsistent research on management control systems (MCS), we develop a research model that links key management roles with informal control systems (self and professional controls). Furthermore, rather than constructing our model based solely on bureaucratic costs associated with administrative controls

(Williamson, 1985), we evoke a theoretical frame that recognizes the importance of social interactions in the process of knowledge generation and organizational learning (Floyd and Lane, 2000; Dwyer, Schurr, and Oh, 1987). Taking such an approach is also in line with recent process-oriented studies (cf. Atuahene-Gima and Li, 2002).

## Conceptual Development and Hypotheses

Because strategic renewal requires both bottom-up learning and organizationally designed experimentation, it is typically considered to be a non-linear, socially complex mechanism (Levinthal and March, 1993). We argue that the most compelling vantage point to study this phenomenon is through the lens of the organizational boundary spanner. Boundary-spanning employees have more access to the external environment and are more likely to understand the strategic problems associated with the firm's capability set (Floyd and Wooldridge, 1997). Furthermore, they have been shown to report higher levels of strategic influence behavior than their nonboundary-spanning counterparts (Astley and Sachdeva, 1984).

Boundary spanners are often considered to be "linking pins" in a similar way to employees who perform similar roles involving management, suppliers, and customers (Dutton et al., 1997; Floyd and Wooldridge, 1992). One important source of boundary-spanning information comes from sales professionals in organizations (Slater and Olsen, 2000). They have been viewed as implementers and/or experimenters of new strategic initiatives. Some scholars have suggested, however, that salespeople engage in autonomous strategic behavior (Hutt, Reingen, and Ronchetto, 1988). In sum, not only do salespeople have access to external information in their boundary-spanning roles, but they can also shape strategy internally through their mid-level position (Slater and Olsen, 2000). By focusing on boundary-spanning salespeople, we expect (a) to better understand how management controls under uncertainty can affect the renewal process, and (b) how mid-level professionals assume key strategic roles in organizations.

### The importance of boundary-spanning activities

The management literature on strategic process provides a long list of strategic roles played by each level of management (cf. Floyd and Lane, 2000) and integrated these activities into various research models (Nonaka, 1994; Bartlett and Ghoshal, 1993). Floyd and Lane's (2000) summary of the literature on strategic roles provides a comprehensive understanding of how these activities operate at various hierarchical levels of management. However, their work does not empirically consider the influence of such activity on individual-level outcomes or if certain employees (i.e., salespeople) participate in roles traditionally reserved for middle managers.

Summarizing Floyd and Wooldridge (1992), key influence activities include championing, synthesizing, facilitating, and implementing. *Championing* is formally defined as the successful promotion of strategic initiatives to superiors, leading to the development of new organizational capabilities or to changes in the use of existing capabilities. *Synthesizing* is defined as the subjective process by which strategic meaning is combined with current operating information and an interpretation of this knowledge is communicated to others within the organization. *Facilitating* refers to the nurturing and development of experimental programs designed to encourage organizational learning and to expand strategy. Finally, *implementing* is defined as the redeployment of organizational capabilities that are often considered to be a top-driven activity.

### Strategic influence activities and control systems

According to transaction cost economics, opportunistic behavior exists, in large part, because of opportunism and information uncertainty (Williamson, 1985). To mitigate the problems associated with opportunism, firms must (i) resort to control systems (Williamson, 1985) and (ii) weigh the costs and benefits of the opportunistic behavior (Hill, 1990). Specifically, sales controls typically are designed to maximize output or certain behaviors, however, we also utilize transaction costs to evaluate how salespersons weigh the cost and benefit of engaging in potentially risky behaviors (i.e., championing new ideas) that extend *past* the traditional role of selling. In conjunction with the transaction cost approach, we also evoke social exchange theory (Blau, 1964). While transaction cost economics has been criticized as "undersocialized" (Ghoshal and Moran, 1996), social exchange theory makes the exchange relationship the unit of analysis and provides us with an opportunity to discern functional-level employees' participation in the "mid-level management" activities.

Most commonly, research in MCS has focused on formal control systems including both process (behavior-based) and output (volume-based) control (Anderson and Oliver, 1987; Marginson, 2002). Another broad focus in the control system domain, however, includes informal control mechanisms (Mintzberg and Waters, 1982; Ramaswami, 1996). As a whole, informal controls do not impose strict procedures and rules to be followed. Instead, the control evolves from a culture supported by management and the firm, in general. In the management literature, research has primarily focused on management styles and clan controls (Ouchi, 1980); however, in other domains informal controls are often bifurcated into "self-control" (i.e., taking pride in one's work, taking responsibility for one's job, etc.) and "professional control" (i.e., shared responsibilities by a group or team).

The focus of self-control falls clearly on the individual assuming responsibility for performance. Given a culture of self-control, we expect employees to take greater risks in order to be recognized as a "star" in the organization. As a result, we expect salespeople operating under self-control to participate in traditional mid-level behaviors including championing, synthesizing, facilitating, and implementing. Armed with the confidence that their performance is under their control, the transaction cost perspective suggests that individuals will seek behaviors that go above and beyond their job description. In addition, social exchange theory suggests that strong and reciprocal relationships can override formal control systems (Blau, 1964). Empowered by cultures of positive reciprocal relationships, self-controls will enable the employee to behave in the best interest of the organization (Flaherty and Pappas, 2000). Thus, both theories suggest that, under conditions of self-control, employees will attempt to influence strategy by engaging in key management behaviors. Stated formally:

H1:    Self-control will be positively associated with the salespeople's participation in championing, synthesizing, facilitating, and implementing.

Conversely, professional control stresses team unity and group decision making in lieu of feelings of individual achievement. According to Williamson (1985), professional controls increase the likelihood of opportunism (i.e., dishonest behavior, distortion of information, and shirking responsibilities). Salespeople must weigh the cost and benefit of engaging in potentially risky behaviors (i.e., championing new ideas) that extend past the traditional role of sales. From a social exchange perspective, professional controls would mask the net benefits of a strong employee–manager dyad. In sum, positive reciprocal relationships (e.g., based in trust) that emanate at the dyadic level will not accrue if the responsibilities are shared (Flaherty and Pappas, 2000). Again, both theories suggest that employees, under conditions of professional control, will be less likely to influence strategy by engaging in key management behaviors. Stated formally:

H2:    Professional control will be negatively associated with the salespeople's participation in championing, synthesizing, facilitating, and implementing.

**How uncertainties moderate the controls–behavior link**

While the first two hypotheses argue that organizations can shape individual's behaviors, research has also suggested that individuals' strategic influence is affected by the degree of uncertainty facing the individual (Floyd and Lane, 2000). It follows, therefore, that alignment of controls to enact strategic renewal requires that individuals are located in places where they can gain information and reduce the associated problems of uncertainty. We introduce two types of uncertainty and posit that they will moderate the controls–behavior linkage. They include employee role conflict (at the individual-group level) and market turbulence (at the firm-industry level).

In stable market conditions, the strategic roles of individuals are, at least to some extent, specific; as turbulence increases, firms are faced with increasing instability and ambiguity (Floyd and Lane, 2000). Taking a transaction cost perspective, turbulent markets will be viewed as uncertain, risky, and problematic to the individual salesperson. When faced with self-control, therefore, individuals will seek to lower exposure to risk and avoid associated costs with behaviors that diverge from the prevailing wisdom of the organization. The social exchange perspective also suggests that market turbulence (or environmental dynamism) will moderate the controls–behavior linkage. As market uncertainty increases, organizations are more likely to foster formalized control systems to minimize the impact of turbulence. Thus, employees will eschew positive reciprocal relationships in favor of goal-oriented (or behavior-oriented) directives. In sum, the positive relationship between self-control and strategic influence activity attenuates in the face of environmental dynamism. Stated formally:

> H3: The relationship between self-control and salespeople's participation in championing, synthesizing, facilitating, and implementing will be diminished, given increased market turbulence.

Professional control suggests that performance is based on group, rather than individual, goals (Ramaswami, 1996). Here, the individual can avoid the costs often associated with dynamic environments by seeking opportunistic behavior shielded by the group (Williamson, 1985). Often cast as a "free rider phenomenon," transaction cost economics suggests that professional controls will mitigate the risk in turbulent markets. Market turbulence would also mitigate the negative influence between professional controls and strategic influence from a social exchange perspective. Stated formally:

> H4: The relationship between professional control and the salespeople's participation in championing, synthesizing, facilitating, and implementing will be enhanced, given increased market turbulence.

Next we consider the role conflict that often emanates from stressful and competing forces *within* individuals (Biddle, 1979). Generally, role conflict occurs when a salesperson feels that the expectations and demands of two or more members of his or her role set are incompatible (Singh, 1998). To the degree that self and professional controls provide direction to the salesperson regarding expectations and job activities, we expect the controls–behavior linkage to be moderated by the degree of role conflict felt by the salesperson.

In the face of increased role conflict therefore, individuals will be unclear about job responsibilities and gravitate toward more formalized, bureaucratic control mechanisms. From a transaction cost approach, this formalized approach will minimize shirking and other opportunistic behavior. From a social exchange lens, increased role conflict will cause managerial values to be less in concert with those of the salesperson, and reciprocal relationships will be less likely. Thus:

> H5: The relationship between self-control and salespeople's participation in championing, synthesizing, facilitating, and implementing will be diminished, given increased role conflict.

> H6: The relationship between professional control and the salespeople's participation in championing, synthesizing, facilitating, and implementing will be enhanced, given increased role conflict.

All of the hypotheses listed are depicted graphically in Figure 13.1.

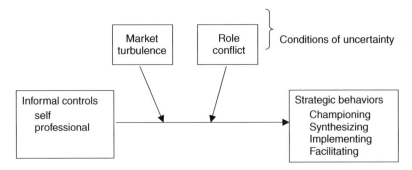

**Figure 13.1**   Summary model of proposed hypotheses

## Research Methods

### Sample and data acquisition

Data on sales organizations were obtained from a national (U.S.) list purchased from a list broker. A random sample of the firms was contacted via initial telephone calls. In the phone conversations, we introduced the study to the sales managers, determined whether or not participation was feasible (e.g., in some instances firms that did not employ salespeople were eliminated), and generated support from the sales managers. Subsequently, sales managers of interested firms were mailed an instruction packet with: (a) a cover letter to sales supervisor; (b) a questionnaire for the sales supervisor; and (c) three salesperson questionnaires to be distributed by the sales supervisor.

The supervisor questionnaire included measures of the firm's market turbulence, product complexity, firm performance, empowerment, and strategic orientation. In addition, supervisors completed a measure of the extent to which they empower employees, as well as performance rankings and participation in the strategic activities for each salesperson. These rankings were matched with the responses from the corresponding salesperson. The salesperson questionnaire included measures of supervisee trust, supervisee control, information sharing, frequency of communication, as well as a host of demographic and background information. The questionnaires were coded to allow for the matching of salespeople to supervisor, as well as back to the master list of companies.

Of 450 firms initially expressing interest and pre-qualifying for participation via phone calls, 132 dyads were received from the first wave of data collection and 25 were received from a second wave resulting in a total of 157 (35 percent) matched dyads. Of the 157 dyads, 98 were obtained from pharmaceutical sales companies, while the remaining 39 were from firms selling proprietaries/sundries within the healthcare industry. A test of differences between the groups across study variables exhibited no significant differences, thus warranting the pooling of these responses. A summary of salesperson characteristics follows: average total income = $93,000; average age = 37; 58 percent male; average length of relationship with current supervisor = 4 years; and 75 percent hold a bachelor's degree or higher.

We tested for non-response bias in a manner consistent with procedures outlined by Armstrong and Overton (1977). We compared responses from the first wave against those from the second wave. No significant differences were determined for the variables in the study. Additionally, comparisons across respondents and non-respondents indicated no significant differences.

### Measures

Pre-existing measures were used for all constructs. Where necessary the measures were adapted slightly in wording to fit the context of the current study. Of the measures completed by the salespeople, most were seven-point Likert-type multi-item scales. Specifically, these measures included a four-item measure of self-control, and a five-item measure of professional control from Ramaswami (1996). Measures of uncertainty were collected using Singh's (2000) six-item measure of role conflict. To determine participation in strategic activities, we closely followed the procedure from Floyd and Wooldridge's (1992) 20-item measure that used five-point Likert-type scales. Other background variables were collected as well. These included age, education, and length of time working with the current supervisor. Reliabilities for constructs are noted in the correlation matrix (Table 13.1). All measures have been used in previous studies and have been found to be both reliable and valid.

## Analyses and Results

Hierarchical moderated regression analysis was used to test H1 through H6. We estimated an initial regression equation including informal controls (self and professional) with each of the four management behaviors (championing, synthesizing, facilitating, implementing). Moderating variables included market turbulence and role conflict while control variables included length of relationship, level of education, and age. In the second model, the hypothesized interactions were added. Prior to doing so, the constituent variables were mean-centered in order to eliminate multicollinearity (Aiken and West, 1991). Variance inflation factors were below the cutoff of 10, ranging from 1.5 to 3.2, thus suggesting that multicollinearity was not a problem. Separate regression equations were estimated for each dependent variable (i.e., championing, synthesizing, implementing, facilitating, and role conflict).

The results presented in Table 13.2 indicate support for many of the hypothesized moderation effects. In hypothesis 1 and 2, we posited that there would be a main effect of informal controls on the salesperson's participation in strategic activity. Results show strong support in each of the four management behaviors in the anticipated direction – self-control was positively related to management activities and professional controls were negatively associated with management activities. Next, we expected that the positive linkage between self-control and management activity would be diminished in the presence of market turbulence (H3) and role conflict (H5). In the face of a turbulent environment, the interaction between self-control and market turbulence was statistically significant for synthesizing information and implementing strategy and in the expected direction for all four activities. The interaction

**Table 13.1**  Variable means, standard deviations, and intercorrelations

| | 1 | 2 | 3 | 4 | 5 | 6 | 7 | 8 | 9 | 10 | 11 |
|---|---|---|---|---|---|---|---|---|---|---|---|
| 1. Market turbulence | — | | | | | | | | | | |
| 2. Self-control | .049 | (.80) | | | | | | | | | |
| 3. Professional control | .010 | .653** | (.94) | | | | | | | | |
| 4. Role conflict | −.172* | −.467** | −.352** | (.86) | | | | | | | |
| 5. Synthesizing | .250** | .352** | .105 | −.330** | (.89) | | | | | | |
| 6. Championing | .258** | .332** | −.001 | −.363** | .868* | (.88) | | | | | |
| 7. Implementing | .165* | .398** | .148 | −.299** | .823** | .734** | (.89) | | | | |
| 8. Facilitating | .359** | .277** | .079 | −.286** | .777** | .805** | .723** | (.77) | | | |
| 9. Age | .148 | .299** | .282** | −.199* | .173 | .106 | −.264** | .198* | — | | |
| 10. Length | .106 | .127 | .214** | .101 | .166* | .027 | .182* | .119 | .363* | — | |
| 11. Education | .367** | −.034 | .022 | .014 | .106 | .090 | .080 | .184* | −.119 | .019 | — |
| | | | | | | | | | | | |
| N | 187 | 150 | 150 | 151 | 178 | 178 | 178 | 178 | 130 | 149 | 149 |
| Mean | 4.65 | 4.94 | 4.91 | 3.61 | 3.27 | 3.10 | 3.23 | 3.01 | 10.78 | 46.95 | 3.97 |
| Standard deviation | 1.36 | 1.24 | 1.61 | 1.19 | 1.02 | 1.05 | 0.91 | 0.84 | 37.00 | 43.4 | 0.95 |

*Note:* Reliabilities shown in bold in the diagonal.
** Correlation is significant at the 0.01 level (two-tailed).
* Correlation is significant at the 0.05 level (two-tailed).

for role conflict was not present, however, results indicate a strong negative main effect of role conflict on each of the four management activities.

We also predicted that the negative linkage between professional control and management activity would be increased in the presence of market turbulence (H4) and role conflict (H6). In the face of a turbulent environment, the interaction between professional control and market turbulence was statistically significant for championing at the $p < .01$ level and was in the expected positive direction for all four activities. The interaction for role conflict was marginally significant for championing. The implications of these findings will be discussed in the following section.

## Discussion

The notion of mid-level strategic influence in organizations has received a great deal of attention in recent years. Specifically, researchers have focused on myriad behaviors that organizational actors undertake to achieve strategic renewal (Floyd and Lane, 2000). While research indicates that the process of achieving renewal requires that organizational actors go above and beyond formal job descriptions, we also suggest that strategic renewal can be affected by informal management controls, shared beliefs, and the degree of uncertainty facing the firm (Chakravarthy et al., 2003). A brief summary of key findings follows:

1. We found that informal control systems are strongly related to boundary-spanning salespersons participation in strategic activities – or those activities that are often associated with strategic renewal (Floyd and Lane, 2000). Traditionally, the majority of work in MCS has focused on the formal mechanisms that can enhance performance. Here, we argue that salespeople seek riskier behavior if informal controls are based on individual responsibility. When the controls were based on group norms, on the other hand, we found that employees sought to minimize the adverse effects of opportunism. In short, professional controls were negatively related to all four management activities.
2. We found that under conditions of uncertainty the controls–behavior linkage was moderated. When reported levels of market turbulence increased, the influence of self-control becomes detrimental to participation in the activities. This finding was significant for synthesizing and implementing, or what Floyd and Wooldridge (1992) referred to as "integrative" activities. On the other hand, the influence of professional control is enhanced by increased market turbulence for championing new ideas. In this case, it appears that employees feel shielded by group norms – similar to the free-rider phenomenon – and exhibit higher levels of championing new ideas to upper management teams. The impact of role conflict as a moderator was not found to be significant and is covered in depth below.
3. Contrary to expectations, the role conflict–informal controls interaction effect was not statistically significant. However, role conflict did have a significant main effect across all four management behaviors. Research suggests that this negative association might stem from stressful and competing forces within individuals

**Table 13.2** Moderated regression analysis: the effect of control on strategic activities

| | Championing | | | | Synthesizing | | | | Implementing | | | | Facilitating | | | |
| | Model 1 | | Model 2 | | Model 1 | | Model 2 | | Model 1 | | Model 2 | | Model 1 | | Model 2 | |
| | β | t-value | β | t-value | β | t-value | β | t-value | β | t-value | β | t-value | β | t-value | β | t-value |
|---|---|---|---|---|---|---|---|---|---|---|---|---|---|---|---|---|
| *Independent variables* | | | | | | | | | | | | | | | | |
| Self-control | .428 | 3.847** | 1.405 | 2.133* | .361 | 3.128** | 1.563 | 2.266* | .384 | 3.355** | 1.107 | 1.618 | .218 | 1.859^ | .566 | .795 |
| Professional control | -.451 | -4.293*** | -2.833 | -3.508** | -.302 | -2.764** | -1.991 | -2.354* | -.251 | -2.316* | -.453 | -.540 | -.234 | -2.106* | -1.214 | -1.392 |
| Role conflict | -.339 | -3.783** | -.664 | -2.610** | -.302 | -3.241** | -.585 | -2.197* | -.225 | -2.434* | -.345 | -1.306 | -.271 | -2.861** | -.646 | -2.35* |
| Market turbulence | .162 | 1.985* | -.430 | -1.134 | .117 | 1.386 | .253 | .637 | .154 | 1.833^ | .823 | 2.091* | .219 | 2.547* | .125 | .306 |
| *Interactions* | | | | | | | | | | | | | | | | |
| Market turbulence X Self | | | -1.403 | .163 | | | -1.575 | -2.228* | | | -1.515 | -2.162* | | | -.809 | -1.109 |
| Market turbulence X Professional | | | 2.092 | 2.890** | | | 1.438 | 1.897^ | | | .414 | .551 | | | 1.007 | 1.288 |
| Role conflict X Self | | | -.507 | -1.105 | | | -.264 | -.550 | | | .335 | .704 | | | .196 | .395 |
| Role conflict X Professional | | | .995 | 1.925^ | | | .745 | 1.377 | | | -.141 | -.263 | | | .271 | .486 |
| *Control variables* | | | | | | | | | | | | | | | | |
| Education | .052 | .659 | .047 | .604 | .085 | 1.050 | .081 | 1.004 | .067 | .828 | .056 | .697 | .153 | 1.852^ | .147 | 1.77^ |
| Length of relationship | .097 | 1.112 | .030 | .335 | .196 | 2.168* | .121 | 1.280 | .145 | 1.617 | .108 | 1.153 | .103 | 1.119 | .050 | .515 |
| Age | -.044 | -.497 | .007 | .076 | -.020 | -.214 | .021 | .231 | .070 | .771 | .090 | .984 | .055 | .588 | .080 | .837 |
| $R^2$ | .312 | | .367 | | .258 | | .306 | | .270 | | .318 | | .233 | | .261 | |
| Adjusted $R^2$ | .271 | | .306 | | .214 | | .239 | | .227 | | .252 | | .187 | | .190 | |
| Incremental $R^2$F-value | | | 2.484* | | | | 1.962^ | | | | 1.980^ | | | | 1.08 | |

** $p < .01$ (two-tailed); * $p < .05$ (two-tailed); ^ $p < .10$ (two-tailed).

(Biddle, 1979). We believe that the individual-level problem of role conflict forces employees to avoid the individual-level activities associated with strategic renewal. These three findings are explored in greater depth below along with limitations and future avenues for research in this important area.

## Conclusions

Based on their boundary-spanning location in organizations, salespeople are expected to understand and anticipate market changes and take entrepreneurial risks (Slater and Olson, 2000). Our results lend strong support to the notion that employees will participate in strategic influence activities when the employee derives success and meaning intrinsically (i.e., through self-control). It appears, on the other hand, that when performance is based on group efforts, salespeople do not pursue key strategic behaviors. Acknowledging the importance of knowledge sharing in the strategic decision-making process (Schwarz, 2003; Nonaka, 1994), we contend that in conditions of uncertainty, informal controls enhance mid-level strategic roles.

In sum, we suggest that the relationship between strategic influence activities and performance be more fully explored. This includes performance at the individual level as well as firm performance. While much of our study adopts Floyd and Wooldridge's (1992) middle management roles, a more robust examination of strategic roles could include 10 or more constructs that were not included here (cf. Floyd and Lane, 2000). Another interesting avenue of potential research would be to identify control combinations. That is, how much and under what conditions, should managers combine both formal and informal control systems? This line of research could uncover interesting nuances about the employee–supervisor dyad and/or keys to tapping into the social network of an organization. These possibilities could certainly enhance the literature on MCS as well as the growing field of strategic renewal.

## References

Aiken, L.S. and West, S.G. 1991. *Multiple Regression: Testing and Interpreting Interactions.* Newbury Park, CA: Sage.

Anderson, E. and Oliver, R. 1987. Perspectives on behavior-based versus outcome-based salesforce control systems. *Journal of Marketing*, **51**: 76–88.

Armstrong, J.C. and Overton, T.S. 1977. Estimating non-response bias in mail surveys. *Journal of Marketing Research*, **14**: 396–400.

Astley, W.G. and Sachdeva, P.S. 1984. Structural sources of intraorganizational power. *Academy of Management Review*, 9(1): 104–13.

Atuahene-Gima, K. and Li, H. 2002. When does trust matter? Antecedents and contingent effects of supervisee trust on performance in selling new products in China and the United States. *Journal of Marketing*, **66**: 61–81.

Bartlett, C.A. and Ghoshal, S. 1993. Beyond the M-form: Toward a managerial theory of the firm. *Strategic Management Journal*, Winter: 23–46.

Biddle, B.J. 1979. *Role Theory: Expectations, Identities, and Behaviors.* New York: Academic Press.

Blau, P.L. 1964. *Exchange and Power in Social Life.* New York: Wiley.

Burgelman, R.A. 1991. Interorganizational ecology of strategy making and organizational adaptation: Theory and field research. *Organization Science*, **2**: 239–62.

Chakravarthy, B.S., Mueller-Stewens, G., Lorange, P., and Lechner, C. 2003. *Strategy Process: Shaping the Contours of the Field*.Oxford, UK: Blackwell.

Dutton, J.E., Ashford, S.J., O'Neil, R.M., Hayes, E., and Weirba, E.E. 1997. Reading the wind: How middle managers assess the contest for selling issues to top managers. *Strategic Management Journal*, **18**(5), 407–25.

Dwyer, F.R., Schurr, P.H., and Oh, S. 1987. Developing buyer–seller relationships. *Journal of Marketing*, **51**: 11–28.

Flaherty, K.E. and Pappas, J.M. 2000. The role of trust in salesperson–sales manager relationships. *Journal of Personal Selling and Sales Management*, **20**(4): 271–8.

Floyd, S.W. and Lane, P.J. 2000. Strategizing throughout the organization: Managing role conflict in strategic renewal. *Academy of Management Review*, **25**(1): 154–77.

Floyd, S.W. and Wooldridge, W. 1992. Middle management involvement in strategy and its association with strategic type. *Strategic Management Journal*, **13**: 153–67.

Floyd, S.W. and Wooldridge, W. 1997. Middle management's strategic influence and organizational performance. *Journal of Management Studies*, **34**: 465–85.

Floyd, S.W. and Wooldridge, W. 2000. *Building Strategy from the Middle*. Thousand Oaks, CA: Sage.

Ghoshal, S. and Moran, P. 1996. Bad for practice: A critique of the transaction cost theory. *Academy of Management Review*, **21**(1): 13–47.

Hill, C.W. 1990. Cooperation, opportunism, and the invisible hand: Implications for transaction cost theory. *Academy of Management Review*, **15**(3): 500–13.

Hutt, M.D., Reingen, P.H., and Ronchetto, J.R 1988. Tracing emergent processes in marketing strategy formation. *Journal of Marketing*, **52**: 4–19.

Levinthal, D.A. and March, J.G. 1993. The myopia of learning. *Strategic Management Journal*, **14** (Special Issue): 95–112.

Marginson, D.E.W. 2002. Management control systems and their effects on strategy formation at the middle-management levels: Evidence from a U.K. organization. *Strategic Management Journal*, **23**(11): 1019–31.

Mintzberg, H. and Waters, J.A. 1982. Tracking strategy in an entrepreneurial firm. *Academy of Management Journal*, **25**(3): 465–99.

Nonaka, I. 1994. A dynamic theory of organizational knowledge creation. *Organization Science*, **5**: 14–37.

Ouchi, W.G. 1980 Markets, bureaucracies, and clans. *Administrative Science Quarterly*, **25**: 120–42.

Ramaswami, S.N. 1996. Marketing controls and dysfunctional employee behaviors: A test of traditional and contingency theory postulates. *Journal of Marketing*, **60**: 105–23.

Schwarz, M. 2003. A multilevel analysis of the strategic decision process and the evolution of shared beliefs.In B.S. Chakravarthy, G. Mueller-Stewens, P. Lorange, and C. Lechner (eds.), *Strategy Process: Shaping the Contours of the Field*, pp.110–36. Oxford, UK: Blackwell.

Singh, J. 1998. Striking a balance in boundary-spanning positions: An investigation of some unconventional influences of role stressors and job characteristics on job outcomes of salespeople. *Journal of Marketing*, **62**(3): 69–86.

Singh, J. 2000. Performance productivity and quality of frontline employees in service organizations. *Journal of Marketing*, **64**(2): 15–34.

Slater, S.F. and Olson, E.M. 2000. Strategy type and performance: The influence of sales force management. *Strategic Management Journal*, **21**: 813–29.

Thompson, J.D. 1967. *Organizations in Action*. New York: McGraw-Hill.

Williamson, O.E. 1985. *The Economic Institution of Capitalism: Firms, Markets, and Relational Contracting*. New York: The Free Press.

# CHAPTER FOURTEEN

# The Role of the Social Context for Strategy Making: Examining the Impact of Embeddedness on the Performance of Strategic Initiatives

Karolin Marx, Christoph Lechner

The evolutionary perspective on strategy process conceptualizes an organization as an ecology of strategic initiatives (Burgelman, 1991, 1994, 2002; Floyd and Wooldridge, 2000; Lovas and Ghoshal, 2000; Chakravarthy *et al.*, 2003). As discrete, proactive undertakings, strategic initiatives either reinforce the current strategy or alter it in order to realign the organization with changed environmental conditions. It has been argued that their evolution is shaped and determined by the organizational context; this context mirror images the conditions of the external market environment and acts therefore as an internal selection mechanism (Burgelman, 1991; Lovas and Ghoshal, 2000). According to Barnett and Burgelman (1996: 7):

> [E]xternal selection and internal selection, together, determine the fates of organizations. Those that continue to survive have an internal selection environment that reflects the relevant selection pressures in the external environment and produces externally viable new strategic variations that are internally selected and retained.

While previous work has mainly focused on the role of the so-called structural and strategic context (Bower, 1970; Burgelman, 1983a,b, 1991), we introduce in this chapter the notion of a social context in which these initiatives are embedded. As initiatives are pursued by formal groups (or informal coalitions), it is reasonable to assume that the type and quality of their social relations to other organizational actors matters substantially for their survival. However, considering the literature on social network research, it is ambiguous what the effect of these social linkages for the selection of initiatives might actually be. On the one hand, it has been shown that social relations have the potential to facilitate innovative activity and gain support and assistance (Nahapiet and Ghoshal, 1998; Tsai and Ghoshal, 1998; Tsai, 2001). On the other hand, it has been argued that there might also be negative consequences. For example, the phenomenon of "over-embeddedness" points to the tendency that social relationships might also constrain an actor's ability to act efficiently (Uzzi, 1996, 1997).

The purpose of this chapter is to sort out these inconsistencies about the effects of social linkages and to develop a theoretical model that is able to grasp the relationship between social context (represented by the embeddedness of initiative groups in the intrafirm network) and the performance of strategic initiatives. In particular we want to achieve three things: First, we want to demonstrate the general significance of social context for strategy making. Second, building upon the distinction of relational, structural, positional, and cognitive embeddedness, we will show that these four embeddedness dimensions have a curvilinear relationship to the performance of initiatives. In our eyes, these curvilinear relations are key in disentangling contradictions in social network research. And third, we will extend this research by integrating the type of the initiative as a key contingency. Based upon the distinction of exploration/exploitation (March, 1991), we show that exploratory undertakings require a different social setting and therefore a different management approach than their exploitive counterparts. In sum, we hope to extend the notion of organizational context in strategy process research by incorporating its under-investigated "social side".

## Theoretical Background

Strategic initiatives have received increasing attention as the core building blocks of strategy making (Bower, 1970; Burgelman, 1983a,b, 1991, 1994, 2002; Floyd and Wooldridge, 2000; Lovas and Ghoshal, 2000). For our purpose, we define strategic initiatives as discrete proactive undertakings that are launched by ideas, composed of groups, and reinforce or alter the current strategy of the firm. This definition incorporates both formal and informal initiatives. It also encompasses initiatives triggered by top, middle, lower management or combinations of them. Further, based upon an evolutionary perspective, we define the performance of initiatives in terms of their survival in the organizational ecology. This implies that corporate resources and top managers' attention are allocated to the initiative and that the initiative is integrated in the current strategy of the firm, thereby reinforcing or altering it.

### The structural and strategic context of initiatives

Although researchers have emphasized the importance of the organizational context for strategy making, so far their attention has mainly focused on the impact of the structural and strategic context (Bower, 1970; Burgelman, 1983a,b, 1991). The structural context encompasses all administrative systems and processes, such as planning or budgeting systems. These steer the allocation of resources towards initiatives (Noda and Bower, 1996). It has been broadly defined as "various organizational and administrative mechanisms" (Noda and Bower, 1996: 160). Top management can directly set those management systems in place and use them to steer the subsequent selection of new initiatives. Because the structural context is in line with the officially espoused strategy of a firm, all selected initiatives are tightly coupled to this strategy as well. Therefore, the structural context is perceived as a quite strict and rigid selection mechanism picking just those initiatives that fit to the predefined requirements.

Besides this, the strategic context allows autonomous initiatives, operating outside the domain of the current strategy, to receive top management attention and to amend the corporate strategy (Burgelman, 1983a,b, 1991, 2002). The strategic context involves few rules, many interactions, and a political process and is therefore more of an informal context (Burgelman, 1983b, 1991). While the structural context affects all initiatives, the strategic context refers to only those initiatives that deviate from the current strategy and represent autonomous strategic behavior within the organization. These initiatives again compete for scarce resources and top management attention, but are only able to gain those through micro-political processes of negotiation, persuasion, or coalitions building. In contrast to the structural context, top management is not able to directly steer this selection mechanism due to the political ambiguities of this process. However, it can indirectly influence this context by creating an environment that gives space and allows for the development of such autonomous undertakings.

### The social context of initiatives: An embeddedness perspective

In extension to these thoughts, we introduce the notion of the social context. This context focuses on formal and informal social relationships. It deals with norms and values that either support or impede the survival of new initiatives. More specifically, it is conceptualized as the embeddedness of the initiative team in the intrafirm network. It starts from the premise that those initiatives that create a particular social context are able to gain scarce corporate resources and top managers' attention, and can therefore survive in an evolutionary sense. In contrast, initiatives that do not create the appropriate social context are less likely to survive. Hence, the social context serves as an internal selection mechanism in the same way as the structural and strategic context. However, in contrast to the structural context, top management can only indirectly influence the selection process of this context.

A key insight of research on social embeddedness is the recognition that purposeful behavior of social actors is influenced by the concrete and enduring social relationships in which these actors are embedded (Granovetter, 1985; Zukin and DiMaggio, 1990; Uzzi, 1996; 1997; Dacin, Ventresca, and Beal, 1999). For our purpose, the relationship between social context, represented by intrafirm network embeddedness, and the performance of strategic initiatives is confronted with two major challenges that are neither theoretically nor empirically fully resolved. The first is based on divergent opinions about the effects of embeddedness. While most scholars emphasize its positive side in terms of access to information, resources, or support (Granovetter, 1985; Zukin and DiMaggio, 1990; Tsai and Ghoshal, 1998; Tsai, 2001), others are more doubtful about its merits and consider negative effects as well (Uzzi, 1996, 1997; Gargiulo and Benassi, 2000; Chung, Singh, and Lee, 2000).

The second challenge is related to the embeddedness construct itself. Studies differ widely with regards to the dimensions of the construct. In order to capture the role of embeddedness in the performance of strategic initiatives, we propose four dimensions of embeddedness that have received broad theoretical and empirical support, namely relational, structural, positional, and cognitive embeddedness (Zukin and DiMaggio, 1990; Granovetter, 1992; Gulati and Gargiulo, 1999; Nahapiet and Ghoshal, 1998; Tsai and Ghoshal, 1998; Simsek, Lubatkin, and Floyd, 2003). Relational embeddedness focuses on assets rooted in the quality of relationships, such as the level of trust and friendship. Structural embeddedness refers to the structure of relations around the focal group and the configuration of ties that make up the unit's network (Zukin and DiMaggio, 1990). Positional embeddedness refers to the position a particular unit occupies in the network, independent of the characteristics of its partners (Gulati and Gargiulo, 1999). And finally, cognitive embeddedness refers to similarity in the mental representations, interpretations, mental models, and worldviews shared by the focal group with the other actors in organization (Nahapiet and Ghoshal, 1998).

## Embeddedness and Strategic Initiatives

Based on these considerations, we propose a theoretical framework that examines the impact of social context on the performance of strategic initiatives. The framework is based on four assumptions. First, as already indicated, strategic initiatives are the core vehicle for strategy making, by either reinforcing or altering the existing strategy (Bower, 1970; Burgelman, 1983a,b, 1991; Lovas and Ghoshal, 2000). Second, the social context is represented by the embeddedness of the groups pursuing initiatives in the intrafirm network. As initiatives are fostered by formal groups or informal coalitions, their network of social relations is expected to have a direct impact on the outcome of new initiatives. Third, we focus on inter-unit relationships within an organization, where the relevant network is composed of the linkages between initiative groups and all other relevant organizational units/actors. As strategy processes often cycle through several management levels, social actors of various types and on various levels may be part of the network. Fourth, as argued by other researchers (Powell, Koput, and Smith-Doerr, 1996; Miller, 1996), the four theoretical dimensions of embeddedness are too broad to lend themselves to the development of refutable research propositions. Therefore, we focus on more specific variables: relational embeddedness as tie strength, structural embeddedness as structural autonomy, positional embeddedness as centrality, and cognitive embeddedness as shared vision. The effects of these four dimensions on initiative performance are summarized in Figure 14.1. In the following paragraphs, we examine these relationships in detail.

### Impact of tie strength (relational embeddedness)

Granovetter (1973: 1361) introduced the idea of tie strength and defined it as a "combination of the amount of time, the emotional intensity, the intimacy (mutual confiding), and the reciprocal services which characterize the tie." Several arguments speak for its positive effects. First, strong ties facilitate the transfer of fine-grained

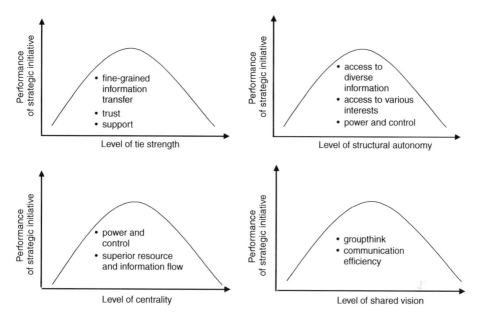

**Figure 14.1**   The controversial effects of embeddedness on the performance of strategic initiatives

information and tacit knowledge (Uzzi, 1996) as they create a channel through which knowledge and information can flow easily. Hansen (1999) shows, for example, that new product development groups with strong ties to other actors are more efficient in transferring non-codified (tacit) knowledge. Strong ties to a large number of other organizational actors, therefore, enable an initiative group to develop the information and knowledge base associated with initiative success more efficiently.

Increasing tie strength is also likely to increase the levels of trust between the initiative group and the other organizational actors (Krackhardt, 1992; Gulati, Nohria, and Zaheer, 2000). Higher trust further increases the success of transferring information and knowledge (Szulanski, 1996) and reduces the search costs involved in such transfers (Gulati, Nohria, and Zaheer, 2000). Levinthal and March (1993) argue that trust enhances the capacity of actors to learn from one another. Similarly, Rangan (2000) argues that exchanges between actors with strong, trusting ties are more efficient because more information leads to better resource allocation and because trust reduces the need for formal contracts.

The third effect stemming from tie strength is increased levels of support between the initiative group and other organizational actors. Strong ties to the rest of the organization are likely to increase the initiative group's connection to key stakeholders, thereby enhancing the perceived desirability and acceptability of the initiative within the organization and thus its likelihood for success (e.g. McAllister, 1995; Nelson, 1989; Floyd and Wooldridge, 1999; Krackhardt, 1992).

At a certain point, however, each marginal increase in the strength of existing ties is likely to have diminishing returns to the information or knowledge base of the initiative group. The more information exchanged between the group and other organizational actors, the higher the probability that additional exchanges produce decreasing marginal benefits for the initiative group (Gulati, 1995; Chung, Singh, and Lee, 2000; Gargiulo and Benassi, 2000).

Moreover, strongly tied initiative groups are less likely to search for links to new actors (Hansen, 1999), due to feelings of familiarity and trust with the existing partners (Gulati, 1995). This is likely to diminish an initiative group's access to information and hence its flexibility in the face of change. Further, at a high level of tie strength the initiative group is not only less willing but also less able to change its partner portfolio (Marsden and Campbell, 1984; Hansen, 1999). Feelings of friendship and obligation can become so strong that effective actions are constrained or original goals derailed (Gimeno and Woo, 1996; Uzzi, 1997; Portes and Sensebrenner, 1993). Partners may become locked in endless mutual exchanges that have little economic value (Gargiulo and Benassi, 2000). This limits access to new information and the group's ability to seek out new sources of support, which is likely to diminish the performance of the initiative.

Summing up, we have argued that with an increasing level of tie strength, the positive effects are diminishing and the negative effects are increasing, which is why we propose a curvilinear inverted U-shaped relationship between tie strength and the performance of strategic initiatives.

> P1:   There is an inverted U-shaped relationship between the degree of tie strength (in terms of the initiative groups and other organizational actors) and the performance of strategic initiatives.

### The impact of structural autonomy (structural embeddedness)

Structurally autonomous initiative groups have links to organizational actors that are not connected to one another (Burt, 1992). Structural autonomy increases access to diverse information (Burt, 1992; Gnyawali and Madhavan, 2001; Koka and Prescott, 2002), which is important because diversity is associated with a broader knowledge base. This breadth, in turn, increases the likelihood that proposals coming out of such a group represent higher quality alternatives. Much as they are exposed to a greater variety of information, structural autonomous initiative groups get to know a greater variety of interests and concerns within the network (Gulati, 1995; Gulati and Gargiulo, 1999). This allows the group to integrate more of these issues into their proposals; thereby increasing the amount of organizational support for the initiative and reducing the possibility that others will attempt to undermine it. The structural autonomous initiative group is also in a position to control the flow of information within the network (Burt, 1992), making the unconnected actors dependent on the autonomous group. Such dependency creates power that can be used to gain additional support, information, and resources, which increases the likelihood for success.

There are also negative effects at high levels of structural autonomy. If the group internalizes too much diverse information, it may focus on exploring new capabilities at the expense of exploiting existing ones (Koka and Prescott, 2002). Groups that engage only in seeking new information will suffer from never capitalizing on their discoveries (Levinthal and March, 1993; McGrath, 2001). In addition, having access to a diverse information base and a broad range of interests increases the risk of confusion within the group, and at high levels, this may lead to ineffective and inefficient actions. Moreover, the more any group monopolizes power within a network the greater the probability that dependant actors will try to change the network structure in order to overcome the monopolistic situation (Gnyawali and Madhavan, 2001).

As the benefits decrease and the costs increase with an increasing level of structural embeddedness, the net effect is a curvilinear, inverted U-shaped relationship between structural autonomy and the performance of strategic initiatives. Thus, we propose:

> P2:   There is an inverted U-shaped relationship between the level of the initiative group's structural autonomy (with regards to other organizational actors) and the performance of strategic initiatives.

## The impact of centrality (positional embeddedness)

Centrality describes the amount of contacts the group has with other organizational actors. First, centrally located initiative groups have more control and power within the firm (Burt, 1992; Brass and Burckhardt, 1992; Ibarra, 1993). This allows the initiative group to pursue its ideas more easily, as it is confronted with less resistance and more support within the organization.

The second effect of centrality is superior access to critical information and resource flows, due to the group's connection to many other organizational actors (Gulati, Nohria, and Zaheer, 2000; Gnyawali and Madhavan, 2001). Such resources and information increase the initiative group's innovative activity (Tsai, 2001), its flexibility, and its chances to successfully pursue the initiative (e.g. Bower, 1970). As central actors are likely to gain information about new developments and external changes sooner than others (Valente, 1995), they can react to those changes earlier and outperform competing undertakings.

On the negative side, a powerful position increases the risk that the peripheral actors withhold valuable information, resources, and support (Sparrowe *et al.*, 2001) and that they try to change the network structure (Uzzi, 1997). Both activities reduce the influential position of the centrally located initiative group and influence the performance of the initiative negatively. Moreover, as groups reach the limits of their ability to process information, increasing access needlessly consumes time. The group may become overconfident, believing that its existing network provides all relevant and valuable information (Koka and Prescott, 2002; Stevenson and Greenberg, 2000). Finally, each additional tie becomes another potential leakage point, i.e. a point through which valuable information may be conveyed to others (Gnyawali and Madhavan, 2001). Based on these arguments, we propose:

> P3:   There is an inverted U-shaped relationship between the level of an initiative group's centrality (with regards to other organizational actors) and the performance of strategic initiatives.

## The impact of shared vision (cognitive embeddedness)

Shared vision refers to the degree that the initiative group shares common goals and aspirations with other organizational actors in the organization (Nahapiet and Ghoshal, 1998; Tsai and Ghoshal, 1998; Simsek, Lubatkin, and Floyd, 2003). First, if the group and the other actors have a collective understanding of the environment, the company, and specific problems, the initiative is more likely to gain legitimacy within the firm (Baum and Oliver, 1991; Gavetti and Levinthal, 2000). Another positive effect of shared vision is the increasing communication efficiency between the initiative group and the actors (Tsai and Ghoshal, 1998; Szulanski, 1996). Similarly, Scott (2001) argues that shared beliefs enable different actors to quickly develop a common definition of the situation. Efficient communication allows the initiative group to transfer information rapidly and to capture small nuances and tacit components of knowledge of other actors' know how. Thus, the group may develop an initiative based on a richer, more complex information base. Assuming that such complexity is mirrored in the intra-organizational and extra-organizational environment, a more complex picture of the situation within the group likely improves its effectiveness and enhances the performance of the initiative.

On the negative side, however, if a shared vision is too strong, it may create a mind set very close to groupthink (Janis, 1972) – the well-known risk that like-minded decision-making groups fail to recognize or take account of new or discrepant information. Mental models limit search and reduce the number of alternatives considered (e.g. Barr, Stimpert, and Huff, 1992; Oliver, 1996; Leonard-Barton, 1992). When this happens initiative groups are likely to ignore important information, make poor choices, and ultimately, completely lose support within the network. Moreover, an initiative group occupied with integrating more and more marginally informative input, is not likely to be very creative (Hurst, Rush, and White, 1989), and when the initiative encounters unanticipated obstacles, novel solutions may not be forthcoming in a timely manner (e.g. Simsek, Lubatkin, and Floyd, 2003).

Drawing on these arguments, the optimal level of cognitive embeddedness is likely to be between extreme homogeneity and heterogeneity.

> P4: There is an inverted U-shaped relationship between the level of shared vision between the initiative group and other organizational actors and the performance of strategic initiatives.

## The degree of exploration as key contingency

The above arguments suggest an optimal point along the curves defining the relationship between the four dimensions of embeddedness and the performance of strategic initiatives. We would argue that the type of an initiative influences the level at which such optimal effects arise. For example, if an initiative builds on existing capabilities, it makes sense to exploit these similarities and to create strong ties around the initiative. However, if an initiative taps into an unfamiliar market or requires innovative approaches, it makes sense to assume that it requires a different social setting.

Based on this reasoning, we argue that the distinction between exploration/exploitation (March, 1991) offers a basis for conceptualizing the task-related contingencies associated with optimal levels of each dimension of embeddedness.

Exploratory initiatives are about "search, variation, risk taking, experimentation, play, flexibility, discovery, innovation" (March, 1991: 7). They are intended to create or develop new capabilities. To succeed, groups pursuing such initiatives need to generate new knowledge and to gain power. A broad knowledge base enables the group to adapt to the environment more effectively (McGrath, 2001). This increases the likelihood that it will produce externally viable solutions (Burgelman, 1991; Floyd and Wooldridge, 1999). In addition, a group exploring a radically new approach needs power to influence the resource allocation and agenda-building processes. Because exploratory initiatives lie outside the existing capability set of the firm, they face more resistance within the organization (Burgelman, 1983b). We argue that the combination of a low level of tie strength and shared vision and a high level of centrality and structural autonomy is beneficial for the success of exploratory initiatives.

Stronger ties decrease the group's willingness and ability to change its partner portfolio (Gulati, 1995). This in turn reduces access to new information and the ability to create new knowledge. A lower level of tie strength, on the other hand, enables the group to change its partner portfolio frequently and increase its knowledge base. Similarly, a strong shared vision between the initiative group and other organizational actors decreases the group's desire for new information. The company as a whole already agrees to a dominant logic (Prahalad and Bettis, 1986) and therefore sees little need to integrate new knowledge or search for additional alternatives (Barr, Stimpert, and Huff, 1992). At a lower level of shared vision, diversity exists, and the focal unit is more likely to increase its knowledge base. On the other hand, increasing structural autonomy increases the unit's possibility to gain diverse information and access to various interests, broadening its knowledge base. Similarly, a higher level of centrality makes the focal group better off. By occupying a central position in the network the initiative group can access various strategic resources, which again increase the unit's knowledge base (Tsai, 2001). Further a high level of centrality and structural autonomy increases the power of the initiative group. However, the level of centrality and structural autonomy should not be too high as this again decreases the group's performance.

Exploitive initiatives are about "refinement, choice, production, efficiency, selection, implementation, execution" (March, 1991: 7). They focus on the improvement of existing capabilities. Initiative groups pursuing such initiatives need to focus and be efficient in order to achieve high performance. Integrating new knowledge may even hinder their performance (McGrath, 2001), as this reduces the coherence of the proposals with the existing knowledge base (Bower, 1970; Burgelman, 1991). Further, exploitive initiatives need to be efficient in order to survive. As an interviewee of Burgelman in Intel (1991: 244) states: "Focus on a few things and do them right". We argue that a combination of a high level of tie strength and shared vision and a low level of centrality and structural autonomy is associated with high performance of exploitive initiatives.

If tie strength increases, the initiative group is more likely to gain fine-grained information, support, and trust, which enables the unit to deepen its focus on the existing knowledge base. Further, increasing shared vision increases the group's ability

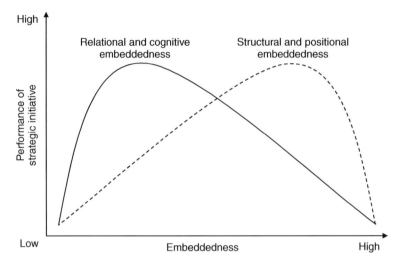

**Figure 14.2** Embeddedness–initiativeperformance relationship moderated by exploratory initiatives (vice versa for exploitative initiatives)

to integrate existing values and norms within the initiative; it also increases the communication efficiency between the group and other organizational actors. However, the level of tie strength and shared vision should not be too high as this might again reduce the performance of the group. On the other side, the focal group is better off if it is located at a less central position because increasing centrality decreases the time available in the group to pursue the development of the initiative. Also, an increasing level of structural autonomy decreases the group's ability to focus on existing knowledge and decreases its performance.

In short, for exploratory initiatives the goal is to create or develop new capabilities. Thus, new knowledge and power are important and maximum initiative performance stems from a higher level of centrality and structural autonomy and a lower level of tie strength and shared vision. For exploitive initiatives the goal is to improve and refine existing knowledge. Thus, focusing and efficiency are important and maximum initiative performance is based on a higher level of tie strength and shared vision and a lower level of centrality and structural autonomy. This discussion suggests that the degree of exploration influences the apex, or the performance-optimizing point of the curve defining the aggregate effects of embeddedness on initiative performance, as demonstrated in Figure 14.2.

Thus, for exploratory and exploitive initiatives there appears to be a certain optimum level of embeddedness along all four dimensions that maximizes initiative performance. Such a formulation reflects what Schoonhoven (1981: 354) labeled "a 'matching' or 'maximizing' theory" (Priem, 1990). Summarizing these arguments, we propose:

> P5:  For exploratory initiatives, lower levels of tie strength and shared vision and higher levels of centrality and structural autonomy are associated with high initiative performance.

P6: For exploitive initiatives, higher levels of tie strength and shared vision and lower levels of centrality and structural autonomy are associated with high initiative performance.

## Discussion and Conclusion

In this chapter, we argued for inverted U-shaped effects of embeddedness on initiative performance. While the benefits of embeddedness increase at lower levels, the costs increase at higher levels. Further, we argued that the optimal level of embeddedness differs with respect to the type of the initiatives. For exploratory initiatives, a lower level of relational and cognitive and a higher level of structural and positional embeddedness are likely to be associated with high initiative performance. For exploitive initiatives, a higher level of relational and cognitive and a lower level of structural and positional embeddedness are likely to be associated with high initiative performance.

### Implications

This model complements previous research that has emphasized the role of the structural context (Bower, 1970; Burgelman, 1983a,b, 1991; Lovas and Ghoshal, 2000) and strategic context determination (Burgelman, 1983a,b) by introducing social relations as an additional, so far under-researched context that is relevant to the success of initiatives. Moreover, by elaborating the contingencies between context, initiative type, and performance, our research points towards certain optimal combinations across these factors. Different types of initiatives require varying social contexts in order to develop and to survive.

It is widely assumed that exploration/exploitation should be balanced in order to ensure the long-term survival of the organization (March, 1991). However, it is difficult to maintain this balance, as companies tend to focus on one side or the other and have problems switching modes. Some researchers argue that the only way to balance exploration and exploitation is to implement them sequentially (e.g. Nonaka, 1994). However, our research offers another possibility. By fostering two distinctive internal selection environments, which facilitate the development and survival of exploratory and exploitive initiatives, firms might be able to master this challenge.

The present model also has implications for social network research. Prior research on intra-firm networks has highlighted the positive side of social relationships, arguing on a "more is better" basis (e.g. Tsai and Ghoshal, 1998; Ghoshal and Bartlett, 1990; Nahapiet and Ghoshal, 1998). Our research highlights not only decreasing returns to social factors, but also the possibility that these factors may actually impede the progress of initiatives.

Overall, research on the social context of strategy processes is just at the beginning. As our arguments suggest, the causal linkages in this area reveal a complex set of relationships requiring further conceptual and empirical work. We hope that our study is a first step in disentangling these linkages.

## References

Barnett, W.P. and Burgelman, R.A. 1996. Evolutionary perspectives on strategy. *Strategic Management Journal*, **17**(summer special issue): 5–19.

Barr, P., Stimpert, L., and Huff, A. 1992. Cognitive change, strategic action, and organizational renewal. *Strategic Management Journal*, **13**(summer special issue): 15–36.

Baum, J.A.C. and Oliver, C. 1991. Institutional linkages and organizational mortality. *Administrative Science Quarterly*, **36**: 187–218.

Bower, J.L. 1970. *Managing the Resource Allocation Process*. Boston, MA: Harvard University Press.

Brass, D.J. and Burkhardt, M.E. 1992. Centrality and power in organizations, In N. Nohria and R.G. Eccles (eds.), *Networks and Organizations: Structure, Form and Action*, pp. 191–215. Boston, MA: Harvard Business School Press.

Burgelman, R.A. 1983a. A model of the interaction of strategic behavior, corporate context, and the concept of strategy. *Academy of Management Review*, **8**: 61–70.

Burgelman, R.A. 1983b. A process model of internal corporate venturing in the diversified major firm. *Administrative Science Quarterly*, **28**: 223–44.

Burgelman, R.A. 1991. Interorganizational ecology of strategy making and organizational adaptation: Theory and field research. *Organization Science*, **2**: 239–62.

Burgelman, R.A. 1994. Fading memories: A process theory of strategic business exit in dynamic environments. *Administrative Science Quarterly*, **39**: 24–56.

Burgelman, R.A. 2002. Strategy as vector and the inertia of coevolutionary lock-in. *Administrative Science Quarterly*, **47**: 325–57.

Burt, R.S. 1992. *Structural Holes: The Social Structure of Competition*. Cambridge, MA: Harvard University Press.

Chakravarthy, B., Mueller-Stewens, G., Lorange, P., and Lechner, C. 2003. Defining the contours of the strategy process field. In B. Chakravarthy, G. Mueller-Stewens, P. Lorange, and C. Lechner (eds.), *Strategy Process: Shaping the Contours of the Field*, pp. 3–18. Oxford, UK: Blackwell.

Chung, S., Singh, H., and Lee, K. 2000. Complementarity, status similarity and social capital as drivers of alliance formation, *Strategic Management Journal*, **21**: 1–22.

Dacin, M.T., Ventresca, M.J., and Beal, B.D. 1999. The embeddedness of organizations: Dialogue and directions. *Journal of Management*, **25**: 317–56.

Floyd, S.W. and Wooldridge, B. 1999. Knowledge creation and social networks in corporate entrepreneurship: The renewal of organizational capability. *Entrepreneurship Theory and Practice*, Spring: 123–43.

Gargiulo, M. and Benassi, M. 2000. Trapped in your own net? Network cohesion, structural holes, and the adaption of social capital. *Organization Science*, **11**: 183–96.

Gavetti, G. and Levinthal, D. 2000. Looking forward and looking backward: Cognitive and experiential search. *Administrative Science Quarterly*, **45**: 113–37.

Ghoshal, S. and Bartlett, C. 1990. The multinational corporation as an interorganizational network. *Academy of Management Review*, **15**: 603–25.

Gimeno, J. and Woo, C. 1996. Economic multiplexity: The structural embeddedness of cooperation in multiple relations of interdependence. *Advances in Strategic Management*, **13**: 323–61.

Gnyawali D.R. and Madhavan, R. 2001. Cooperative networks and competitive dynamics: A structural embeddedness perspective. *Academy of Management Review*, **26**: 431–45.

Granovetter, M.S. 1973. The strengths of weak ties. *American Journal of Sociology*, **78**: 1360–80.

Granovetter, M.S. 1985. Economic action and social structure: The problem of embedded-ness. *American Journal of Sociology*, **91**: 481–510.

Granovetter, M.S. 1992. Problems of explanation in economic sociology. In N. Nohria, and R.G. Eccles (eds.), *Networks and Organizations: Structure, Form and Action*, pp. 25–56. Cambridge, MA: Harvard University Press.

Gulati, R. 1995. Social structure and alliance formation patterns: A longitudinal analysis. *Administrative Science Quarterly*, **40**: 619–52.

Gulati, R. and Gargiulo, M. 1999. Where do interorganizational networks come from? *American Journal of Sociology*, **104**: 1439–93.

Gulati, R., Nohria, N., and Zaheer, A. 2000. Strategic networks. *Strategic Management Journal*, **21**: 203–15.

Hansen, M.T. 1999. The search-transfer problem: The role of weak ties in sharing knowledge across organization subunits. *Administrative Science Quarterly*, **44**: 82–111.

Hurst, D.K., Rush, J.C., and White, R.E. 1989. Top management team and organizational renewal. *Strategic Management Journal*, **10**: 87–105.

Ibarra, H. 1993. Network centrality, power, and innovation involvement: Determinants of technical and administrative roles. *Academy of Management Journal*, **36**: 471–501.

Janis, I.L. 1972. *Victims of Groupthink*. Boston, MA: Houghton Mifflin.

Koka, B.R. and Prescott, J.E. 2002. Strategic alliances as social capital: A multidimensional view. *Strategic Management Journal*, **23**(9): 795–816.

Krackhardt, D. 1992. The strengths of strong ties: The importance of philos in organizations, In N. Nohria and R.G. Eccles (eds.), *Networks and Organizations: Structure, Form and Action*, pp. 216–39. Cambridge, MA: Harvard University Press.

Leonard-Barton, D. 1992. Core capabilities and core rigidities: A paradox in managing new product development. *Strategic Management Journal*, **13**(summer special issue): 111–25.

Levinthal, D.A. and March, J.G. 1993. The myopia of learning. *Strategic Management Journal*, **19**: 439–59.

Lovas, B. and Ghoshal, S. 2000. Strategy as guided evolution. *Strategic Management Journal*, **21**: 875–96.

March, J.G. 1991. Exploration and exploitation in organizational learning. *Organization Science*, **2**(Special Issue): 71–87.

Marsden, P.V. and Campbell, K.E. 1984. Measuring tie strengths. *Social Forces*, **63**: 482–501.

McAllister, D.J. 1995. Affect- and cognition-based trust as foundations for interpersonal coop-eration in organizations. *Academy of Management Journal*, **38**(1): 24–59.

McGrath, R.G. 2001. Exploratory learning, innovative capacity, and managerial oversight. *Academy of Management Journal*, **44**: 118–31.

Miller, D. 1996. The embeddedness of corporate strategy: Isomorphism vs. differentiation. *Advances in Strategic Management*, **13**: 283–91.

Nahapiet, J. and Ghoshal, S. 1998. Social capital, intellectual capital, and the organizational advantage. *Academy of Management Review*, **23**: 242–66.

Nelson, R.E. 1989. The strengths of strong ties: Social networks and intergroup conflict in organizations. *Academy of Management Journal*, **32**: 377–401.

Noda, T. and Bower, J.L. 1996. Strategy making as iterated processes of resource allocation. *Strategic Management Journal*, **17**: 159–92.

Nonaka, I. 1994. A dynamic theory of organizational knowledge creation. *Organization Science*, **5**: 14–37.

Oliver, C. 1996. The institutional embeddedness of economic activity. *Advances in Strategic Management*, **13**: 163–86.

Portes, A. and Sensebrenner, J. 1993. Embeddedness and immigration: Notes on the social determinants of economic action. *American Journal of Sociology*, **98**: 1320–50.

Powell, W.W., Koput, K., and Smith-Doerr, L. 1996. Interorganizational collaborations and the locus of innovation: Networks of learning in biotechnology. *Administrative Science Quarterly*, **41**: 116–45.

Prahalad, C.K. and Bettis, R. 1986. The dominant logic: A new linkage between diversity and performance. *Strategic Management Journal*, 7: 485–501.

Priem, R.L. 1990. Top management team group factors, consensus and firm performance. *Strategic Management Journal*, **11**: 469–78.

Rangan, S. 2000. The problem of search and deliberation in economic action: When social networks really matter. *Academy of Management Review*: 813–28.

Schoonhoven, C.B. 1981. Problems with contingency theory: Testing assumptions hidden within the language of contingency "theory". *Administrative Science Quarterly*, **26**: 349–77.

Scott, W.R. 2001. *Institutions and Organizations*, 2nd edition. Thousand Oaks, CA: Sage.

Simsek, Z., Lubatkin, M.H., and Floyd, S.W. 2003. How interorganizational networks influence entrepreneurial behavior: A structural embeddedness perspective. *Journal of Management*, **29**: 427–42.

Sparrowe, R.T., Liden R.C., Wayne, S.J., and Kraimer, M.L. 2001. Social networks and the performance of individuals and groups, *Academy of Management Journal*, **44**: 316–25.

Stevenson, W.B. and Greenberg, D. 2000. Agency and social networks: Strategies of action in a social structure of position, opposition, and opportunity, *Administrative Science Quarterly*, **45**: 651–78.

Szulanski, G. 1996. Exploring internal stickiness: Impediments to the transfer of best practice within the firm. *Strategic Management Journal*, **17**(Winter Special Issue): 27–43.

Tsai, W. 2001. Knowledge transfer in intraorganizational networks: Effects of network position and absorptive capacity on business unit innovation and performance. *Academy of Management Journal*, **44**: 996–1004.

Tsai, W. and Ghoshal, S. 1998. Social capital and value creation: The role of intrafirm networks. *Academy of Management Journal*, **41**: 464–76.

Uzzi, B. 1996. Embeddedness and economic performance: The network effect. *American Sociological Review*, **61**: 674–98.

Uzzi, B. 1997. Social structure and competition in interfirm networks: The paradox of embeddedness. *Administrative Science Quarterly*, **42**: 35–67.

Valente, T.W. 1995. *Network Models of the Diffusion of Innovations*. Cresskill, NJ: Hampton Press.

Zukin, S. and DiMaggio, P. 1990. Introduction. In S. Zukin and P. DiMaggio (eds.), *Structures of Capital: The Social Organization of the Economy*, pp. 1–36. New York: Cambridge University Press.

# CHAPTER FIFTEEN

# Strategic Consensus and Constructive Confrontation: Unifying Forces in the Resource Accumulation Process

Franz W. Kellermanns, Steven W. Floyd

Since the late 1960s (Stagner, 1969), researchers have been interested in the subject of strategic consensus, which broadly describes the "agreement among top-, middle-, and operating-level managers on the fundamental priorities of the organization" (Floyd and Wooldridge, 1992: 28). Research generally assumes a positive association between strategic consensus and performance (e.g., Bourgeois III, 1980; Iaquinto and Fredrickson, 1997), but not all studies have supported this relationship (e.g., West Jr. and Schwenk, 1996). Moreover, with the exception of two more process-oriented studies (Iaquinto and Fredrickson, 1997; Markoczy, 2001), existing research has focused on competitive strategies and near-term resource allocation priorities as the content of strategic consensus.

To date, however, scholars have not explored the question of whether consensus on the organization's longer term resource, *accumulation* priorities, influences the quality or consistency of resource flow decisions (i.e. decisions to invest in certain kinds of resources). This lack of research is surprising because as Dierickx and Cool (1989: 1510) argue: "to explain performance differences among firms on the basis of current strategic expenditures only, is pointless and likely to lead to conflicting results." Thus, one explanation for the inconsistent findings in the research on the consensus performance relationship may be the failure to account for consensus on resource accumulation priorities. Such consensus likely increases both the consistency and quality of resource flows, and this, in turn, can be expected to lead to the accumulation of superior stocks of assets and unique resource bundles within the organization (Barney, 1991; Dierickx and Cool, 1989; Wernerfelt, 1997).

The purpose of this chapter is to explain the antecedents and effects of resource accumulation consensus. We define resource accumulation consensus *as shared understanding about and commitment toward the resources needed to create a superior resource stock*. Based on the premise that such consensus increases the likelihood that superior assets stocks will be accumulated, we would argue that subsequent decisions to deploy such resources are more likely to result in competitive advantage. Our explanation of where such consensus comes from begins with the proposition that resource accumulation occurs as a part of information exchange and decision making among central actors within the intra-organizational network (Floyd and Lane, 2000; Nahapiet and Ghoshal, 1998). This group is likely to include middle and operating-level managers, as well as members of top management. Based on the need to engage this broad range of actors, we argue that the decision-making processes preceding resource accumulation consensus are likely to include both cognitive and affective forms of conflict at the network level of analysis. Theory suggests that if consensus is to form under such circumstances, there is a need to encourage a certain degree of cognitive conflict without triggering dysfunctional levels of affective conflict (Amason, 1996), a process termed here and elsewhere as "constructive confrontation" (Burgelman, 1994; Danneels, 2003). The argument thus turns to how structural and relational characteristics of the intra-organizational network are likely to influence the development of constructive confrontation. In particular, we offer a series of propositions on network centralization and structural equivalence as antecedents of constructive confrontation. Finally, the discussion traces broader implications for the quality of strategic decisions and the development of competitive advantage.

This chapter contributes to the strategy process literature in three ways. First, it defines a new type of strategic consensus, one that forms around network central actors and is related to how organizations accumulate resources and create competitive advantage (Barney, 1991). Second, it provides a rigorous description of the social context within which decisions about resource accumulation occur (Burgelman, 1991, 1994). While constructive conflict has been investigated as an antecedent of group decisions (Amason, 1996; Jehn, 1997a), the construct has received almost no theoretical attention at the organizational or network levels of analysis; Burgelman (1994) and Danneels (2003) are exceptions. Third, this chapter extends prior work by articulating specific relationships between characteristics of intra-organizational networks and the critical information exchanges associated with resource accumulation and organizational learning (Floyd and Lane, 2000; Nahapiet and Ghoshal, 1998; Tsai, 2001).

## Theoretical Background

The formation of consensus relative to the organization's resource base represents a different domain of managerial decision making than that studied in prior research – where the emphasis has been on environmental conditions, strategic goals, and competitive strategies. We begin therefore with a fuller elaboration of what we mean by resource accumulation consensus, how it differs from other forms of strategic consensus and related organizational constructs, why achieving it is important to organizational performance, and why doing so is likely to be difficult.

A process perspective on the resource-based view suggests a distinction between the accumulation of resources and their deployment (Dierickx and Cool, 1989; Floyd and Wooldridge, 2000). Consistent with Dierickx and Cool (1989: 1507), we see the accumulation process as composed of the flow decisions determining investments in assets and skills over a period of time, which will build a resource stock for the organization. The deployment process, on the other hand, consists of decisions to implement strategies by deploying available resource stocks (Barney, 1991). To date, most research on strategic consensus has focused on the allocation or deployment of resources by the top management team (e.g. Bourgeois III, 1980; West Jr. and Schwenk, 1996).

Recently, however, researchers have begun to focus on how organizations accumulate resources. Collectively, they have described resource accumulation as a social learning process involving information exchanges between managers at multiple organizational levels (Burgelman, 1994; Floyd and Lane, 2000). More specifically, Floyd and Lane (2000) describe resource accumulation as a system of decision-making roles and social exchanges at the operating, middle, and top levels of the managerial hierarchy.

As Dierickx and Cool (1989) observe, the accumulation of resource stocks occurs as the result of decisions that managers make over time to invest in particular assets and skills. When these resource flows are purposeful, they are guided by managers' intentions to maintain or accumulate certain asset stocks. The above-presented definition of resource accumulation consensus thus reflects the need for high quality and consistent decisions about: (i) which resources to accumulate in order to maintain and improve the deployment of existing competencies in pursuit of current strategies; and (ii) which resources to accumulate in order to develop new competencies to pursue future strategies. Consistent with Dierickx and Cool (1989), the basis for a relationship between resource accumulation consensus and economic performance, then, is that consensus produces high quality and consistent decisions to accumulate a particular set of assets and skills. These resource flows, in turn, lead to asset stocks, including core competencies, which are superior to those that would result from unfocused resource flows.

Many resource accumulation decisions are "autonomous," i.e. untethered to official strategy (Burgelman, 1983). They emerge from the unique information and expertise that are available at middle and lower levels of the organization. Such influence is likely to increase upside variance in the set of alternatives being considered, thereby enhancing the value of the organization's real options (McGrath, 1999). Rather than top-down, resource accumulation has been described as a bottom-up or middle-up-down process (Floyd and Wooldridge, 1999; Nonaka, 1988). It relies on social interactions both within and outside the system of formal authority and communication (Kanter, 1983). Therefore, it is important to conceptualize resource accumulation consensus as the level of agreement among influential managers at multiple levels of the hierarchy on which resources build.

According to social network theory, those who are more centrally located within the intra-organization network are likely to be more influential than those less centrally located. Central actors link other actors within the network and act as brokers between internal and external actors. This provides them with: (i) access to valuable information (Burt, 1992); (ii) more frequent internal and external communication linkages (Rapert, Velliquette, and Garretson, 2002) and (iii) the ability to diffuse decision-making criteria better and more efficiently than other organization members(Brass, Butterfield, and Skaggs, 1998; Freeman, 1979). Individually, then, central actors are in a better position than others to judge organizational needs, and if they reach consensus on the basis of free and open exchange, the decision outcome is likely to be influenced by a high quality information base (Burt, 1992). Thus, resource accumulation decisions grounded in consensus among network central actors are likely to be of high quality, i.e. identify a set of resources likely to support competitive advantage.

The quality of resource flow decisions may be compromised by poor execution without a common commitment to, as well as shared understanding of, resource accumulation priorities (Wooldridge and Floyd, 1989). When actors, such as middle managers, are not committed to a set of priorities, their perceptions of self-interest or sub-unit interest are likely to over-ride what they perceive as organizational interests. This may lead to filtering information, foot-dragging, or even sabotage, even if managers understand what the intended priorities are (Guth and MacMillan, 1986).

In sum, higher levels of consensus on resource accumulation based on free and open exchange among network central actors is positively associated with: (i) higher quality decisions that reflect the needs of the organization (because they have been informed by a high quality information base); and (ii) more highly focused and consistent resource accumulation decisions throughout the organization. Greater consistency and better quality decisions in resource accumulation decisions, in turn, suggest that the organization is more likely to develop a superior set of organizational resources. More formally:

> **Proposition 1:**   Resource accumulation consensus among network central actors is positively related to the accumulation of a superior resource stock.

There are at least three reasons to believe that creating such consensus is difficult. First, the relationship between resources and competitive advantage is causally ambiguous (Reed and DeFillippi, 1990). This means that network central actors are likely to hold a wide range of opinions about which resources are important (King and Zeithaml, 2001). Second, since the decisions associated with resource accumulation may be made by central actors at different levels and in different sub-units (Burgelman, 1994; Floyd and Lane, 2000; Nonaka, 1991), a large number and diversity of perspectives are likely to be introduced into the decision-making process. As this diversity increases, consensus becomes more difficult to achieve (Amason, 1996; Floyd and Lane, 2000). Third, resource accumulation priorities affect resource flows into or out of organizational sub-units, thereby influencing the distribution of intra-organizational power (Hinings et al., 1974). This increases the potential that self-interest and political behavior will over-ride higher order goals among individual actors (Guth and MacMillan, 1986), and to this extent, reduces the potential for consensus. Since it is likely to develop from diverse perspectives of many different actors, under ambiguous conditions, and in the context of power differences, resource accumulation consensus likely forms in an environment with a high potential for both cognitive and affective conflict. As a result, creating resource accumulation consensus appears to depend on how decision making among network central actors balances cognitive conflict, which is associated with positive outcomes, and affective conflict, which is associated with negative outcomes – a process described as constructive confrontation.

## The Antecedents of Resource Accumulation Consensus

Figure 15.1 traces the relationships discussed in this chapter. As the figure shows, our model is longitudinal. We focus on the structural features of an organizational network necessary to generate adequate levels of cognitive conflict without triggering affective conflict, i.e. constructive confrontation. We examine the network's structural dimensions as part of a deeper level diversity (Harrison and McLaughlin, 1996) and as important antecedents of rich information exchange (Daft and Lengel, 1996; Harrison and McLaughlin, 1996). In particular, we argue that moderate levels of centralization and low structural equivalence are the network conditions most likely to produce constructive confrontation. The open expression and exchange of diverse information that occurs as a result are likely to produce consensus within the network on a set of resource accumulation priorities. As the figure suggests, such consensus is expected to lead to a high quality stream of resource flow decisions and the accumulation of superior resource stocks, which, when deployed, will eventually lead to higher levels of economic performance.

### Conflict and consensus in groups and organizational networks

There are two types of conflict. Affective conflict deals with disagreement that is perceived as personal and that is generally perceived to be dysfunctional (Amason, 1996). Affective conflict is harmful to decision quality and may even destroy any positive group dynamics (Wall Jr., Galanes, and Love, 1987). Cognitive conflict, on the other hand, mainly deals with task-oriented problems and focuses on judgmental differences about how to achieve a common goal (Amason, 1996; Jehn, 1997b; Priem and Price, 1991). Cognitive conflict is beneficial to decision quality because it increases the number of options considered, prevents premature consensus, and enhances the motivation of those involved ( Wall Jr., Galanes, and Love, 1987).

Much of the research on affective and cognitive conflict focuses on groups or teams. Consistent with an emphasis on the internal selection environment (Burgelman, 1994; Floyd and Wooldridge, 2000; Nahapiet and Ghoshal, 1998; Tsai, 2001), however, in this chapter we describe the dynamics of the two types of conflict and their antecedents at the network and organizational levels of analysis.

Adapting the logic for conflict's effects in decision-making groups to the organizational level of analysis, we argue that cognitive conflict increases the heterogeneity of

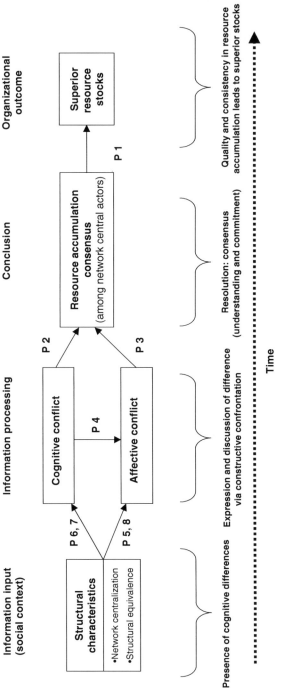

Figure 15.1 Antecedents and effects of resource accumulation

information within an intra-organizational network and that this heterogeneity improves decision making in the resource accumulation process (Fisher, 1980). Consistent with work done in groups, however, it is likely that an extremely high level of cognitive conflict can be counterproductive (e.g., Jehn, 1995). Intense conflict of any kind inhibits consensus, and prevents the actors involved from being able to move to other important topics (Ghoshal and Moran, 1996). In contrast, low cognitive conflict in resource accumulation decisions is likely to cement the status quo and facilitate groupthink (Janis, 1972, 1983). In groups it has been shown that moderate levels of cognitive conflict lead to more stimulating discussions and better utilization of members' capabilities, increasing the level of understanding and commitment to decisions (Amason, 1996; Jehn, 1995).

Projecting these results to the network level, it seems likely that extreme levels of cognitive conflict will decrease the likelihood or degree of resource accumulation consensus, whereas moderate levels will increase it. We therefore propose:

> Proposition 2:   There is a curvilinear relationship between cognitive conflict in the resource accumulation process and the degree of resource accumulation consensus. Specifically, low and high levels of cognitive conflict are associated with lower degrees of consensus than moderate levels of cognitive conflict.

In addition to cognitive conflict, the potential for shifts in resources and status among individual managers means that emotional responses must also be considered (Eisenhardt, 1989a, 1989b; Guth and MacMillan, 1986; Korsgaard, Schweiger, and Sapienza, 1995). When managerial behavior is interpreted as political gamesmanship, or if behavior is perceived as not serving organizational goals, high levels of affective conflict are likely to be experienced (Amason, 1996; Eisenhardt and Bourgeois, 1988). Affective conflict leads to defensiveness, blaming, off-task behavior, and the loss of focus (Jehn, 1997b). The higher the levels of affective conflict, the lower the potential for later consensus (Jehn, 1997b).

Once affective conflict begins, it is likely to become negative and sustained, since the consensus-finding process in regard to resource accumulation decisions takes place over relatively long periods of time (Barney, 1991; Hall, 1992). The stakes for the people involved are typically high. In this situation, disagreement may even become institutionalized – what Mintzberg (1987) describes as a "complete political arena." In such situations, managers' differences on issues and priorities become frozen, and hostile relationships drive rationality out of decision making. In short, without a willingness to consider other viewpoints, the potential for reaching an informed consensus on resource accumulation issues is extremely unlikely. We therefore propose a negative relationship between affective conflict and the level of resource accumulation consensus.

> Proposition 3:   There is a negative relationship between affective conflict and the degree of resource accumulation consensus.

Previous research shows high correlations between cognitive and affective conflict (Simons and Peterson, 2000). The encouragement of one without the other, such as Burgelman (1994) suggests by the phrase "constructive confrontation," is therefore not a simple prescription. In particular, there are a number of ways that cognitive conflict may lead to affective conflict. First, cognitive conflict may be perceived as political gamesmanship (Eisenhardt and Bourgeois, 1988; Finkelstein, 1992) or self-serving behavior (Pinto, Pinto, and Prescott, 1993; Pondy, 1967). Second, divergent points of view may generate heated discussions and the use of harsh language, thereby creating negative affect within the organization (Pelled, 1996; Simons and Peterson, 2000). Third, information asymmetries may produce the appearance of self-serving behavior (Pinto, Pinto, and Prescott, 1993), even if the intent was not self-serving at all. Thus, it seems likely that cognitive conflict may lead to affective conflict in the resource accumulation process.

> Proposition 4:   There is a positive association between cognitive conflict and affective conflict in the resource accumulation process.

This association has negative consequences for consensus because the negative effects of affective conflict appear to be an inevitable accompaniment to the positive effects of cognitive conflict. It is, therefore, important to understand how the positive relationship between the two can be mitigated, i.e. how to foster constructive confrontation. Because the relevant unit of analysis in resource accumulation consensus is a group of central actors, our explanation centers on the structural features of social context, i.e. the intra-organizational network, that are in part responsible for both the cognitive and emotional dispositions among actors at a particular point in time.

### Structural and relational antecedents of constructive confrontation

As suggested above, creating constructive confrontation among central actors in an intra-organizational network appears to be a difficult challenge, largely due to the tendency of cognitive conflict becoming tainted by negative affect. Structurally, centralization and structural equivalence are identified here as critical factors because they capture different qualities of information exchange. Centralization refers to the number of individuals and the scope of their decisions; it therefore captures the overall breadth and quantity of social exchanges in resource decisions. Structural equivalence, on the other hand, captures the diversity of information exchanged (Degenne and Forse, 1999).

Each of these two variables can be expected to have direct effects on the level and type of conflict in resource accumulation decisions. The following argument, therefore, outlines the main effects of network structure on the two types of conflict.

*Centralization.*    Centralization refers to the hierarchical levels and the distribution of power within a network (Brass and Burkhardt, 1993). Prior research has shown that power asymmetries are associated with sustained conflict (Cliff, 1987; Pfeffer, 1981). Consistent with this, Eisenhardt and Bourgeois (1988) found that high levels of conflict developed within top management teams when power was concentrated in the hands of CEOs, but not in TMTs where the power was more evenly distributed. Moreover, the qualitative data in their study (Eisenhardt and Bourgeois, 1988) suggested that such conflict included negative affect and political gamesmanship. Menon and Bharadwaj (1996) also found a positive relationship between concentrations of authority and affective conflict. Yukl, Guinan, and Sottolano's (1995) results suggest that negative affect would be particularly likely in cases where decisions were perceived as unjustified or due mainly to the inequality of power. Accordingly, higher centralization in intra-organizational networks is likely to produce affective conflict in the resource accumulation process.

> **Proposition 5:**   Network centralization will be positively associated with affective conflict in the resource accumulation process.

Lower levels of network centralization, on the other hand, lead to broader participation in decision making and a greater diversity of ideas (Ruekert and Walker, 1987). Low network centralization has also been associated with an organization's response to uncertainty, innovation, cooperation, and entrepreneurship (Caruana, Morris, and Vella, 1998; Olson, Walker Jr., and Ruekert, 1995; Sparrowe *et al.*, 2001). These positive effects are the outcome of increased influence from a larger number of organizational actors and a greater diversity of perspectives, which, in turn, results in a higher level of cognitive conflict (Amason and Schweiger, 1994). Indeed, in prior research, lower network centralization has been associated with positive performance effects (e.g., Love, Priem, and Lumpkin, 2002).

> **Proposition 6:**   Network centralization will be negatively associated with cognitive conflict in the resource accumulation process.

*Structural equivalence.*   Structural equivalence is a product of one's position within the organizational network and refers to the similarity of exposure to information (Burt, 1987). People high in structural equivalence occupy similar positions in the social network and have similar patterns of interactions with other actors in the network (Burt, 1987). When actors share a common set of interactions (i.e. when they interact with the same people), they tend to be exposed to the same information and therefore become similarly socialized (Burt, 1987). Even if some of the common ties are indirect, the result of sharing the same set of relationships is a homogenization of attitudes and behaviors (Burkhardt, 1994).

Similar socializing and communication with similar actors reinforces common opinions and leads to similar evaluations of ambiguous objects (Burt, 1983). Although resource accumulation can be characterized as an ambiguous process (Dierickx and Cool, 1989), it is likely that structural equivalence will lead to a similarity of perspectives among actors and thereby reduce the level of cognitive conflict experienced in the network. Similarity in attitudes and behavior is also likely to lead to a reduced level of affective conflict. This assertion corresponds with Pelled (1996) who found that more homogeneous groups experience less affective conflict. The dampening effect of low structural equivalence on affective conflict is also supported by Jehn and Mannix (2001) who found a negative correlation between value consensus and affective conflict.

> Proposition 7:   Structural equivalence is negatively associated with cognitive conflict in the resource accumulation process.

> Proposition 8:   Structural equivalence is negatively associated with affective conflict in the resource accumulation process.

## Discussion

The difficulties organizations face in acquiring resources and learning new competencies has been identified as a critical area of opportunity for future research (Danneels, 2003; Priem and Butler, 2001). In this chapter, we described one aspect of this socially complex and longitudinal process, arguing that resource accumulation consensus involves strategic actors positioned centrally in the intra-organizational network. Our premise is that consensus among network central actors leads to consistent accumulation of resources and produces superior asset stocks. This, in turn, facilitates organizational adaptation and the potential to earn superior economic rents.

### Implications for theory and research

One implication of this argument is how it speaks to the inconsistent research results on the consensus performance relationship. Whereas some studies support the existence of a positive relationship (e.g. Hrebiniak and Snow, 1982; Iaquinto and Fredrickson, 1997), other studies show no negative effects (e.g. West Jr. and Schwenk, 1996; Wooldridge and Floyd, 1990). Based on the analysis here, we suspect that the narrow focus of consensus research on the resource allocation or deployment process within top teams serves as part of the explanation for the inconsistent findings. When resource accumulation consensus is low, needed resources may not be accumulated, and this inhibits performance, even if other conditions are normative.

By describing organizational conditions leading to the accumulation of superior asset stocks, we have tried to contribute to the broader literature of resource-based advantage. Recently, there have been criticisms of the theory on the basis that it offers little explanation for where resources come from (Priem and Butler, 2001). The explanation here is that resource differences arise because of differences in network structures and the process associated with making resource accumulation decisions. If viewed in resource-based terms, the ability to develop consensus among network central actors on a high quality set of resource accumulation decisions may be seen as a higher level organizational capability (Conner, 1991; Dierickx and Cool, 1989), which increases the chances for superior performance.

In conclusion, our chapter offers a new perspective on strategic consensus. We hope that broadening the scope of inquiry in this way contributes constructively to the theoretical dialogue in this research stream. In addition, we hope the discussion in the chapter serves as a stimulus for future theoretical and empirical research on the broader strategy process.

## References

Amason, A.C. 1996. Distinguishing the effects of functional and dysfunctional conflict on strategic decision making: Resolving a paradox for top management teams. *Academy of Management Journal*, **39**(1): 123–48.

Amason, A.C. and Schweiger, D.M. 1994. Resolving the paradox of conflict, strategic decision making and organizational performance. *International Journal of Conflict Management*, **5**: 239–53.

Barney, J. 1991. Firm resources and sustained competitive advantage. *Journal of Management*, **17**(1): 99–120.

Bourgeois III, L.J. 1980. Performance and consensus. *Strategic Management Journal*, **1**: 27–48.

Brass, D.J. and Burkhardt, M.E. 1993. Potential power and power use: An investigation of structure and behavior. *Academy of Management Journal*, **35**: 441–70.

Brass, D.J., Butterfield, K., and Skaggs, B.C. 1998. Relationships and unethical behavior: A social network perspective. *Academy of Management Review*, **23**(1): 14–31.

Burgelman, R.A. 1983. A model of the interaction of strategic behavior, corporate context, and the concept of strategy. *Academy of Management Review*, **8**(1): 61–70.

Burgelman, R.A. 1991. Intraorganizational ecology of strategy making and organizational adaptation: Theory and field research. *Organization Science*, **2**(3): 239–62.

Burgelman, R.A. 1994. Fading memories: A process theory of strategy business exit in dynamic environments. *Administrative Science Quarterly*, **39**: 24–56.

Burkhardt, M.E. 1994. Social interaction effects following a technological change: A longitudinal investigation. *Academy of Management Journal*, **37**(4): 869–98.

Burt, R.S. 1983. Cohesion versus structural equivalence as a basis for network subgroups. In R.S. Burt and M.J. Minor (eds.), *Applied Network Analysis*, pp. 262–82. Beverly Hills, CA: Sage.

Burt, R.S. 1987. Social contagion and innovation: Cohesion versus structural equivalence. *American Journal of Sociology*, **92**: 1287–335.

Burt, R.S. 1992.*Structural Holes: The Social Structure of Competition*. Cambridge, MA: Harvard University Press.

Caruana, A., Morris, M.H., and Vella, J. 1998. The effect of centralization and formalization on entrepreneurship in export firms. *Journal of Small Business Management*, **36**(1): 16–29.

Cliff, G. 1987. Managing organizational conflict. *Management Review*, **70**(5): 51–3.

Conner, K.R. 1991. A historical comparison of resource-based theory and five schools of thought within industrial organization economics: Do we have a new theory of the firm? *Journal of Management*, **17**(1): 121–54.

Daft, R.L. and Lengel, R.H. 1996. Organizational information requirements, media richness and structural design. *Management Science*, **32**: 554–71.

Danneels, E. 2003. Organizing for renewal: Antecedents of second-order competences. *Working Paper: Worcester Polytechnic Institute*.

Degenne, A. and Forse, M. 1999.*Introducing Social Networks*. London: Sage.

Dierickx, I. and Cool, K. 1989. Asset stock accumulation and sustainability of competitive advantage. *Management Science*, **35**(12): 1504–14.

Eisenhardt, K.M. 1989a. Agency theory: An assessment and review. *Academy of Management Journal*, **14**(1): 57–74.

Eisenhardt, K.M. 1989b. Making fast decisions in high velocity environments. *Academy of Management Journal*, **32**: 543–76.

Eisenhardt, K.M. and Bourgeois, L.J. 1988. Politics of strategic decision making in high-velocity environments: Towards a midrange theory. *Academy of Management Journal*, **31**(4): 737–70.

Finkelstein, S. 1992. Power in top management teams: Dimensions, measurement, and validation. *Academy of Management Journal*, **35**(3): 505–38.

Fisher, B.A. 1980. *Small Group Decision Making*. New York: McGraw-Hill.

Floyd, S.W. and Lane, P.J. 2000. Strategizing throughout the organization: Managing role conflict in strategic renewal. *Academy of Management Review*, **25**(1): 154–77.

Floyd, S.W. and Wooldridge, B. 1992. Managing strategic consensus: The foundation of effective implementation. *Academy of Management Executive*, **6**(4): 27–39.

Floyd, S.W. and Wooldridge, B. 1999. Knowledge creation and social networks in corporate entrepreneurship: The renewal of organizational capability. *Entrepreneurship: Theory and Practice*, **23**(3): 123–43.

Floyd, S.W. and Wooldridge, B. 2000. *Building Strategy from the Middle: Reconceptualizing Strategy Process*. Thousand Oaks, CA: Sage.

Freeman, L.C. 1979. Centrality in social networks: Conceptual clarifications. *Social Networks*, **1**: 215–39.

Ghoshal, S. and Moran, P. 1996. Bad for practice: A critique of the transaction cost theory. *Academy of Management Review*, **21**(1): 13–47.

Guth, W.D. and MacMillan, I.C. 1986. Strategy implementation versus middle management self-interest. *Strategic Management Journal*, **7**: 313–27.

Hall, R. 1992. The strategic analysis of intangible resources. *Strategic Management Journal*, **13**(2): 135–44.

Harrison, D.A. and McLaughlin, M.E. 1996. Structural properties and psychometric qualities of organizational self-reports: Field test of connections predicted by cognitive theory. *Journal of Management*, **22**(2): 313–38.

Hinings, C., Hickson, D., Pennings, J., and Schenk, R. 1974. Structural conditions in interorganizational power. *Administrative Science Quarterly*, **19**: 22–44.

Hrebiniak, L.G. and Snow, C.C. 1982. Top-management agreement and organizational performance. *Human Relations*, **35**(12): 1139–58.

Iaquinto, A.L. and Fredrickson, J.W. 1997. TMT agreement about the strategic decision process: A test of some of its determinants and consequences. *Strategic Management Journal*, **18**(1): 63–75.

Janis, I.L. 1972. *Victims of Groupthink*. Boston, MA: Houghton Mifflin.

Janis, I.L. 1983. *Groupthink: Psychological Studies of Policy Decisions and Fiascoes*. Boston, MA: Houghton Mifflin.

Jehn, K.A. 1995. A multimethod examination of the benefits and detriments of intragroup conflict. *Administrative Science Quarterly*, **40**: 256–82.

Jehn, K.A. 1997a. Affective and cognitive conflict in work groups: Increasing performance through value-based intragroup conflict. In D. Dreu and E. Van de Vliert (eds.), *Using Conflict in Organizations*, pp. 87–100. London: Sage.

Jehn, K.A. 1997b. A quantitative analysis of conflict types and dimensions in organizational groups. *Administrative Science Quarterly*, **42**(3): 530–58.

Jehn, K.A. and Mannix, E.A. 2001. The dynamic nature of conflict: A longitudinal study of intragroup conflict and group performance. *Academy of Management Journal*, **44**(2): 238–51.

Kanter, R.M. 1983. *The Change Masters*. New York: Simon and Schuster.

King, A.W. and Zeithaml, C.P. 2001. Competencies and firm performance: Examining the causal ambiguity paradox. *Strategic Management Journal*, **22**: 75–99.

Korsgaard, M.A., Schweiger, D.M., and Sapienza, H.J. 1995. Building commitment, attachment, and trust in strategic decision-making teams: The role of procedural justice. *Academy of Management Journal*, **38**(1): 60–84.

Love, L.G., Priem, R.L., and Lumpkin, G.T. 2002. Explicitly articulated strategy and firm performance under alternative levels of centralization. *Journal of Management*, **28**(5): 611–27.

Markoczy, L. 2001. Consensus formation during strategic change. *Strategic Management Journal*, **22**: 1013–31.

McGrath, R.G. 1999. Falling forward: Real options reasoning and entrepreneurial failure. *Academy of Management Review*, **24**(1): 13–30.

Menon, A. and Bharadwaj, S.G. 1996. The quality and effectiveness of marketing strategy: Effects of functional and dysfunctional conflict in intraorganizatinal relationships. *Journal of the Academy of Marketing Science*, **24**(4): 299–313.

Mintzberg, H. 1987. Crafting strategy. *Harvard Business Review*, 4: 66–75.

Nahapiet, J. and Ghoshal, S. 1998. Social capital, intellectual capital, and the organizational advantage. *Academy of Management Review*, **23**(2): 242–66.

Nonaka, I. 1988. Toward middle-up-down management: Accelerating information creation. *Sloan Management Review*, **29**: 9–18.

Nonaka, I. 1991. The knowledge-creating company. *Harvard Business Review*, **69**: 96–104.

Olson, E.M., Walker Jr., O.C., and Ruekert, R.W. 1995. Organizing for effective new product development: The moderating role of product innovativeness. *Journal of Marketing*, **59**(1): 48–62.

Pelled, L. 1996. Demographic diversity, conflict, work group outcomes: An intervening process theory. *Organization Science*, 7: 615–31.

Pfeffer, J. 1981. *Power in Organizations*. Boston, MA: Pitman.

Pinto, M., Pinto, J., and Prescott, J. 1993. Antecedents and consequences of project team crossfunctional cooperation. *Management Science*, **39**: 1281–97.

Pondy, L.R. 1967. Organizational conflict: Concept and models. *Administrative Science Quarterly*, **12**(2): 296–320.

Priem, R.L. and Butler, J.E. 2001. Is the resource-based "view" a useful perspective for strategic management research? *Academy of Management Review*, **26**(1): 22–40.

Priem, R.L. and Price, K. 1991. Process and outcome expectation for the dialectic inquiry, devil's advocacy, and consensus techniques of strategic decision making. *Group and Organization Studies*, **16**: 206–25.

Rapert, M.I., Velliquette, A., and Garretson, J.A. 2002. The strategic implementation process. Evoking strategic consensus through communication. *Journal of Business Research*, **55**: 301–10.

Reed, R. and DeFillippi, R. 1990. Causal ambiguity, barriers to imitation, and sustainable competitive advantage. *Academy of Management Review*, **15**: 88–102.

Ruekert, R.W. and Walker, O.C., Jr. 1987. Interactions between marketing and R&D departments in implementing different business strategies. *Strategic Management Journal*, **8**: 233–48.

Simons, T.L. and Peterson, R.S. 2000. Task conflict and relationship conflict in top management teams: The pivotal role of intragroup trust. *Journal of Applied Psychology*, **85**(1): 102–11.

Sparrowe, R.T., Linden, R.C., Wayne, S.J., and Kramer, M.L. 2001. Social networks and the performance of individuals and groups. *Academy of Management Journal*, **44**(2): 316–25.

Stagner, R. 1969. Corporate decision making: An empirical study. *Journal of Applied Psychology*, **53**(1): 1–13.

Tsai, W. 2001. Knowledge transfer in intraorganizational networks: Effects of network position and absorptive capacity on business unit innovation. *Academy of Management Journal*, **44**(5): 996–1004.

Wall Jr, V.D., Galanes, G.J., and Love, S.B. 1987. Small, task-oriented groups: Conflict, conflict management, satisfaction, and decision quality. *Small Group Behavior*, **18**(1): 31–55.

Wernerfelt, B. 1997. Methodological challenges facing the resource-based view of the firm: An agenda for future research. Remarks presented at the Academy of Management annual meeting, Boston, MA.

West Jr., C.T. and Schwenk, C.R. 1996. Top management team strategic consensus, demographic homogeneity and firm performance: A report of resounding nonfindings. *Strategic Management Journal*, **17**: 571–6.

Wooldridge, B. and Floyd, S.W. 1989. Research notes and communications strategic process effect on consensus. *Strategic Management Journal*, **10**: 295–302.

Wooldridge, B. and Floyd, S.W. 1990. The strategy process, middle management involvement, and organizational performance. *Strategic Management Journal*, **11**: 231–41.

Yukl, G., Guinan, P.J., and Sottolano, D. 1995. Influence tactics used for different objectives with subordinates, peers, and superiors. *Group and Organization Management*, **20**: 272–96.

# Innovative Models of Strategy Process

# CHAPTER SIXTEEN

# What Really is Strategic Process?

## Mark Kriger

Strategic process can be conceived of as the sum total of purposes, plans, and action sequences by which an organizational entity commits human and financial resources, time, and energy to shape its long-term future in relevant competitive environments (Mintzberg, 1994). A strategy is also a theory about how to create competitive advantage (Porter, 1980, 1996).

For several thousand years organizations of all sizes have been creating and exercising strategies to attain organizational objectives. The earliest works on strategy such as those by Sun Tzu (China), Miyumoto Musashi (Japan), and Alexander the Great (Greece), to name a few, were written by military strategists. It is only in the second half of the twentieth century with Drucker, Ohmae, Ansoff, Andrews, and more recently with Porter, Mintzberg, Quinn, and others that an extensive literature addressing the question "what is strategy?" has arisen.

This conceptual note aims to redress a growing myth, adopted in a number of articles but exemplified in a seminal *Harvard Business Review* article by Porter entitled, "What is Strategy?". The myth, succinctly stated, is that strategy, whether at the business or organizational level, is a single subject that involves a single monolithic construct, which, at its base, should primarily be constructed from an economic paradigm.

Although strategy is one word we propose that it involves at least three distinct constructs under the guise of one term. Until we recognize this, the direction of the strategy field will continue to be stuck in irreconcilable turf warfare and consequent confusion. The three constructs are:

1. explicit strategy formulation;
2. tacit strategizing; and
3. the methods and processes by which explicit strategies are realized via deeply embedded tacit knowledge and organizational routines.

These three strategy constructs are used and promulgated in differing ways, consciously and unconsciously, by three core constituencies: academic strategists (A);

**Table 16.1**   The ABCs and their strategic process interest sets

| Constituency | Strategic process interests and activities |
| --- | --- |
| Academic strategists | • Making generalizations about explicit knowledge of strategy (*creating frameworks and models*)<br>• Creating and extending theories about the components, categories, causal relationships between constructs and subareas of strategy (*theory generation*)<br>• Observing and recording of strategic process and strategizing-in-use (*industry and business cases*)<br>• Testing theories of strategy (*empirical research*) |
| Business strategists | • Using and deploying tacit knowledge of strategic process made partially explicit in order to inform, manage, and educate key stakeholders, especially other managers and internal employees<br>• Understanding strategic process from first-hand experience, often supplemented with reports and studies by consultants |
| Strategy consultants | • Developing conceptual frameworks, methods, case descriptions and tools for the analysis and formulation of strategy<br>• Benchmarking and generating best practice advice<br>• Understanding both explicit and tacit knowledge of strategy with a client focus<br>• Identifying and translating explicit to explicit strategic knowledge and tacit to explicit strategic knowledge in order to meet client needs, objectives, and expectations |

business managers and leaders (B); and strategy consultants (C); the so-called ABCs of the Strategic Management Society. Sometimes, though rarely, individual professionals engage in all three types of strategizing activities. An important question to be addressed is: How can we bridge what are essentially three differing preferred sets of activities and language systems in use which exist among the three groups of strategy professionals? (See Table 16.1 for an overview of these interest sets.)

In order to address the preceding question we shall relax the usually sacrosanct assumption of Occam's Razor in order to display and discuss the subject at a level closer to the true complexity of the ongoing puzzle of strategic process. Occam's Razor, arising back in the Middle Ages, essentially states that all things being equal, it is important in theory generation to reduce as far as possible the explanatory factors in a model or framework to the least number required to explain a phenomenon.

## The Importance of the Subject

The importance of this subject lies in the fact that until we begin to understand the nature of the complexity of what strategic process really is, we shall continue to create barriers of misunderstanding between the three major constituencies represented in the field.

The premise behind this chapter is that the strategy literature has so far failed to generate a theory about what strategy really is. If we ask, "Why?" a number of authors have noted fundamental differences in the way in which strategy is both investigated and written about (Farjoun, 2002; Porter, 1996). The various camps of theorists are onto one aspect or another of the ongoing dilemma, however, most are missing crucial components which are less rational but underpin the creation of all intended strategies, realized and unrealized (see Damasio, 1994, for a supportive argument regarding the necessity of human feelings for the understanding of how decision making takes place at the individual level).

Most of the progress in the field of strategy has taken place to date in the formulation area. Porter (1980, 1985, 1991, 1996) has notably achieved a well-recognized set of understandings about strategy formulation and Brandenburger and Nalebuff (1996) extended this to include the concept of *complementors* using game theory. The now well-known resource-based view of strategy is a theory about how to create a sustainable competitive advantage (Barney, 1986, 1991). But what virtually all strategy formulation academics fail to observe is that prior to a cognitively well-formulated strategy there is a set of underlying purposes, intentions, and feelings about the strategy that, though often unarticulated, both shape *and* constrain subsequent strategic process.

Strategy formulation emerges from a complex set of largely tacit knowledge and unarticulated feelings. The key to creating a shared strategy is to create in others a common set of feelings, perceptions, and beliefs and then to articulate a corresponding set of purposes and directions. In the race by many strategy academics to make strategy mainly a cognitive field, where generalizations and predictions are most valued, this essential aspect of strategy has been largely overlooked, even denied.

## Towards an Understanding of the Complexities of Strategic Process

There are currently several existing schools or views of strategy, most notably the *resource-based* (Barney, 1991; Hamel and Prahalad, 1994; Grant, 1996), the *activity-based* (Porter, 1985), and more recently the *knowledge-based* (Nonaka and Takeuchi, 1995; Spender, 1996; Stewart, 1997; Boisot, 1998; Choo, 1998; Nonaka and Konno, 1998), and *micro-strategizing* approaches (Johnson, Whittington, and Melin, 2003). In complex human systems, such as strategic processes and executive leadership, practitioners and academics need to think, analyze, and make decisions based on a number of rarely acknowledged complexities. These complexities include the following areas and aspects.

### Multiple logics, paths, causes, and alternative frameworks

1. The presence of causal loops and continuous co-alignment between the firm and its environment (Farjoun, 2002) as well as the pervasiveness of multiple causes and moderating variables (Senge, 1989).
2. The existence of alternative models and frameworks that fit depending upon situational contingencies (Mintzberg, 1979, 1994).

3. The significance of small deviations in initial conditions resulting in potentially large eventual effects (see complexity and chaos theory, Thietart and Forgues, 1995; Prigogine, 1980; Stacey, 1992).
4. The existence of equi-finality – where multiple paths can lead to the same end state or goal (Senge, 1989).
5. The salience of "and–also" in addition to "either–or" logics (Roethlisberger, 1977; Barnes and Kriger, 1986).

## Multiple levels of scale, decision levels, and categories of time

6. Organizational/strategic decision making consisting of nested "decision levels" (Kriger and Barnes, 1992; Langley *et al.*, 1995) and nested levels of scale (Jaques, 1986).
7. Simultaneously interacting levels of scale with multiple levels of phenomena that are nested as "holons" (Wilber, 1996, 1999), for example, macro-economy–industry–company–business–group–interpersonal–individual. In a holon each higher level system includes each lower level system.
8. Multiple time frames with varying cycles of time-based phenomena (Jaques, 1986; Kriger and Barnes, 1992).
9. Differing concepts of time: *kairos–chronos*, entrainment processes, monochronicity–polychronicity (Carse, 1986; Brand, 1999).
10. Developmental stages of organizations, groups, and individuals (Kohlberg, 1969; Loevinger, 1976; Kegan, 1982; Fisher, Rooke, and Torbert, 2000).
11. The simultaneity of goal setting and planning cycles at the same time as longer term visioning processes (Schaefer and Voors, 1986; Westney and Mintzberg, 1989; Nutt and Backoff, 1997).
12. Simultaneous finite and infinite games. Most business organizations operate as finite games but are unaware that they are embedded within "infinite" games. In a finite game the purpose is winning and to defeat one's opponents; in an infinite game, such as culture, families, governance, and nature, the purpose is to continue the game and to extend it as long as possible. In infinite games the rules are changed, as needed, to keep the game ongoing and improving. (Carse, 1986; Hampden-Turner and Trompenaars, 1997; Brand, 1999).

## Knowledge, managerial wisdom, and emotional intelligence

13. The importance of intangible assets, especially knowledge, both tacit and explicit (Polanyi, 1958, 1966; Dierickx and Cool, 1989; Hedlund, 1994; Leonard-Barton, 1995; Nonaka and Takeuchi, 1995; Spender, 1996; Sanchez and Heene, 1997; Stewart, 1997; Boisot, 1998; Choo, 1998; Leonard and Sensiper, 1998; Nonaka and Konno, 1998; von Krogh, 1998).
14. The development of managerial wisdom to understand how to balance long-term trends and short-term challenges (Bigelow, 1992; Kriger and Malan, 1993; Malan and Kriger, 1998; Kriger and Hanson, 1999).
15. The cognitive complexity of individuals (Jaques, 1986, 1989; Streufert, 1997; Wilber, 1999; Fisher, Rooke, and Torbert, 2000).

16. The simultaneity of intuitive and rational forms of judgment (Bastick, 1982; Parikh, 1994).
17. The salience of emotional intelligence for long-term organizational effectiveness and success (Salovey and Mayer, 1990; Goleman, 1995, 1998; Bar-On, 2000; Goleman, Boyatzis, and McKee, 2002).
18. The pervasiveness of and ability to perceive holistic patterns of relationships (Bohm, 1980; Bradley, 1998; Marion, 1999).

**Paradoxical tensions, opportunities, and values**

19. Alternative scenarios, which do not allow one to strictly predict, but do prepare the organization for alternative possibilities (see Schwartz, 1991 – especially "Steps to Developing Scenarios," pp. 226–34; Van de Heijden, 1996).
20. The expectation of surprises and learning to see them as opportunities rather than threats (D'Aveni, 1994; Grove, 1996).
21. The presence of paradoxical tensions and competing values (Quinn, 1988) such as:

>adaptability *and* stability
>flexibility *and* control
>decentralization *and* centralization
>differentiation *and* integration
>productivity and efficiency *and* morale
>internal focus *and* external focus
>planning *and* visioning.

22. The presence of and necessity of collecting and utilizing "soft" (qualitative) as well as "hard" (quantitative) data (Kriger and Malan, 1993).

**The role of middle managers, absorptive capacity, and micro-strategizing**

23. The importance of the role of middle managers in initiating autonomous strategic processes, often autonomously from top management (see Nonaka, 1988; Burgelman, 1983, 2002; Floyd and Lane, 2000; Floyd and Wooldridge, 1997, 2000).
24. The level of the absorptive capacity of the firm and its sub-units (Zahra and George, 2002).
25. Micro-strategizing and the need to deal with forces of continuous change (Hurst, 1995; Brown and Eisenhardt, 1997; Johnson, Whittington, and Melin, 2003).

## Towards a Model of Strategic Process

In an attempt to integrate the preceding we propose the overall framework in Figure 16.1. Following the upper loop in the figure, cycle A, consists of a process of looking for pattern matches or disconfirmations between previously developed theories or predictions and dynamically changing data, internal and external to the organization. The governing processes in cycle A are largely rational with clearly specifiable

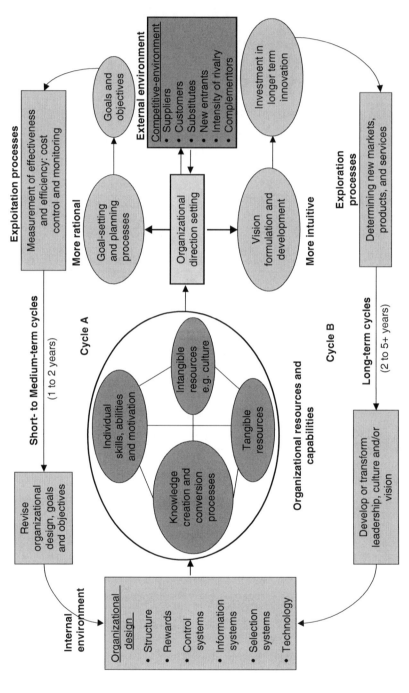

Figure 16.1   Strategic Process and Direction Setting

steps, benchmarks, and control systems that allow the tracking of deviations from predictions made *ex ante*. Adjustments in the deployment of organizational of resources are made based on the deviations from plans or goals. Cycle A, when it predominates in an organization, tends to result in organizations that are more like machine bureaucracies (Mintzberg, 1979), with well-specified roles and reporting relationships. It works best in environments that are stable, have areas of predictability with few discontinuities in terms of markets and technological evolution.

Organizational direction setting in the lower loop in Figure 16.1, cycle B, consists largely of searching for new directions, markets, products, and services that currently do not exist and often are only partially perceived or felt. Resource allocation of finances and people takes place incrementally based on a complex mix of intuition, feelings, and reasoning. Alignment of individuals tends to take place by virtue of shared values, cultural affinities, and feelings that are often only partially conscious to organizational members. Cycle B, on the whole, is highly entrepreneurial in nature and attracts individuals who want to do things differently or to create products and services that have not been created before.

Especially, in today's turbulent social, economic, political, and technological environments most organizations need both cycles to be operating, within different parts of the value chain and functional areas. A major organizational challenge for managers is to value and reward both exploitation processes (cycle A) and exploration processes (cycle B) and to find ways to integrate the two, rather than to collapse into an "either–or" of planning versus incrementalism, into goal setting without vision development, or vision formation without goals by which to benchmark (March, 1991). It is the tension and movement between cycles A and B that can produce some of the most dynamic and difficult to imitate organizational capabilities. Unfortunately, it is often only *post hoc* that organizational members can perceive how these dynamic capabilities have been created and nurtured. However, while immersed in these processes, individuals can nonetheless often feel and report on the excitement of the interactions taking place (Kidder, 1981; Burgelman, 2002; Gerstner, 2002).

Some of the theorists who have wrestled with the above problem beginning with Barnard (1938) are: Andrews (1987), Quinn (1980), Fredrickson (1986), Huff and Reger (1987), Mintzberg (1978, 1994), Pettigrew (1985), Van de Ven (1992), Chakravarty and Doz (1992), D'Aveni (1994), and Camillus (1997).

## Conclusion

In the final analysis strategic managers and leaders need to be aware of a number of pervasive pitfalls:

1. The generation of *oversimplifying assumptions*.
2. The tendency to favor and create *false dichotomies* (e.g. the situation is either "good" or "bad", the firm is "effective" or "ineffective" – situations and organizations consist of mixtures of both).
3. A preference for purely logic-based solutions which are not appropriately balanced with intuitive judgment coming from past experience and the understanding of larger competitive patterns.

4. The tendency to avoid encouraging others to ask good (i.e. challenging) questions.
5. A preference towards smoothing over conflict in strategy implementation processes rather than surfacing divergent viewpoints and treating them as opportunities for increasing cognitive variability (Malan and Kriger, 1998).

Strategic process is hardly a simple subject since it relies upon not only the application of economic theories, but also on the use of psychological, social psychological, sociological, and political theories and sense-making models and frameworks. Academics, business people, and consultants, in their having differing language systems for portraying and communicating this complexity, further increase the complexity of what (really) constitutes strategic process.

# References

Andrews, K.R. 1987. *The Concept of Corporate Strategy*, 3rd ed. Homewood, IL: Irwin.
Bar-On, R. 2000. Emotional and social intelligence: Insights from the Emotional Quotient Inventory (EQ-I). In R. Bar-On and J.D.A. Parker (eds.), *Handbook of Emotional Intelligence*, pp. 363–88. San Francisco: Jossey-Bass.
Barnard, C.I. 1938. *The Functions of the Executive*. Cambridge, MA: Harvard University Press.
Barnes, L.B. and Kriger, M.P. 1986. The hidden side of organizational leadership. *Sloan Management Review*, **28**: 15–26.
Barney, J.B. 1986. Organizational culture: Can it be a source of sustained competitive advantage? *Academy of Management Review*, **11**: 656–65.
Barney, J.B. 1991. Firm resources and sustained competitive advantage. *Journal of Management*, **17**: 99–120.
Bastick, T. 1982. *Intuition: How We Think and Act*. New York: Wiley.
Bigelow, J. 1992. Developing managerial wisdom. *Journal of Management Inquiry*, **1**(2): 143–51.
Bohm, D. 1980. *Wholeness and the Implicate Order*. Boston, MA: ARK Paperbacks.
Boisot, M. 1998. *Knowledge Assets: Securing Competitive Advantage in the Information Economy*. New York: Oxford University Press.
Bradley, R.T. 1998. Values, agency, and the theory of quantum vacuum interaction. In K.H. Pribram (ed.), *Brain and Values: Is a Biological Science of Values Possible?* pp. 471–504. Mahwah, NJ: Lawrence Erlbaum.
Brand, S. 1999. *The Clock of the Long Now: Time and Responsibility*. London: Phoenix.
Brandenburger, A.M. and Nalebuff, B.J. 1996. *Coopetition*. New York: Currency Doubleday.
Brown, S.L. and Eisenhardt, K.M. 1997. The art of continuous change: Linking complexity theory and time-paced evolution in relentlessly shifting organizations. *Administrative Science Quarterly*, **42**: 1–34.
Burgelman, R.A. 1983. A model of the interaction of strategic behavior, corporate context, and the concept of strategy. *Academy of Management Review*, **8**: 61–70.
Burgelman, R.A. 2002. *Strategy is Destiny: How Strategy Making Shapes a Company's Future*. New York: The Free Press.
Camillus, J. 1997. Shifting the strategic management paradigm. *European Management Journal*, **15**(1): 1–7.
Carse, J.P. 1986. *Finite and Infinite Games*. New York: Ballantine.
Chakravarthy, B. and Doz, Y. 1992. Strategy process research: Focusing on corporate self-renewal. *Strategic Management Journal*, **13**: 5–14.

Choo, C.W. 1998. *The Knowing Organization*. New York: Oxford University Press.

Damasio, A.R. 1994. *Descartes' Error: Emotion, Reason, and the Human Brain*. London: Macmillan.

D'Aveni, R.A. 1994. *Hypercompetition: Managing the Dynamics of Strategic Maneuvering*. New York: The Free Press.

Dierickx, I. and Cool, K. 1989. Asset stock accumulation and sustainability of competitive advantage. *Management Science*, **35**(12): 1514–31.

Farjoun, M. 2002. Towards an organic perspective on strategy. *Strategic Management Journal*, **23**: 561–94.

Fisher, D., Rooke, D., and Torbert, W. 2000. *Personal and Organizational Transformations through Action Inquiry*. Boston, MA: Edge Work Press.

Floyd, S.W. and Lane, P.J. 2000. Strategizing throughout the organization: Managing role conflict in strategic renewal. *Academy of Management Review*, **25**(1): 154–77.

Floyd, S.W. and Wooldridge, B. 1997. Middle management strategic influence and organizational performance. *Journal of Management Studies*, **34**: 465–85.

Floyd, S.W. and Wooldridge, B. 2000. *Building Strategy from the Middle: Reconceptualizing Strategy Process*. Thousand Oaks, CA: Sage.

Fredrickson, J.W. 1986. The strategic decision process and organizational structure. *Academy of Management Review*, **11**(2): 280–97.

Gerstner, L.V. Jr. 2002. *Who Says Elephants can't Dance? Inside IBM's Historic Turnaround*. New York: HarperBusiness.

Goleman, D. 1995. *Emotional Intelligence: Why it can matter more than IQ*. London: Bloomsbury.

Goleman, D. 1998. *Working with Emotional Intelligence*. New York: Bantam.

Goleman, D., Boyatzis, R., and McKee, A. 2002. *Primal Leadership: Realizing the Power of Emotional Intelligence*. Boston, MA: Harvard Business School.

Grant, R.M. 1996. Toward a knowledge-based theory of the firm. *Strategic Management Journal*, **17**: 109–22.

Grove A.S. 1996. *Only the paranoid survive: How to exploit the crisis points that challenge every company and career*. London: HarperCollinsBusiness.

Hamel, G. and Prahalad, C.K. 1994. *Competing for the Future*. Boston, MA: Harvard Business School Press.

Hampden-Turner, C. and Trompenaars, F. 1997. *Mastering the Infinite Game*. Oxford, UK: Capstone.

Hedlund, G. 1994. A model of knowledge management and the N-form corporation. *Strategic Management Journal*, **15**: 73–90.

Huff, A.S. and Reger, R.K. 1987. A review of strategic process research. *Journal of Management*, **13**: 211–36.

Hurst, D.K. 1995. *Crisis and Renewal: Meeting the Challenge of Organizational Change*. Boston, MA: Harvard Business School Press.

Jaques, E. 1986. The development of intellectual capability: A discussion of stratified systems theory. *Journal of Applied Behavioral Science*, **22**: 361–83.

Jaques, E. 1989. *Requisite Organization*. Arlington, VA: Cason Hall.

Johnson, G., Whittington, R., and Melin, L. 2003. Micro strategy and strategizing: Towards an activity-based view. *Journal of Management Studies*, **40**(1): 3–22.

Kegan, R. 1982. *The Evolving Self*. Cambridge, MA: Harvard University Press.

Kidder, T. 1981. *The Soul of a New Machine*. Boston, MA: Little, Brown.

Kohlberg, L. 1969. Stage and sequence: The cognitive and developmental approach to socialization theory and research. In D.A. Goslin (ed.), *Handbook of Socialization Theory and Research*, Chicago, IL: Rand-McNally.

Kriger, M.P. and Barnes, L.B. 1992. Organizational decision making as hierarchical levels of drama. *Journal of Management Studies*, **29**: 439–57.

Kriger, M.P. and Hanson, B.J. 1999. A value-based paradigm for creating truly healthy organizations. *Journal of Organizational Change Management*, **12**(4): 302–17.

Kriger, M.P. and Malan, L.C. 1993. Shifting paradigms: The valuing of personal knowledge, wisdom, and other invisible processes in organizations. *Journal of Management Inquiry*, **2**(4): 391–8.

Kuhn, T.S. 1970. *The Structure of Scientific Revolutions*. Chicago, IL: University of Chicago Press.

Langley, A., Mintzberg, H., Pitcher, P., Posada, E., and Saint-Macary, J. 1995. Opening up decision making: The view from the black stool. *Organization Science*, **6**: 260–79.

Lawrence, P.R. and Nohria, N. 2002. *Driven: How Human Nature Shapes Our Choices*. Boston, MA: Harvard Business School Press.

Leonard-Barton, D. 1995. *Wellsprings of Knowledge: Building and Sustaining the Sources of Innovation*. Boston, MA: Harvard Business School Press.

Leonard, D. and Sensiper, S. 1998. The role of tacit knowledge in group innovation. *California Management Review*, **40**(3): 112–32.

Loevinger, J. 1976. *Ego Development: Conception and Theories*. San Francisco: Jossey-Bass.

Malan, L.-C. and Kriger, M.P. 1998. Making sense of managerial wisdom. *Journal of Management Inquiry*, **7**(3): 242–51.

March, J.G. 1991. Exploration and exploitation in organizational learning. *Organization Science*, **2**(1): 71–87.

Marion, R. 1999. *The Edge of Organization*. Thousand Oaks, CA: Sage.

Mintzberg, H. 1978. Patterns in strategy formation. *Management Science*, **24**(9): 935–48.

Mintzberg, H. 1979. *The Structuring of Organizations: A Synthesis of the Research*. Englewood Cliffs, NJ: Prentice-Hall.

Mintzberg, H. 1994. *The Rise and Fall of Strategic Planning*. New York: The Free Press.

Nonaka, I. 1988. Toward middle-up-down management: Accelerating information creation. *Sloan Management Review*, **29**: 9–18.

Nonaka, I. and Konno, N. 1998. The concept of "ba": Building a foundation for knowledge creation. *California Management Review*, **40**(3): 40–54.

Nonaka, I. and Takeuchi, H. 1995. *The Knowledge-Creating Company: How Japanese Companies Create the Dynamics of Innovation*. New York: Oxford University Press.

Nutt, P. and Backoff, R. 1997. Crafting vision. *Journal of Management Inquiry*, **6**(4): 308–28.

Parikh, J. 1994. *Intuition: The New Frontiers of Management*. Oxford, UK: Blackwell.

Pettigrew, A.M. 1985. *The Awakening Giant: Continuity and Change in ICI*. Oxford, UK: Blackwell.

Polanyi, M. 1958. *Personal Knowledge*. Chicago, IL: University of Chicago Press.

Polanyi, M. 1966. *The Tacit Dimension*. London: Routledge and Kegan Paul.

Porter, M.E. 1980. *Competitive Strategy: Techniques for Analyzing Industries and Competitors*. New York: The Free Press.

Porter, M.E. 1985. *Competitive Advantage: Creating and Sustaining Superior Performance*. New York: The Free Press.

Porter, M.E. 1991. Towards a dynamic theory of strategy. *Strategic Management Journal*, **12**: 95–112.

Prigogine, I. 1980. *From Being to Becoming: Time and Complexity in the Physical Sciences*. San Francisco: W.H. Freeman.

Quinn, J.B. 1980. *Strategies for Change: Logical Incrementalism*. Homewood, IL: Irwin.

Quinn, R.E. 1988. *Beyond Rational Management: Mastering the Paradoxes and Competing Demands of High Performance*. San Francisco: Jossey-Bass.

Roethlisberger, F.J. 1977. *The Elusive Phenomena*. Boston, MA: Harvard Business School Press.
Salovey, P. and Mayer, J.D. 1990. Emotional intelligence. *Imagination, Cognition, and Personality*, 9: 185–211.
Sanchez, R. and Heene, A. 1997. A competence perspective on strategic learning and knowledge management. In R. Sanchez and A. Heene (eds.), *Strategic Learning and Knowledge Management*, pp. 3–15. Chichester, UK: Wiley.
Schaefer, C., and Voors, T. 1986. *Vision in Action: The Art of Taking and Shaping Initiatives*. Hudson, NY: Lindisfarne Press.
Schwartz, P. 1991. *The Art of the Long View: Planning for the Future in an Uncertain World*. New York: Currency Doubleday.
Senge, P.M. 1989. *The Fifth Discipline: The Art and Practice of the Learning Organization*. New York: Doubleday.
Spender, J.-C. 1996. Making knowledge the basis of a dynamic theory of the firm. *Strategic Management Journal*, 17: 45–62.
Stacey, R.D. 1992. *Managing the Unknowable: Strategic Boundaries between Order and Chaos in Organizations*. San Francisco: Jossey-Bass.
Stewart, T.A. 1997. *Intellectual Capital: The New Wealth of Organizations*. London: Nicholas Brealey.
Streufert, S. 1997. Complexity: An integration of theories. *Journal of Applied Social Psychology*, 27(3): 2068–95.
Thietart, R.A. and Forgues, B. 1995. Chaos theory and organization. *Organization Science*, 6: 19–31.
Van de Ven, A. 1992. Suggestions for studying strategy process: A research note. *Strategic Management Journal*, 13: 169–88.
Van der Heijden, K. 1996. *Scenarios: The Art of Strategic Conversation*. New York: Wiley.
von Krogh G. 1998. Care in knowledge creation, *California Management Review*, 40(3): 133–53.
Westney, E. and Mintzberg, H. 1989. Visionary leadership and strategic management. *Strategic Management Journal*, 10: 17–32.
Wilber, K. 1996. *A Brief History of Everything*. Boston, MA: Shambhala Press.
Wilber, K. 1999. *Integral Psychology*. Boston, MA: Shambhala Press.
Zahra, S. and George, G. 2002. Absorptive capacity: A review, reconceptualization, and extension. *Academy of Management Review*, 27(2): 185–203.

# CHAPTER SEVENTEEN

# Micro Strategy and Strategizing: Implications for Strategy Process Research[1]

## Gerry Johnson, Leif Melin, Richard Whittington

We have previously[1] advanced the argument that while the field of strategy has traditionally concentrated on the phenomenon of organizations, it needs now to attend to much more micro-level phenomena; to the detailed processes and practices which constitute the day-to-day activities of organizational life and yet which relate to strategic outcomes. While our earlier concerns were with the broader strategy field, this chapter focuses more specifically on the process domain. It offers a critique of "strategy process" research from such a micro perspective and suggests benefits of the activity/practice-based view as well as considering some challenges for further research.

## Introduction

This chapter argues for a shift in strategy process research towards a micro perspective on strategizing. More specifically we call for an emphasis on the detailed processes and practices which constitute the day-to-day activities of organizational life *and* which relate to strategic outcomes. Our focus therefore is on the close understanding of those myriad, micro activities of strategizing in practice that, while often invisible to traditional strategy research, nevertheless can have significant consequences for organizations and those who work in them. Indeed we have come to think of such work as an activity-based or practice-based view of strategy.

   The activity-based view that we shall outline starts from the proposition that value lies increasingly in the micro activities of managers and others in organizations. Thus the activity-based view is concerned with the consequential details of organizational work and praxis (Whittington, 2002a). It goes *inside* organizations, their strategies and their processes, to investigate what is actually done and by whom. It is concerned with the activities of *strategizing* (Whittington, 2003). We recognize that this activity-based view is demanding in terms of research and we outline some of the key challenges that face us. However, we believe that there are substantial pay-offs to grasping these micro activities and we take encouragement from the papers that appeared in the special issue of the *Journal of Management Studies* and the growing interest in the field.[2]

## The Legacy of Process Research

Since the 1970s, strategy process research has made substantial contributions to the strategy discipline. The initial steps were taken simultaneously in Canada (Mintzberg, 1973; Mintzberg, Raisinghani, and Theoret, 1976), the UK (Pettigrew, 1973, 1985; Johnson, 1987), and Sweden (Rhenman, 1973; Normann, 1971, 1977; Jönsson and Lundin, 1977; Melin and Hellgren, 1993). We are strongly sympathetic to this process turn in the strategy field and we shall highlight three major contributions that we want to hold on to. However, we shall also identify some significant limitations that help establish our own agenda for the micro strategy and strategizing perspective.

First of all on the credit side, the process school has irrevocably opened up the black box of the organization. Strategy is now recognized as an organizational phenomenon rather than a macro-strategy problem detached from the internal dynamics of the organization. Internal politics (Pettigrew, 1973) and organizational tensions (Normann, 1977) have been introduced into the strategy process, not just as inevitable failings of organizations, but as significant for strategy outcomes, even attributes to be exploited positively for strategy development. We wish to stay inside this black box, indeed delve even further into it.

A second contribution of strategy process research is to have "humanized" the field (Pettigrew, Thomas, and Whittington, 2002: 12). Unlike studies that purport to shed light on key organizational phenomena, such as top teams, by reducing them to sets of demographics, the process research tradition, especially through the application of social construction and cognitive perspectives, has strongly affirmed that strategy is made by human beings. The implications, that we will come back to, are that strategy researchers must be in direct and close contact with the actors, and that theoretical constructs must, figuratively speaking, be filled with people. We want a theory of social action within the strategy context.

A third important contribution of strategy process research is the legitimization of small sample in-depth studies. Single case studies such as Pettigrew's (1985) or the close observation of managerial work by Mintzberg (1973) have proved to be the source of rich and enduring insight. Such an approach allows us to develop the holistic and contextual understanding essential to unpacking the complex driving forces of strategic change and stability (Melin, 1986, 1989). These in-depth studies are not only valid in themselves, but vital complements to the large-scale, aprocessual studies typical of traditional strategy performance studies. In-depth studies will be a necessary feature of the micro-strategy and strategizing perspective as well.

However, we need to be alive to the limitations of the process tradition. There are six points to be made, which together set some tough challenges for our own micro-strategy and strategizing perspective.

### Research from the veranda

First, while they have opened the black box of organizations, the process researchers haven't dug far within. Much of what purports to examine processes of strategy development in organizations is too distant from human action, relying on surrogate measures such as demographics, surveys, or second-hand retrospective reports, given typically by senior executives. Too often they are reminiscent of the early anthropologists' accounts of tribal customs based on conversations with local chiefs on colonial verandas. Progress in anthropology involved ethnographers directly engaging with – indeed living in – the world of action and practice. Something similar is true for management studies. Part of the problem is the level of analysis. Brown and Duguid (2000) have observed that practice is what is *inside* the process. In defining process research as about the systems and processes of organizations as wholes (Chakravarthy and Doz, 1992), the process tradition does not oblige us to probe far into what is going on inside. Process research might tell us a good deal about the overall processes of organizational decision making and organizational change, but it has been less interested in the practical activity and tools necessary to make these processes happen. What managers actually do, and with what techniques or skills, is left obscure. The process tradition has tended to fix upon the organizational level at the expense of the practical activity of those who actually constitute the processes. If we want to grasp the micro activity of practice, we shall need to get off our "verandas" and get a good deal closer to the actual work that makes up the organizational systems and processes of the process tradition.

### Practical implications

A second challenge for process research is the extent of its practical implications. Does it really help managers in their daily strategizing activities, for example, how to engage in everyday strategic debate in a convincing and motivating manner? In so far as the process tradition has been prescriptive, the typical focus has been on the overarching design of strategic change or decision-making processes, remote from what managers are doing in the day to day (Pettigrew and Whipp, 1992; Hickson *et al.*, 1986). Beyond that, process case studies have provided rich descriptions, but largely left to the reader the hard work of interpreting these into practice. We argue that a strong instrumental reason for the importance of a more micro activity-based view of strategy in general and strategy processes in particular is that managers manage activities. If we are to aid management and the managing of organizations we need to achieve a higher degree of reflexivity among those actors about what they are doing at that level and its effects. Much of the influential literature on strategy process, important as it is, has left the manager bereft of insights, let alone guidelines for action, at this micro level.

## The process–content divide

A third limitation in process research is due to its separation from content issues: indeed, the process tradition has tended to define itself as the opposite of content (Chakravarthy and White, 2002). When demonstrating that managers are networking, communicating, politicking, or deciding (Mintzberg, 1973; Kotter, 1982), process studies do not show in what regard. We still know little about the processes of diversifying, structuring, allying, or internationalizing as specific strategic initiatives (Melin, 1992). Yet process has a great deal to do with content studies, which on their own have proved substantially inadequate in explaining the performance outcomes of a range of crucial strategic themes, from diversification through to organizational structure (Grant, 2002; Whittington, 2002b) To take those two areas of empirical inquiry, Grant, Jammine, and Thomas (1988) concluded some time ago that progress in diversification research requires small-sample, fine-grained investigations capable of capturing both the subtlety of economically valuable relationships and their sensitivity to managerial action or inaction. And research on the design of corporate structures has similar limitations especially around the advantages of the multidivisional structure and its fit with various diversification strategies (Whittington, 2002b). Again, there are problems both with crude measures and with the exclusion of action. Structural categories are too static to pick up the continuous structural changes of contemporary business (Galunic and Eisenhardt, 1994; Brown and Eisenhardt, 1997). From our micro perspective, we therefore argue that the distinction between content and process is an unhelpful and unnecessary one and that greater attention to what is going on inside processes and strategies can both remove barriers and enhance explanation.

## Links to outcomes

The fourth limitation derives in part from the separation from the content approach, which has traditionally focused on organizational performance. Although there are notable exceptions (Pettigrew and Whipp, 1992), process research too often lacks explicit links to strategy outcomes. We should recognize that process research is dealing with a complex and ambiguous reality, meaning that we have to deal with networks of mutual causation (Melin, 1987). The same is true for a micro-strategy perspective, but at least it is helpful to be clear about what we are trying to explain and in what terms – a point we take up later.

## The agency issue

Process research has been reluctant to query the role of managerial agency (Pettigrew, 1985). Even if some studies have shown that managers can be central to strategizing (e.g. Hellgren and Melin, 1993), we still need to explore further if, and how, they make a difference. As our principal point of contact, we may easily exaggerate the importance of managers, particularly those at the strategic center, whereas activity at the periphery can have crucial effects (Johnson and Huff, 1998). Moreover, managerial agency is dependent on both general and situational constraints (Whittington, 1988). Managers can be captured in wider belief systems and technologies that constrain their possibilities for action. As both institutionalist theorists (Abrahamson, 1996) and critical theorists (Knights and Morgan, 1991) suggest, micro activities may easily be dominated by societal forces. In exploring how this might be so, an activity-based view can and should be neutral on the question of managerial agency.

**The trap of the particular**

Finally, process researchers who do seek to understand the actual processes within organizations too often employ case studies that become trapped within the particular. The empirical richness of much process research is both a strength and a weakness. We have many thick descriptions, but too few rigorous analyses and systematic comparisons around general theories or issues. The result has been poor accumulation of knowledge. Rather than emphasizing the rich idiosyncrasy of their data, case study researchers should use their empirical observations to establish patterns across similar issues and build theories with greater leverage in the real world. Data in itself is less valuable than theory that can explain why, how, with what consequences, and in what circumstances. Again, this is a challenge we return to later.

In sum, the process tradition has got us some way into the black box of organizations, but we have further to go if we are to truly understand the micro activities that make up organizational processes and contribute to organizational value.

## Towards an Activity-Based View of Strategy and Strategizing

Our argument, then, is that process research can be advanced by taking a more micro perspective attentive to the significant details of what is going on inside the processes: to repeat our opening definition, with "the detailed processes and practices which constitute the day-to-day activities of organizational life *and* which relate to strategic outcomes."

Our agenda is distinct in that it comes at enduring issues in strategy from the bottom-up, from the activities that constitute the substance of strategic management. We acknowledge that others adjacent to the strategy field have a similar agenda. For example, in relation to management and organizational cognition, Walsh (1995) argues that it is necessary to understand it in terms of people's behavior; Weick and Roberts (1993) show that collective cognition is embedded in organizational activities; and Eden and Ackermann (1998) argue for close engagement with practice to understand the relation between cognition and strategy. Within organization theory more widely, Blackler, Crump, and McDonald (2000) have also recently been developing an explicitly activity-orientated approach, based on the activity theory of Engeström. Our argument is parallel, but more specific to strategy. It is time to shift the strategy research agenda towards the micro: to start not from organizations as wholes – corporations, business units, and so on – but from the activities of individuals, groups, and networks of people upon which key processes and practices depend. In so doing, and building on our review of the strategy process field, a number of benefits become clear as do the challenges that need to be faced.

## The benefits

The benefits of an activity-based view of strategy are at least threefold: extending existing traditions of research; transcending divisions within the discipline; and offering practical, actionable guidance to practitioners.

First, and in line with needs expressed in many fields of strategy research, there is a need to link levels of explanations. An activity-based view does not deny the importance of research that has raised to the awareness of managers and researchers alike the broad issues facing strategists. The challenge of achieving and sustaining competitive advantage, of identifying and building on unique organizational assets or competencies, of managing multinational organizations, or diversifying and acquiring businesses successfully are all informed by such work. However, it does respond to the call for the need to extend explanation to the processes and activities that underpin and constitute such phenomena.

In so doing an activity-based view does away with the content/process split which has driven the strategy debate for so many years. The activities and processes that underpin strategy content are equivalent to those that explain strategy development or the management of strategic change. The level of analysis is the same. By emphasizing this activity-based perspective we are able to overcome – indeed the perspective demands we overcome – this established but regrettable divide. We can apply similar lenses to both such classic content issues as diversification and structure and the central process issues of strategic decision making and change.

A third benefit is that it is activities and processes that are the day-to-day stuff of management. It is what managers do and what they manage. It is also what organizational actors engage in more widely. So the research agenda matches the lived world of organizational actors. At least potentially it therefore provides the opportunity to translate research findings into organizational action more directly. As academics, we may make a bigger impact at the micro level than at the traditional macro level.

This does, however, raise an important question, which is the extent to which these processes and activities are actually manageable? On this an activity-based view is agnostic or neutral. It does not presuppose the primacy of managerial agency but rather encourages the exploration of the centrality of management within the complexity of the processes that go to make up and influence organizations. An activity-based view of strategy allows for, but does not commit to, managerial agency. What it does, however, is encourage reflexivity by both academics and managers on the role and effect of managers within the more inclusive notion of organizational activity; and in so doing avoids breaking out the concept of strategy as somehow separate and distinct from that world.

## The challenges

The activity-based view offers an agenda worth following, but there are major challenges ahead: we highlight four.

First, one advantage more traditional research has is that the dependent variable is fairly clear: the aim is to explain organizational performance. This leaves the question of *what is an activity-based view trying to explain*? One legitimate concern is the phenomena that micro activities underpin and in this sense there may be a link to relatively conventional performance measures, if second hand. For example, the debate on competitive advantage informed by the resource-based view poses the challenge of how resources in the form of routines, assets, and processes are configured to provide sustainable rents. It may not be possible to link this directly to organizational performance, but an activity-based view might be able to demonstrate how configurations of such assets take shape. Mapping technologies for identifying such asset-shaping activities have only recently emerged and are now being applied to questions of competitive advantage and sustainability (Eden and Ackermann, 2000; Ambrosini, 2003; Ambrosini and Bowman, 2002; Johnson and Johnson, 2002). Other issues, such as diversification or organizational restructuring, lend themselves equally to a micro analysis of the activities by which they are done.

An alternative focus is for the activity-based view to concentrate on the effectiveness of practices and practitioners in more immediate terms. Just what do managers have to do to make a difference and what is their impact? What works for them and what does not work? Here appropriate measures are not so much overall economic performance as recognition of managerial influence, the adoption of strategic initiatives, or perceived success of strategy-making episodes. A good deal of the literature on leadership already shades into this area by discussing the activities and behaviors of effective leaders (Grint, 1999). We have already noted the difficulties of the mainstream strategy literature in finding consistent economic performance relationships at the organization level. There might be higher returns by extending the leadership tradition to explaining the effectiveness of strategy managers, projects, and techniques.

Of course there are those who would argue that the search for some sort of dependent variable is irrelevant or pragmatically premature. A less ambitious but nonetheless worthwhile aim for an activity-based view might simply be to encourage reflexivity. Research that exposes and explains the consequential complexities of strategic activity is unlikely to yield many easy prescriptions. It can, though, provide moments for reflection. In explaining complexity, the activity-based view may contribute to the formation of "reflective practitioners," more subtle and sensitive in their strategic practice (Schön, 1983).

A second concern is that of *knowledge accumulation*. As noted earlier, a criticism of the case study orientation of process research is it too often fails to accumulate insight and knowledge beyond the specific context of the particular study. The challenge for micro studies of strategy activities is to rise beyond the specific.

An agenda for more cumulative work can be taken directly from prior research in the strategy field. The content tradition gives us major issues to study at the micro level, diversification, restructuring and much more. Process studies have contributed further crucial questions, such as strategic decision making and change. Linking micro studies to such prior empirical work is both possible and desirable. Moreover, micro research can draw on extant bodies of theory to increase their leverage, just as the better process studies have done. There is no shortage of theoretical perspectives upon which to build. Certainly the resource-based view provides a theory relevant to a micro approach for example. But those interested in this field draw on structuration theory, institutional theory, complexity theory, evolutionary economics, social psychology, and cognition. All of these theoretical approaches offer frameworks within which knowledge can cumulate and be systematically compared.

There are also challenges to do with the *design of research*. Almost inevitably micro studies have to be constrained in terms of their scope and unit of analysis. However, it is possible for researchers to identify particular units of analysis that can contribute to the more general. These could include the events or episodes that are typically critical to strategy development, for instance board meetings or away days; activities and processes which commonly underpin and explain competitive advantage, for example the transfer of knowledge; or the ways in which the standard tools and techniques of strategy, from portfolio planning to Porterian analysis, are actually employed. While each of these can be studied quite minutely, wider resonance is given because these are activities that are common and comparable across many organizations. Here it is important that such fine-grained studies are located in their wider context. They need to span levels: the level of individual interaction, the organizational level, and the level of the organization's context. This is a significant challenge. The danger is that studies veer to one extreme or the other: they are so micro – so concerned with explaining detailed processes – that they have little to say about how such processes contribute to general outcomes. Or more commonly, they claim to address micro issues when in fact they are merely deducing them from macro phenomena or outcomes.

Such work also requires a *close engagement with practice* rather than a reliance on surrogate measures. The challenge is to uncover strategic activities in their real rather than just their reported form. Most process studies actually rely on retrospective accounts of process by the actors involved. As anthropologists have long known, such accounts do not always reflect what actually goes on. The onus is on the researcher to provide convincing evidence that such processes and activities have been captured as accurately as possible; or at least that retrospective accounts are convincingly cross-checked. In any case, engaging closely with practice at this micro level will typically require the cooperation of practitioners. The plea to regard organizational actors, not so much as subjects of study, but as research collaborators is growing (Eden and Huxham, 1996; Tranfield and Starkey, 1998). An activity-oriented approach to research will benefit from the joint production of knowledge – not just by studying practice, but by directly involving practitioners.

## Conclusion

Our contention in this chapter, as it was in the Special Issue, is that the field of strategy research and the process field within it need to move on and that the micro activity-based perspective we advocate provides an agenda. It is a direction that draws together the various strands of strategy research under a theme that is practically relevant to managers and provides the promise of greater explanatory power than hitherto. There is already a growing body of research emerging, not least evident in the Special Issue of the *Journal of Management Studies* (Balogun *et al.*, 2003; Hendry and Seidl, 2003; Jarzabkowski, 2003; Maitlis and Lawrence, 2003, Regnér, 2003; Salvato, 2003; Samra-Fredericks, 2003)[3]. Our call now is for debate and proposals on how this agenda might be developed further and how a community of scholars wishing to take up the challenge of this research work can best be built. We believe that the prize is both intellectually distinctive and practically worthwhile.

## Notes

1. This chapter uses extracts from the introductory paper by the same authors, "Micro strategy and strategizing: Towards an activity-based view," in the special issue of the *Journal of Management Studies* edited by them on *Micro Strategy and Strategizing*, **40**(1): 3–22, 2003.
2. Current work in this emerging field can be accessed via the website www.strategy-as-practice.org.
3. All of these papers are to be found in the special issue of *Journal of Management Studies* on *Micro Strategy and Strategizing*, edited by G. Johnson, L. Melif and R. Whittington, **40**(1), 2003.

## References

Abrahamson, E. 1996. Management fashion. *Academy of Management Review*, **21**(1): 254–85.

Ambrosini, V. 2003. *Tacit and Ambiguous Resources as Sources of Competitive Advantage.* Basingstoke, UK: Palgrave Macmillan.

Ambrosini, V. and Bowman, C. 2002. Mapping successful organizational routines. In A.S. Huff and M. Jenkins (eds.), *Mapping Strategic Knowledge*, pp. 19–45. London: Sage.

Blacker, F., Crump, N., and McDonald, S. 2000. Organizing processes in complex activity networks. *Organization*, 7(2), 277–300.

Brown, J.S. and Duguid, P. 2000. *The Social Life of Information*. Boston, MA: Harvard Business School Press.

Brown, S.L. and Eisenhardt, K.M. 1997. The art of continuous change: Linking complexity theory and time-paced evolution in relentlessly shifting environments. *Administrative Science Quarterly*, **42**: 1–34.

Chakravarthy, B. and Doz, Y. 1992. Strategy process research: Focusing on corporate self-renewal. *Strategic Management Journal*, **13**: 5–14.

Charkravarthy, B. and White, R. 2002. Strategy process: Changing and implementing strategies. In A. Pettigrew, H. Thomas, and R. Whittington (eds.), *Handbook of Strategy and Management*. London: Sage.

Eden C. and Ackermann F. 1998. *Making Strategy: the Journey of Strategic Management*. London: Sage.

Eden, C. and Ackermann, F. 2000. Mapping distinctive competencies: A systemic approach. *Journal of the Operational Society*, **51**: 12–20.

Eden, C. and Huxham, C. 1996. Action research for the study of organizations. In S.R. Clegg, C. Hardy, and W.R. Nord (eds.), *Handbook of Organization Studies*, pp. 526–42. London: Sage.

Galunic, C. and Eisenhardt, K. 1994. Renewing the strategy–structure–performance paradigm. *Research in Organizational Behavior*, **16**: 215–55.

Grant, R. 2002. Corporate strategy: Managing scope and strategy content. In A. Pettigrew, H. Thomas, and R. Whittington (eds.), *Handbook of Strategy and Management*. London: Sage.

Grant, R., Jammine, A., and Thomas, H. 1988. Diversity, diversification and performance among British manufacturing firms, 1972–1984. *Academy of Management Journal*, **31**: 771–801.

Grint, K. 1999. *The Arts of Leadership*. Oxford, UK: Oxford University Press.

Hellgren, B. and Melin, L. 1993. The role of strategists' way of thinking. In J. Hendry and G. Johnson (eds.), *Strategic Thinking, Leadership and the Management of Change*. Chichester, UK: Wiley.

Hickson, D.J., Butler, R., Cray, D., Mallory, G. and Wilson, D.C. 1986. *Top Decisions: Strategic Decision Making in Organizations*. San Francisco: Jossey Bass.

Johnson, G. 1987. *Strategic Change and the Management Process*. Oxford: Blackwell.

Johnson, G. and Huff, A. 1997. Everyday innovation/everyday strategy. In G. Hamel, C.K. Prahalad, H. Thomas, and D. O'Neill (eds.), *Strategic Flexibility*. Chichester, UK: Wiley.

Johnson, P. and Johnson, G. 2002. Facilitating group cognitive mapping of core competencies. In A.S. Huff and M. Jenkins (eds.), *Mapping Strategic Knowledge*, pp. 220–36. London: Sage.

Jönsson, S. and Lundin, R. 1977. Myths and wishful thinking as management tools. In P.C. Nystrom and W.H. Starbuck (eds.), *Prescriptive Models of Organizations*. Amsterdam: North-Holland.

Knights, D. and Morgan, G. 1991. Corporate strategy, organizations, and subjectivity. *Organization Studies*, 12(2): 251–74.

Kotter, J. 1982. *The General Managers*. New York: The Free Press.

Melin, L. 1986. The field-of-force metaphor: A study in industrial change. *International Studies of Management and Organization*, 17(1), 24–33.

Melin, L. 1987. Commentary: Understanding strategic change. In A. Pettigrew (ed.), *Management of Strategic Change*, pp. 154–65. Oxford: Blackwell.

Melin, L. 1989. The field-of-force metaphor, *Advances in International Marketing*, pp. 161–79. Greenwich, CT: JAI Press.

Melin, L. 1992. Internationalization as a strategy process. *Strategic Management Journal*, 13: 99–118.

Melin, L. and Hellgren, B. 1993. Patterns of strategic processes: Two typologies. In H. Thomas (ed.), *Building the Strategically Responsive Organization*. Chichester, UK: Wiley.

Mintzberg, H. 1973. *The Nature of Managerial Work*. New York: Harper and Row.

Mintzberg, H., Raisinghani, O., and Theoret, A. 1976. The structure of unstructured decision processes. *Administrative Science Quarterly*, 21: 246–75.

Normann, R. 1971. Organizational innovativeness: Product variation and reorientation. *Administrative Science Quarterly*, June: 203–15.

Normann, R. 1977. *Management for Growth*. New York: Wiley.

Pettigrew, A.M. 1973. *The Politics of Organisational Decision Making*. London: Tavistock.

Pettigrew, A.M. 1985. *The Awakening Giant*. Oxford: Blackwell.

Pettigrew, A.M., Thomas, H., and Whittington, R. 2002. Strategic management: Strengths and limitations of a field. In A. Pettigrew, H. Thomas, and R. Whittington (eds.), *Handbook of Strategy and Management*. London: Sage.

Pettigrew, A.M. and Whipp, R. 1991. *Managing Change for Competitive Success*. Oxford: Blackwell.

Rhenman, E. 1973. *Organization Theory for Long-Range Planning*. London: Wiley.

Schön, D.A. 1983. *The Reflective Practitioner: How Professionals Think in Action*. New York: Basic Books.

Tranfield, D. and Starkey, K. 1998. The nature, social organization and promotion of management research. *British Journal of Management*, 9: 341–53.

Walsh, J.P. 1995. Managerial and organizational cognition: Notes from a trip down memory lane. *Organization Science*, 6(3): 280–321.

Weick, K.E. and Roberts, K.H. 1993. Collective mind in organizations: Heedful interrelating on flight decks. *Administrative Science Quarterly*, 38: 357–81.

Whittington, R. 1988. Environmental structure and theories of strategic choice. *Journal of Management Studies*, 25(6): 1–17.

Whittington, R. 2002a. Practice perspectives on strategy: Unifying and developing a field. *Academy of Management Best Paper Proceedings*, Denver.

Whittington, R. 2002b. Corporate structure: From policy to practice. In A. Pettigrew, H. Thomas, and R. Whittington (eds.), *Handbook of Strategy and Management*. London: Sage.

Whittington, R. 2003. The work of strategizing and organizing: For a practice perspective. *Strategic Organization*, 1(1): 117–25.

# CHAPTER EIGHTEEN

# Strategic Renewal and the Entrepreneurial Mind: The Importance of Cognition and Learning

Andrew C. Corbett

## Introduction

Much of today's strategy research strays from the genesis of strategic management and its original focus on individual action. By viewing strategic management through the lenses of entrepreneurship and psychology, this paper re-examines and reiterates the importance of the individual in the process of strategic renewal. Recent strategy research on invention provides firms with useful prescriptions for overcoming the learning traps associated with generating breakthrough inventions aimed at strategic renewal (Ahuja and Lampert, 2001). However, this same research has found that not all firms use entrepreneurial strategies – leaving researchers to wonder about this variation. Essentially, why do some firms adopt entrepreneurial strategies and others do not?

This article answers this question by examining how individual cognition and learning drive entrepreneurial opportunity generation – the engine of entrepreneurial strategies. This examination should prove to be of importance to both researchers and practitioners of strategic management. For scholars it provides new insights into the entrepreneurial mind and its relationship to strategic renewal. The overarching issue for practitioners is a reminder that strategy making, at its core, is dependent on the individuals who formulate and execute the organization's plans. The origins of all strategic actions can be traced to the learning, creative, and cognitive activities of individuals within the organization. Studying strategic renewal from a firm level is necessary, but not sufficient. Firms that are most successful at strategic renewal recognize the central role that individual learning and cognition play within the process of strategic management.

## The Roots of the Individual within Strategic Management

Strategic management research has traditionally emphasized administrative management behavior, which is in contrast to the entrepreneurial perspective that appears to represent the paradigm toward which the field is evolving (Michael, Storey, and Thomas, 2002). While the fields of strategic management and entrepreneurship have evolved primarily independent of each other (Hitt *et al.*, 2001), many scholars are beginning to argue that strategists must employ entrepreneurial tactics and actions in order to sustain their organizations (McGrath and Macmillan, 2000; Meyer and Heppard, 2000). Building from this research and augmenting it with the entrepreneurial cognition perspective, the current study examines the effects that individual cognitive processing has on organizational strategic renewal.

Recognizing that entrepreneurship and the generation of new ideas start at the individual level (Shaver and Scott, 1991), this research examines the role that individual cognitive abilities play in strategic renewal. Borrowing theory from psychology, this investigation examines how individuals acquire and process new information in order to develop ideas for strategic renewal. Interest in examining the entrepreneurial actions of individuals within the strategy-making process is warranted, but not novel. While most strategy researchers have focused on other issues, pioneers in the field have based the foundation of strategy on the individual and his or her ability to exercise cognitive judgment (Mintzberg, Ahlstrand, and Lampel, 1998; Schendel and Hofer, 1979). Mintzberg and colleagues detail how the three early dominant schools of thought regarding strategy research were centered largely on the decision-making authority and insights of an individual (generally, the CEO). Schendel and Hofer (1979) stress the importance of the individual and the effect that his or her entrepreneurial actions can have on renewal, ". . . A model that fails to place entrepreneurial choice at the center of the managerial universe is one that is incapable of providing a mechanism for renewing the firm beyond its originally intended purpose."

According to Pettigrew (1992), however, the promise of the field has yet to be fulfilled because much of strategic management writing "is an exercise in comparative statistics," as opposed to an investigation of a process. Although the field has moved forward in the years since Pettigrew's critique, recent research illustrates a need for examining the nexus of cognition, entrepreneurship, and strategic management. For example, questions regarding cognitive demands and information overload confound researchers investigating entrepreneurship in large corporations (Ahuja and Lampert, 2001). Concurrently, a recent recognition of the importance of cognition to the entrepreneurial process is emerging (Baron, 1998; Shane and Venkataraman, 2000; Mitchell *et al.*, 2002). This study takes a cue from Shane and Venkataraman by investigating individuals' cognitive abilities in regard to the identification of new opportunities and paths for strategic renewal.

In their study of entrepreneurship in large firms, Ahuja and Lampert (2001) developed a model explaining that large firms create breakthrough inventions by experimenting with novel, emerging, and pioneering technologies. Amid the numerous insights contained in this work, Ahuja and Lampert find that firms can fall into learning traps that inhibit their abilities to discover ideas and inventions for strategic renewal. The authors suggest that "cognitive demands" and "information overload" may explain part of their non-findings, and then pose the question of why some firms vary in their adoption of entrepreneurial strategies. The current work provides a response: as well done as Ahuja and Lampert's study was, it was designed to answer questions about *inventions* at a *firm* level and as such, their research could not provide insights into cognitive issues that occur at the individual level. In order to answer the questions posed by Ahuja and Lampert, this chapter examines *innovation* at an *individual* level. Specifically, the current research investigates cognition in regard to how individuals within organizations examine inventions as a means to generate opportunities for innovation and strategic renewal.

## Theory and Hypotheses

Theory from psychology provides us with distinct perspectives from which to view the domain of learning and provides an appropriate theoretical foundation for this study. This perspective corresponds to three well-established views of learning: empiricist, rationalist, and pragmatist-sociohistoric (Case, 1992; Packer, 1985); today these three perspectives are generally referred as the behaviorist, cognitive, and the situative perspectives (Greeno, Collins, and Resnick, 1996). The consistent themes that emerged from interviews conducted to support this study were the importance of individual learning and cognitive processing abilities, and their relationship to generating new venture ideas for strategic renewal. As such, the cognitive perspective of learning was followed to support this research.

The cognitive perspective of learning is focused on issues such as reasoning, problem solving, planning, and comprehending language. It emphasizes the understanding of concepts and theories in different domains. "Learning is understood as a constructive process of conceptual growth, often involving reorganization of concepts in the learner's abilities such as problem-solving strategies and metacognitive processes" (Greeno, Collins, and Resnick, 1996: 16). Social learning theory (Bandura, 1977) captures the importance of this perspective as it relates to the generation of ideas for new strategic breakthroughs. This theory is constructed primarily upon cognitive learning. Bandura emphasizes that learning is a self-regulatory process in which individuals have some measure of control over the environment and what influences them, "People are not simply reactors to external influences. They select, organize, and transform the stimuli that impinge upon them" (1977: vii).

This type of learning emphasizes the fact that individuals organize information in their own unique manner, which reflects one of the classic tenets of the field of psychology – that behavior is a function of both the person and the environment. An investigation of the cognitive learning processes of individuals involved in strategic renewal allows us to supplement content-based strategic management research that focuses on firm-level issues. Further, investigations examining issues derived from social learning theory allow us to answer questions regarding cognition and information overload asked by previous researchers (Ahuja and Lampert, 2001). The entrepreneurship literature has begun to demonstrate the usefulness of such an approach. For example, Baron (1998) theorizes that the determining factor in why some people are able to recognize entrepreneurial opportunities and others are not is due to cognitive differences, e.g., because some are more optimistic (Shepperd, Ouellette, and Fernandez, 1996), some have a higher tolerance for risk (Kahnemann and Lovallo, 1994), and others rely on a higher level of self-efficacy (Markman, Balkin, and Baron, 2001). Busenitz and Barney (1996) show that successful entrepreneurs differ from corporate managers in their use of heuristics and biases, because their cognitive frameworks and "mental shortcuts" allow them to recognize and take advantage of new venture opportunities.

The current study examines similar phenomena within the context of strategic renewal. The question at hand is, "How does individual cognition affect the recognition of opportunities for strategic renewal?" Specifically, I look at the following individual learning variables: general human capital (existing knowledge and experience), specific human capital (knowledge in a specific domain), cognitive style (the manner in which one processes new information), and learning orientation (the manner in which one acquires new information). Each of these variables was developed from interviews conducted with individuals involved with strategic renewal projects. The data from these interviews, in concert with theory, allow me to construct the four hypotheses detailed below. Prior to the formal statement of each hypothesis, I develop rationale from theory and support from interview data. The first two hypotheses examine human capital.

Becker (1964) developed the concept of human capital by extending microeconomic analysis to a wide range of human behavior. He popularized the idea that education and training are investments, just like a company's purchase of a new plant or equipment. He argued that through learning and updating one's knowledge base, one's human capital is increased. Most importantly, this accumulation of new attributes can be linked to increased productivity. The importance of human capital to strategic renewal is its inimitability and the resulting potential for sustained competitive advantage that it provides (Barney, 1991; Wernerfelt, 1984).

The literature on renewal and entrepreneurial process is replete with studies examining the effects of human capital and entrepreneurial action. Greene and Brown (1997) provide a typology of firms and stress the importance of human capital across every type of enterprise. Others have looked at specific types of human capital, including reputation (Dollinger, 1995), age (Cressy and Storey, 1995), industry know-how (Cooper, Gimeno-Gascon, and Woo, 1994), and management experience (Cooper, 1981, 1985; Westhead, 1995). Perhaps most importantly for the current study, Ucbassaran et al. (2004) state that one's ability to successfully sort through and use dense information to identify opportunities is highly dependent on one's level of human capital. It is important to note that previous research (Brüderl, Preisendorfer, and Zeigler, 1992; Cooper, Gimeno-Gascon, and Woo, 1994) has delineated the differences between general human capital (basic skills and experience) and industry-specific human capital (expertise). Some researchers detail the importance of experience (Cohen and Levinthal, 1990). In contrast, others (Hamel and Prahalad, 1996) suggest that with the rapid pace of change, experience and related basic skills are less likely to help individuals with the new challenges that confront them. Additionally, Dawes (1988) states that experience is not always a good teacher. He details eight specific biases and problems that may result from a reliance on experience and then suggests that specific expertise may be a better tool to recognize ideas for strategic renewal. In this study, the effects of general human capital (basic skills and experience) and specific human capital (knowledge on a specific domain) are tested in a rapidly changing environment. Specific human capital is measured as an individual's knowledge of, and expertise with, an emerging technology (Ahuja and Lampert, 2001). The interviews done in this study provide support for both experience and expertise. An aerospace executive interviewed for the study explained:

> To recognize true opportunities, you have to have the experience and knowledge to know what's what. What's serious and what isn't. If it sounds, or you get an idea or a problem that sounds like there might be something to it, you follow it.

A wireless firm CEO stated that to learn more about a potential opportunity for renewal one's specific human capital is crucial:

> . . . Being familiar with the technology. Being comfortable that we could go and talk to people in the marketplace and we could talk to the customers and learn more.

Based on theory and field interviews, the following hypotheses are offered in support of general human capital (basic skills and experience) and specific human capital (expertise).

> H1   There will be a positive relationship between an individual's level of general human capital and the number of innovative opportunities identified for strategic renewal.

> H2   There will be a positive relationship between an individual's level of specific human capital and the number of innovative opportunities identified for strategic renewal.

Hypotheses one and two examine an individual's existing stock of knowledge. In addition to investigating individuals' existing knowledge base, I examine how they process information. Individuals tend to gravitate toward a habitual preference for organizing and processing information (Streufert and Nogami, 1989) – a preference referred to as their cognitive style. Cognitive style develops from a reliance on organizing and processing information in either a more "right-brain" or "left-brain" manner (Allinson and Hayes, 1996). Allinson and Hayes explain that, "Intuition, characteristic of the right brain orientation, refers to immediate judgment based on feeling and the adoption of a global perspective. Analysis, characteristic of the left brain orientation, refers to judgment based on mental reasoning and a focus on detail" (1996: 122). Essentially, the cognitive processes of Allison and Hayes' "analyst" work in a straightforward, logical pattern; whereas, their "intuitivist" takes a broader perspective and incorporates many different inputs at once.

With respect to recognizing opportunities for strategic renewal, I hypothesize that the linear approach of the analyst, which usually results in this person searching for one "right" solution, will result in a relatively low number of opportunities identified.

Conversely, the intuitivist's non-linear approach generally results in this person evaluating many different solutions to a problem. One wireless firm's CEO comments supplemented the theory and informed my thinking:

> To recognize them (opportunities for a new strategic direction) you have to be creative enough to realize them, to think differently – you see a new technology or you see that something profoundly different coming about that you can now apply to that space. Or, you see something that has occurred in a different industry and you can now take over and put into that space. Or you can just see some need that is unfulfilled or some service that is truly unique.

Therefore, when put in the context of this study and based on the broader and more varied cognitive perspective of the intuitivist, the following hypothesis is offered:

H3   The more intuitive an individual's cognitive style, the greater the number of innovative opportunities identified for strategic renewal.

While cognitive style relates to individual preference for processing information when carrying out learning activities (Valley, 1997), a learning orientation describes how people initially acquire information (Kolb, 1984). The last hypothesis examines the relationship between an individual's learning orientation and his or her ability to identify opportunities. Kolb (1984) states that most people develop a preferred learning orientation based on their heredity, life experience, and the demands of their current environment. All individuals vary on these three inputs to learning orientation, therefore learning orientation contributes significantly to the variance in human learning (Kolb, 1984; Levy, 1980). Kolb submits that through various forms of socialization, people tend to build a reliance on one of the two basic forms of grasping information: apprehension and comprehension.

When individuals acquire information through comprehension, they are relying on their ability to think through abstract concepts and reinterpret prior information. When individuals acquire information through apprehension, they rely on their feelings to digest the direct, concrete occurrence that they are currently experiencing. Table 18.1 summarizes the differences in learning orientation with regard to each orientation's perspective toward time, objectivity, and the type of knowledge that results.

Applying this theory in the current context, a difference in the ability to recognize new strategic ideas may result from the fact that individuals tend to rely on one of these contrasting modes. While the process of apprehension develops unique personal knowledge, this learning orientation is restrictive, relative to the mode of comprehension. Individuals who rely on the apprehension mode would be less discerning than their comprehension counterparts. Those relying on comprehension have a forward-looking schema that uses past knowledge to help make sense of newly acquired information. Their more critical eye also leads me to propose that they would have an advantage over those who rely on apprehension to recognize opportunities for strategic renewal.

**Table 18.1**  Differences in learning modes

| Learning mode | Apprehension | Comprehension |
|---|---|---|
| Present/Past | Occurs in the here and now, exists in continuously unfolding events | Record of the past that helps to seek to define future events |
| Acritical/Critical | A registrative process transformed by appreciation | An interpretive process transformed by criticism |
| Personal/Social knowledge | Personal subjective process that cannot be known by others | An objective social process based on words, symbols, and images |

The CFO of a technology start-up firm unwittingly endorsed Kolb's thoughts on the different learning orientation of individuals and their potential effects on developing new strategic ideas:

> Well, I think that the opportunity that we went after was much more a concept that I could understand (than other options). It was specific to a product and market and it was more of like a real thing. I learn much more by compartmentalizing things ... The other possibilities were very conceptual, theoretical and it wasn't as real world to me.

The formal statement of the hypothesis is as follows:

> H4  The more an individual's learning orientation tends toward comprehension, the greater the number of innovative opportunities identified for strategic renewal.

## Methodology

### Instrument and sample

McCracken (1988) states that while quantitative methods survey the terrain, qualitative methods mine it. In the case of the present study, it was necessary to both mine and then survey the terrain. First, I investigated idea and opportunity generation within the strategic renewal process by conducting a number of long interviews. The interview was the most appropriate qualitative technique for my purposes, as it is deliberately more efficient and less obtrusive than other ethnographic techniques. "The long interview gives us the opportunity to step into the mind of another person, to see and experience the world as they do themselves" (McCracken, 1988: 9).

Sixteen semi-structured interviews of high technology professionals were conducted to gain an understanding of what individual-level factors are important in the process of strategic renewal. The individuals interviewed were from various levels of their organizations, including founders, owners, top management team members, engineers, and researchers. Through analysis of the interviews, a pattern emerged that suggests that differences in cognition and individual learning may play an important role in how individuals contribute to strategic renewal initiatives. These interviews ultimately focused on reoccurring descriptions of how knowledge, cognition, and learning effect idea generation within the process of strategic renewal. The insight gained from these interviews was then used in the development of the quantitative instrument.

This instrument included a number of scales regarding learning and cognition as well as a cognitive task that required participants to identify opportunities for strategic renewal based on a recent invention. A random sample of 1,592 founders, owners, top management team members, engineers, and researchers of technology-based firms was used in this study. The sample came from the 2002 Rocky Mountain High Technology Directory. This four-step total design method process (Dillman, 2000) yielded 312 completed surveys and 83 returns of incorrect addresses (a response rate of 21 percent).

## Dependent variable

The dependent variable, the number of innovative opportunities recognized, was captured from respondents' answers from the quasi-experiment. In the experiment, subjects were asked to list as many ideas for strategic renewal as they could, based upon a detailed description of a new technological protocol (the Bluetooth wireless protocol). The respondents listed 1,454 ideas. These statements were then judged for their viability as true opportunities for strategic renewal by three independent raters, all of whom have experience and expertise in high technology venture development. The judges were given explicit instructions and detailed rating sheets. They were also provided with previous research that discussed the concepts of ideas, opportunities, and true viability. The judgment of the three raters had an initial inter-rater reliability of 89.1 percent. Subsequently, the raters further discussed the items that were in disagreement until they reached 100 percent agreement.

## Independent variables

In this study human capital was measured in two separate ways, as general human capital and as specific human capital. General human capital was measured by an index composed of a number of different variables. Becker (1964) states that experience and job training are two of the most important aspects of general human capital. As such, I developed a human capital index comprising each individual's age, job level, years in their current job, years with their current firms, and years in their current industry. Specific human capital was measured by self-report on Likert-type scale items that inquired about each individual's level of knowledge and familiarity with the Bluetooth protocol (the protocol that was to be used in the experiment). Cognitive style was measured using Allinson and Hayes' (1996) cognitive style index (CSI). Using 38 questions, the CSI measures the general intuition-analysis dimension of an individual's cognition. Learning orientation was captured using a normative version (Geiger, Boyle, and Pinto, 1993) of Kolb's learning style inventory (1984), which is composed of 48 independent statements regarding one's preferred learning orientation.

**Table 18.2**  Descriptive statistics and correlations

|  | Mean | SD | 1 | 2 | 3 | 4 |
|---|---|---|---|---|---|---|
| 1. Opportunities recognized | 3.81 | 2.67 | — | | | |
| 2. Specific human capital | 1.92 | .976 | .179** | — | | |
| 3. General human capital | 17.10 | .687 | .045 | .011 | — | |
| 4. Cognitive style | 38.02 | 12.6 | −.114* | −.132** | .168** | — |
| 5. Learning orientation | 3.28 | 8.05 | −.108* | −.011 | −.026 | −.453** |

$*p < .05;$ $**$ $p < .01$

**Table 18.3**  Regression analysis of opportunities recognized

|  | Independent effects |
|---|---|
| Specific human capital | .151** |
| General human capital | .071 |
| Cognitive style | −.192** |
| Learning orientation | .178** |
| $R^2$ | .072** |

$**$ $p < .01$

## Results

Tables 18.2 and 18.3 provide descriptives, correlations, and results of the regression analysis. As hypothesized, specific human capital, cognitive style, and learning mode are each significantly related to the number of innovative opportunities identified, providing support for Hypotheses 2, 3, and 4. No support was found for the proposed relationship between general human capital and the number of opportunities identified (Hypothesis 1).

## Discussion and Implications

As the fields of strategic management and entrepreneurship continue to develop a symbiotic relationship, the role of individual behavior and entrepreneurial action needs to once again become a focal point of strategic management research (Pettigrew, 1992; Hitt *et al.*, 2001). While teams can carry out new initiatives, the generation of initial ideas begins with the individual (McGrath and MacMillan, 2000; Shaver and Scott, 1991). The results of this research demonstrate the importance of the individual's cognitive schema to strategy making. This is to say that firm-level effects tell us only part of the story. To gain a greater understanding of strategy process, researchers must investigate individuals within the firm.

This point was brought to the fore by Ahuja and Lampert's (2001) research into entrepreneurship in large organizations. This work showed that firms must experiment with novel, emerging, and pioneering technologies in order to develop breakthrough inventions for strategic renewal. However, Ahuja and Lampert were unable to expound upon why some firms, and not others, adopt entrepreneurial strategies. The current study augments Ahuja and Lampert's work by showing that much of the impetus for adopting entrepreneurial strategies begins with the individuals charged with making strategy. The results of this study suggest that the process of strategic renewal is dependent upon individuals who have certain knowledge, learning, and cognitive predilections.

## Cognitive factors

Many studies in entrepreneurship suggest that experience is a crucial factor in finding and developing new venture ideas (Vesper, 1980; Ronstadt, 1988; Gilad, Kaish, and Ronen, 1988). However, Hamel and Prahalad (1996) argue that moving people away from a reliance on experience and toward a broader view will help them discover opportunity.

> In a world of discontinuous change, shouldn't authority rest not only on experience, but also on the capacity to learn and adapt? In such an environment, what is the value of experience gained solely within one industry context? . . . Might the capacity to think across industry boundaries – to spot opportunities at the juncture of two or more industries; to draw relevant analogies from seemingly unrelated industries – be as valuable as deep experience on a single sector? If so, how does one breed managers with the capacity to escape the conventions of the past and build entirely new industries? (1996: 240)

The findings of this study, in regard to general human capital and expertise, bring a finer point to the earlier studies of opportunity development and strategic renewal. My results suggest that general experience is not significantly related to one's ability to identify opportunities for new ventures or strategic renewal. This finding is in contrast to earlier work (Vesper, 1980; Ronstadt, 1988; Gilad, Kaish, and Ronen, 1988). Conversely, the positive relationship between specific human capital (expertise) and the number of opportunities identified supports the thesis of Hamel and Prahalad. Their points about learning and adapting are sound, and their suggestion that individuals must balance knowledge from many disparate places is well placed. However, the first two results from this study suggest that we must be careful not to let the pendulum swing too far toward broad accumulation of knowledge and experience. Individuals still must have in-depth, specific knowledge to find initial ideas for strategic renewal. This is particularly important in the technical arenas investigated in this study. While general capabilities may be important in developing and exploiting a strategic initiative, the specific knowledge cultivated by the individual is necessary to find the opportunity in the first place.

This study also demonstrates that it is not just one's use of current knowledge and expertise that is of value, but also how one acquires and processes new information that makes a difference in initiating ideas for strategic renewal. Learning orientation refers to the two primary ways in which an individual can acquire information as part of the cognitive process, either through direct experience or through a re-creation of experiences. This study found that individuals who rely more on the latter, *comprehension* (a reliance on new information critically reinterpreted with prior information), recognized more opportunities than those who rely on the former, *apprehension* (a reliance on tangible, immediate experience).

Similarly, this study found that an individual's cognitive style is significantly related to one's ability to recognize innovative ideas for strategic renewal. Using the cognitive style index developed by Allinson and Hayes (1996), this study found support for the hypothesis that individuals who use an intuitive cognitive style – one that relies on immediate judgment based on feelings and a global view – will recognize a greater number of opportunities than individuals who rely on a more analytical style (judgment based on mental reasoning and a focus on detail). Previous findings (Allinson and Hayes, 1996) have stated that having individuals with both analytical and intuitive styles in your organization is important to balance certain tasks. However, the results of this study suggest that when the critical issue at hand is how to develop new products or services for strategic renewal, a preponderance of individuals with an intuitive style is preferred.

## Implications

Shane and Venkataraman (2000) theorize that cognitive abilities may play a crucial role in developing entrepreneurial opportunities. Similarly, Ahuja and Lampert (2001) pondered what cognitive forces might affect a firm's decisions about whether or not to employ entrepreneurial strategies. Indeed, initiating strategic renewal by developing new products and services is a multifaceted endeavor. This study illustrates that how individuals acquire and process information as part of the learning process is a very important part of the strategic process. In part, this research verifies the theoretical conjecture of Shane and Venkataraman, while also providing some answers to the questions of Ahuja and Lampert.

In addition to the implications for scholars, this study makes contributions for the practicing strategist. The results of this study may be most important for human resource professionals involved in the hiring of process or team leaders who are responsible for building ad hoc teams charged with leading strategic renewal. The results of this work suggest that cognitive measures might be incorporated into the screening process when composing teams that will be focused on strategy making and strategic renewal. Additionally, this study suggests that individuals who tend to be specialists as opposed to generalists may be better suited for strategic renewal initiatives (at least in the beginning stages). This is important for practice, especially for fledgling start-ups or large firms trying to find new services to offer. While the generalist may be an excellent candidate to run an ongoing operation, the results from this study suggest specialists are better suited to help develop new initiatives or new operations.

In sum, the results of this study suggest that individual learning and cognitive behaviors have an important role within the strategic renewal process. Whereas strategy research has meandered away from investigations of the individual (Pettigrew, 1992), this study demonstrates the importance of investigating the role of individuals in the strategy renewal process, which brings us closer to the original intention of strategy research (Schendel and Hofer, 1979).

# References

Ahuja, G. and Lampert, C.M. 1996. Entrepreneurship in the large corporation: A longitudinal study of how established firms create breakthrough inventions. *Strategic Management Journal*, 22(6–7): 521–43.

Allinson, C.W. and Hayes, J. 1996. The cognitive style index: A measure of intuition analysis for organizational research. *Journal of Management Studies*, 1: 119–35.

Bandura, A. 1977. *Social Learning Theory*. Englewood Cliffs, NJ: Prentice Hall.

Barney, J. 1991. Firm resources and sustained competitive advantage. *Journal of Management*, 17(1): 99–120.

Baron, R. 1998. Cognitive mechanisms in entrepreneurship: Why and when entrepreneurs think differently than other people. *Journal of Business Venturing*, 13(4): 275–94.

Becker, G.S. 1964. *Human Capital*. Chicago, IL: University of Chicago Press.

Brüderl, J., Preisendorfer, P., and Zeigler, R. 1992. Survival chances of newly founded business organizations. *American Sociological Review*, 57(2): 227–42.

Busenitz, L. and Barney, J. 1996. Differences between entrepreneurs and managers in organizations: Biases and heuristics in strategic decision making. *Journal of Business Venturing*, 12(1): 9–30.

Case, R. 1992. Neo-Piagetian theories of cognitive development. In R.J. Sternberg and C.A. Berg (eds.), *Intellectual Development*. New York: Cambridge University Press.

Cohen, W.M. and Levinthal, D. 1990. Absorptive capacity: A new perspective on learning and innovation. *Administrative Science Quarterly*, 35: 128–52.

Cooper, A.C. 1981. Strategic management, new entrants and small business. *Long Range Planning*, 14: 39–45.

Cooper, A.C. 1985. The role of incubator organizations in the founding of growth-oriented firms. *Journal of Business Venturing*, 1(1): 75–87.

Cooper, A.C., Gimeno-Gascon, F.J., and Woo, C.Y. 1994. Initial human capital and financial capital as predictors of new venture performance. *Journal of Business Venturing*, 9: 371–95.

Cressy, R. and Storey, D. 1995. *New Firms and their Bank*. London: National Westminster Bank PLC.

Dawes, R. 1988. *Rational Choice in an Uncertain World*. San Diego: HBJ.

Dillman, D.A. 2000. *Mail and Internet Surveys*. New York: Wiley.

Dollinger, M.J. 1995. *Entrepreneurship: Strategies and Resources*. Upper Saddle River, NJ: Prentice Hall

Geiger, M.A., Boyle, E.J., and Pinto, J.K. 1993. An examination of ipsative and normative versions of Kolb's learning style inventory. *Educational and Psychological Measurement*, 53: 717–26.

Greene, P.G. and Brown, T.E. 1997. Resource needs and the dynamic capitalism typology. *Journal of Business Venturing*, 12: 161–73.

Greeno, J.G., Collins, A.M., and Resnick, L.B. 1996. Cognition and learning. In D.C. Berliner and R.C. Calfee (eds.), *Handbook of Educational Psychology*. New York: Macmillan.

Gilad, B., Kaish, S., and Ronen, J. 1988. The entrepreneurial way with information. In S. Maital (ed.), *Applied Behavioral Economics*, Vol. 2, pp. 481–503. New York: New York University Press.

Hamel, G. and Prahalad, C.K. 1996. Competing in the new economy: Managing out of bounds. *Strategic Management Journal*, 17: 237–42.

Hitt, M.A., Ireland, R.D., Camp, S.M., and Sexton, D.L. 2001. Strategic entrepreneurship: Entrepreneurial strategies for wealth creation. *Strategic Management Journal*, 22(6–7): 479–91.

Kahneman, D. and Lovallo, D. 1994. Timid choices and bold forecasts: A cognitive perspective on risk-taking. In R. Rumelt, R. Schendel, and D. Teece (eds.), *Fundamental Issues in Strategy: A Research Agenda*, pp. 71–96. Boston, MA: Harvard Business School Press.

Kolb, D.A. 1984. *Experiential Learning: Experience as the Source of Learning and Development.* Englewood Cliffs, NJ: Prentice Hall.

Levy, J. 1980. Cerebral asymmetry and the psychology of man. In M. Wittrock (ed.), *The Brain and Psychology.* New York: Academic Press.

Markman, G.D., Balkin, D.B., and Baron, R.A. 2001. Inventors' cognitive mechanisms as predictors of new venture performance. Paper presentation at the meetings of the *Academy of Management*, Washington, DC.

McCracken, G. 1988. *The Long Interview.* Newbury Park, CA: Sage.

McGrath, R. and MacMillan, I. 2000. *The Entrepreneurial Mindset.* Cambridge, MA: Harvard University Press.

Meyer, G.D. and Heppard, K.A. 2000. *Entrepreneurship as Strategy: Competing on the Entrepreneurial Edge.* Thousand Oaks, CA: Sage.

Michael, S., Storey, D., and Thomas, H. 2002. Discovery and coordination in strategic management and entrepreneurship. In M.A. Hitt, R.D. Ireland, S.M. Camp, and D.L. Sexton (eds.), *Strategic Entrepreneurship.* Oxford, UK: Blackwell.

Mintzberg, H., Ahlstrand, B., and Lampel, J. 1998. *Strategy Safari: A Guided Tour Through the Wilds of Strategic Management.* New York: The Free Press.

Mitchell, R.K., Busenitz, L., Lant, T., McDougall, P.P., Morse, E.A., and Brock Smith, J. 2002. Toward a theory of entrepreneurial cognition: Rethinking the people side of entrepreneurship research. *Entrepreneurship: Theory and Practice*, Winter: 93–104.

Packer, M.J. 1985. Hermeneutic inquiry in the study of human conduct. *American Psychologist*, **40**: 1081–93.

Pettigrew, A. 1992. The character and significance of strategy process research. *Strategic Management Journal*, **13**: 39–60.

Ronstadt, R. 1988. The corridor principle. *Journal of Business Venturing*, **3**: 31–40.

Schendel, D. and Hofer, C. 1979. *Strategy Management: A New View of Business Policy and Planning.* Boston, MA: Little, Brown.

Shane, S. and Venkataraman, S. 2000. The promise of entrepreneurship as a field of research. *Academy of Management Review*, **25**(1): 217–26.

Shaver, K.G. and Scott, L. R. 1991. Person, process, choice: The psychology of new venture creation. *Entrepreneurship Theory and Practice*, Winter: 23–42.

Shepperd, J., Ouellette, J., and Fernandez, J. 1996. Abandoning unrealistic optimistic performance estimates and the temporal proximity of self-relevant feedback. *Journal of Personal Psychology*, **70**: 844–55.

Streufert, S. and Nogami, G.Y. 1989. Cognitive style and complexity: Implications for I/O psychology. In C.L. Cooper and I. Robertson (eds.), *International Review of Industrial and Organisational Psychology.* Chichester, UK: Wiley.

Ucbassaran, D., Wright, M., Westhead, P., and Busenitz, L. 2004. In J. Katz and D. Shepherd (eds.), *Advances in Entrepreneurship, Firm, Emergence, and Growth.* Greenwich, CT: JAI Press.

Valley, K. 1997. Learning styles and courseware design. *Association for Learning Technology Journal*, **5**(2): 42–51.

Vesper, K.H. 1980. *New Venture Strategies.* Englewood Cliffs, NJ: Prentice Hall.

Wernerfelt, B. 1984. A resource-based view of the firm. *Strategic Management Journal*, **5**: 171–80.

Westhead, P. 1995. Survival and employment growth contrasts between types of owner-managed high-technology firms. *Entrepreneurship: Theory and Practice*, **20**(1): 5–27.

# CHAPTER NINETEEN

# Emotional Attachment and Conflict in Strategic Decision Making in New Ventures

Otto Koppius, Fedde Germans, Rogier Vos

## Introduction

Consider the following verbatim exchange that occurred during a meeting of a top management team (TMT) of a software firm, where three people (Marketing, Content, and Development) have to make a strategic decision regarding their main product. The discussion centers around whether or not they should adopt a specific technological standard (called Library E) for their product or alternatively, remain platform-independent (and offer their product based on Library C as well as Library E):

*Marketing*: We suggest being independent because of two reasons: First, we are afraid of betting on the wrong horse when we choose for one particular library. The dominant design hasn't manifested itself yet so if we bet on the wrong horse, we could end up empty handed. Second . . .

*Development*: Do you really think Library C will eventually be the dominant design? When the industry uses Library C they will soon found out that it cannot help them solve their communication problems.

*Marketing*: But what if Library C solves their problems? It may be too concise, but if that's what they want, they will be satisfied with Library C. And second, if I may finish my statement, how can we win credibility if we want to stimulate the industry to standardize their communication and offer them only one alternative? Then we don't want them to standardize, but we want them to use Library E to standardize? It's like saying: "Hey, you have to standardize, but only with Library E."

*Content*: I have been working on Library E for decades and it is the best available at the moment. The only problem is that the industry doesn't know that yet.

*Development*: That's true, the market is like a woman, you never know where she is heading!

*Marketing*: That might be true and therefore we want to be independent, because the market is unsure, we can better choose the most secure option: independency. We too believe Library E is qualitatively the best, but I'll do what my customers pay me to do: implement the library they want.

*Development*: Oh, come on, what do you know about the market? I just know the market will choose for Library E, believe me, I have been walking around there for some while, so I can tell.

If we were to imagine how a discussion in a TMT regarding the adoption of a technological standard would unfold, the exchange above is probably not what immediately comes to mind. Given the importance of strategic decisions, we would expect a comprehensive search for relevant information (Fredrickson and Mitchell, 1984; Eisenhardt, 1989), a careful weighing of the argument's pros and cons (Schweiger, Sandberg, and Rechner, 1989) from all parties involved (Dean and Sharfman, 1996; Kim and Mauborgne, 1993) based on task-relevant arguments (Amason, 1996; Simons and Peterson, 2000), hopefully leading to a consensus (Dooley, Fryxell, and Judge, 2000; Knight *et al.*, 1999) about the course of action for implementation. This is not to say that the strategic decision-making process partly described above does not have these elements, but rather that there appear to be other factors at play as well. This chapter will investigate some of these factors, focusing in particular on the role of emotional attachment and conflict.

## Emotions and Emotional Attachment in Organizations

Just as other people feel emotions in everyday life, so do people in organizations (Hochschild, 1983; Isen and Baron, 1991; Fineman, 1993). While these and other studies have investigated how emotions[1] influence day-to-day work behavior (e.g. Jehn, 1997; Forgas and George, 2001), comparatively little work has been done within a strategy context. Huy (2002) described the constructive role of emotions and emotion management by middle managers in facilitating strategic change throughout an organization. Specifically in a strategic decision-making context, Kisfalvi and Pitcher (2003) analyzed how a CEO's character and emotions prevented constructive debate in a family-run firm.

The role of emotions in strategic decision-making is perhaps a somewhat double-edged sword. On one hand, we would expect that the high stakes of a strategic decision would ensure a decision process of careful deliberation based on substantiated arguments. On the other hand, however, these same high stakes may cause strategic decision-makers to experience strong personal feelings about certain issues because they have become emotionally attached to the organization, given their deep involvement and commitment to it (Baron, 1998) and this could subsequently influence their decision processes (Forgas, 1995). It is necessary to distinguish this emotional attachment from specific emotions, because there is an important conceptual difference. Following the works of Marris (1986) and Bowlby (1969) in psychology, we view emotional attachment as providing people with a basic frame for meaning and relatedness (see also Abelson's (1988) discussion of ego involvement in developing conviction). In other words, emotional attachment is *not* an emotion in itself, but rather a *condition* from which emotion arises (see also Vince and Broussine, 1997). The same emotional attachment can give rise to different emotions depending on the circumstances, so there is not a one-to-one mapping from emotional attachment to emotion. This more abstract level of analysis is different from the traditional literature on emotions in organizations that focuses on specific emotions such as happiness or anger of employees (e.g. Fineman, 1993).

Although not their specific focus and therefore not elaborated on by the authors, two articles in the strategy literature offer a glimpse of the role that this emotional attachment may play in strategic decision making. In his study on the global bearings industry, Collis (1991) discussed SKF's European production restructuring during the 1970s and stated that it was partly based on:

> ... special *emotional attachment*, e.g. the Göteborg plant management was committed to spherical roller bearings because that product had been invented in Sweden (Collis, 1991: 64, emphasis added).

In his study of Intel's strategy, Burgelman (1994) noted a similar phenomenon when discussing Intel's slow exit from the DRAM business:

> *Emotional attachment* by many top managers to the product that had "made Intel" was also part of the inertial force. In the course of the interviews, most managers mentioned emotional factors to explain why it had taken so long for Intel to get out of the DRAM business. One middle manager, for instance, said that Intel had lived on DRAMs and that it was therefore difficult to get out: "It was kind of like Ford deciding to get out of cars" (Burgelman, 1994: 41, emphasis added).

These quotes suggest that emotional attachment may be an important factor driving certain strategic decisions and in this chapter we investigate this phenomenon in more detail. Using an inductive study of four strategic decisions in a new venture, two in which one or more decision makers were emotionally attached to the issue being decided upon and two in which no decision makers were emotionally attached, we formulate three propositions regarding the effect of emotional attachment on strategic decision-making. The evidence from this multiple case study suggests that emotionally attached decision makers frame the issue from a personal perspective instead of an organizational perspective. When arguing their position, they are more likely to use principled arguments and opinions instead of logical arguments and facts and they are more likely to discuss in terms of values and goals instead of specific measures and steps to be taken. If emotional attachment is present, the strategic decision-making process will have more affective conflict between decision-makers. Overall, this suggests that emotional attachment is an influential factor in the strategic decision-making process.

The following section briefly describes the company background, the multiple case study methodology employed here, and the four specific strategic decisions studied. We then discuss each proposition in more detail and provide empirical grounding from the four cases. We close with a discussion on the limitations and generalizability of our conclusions and we make suggestions for a more encompassing theory of strategic decision-making.

**Table 19.1**   Esperanto characteristics

| Company | Marketing | Development | Content |
|---|---|---|---|
| Number of members | 9 | 1 | 1 |
| Number of members in Esperanto | 4 | 1 | 1 |
| Function | Marketing and sales | Technical | Technical |
| Average experience in industry (years) | 4 | 12 | 30 |
| Number of votes | 1 | 1 | 1 |
| Financially dependent on Esperanto | No | Yes | No |

## Company Background

The Dutch venture we studied, called Esperanto (an alias), is an alliance between three Dutch companies in the petrochemical industry: Marketing, Content, and Development. Esperanto defines as its mission: "Stimulating the industry to use a communication standard in designing and maintenance of objects." This communication standard can be seen as a computer language through which information systems communicate with each other. In the industry, two sorts of libraries are being used for this language: Library Extensive (Library E) and Library Concise (Library C), but no dominant design has emerged yet. Marketing, Development, and Content formed the joint venture in 2000 in order to offer the industry a "one-stop shop" for implementing a library by offering applications, error-free libraries, and implementation services. Esperanto does not have a central office and the different companies are spread around the center of the Netherlands. Voting in the TMT is done on an equal base per company although Marketing has four members involved in Esperanto and Content and Development only one.

Marketing consists of nine people and has a background in integrating information systems in the industry for three years. It performs the marketing and sales function as well as being the webmaster for Esperanto. Four people from Marketing join Esperanto's meetings and the members are two programmers and two marketers with an average age of 31. Content consists of one person who retired from the industry, is not financially dependent on Content, and has 30 years of experience in the industry. Content was closely involved in developing Library E from the early start and performed the role of library manager within the industry. Content performs the function of library manager in Esperanto, which consists of keeping the library up to date and scanning the library for errors or contradictions. Development, as well as Content, consists of one person. The developer founded his company as a freelance consultant and is financially dependent on it. Development was also closely involved in the development of Library E and performs the role of application developer in Esperanto. In Table 19.1, the different characteristics of the three parties are depicted.

## Research Methodology

We studied Esperanto over a period of 19 months in 2001–2002. The study followed an embedded multiple-case design (Yin, 1984) in which we studied four strategic decisions within a single firm. Decisions were selected during an exploratory phase in which the TMT members indicated in interviews what the most important strategic decisions were that they had taken during Esperanto's existence. One of the researchers worked at Marketing and was involved in Esperanto as an employee from March 2001 until September 2002. He observed and took notes of many conversations about strategic decisions and other issues between Marketing and Content and Marketing and Development (but not between Content and Development). Although he was not formally involved in the strategic decision-making process in Esperanto, he attended 17 of the 24 Esperanto management team meetings that occurred during the period studied. All Esperanto employees were interviewed by one of the other researchers together with a research assistant. The researcher employed by Marketing/Esperanto was not involved in these interviews to emphasize the neutrality of the procedure. Given the frankness of the answers we received, we do not believe that social desirability played a large role in the interviews. Also, Esperanto was keen to get an objective overview of its strategic decision-making processes and thus had less incentive to mask the reality of it. Additionally, we had access to meeting minutes, company memos, and internal email correspondence, which allowed for a crosscheck of the interview data. It also gave us insight into the actual process that preceded the decision, because we could observe decision makers arguing back and forth over email. Field notes of phone conversations and discussions during management team meetings further triangulated this data.

## The Four Strategic Decisions

### The founding of Esperanto

Since the beginning of 1999, members of Marketing, Content, and Development had a seat in the independent committee, which was involved in stimulating the use of a standard communication language in the industry. Because all members had their own companies, which have major stakes in a broad use of a communication standard in the industry, they suggested the idea of founding a joint venture. It had the same goal as the independent committee, but would stimulate the acceptance of the standard from a commercial point of view. For all parties involved, it was a logical decision given the aims of the committee that the joint venture emerged from and their goal of profiting from the standardization.

### Being dependent on Library E or being independent

In the beginning of 2001, Content suggested a meeting to decide whether Esperanto would only sell applications based on Library E, or would be an independent player and offer whatever library the industry asked for. This is the strategic issue that prompted the discussion quoted in the introduction. After a long discussion, consensus was reached that Esperanto would be independent. We argue that Content and Development had strong emotional attachment to this issue, as both had been working on Library E for many years. For them, it became part of their personal identity. Marketing said in an interview: "Being independent meant that Development and Content managers needed to abandon their baby they had been working on for years.

**Table 19.2**   Four strategic decisions and typical quotes

| Decision | Emotionally attached | | |
| | Marketing | Development | Content |
|---|---|---|---|
| 1   Foundation of Esperanto | No | No | No |
| 2   Independency | No | Yes | Yes |
| 3   Free delivery of library | No | No | No |
| 4   Change of mode of cooperation | Yes | Yes | Yes |

In fact, they wouldn't abandon their baby, but simply adopt a new one." Marketing was a relative newcomer to the field and experienced no such emotional attachment, for them it was more or less one of the projects in their portfolio.

### Free delivery of library or billable content

A meeting at the headquarters of Marketing was scheduled in March 2002, during which it was discussed whether or not to charge for the library itself (regardless of which library) that had been freely available until then. Within an hour it was decided that the libraries should be delivered for free to the customer based on the argument that the libraries are public domain and that Esperanto should make money on the implementation. As the decision centered not around a specific library, the link to the personal identities of Content and Development was absent and they were not likely to be very emotionally attached to this issue.

### Change of mode of cooperation

Revenue was lacking during 2001 and the first half of 2002. In June 2002, a meeting about operational issues was held at the headquarters of Marketing. At the beginning, Content introduced a memo stating that Marketing, after several meetings promising to meet its commitments, still did nothing about acquisition. A recess was held and after drinking some coffee it was suggested to either quit or change the mode of cooperation into a much looser structure with more independence for each of the constituting companies in the joint venture. The latter was eventually decided on. As Esperanto through its (short) history had become an important part of each of the decision-maker's personal identities, all three parties were likely to be emotionally attached to the issue of what effectively amounted to the dissolution of Esperanto. See Tables 19.2 and 19.3 for descriptions and typical quotes of the four decisions and the associated emotional attachment.

## Emotional Attachment and the Personal Perspective

The traditional view of strategic decision-making processes is based on "a common model of rational action" (Eisenhardt and Zbaracki, 1992). It is focused on judgmental

**Table 19.3** Typical quotes

| | Decision | Conflict | Durance of process | Start date | End date | Remarkable quote |
|---|---|---|---|---|---|---|
| 1 | Foundation of Esperanto | No | 12 weeks | August 1, 2000 | October 31, 2000 | "Together we can convince the market to use standard X" |
| 2 | Independency | Yes | 1 month | January 7, 2001 | February 7, 2001 | "The market is simply too stupid to understand that standard X is the richest" |
| 3 | Free delivery of library | No | 2 weeks | March 6, 2001 | March 20, 2001 | "A standard can never become a standard if it isn't free" |
| 4 | Change of mode of cooperation | Yes | 1 day | June 20, 2002 | June 20, 2002 | "Even worse: I worked my butt off for zip!" |

differences about how best to achieve common objectives – the cognitive conflict (Amason, 1996). The members involved in a strategic decision process have to decide to take an organizational perspective without any personal interests, and using factual information as much as possible. The cases in this research indicate a different view. When one or more decision-makers were emotionally involved, they used arguments based on their own goals and values instead of arguments based on what might be the best for the organization. Deciding on factual information only happened when nobody was emotionally attached to a decision. This leads to:

> **Proposition 1:** Decision makers who are emotionally attached to an issue will frame the decision from a personal perspective, not from an organizational perspective.

The foundation of Esperanto was a fully joint decision of the three participants. At the moment they decided on Esperanto no emotional attachment was involved. They were willing to cooperate to achieve the proposed goals for each of the companies.

The emotional involvement with the standardization decision resulted in undermining the strategic independency decision, because customers never see another standard other than the Development standard (Library E). In interviews Content and Development said: "We just act like being independent, but always push our customers into our standard." This implies that the decision is made out of a personal perspective of the both parties. Although they agreed with the independence, so Marketing could sell the concept to customers easier, they were convinced about their "best" Library E and on Library E based tools.

The third decision about providing the library for free was fairly straightforward, because the circumstances pushed the decision in that direction: one of the market leaders and potential global users would only contribute when providing it for free.

Even the parties, who had to invest and work on a library that would be provided for free, did not influence the decision in a disturbing way. They took an organizational perspective and saw this was the only way a "standard" could become a success:

> *Marketing*: A standard can never become a standard if it isn't free.

In the case about changing the mode of cooperation, personal interests were the basis of the conflict. In the decision-making process the parties were throwing a lot of accusations towards each other like:

> Content: Only after making lots of noise you began in action to save Esperanto, my input in the potential customer approach is ignored.

Personal perspective taking and personal attacks abounded.

## Principled or Logical Arguments in Decision Making

Arguments based on facts are emphasized when taking strategic decisions (Welcomer, Gioia, and Kilduff, 2000; Sillince, 2000) This implies that only logical arguments are used during conflicts, which can be considered the opposite of principled arguments. Principled arguments are arguments based on personal opinions and values that are more or less statements that cannot be argued upon. Therefore, people who are emotionally attached to a certain issue are more likely to use principled arguments instead of logical arguments and discuss in terms of goals and values instead of specific measures, actions, and plans. The results of this research support this proposition. Principled arguments were used very often when one of the decision makers was emotionally attached to a decision.

In formal terms:

> Proposition 2: When persuading others, decision makers who are emotionally attached to an issue, will use more principled arguments and fewer logical arguments than decision makers who are not emotionally attached to the issue.

When looking at the foundation decision, no conflicts emerged during the decision-making process. Arguments for founding Esperanto were very well gathered and presented in the meeting. Company goals were set and in October 2000, Esperanto was founded. The three parties decided to gain a modest turnover of €20,000 in the first year, to see if the cooperation was profitable. When deciding whether to be independent or to focus on Library E, many defendable arguments were used in favor of independence by Marketing.

> *Marketing*: A small player like Esperanto doesn't have the power to force the market to use Library E, so we have to focus on market pull instead of technology push with both libraries.
> *Development*: The market is too stupid to be able to decide which standard is the best.

The decision process about delivering the library for free progressed smoothly. In order to become a standard it must be offered for free, otherwise the market will not adopt it. No conflicts emerged during the decision-making process and rational arguments were being used.

> *Development*: I think we better can deliver the Library for free and make money on the implementations and the applications. We cannot let our customers pay for the library because actually it is public domain.

When focusing on this analysis, it can be concluded that the non-emotional attachment of a decision maker to an issue leads to a more constructive decision-making process. Arguments are logical and can be substantiated or used to attack other arguments. However, when deciding on the dependency or change of form of cooperation, it was found that decision makers who were emotionally attached to an issue used principled arguments in persuading the other parties.

## Emotional Attachment and Conflict

Prior research has shown that when a conflict is affective, it tends to be emotional and focused on personal incompatibilities or dispute (Amason, 1996). Affective conflicts are a result of cognitive disagreements and are perceived as personal criticism. When decision makers feel emotionally attached to a particular decision, they are more likely to perceive every sign of criticism, whether it is cognitive or affective criticism, as being personal. This implies that when the decision maker is emotionally attached the chance that an affective conflict occurs increases. The data collected during this research points in this direction. Especially in the last few months of the research, many affective conflicts seemed to arise out of the blue, which sometimes were not related to the decision itself. The proposition is formulated as follows:

> **Proposition 3:** If one of the decision makers is emotionally attached to an issue, the more likely an affective conflict will emerge during the decision-making process.

During the second decision, affective conflicts emerged from the start of the meeting. While starting on a cognitive basis, conflicts soon became out of hand.

> *Marketing*: In order to stimulate the market into using a standard, we must be independent. By doing so, the market simply cannot ignore us when doing a standardization project. Besides, when the dominant design emerges, we will always be on the right side.
> *Development*: How can I be independent? Library C is not worth being a standard. Even Little Red Riding Hood is more interesting than Library C! Do you really think I can be independent? Are you really that ignorant?

Even though every party agreed that Library E was the richest, they finally agreed that they would be independent. But if customers ask which library Esperanto preferred, they would advise on Library E.

This conflict and especially the outcome of the decision would be the basis of many affective conflicts in the future. When Marketing engaged in a project, using Library C, Development and Content managers blamed Marketing for being independent and undermining Esperanto's base of existence. When Marketing replied: "How can you blame me for being independent? We agreed on being independent." Content and Development replied in an email with the following principled argument: "But Marketing, the whole world knows we are not independent, don't argue on this subject again." Marketing countered: "On our website the customer can read: 'Esperanto is an independent platform for …'", to which Content and Development effectively ended the discussion with "I have never understood why we said that."

In the third decision, consensus was achieved very soon. A standard cannot be a standard when it is not offered for free, however the implementation of the decision shows another result. When Marketing was in an acquisition process, the customer said it wanted Library E in the application. The total sum was no more than €10,000. However, Content replied:

> *Content*: Very well, can you add €200,000? I have been working on Library E for two years, but didn't get paid for it. If they want it, they can have it for €200,000.
> *Marketing* (by phone): I cannot ask that. Library E is free, so we will definitely lose this project if I do that. Besides, we agreed that we would offer every library for free. And apart from this, nobody gave you the assignment to continue working on the maintenance of Library E. How can you ask such an amount for work, the customer didn't give you an assignment for?
> *Content*: Do you think I did all this work for nothing? Maybe you spent about eight hours a week on Esperanto doing nothing, but I did more.

Or consider the following exchange of blame between Development and Marketing:

> *Development*: You (Marketing) are responsible for sales but you didn't do squat!
> *Marketing*: You are right we didn't do enough, but you are not supporting me. You talk to potential customers without informing me, and you blame me when we use Library C for our own projects while we decided to be library independent.

The results support the proposition that emotional attachment increases affective conflicts. When decision-makers were emotionally attached to an issue, the results show that out of two of the four decisions affective conflicts emerged from emotional attachment. In addition, it can be seen that commitment to decisions resulted in a lack of common supported direction for action. Regarding the decision to be independent, commitment to the decision was never achieved and the decision became the target of cynicism and counter-effort (Guth and MacMillan, 1986).

## Discussion

In the previous section, we attempted to substantiate the propositions we derived from the case data. In this section, we will consider some alternative interpretations of our data and discuss some factors that may limit the ability to generalize in our conclusions. An issue that is not immediately obvious from the data, but did come up in various comments on a number of occasions, is the relatively low commitment of Marketing to Esperanto. Marketing does not depend on Esperanto for its revenue and in fact, Marketing's largest external investor is only supportive of Marketing's involvement in Esperanto as long as it does not interfere with Marketing's core activities. Another contributing factor was that although Marketing initially insisted on writing a business plan, Development and Content voted against this proposal because they felt it was unnecessary given their extensive industry experience. This led to less commitment of Marketing to the goals that were set: "We don't depend on the turnover that Esperanto will generate and because no rigid goals were set on paper, we simply didn't put it on our agenda as a hard target." Development and Content in particular felt this as a lack of commitment. In the interview, Content said that he had set up a test case for Marketing's commitment: although Marketing was responsible for launching updates on the online web-browser, Marketing never published the new updates delivered by Content. In addition, the "find function" was not built into the browser, even though all parties agreed that it was necessary. The Marketing employee who had to execute the browser updates had no time, because he was busy with other (non-Esperanto) projects, i.e. having other priorities than Esperanto. For Content, this case showed the attitude of Marketing towards Esperanto. In the end, Marketing did admit to its lack of commitment from the beginning. However, although the commitment imbalance is what triggered the conflicts in the decision to change the mode of cooperation and it played a role in the independence decision as well, we believe that it is not the root cause. We feel that the imbalance in commitment to Esperanto was caused by Marketing's low emotional attachment to Esperanto's product, as it was never a part of its core activities. Content and Development were much more emotionally attached to Library E, since they had been developing it for the last few years, and were therefore much more committed to persist in developing it further and seeing it implemented in industry. This also suggests that emotional attachment may not necessarily be an entirely bad thing. It could be that a certain amount of emotional attachment (just like a certain amount of overconfidence, e.g. Baron (1998)) is necessary to persist in the face of the adversity that any young firm will encounter (similar to the link made between emotional attachment and escalation of commitment by Keil (1995)). The question of what this optimal amount of emotional attachment could be, is left for future research.

Another alternative explanation for our results may be that it is simply due to the specific personalities involved. Perhaps the personalities of the decision makers were such that they were bound to clash at some point, regardless of the decision issue and therefore our results do not generalize to cover strategic decision-making situations in other organizations. As we did not administer any personality tests, we cannot refute this claim. However, this also means that the counterclaim that the personalities involved were indeed representative for other strategic decision-making situations cannot be refuted either. A more serious limitation to the ability to generalize is the fact that Esperanto is an extremely small organization without central headquarters, and composed of three separate organizations. The fact that three separate organizations were involved in Esperanto meant that, despite the agreed-upon goals, there was a distinct possibility that the interests of the member organizations might be put before Esperanto's interests, which is more difficult to do in a regular organization. Not having a central headquarters and thus only having infrequent face-to-face meetings (most communication within Esperanto occurred via email and phone) meant that conflict resolution was more difficult and the potential for covert action and political behavior increased. This could lead to a decrease in decision-making performance (Eisenhardt and Bourgeois, 1989), independently of emotional attachment playing a role.

## Conclusions and Implications

Because of their high involvement in the organization, top management may experience intense emotions regarding their organization. Eisenhardt suggested that emotions are central to the strategic decision-making process (Eisenhardt, 1989; Eisenhardt and Bourgeois, 1989), but so far this has not been investigated empirically. In this study, we heed this call and empirically investigate how this emotional attachment affects the strategic decision-making process. Through a detailed case study of several strategic decisions in a new venture, we show that decision makers that are emotionally attached to a particular issue frame the problem in a different way than non-emotionally attached decision-makers. Emotionally attached decision-makers try to convince the others in a different style and use different types of arguments. Emotional attachment of one of the decision-makers also gives rise to more affective conflict; it reduces the quality of the decision process and can yield less commitment to the decision, which in turn could make implementation more difficult.

These findings have implications for most theories of strategic decision-making processes. Most theories emphasize rational aspects or political aspects (Eisenhardt and Zbaracki, 1992), but this study shows that emotional aspects have to be taken into account as well. However, we do not want to propose an emotional theory of strategic decision making as we feel that would be a very limited view indeed. Instead, we would like to call for broader, more encompassing theories that take into account all the aspects mentioned here. One issue in particular that warrants further investigation is the establishment of conditions under which rational, political, emotional, or other aspects dominate the process. In closing, we will briefly discuss how we think managers could deal with emotional attachment and perhaps even profit from it. First managers have to realize that decision-makers are humans who have emotions. Ignoring the problem will not make it go away: it must be dealt with. We think the worst you can do is attack emotionally attached decision-makers on their motives or principled arguments. While a full analysis of conflict-handling techniques is beyond the scope of this chapter, data from the cases suggest that Marketing's approach, i.e. attempting to defuse the arguments through logical arguments, may have actually backfired. By arguing this way you cannot expect any flexibility from the emotional attached decision-maker as admitting to the logical arguments would mean a severe loss of face because he would have to admit to overseeing (often simple) logic. Therefore, his point of view may become more rigid than ever before. Emotionally attached decision-makers in most cases see only one solution to comply to their emotional attachment while in practice more often other alternatives can be generated. Therefore managers have to understand the grounds for these emotions and find a solution for these grounds so emotions can become dissociated from the particular issue on which they are focused in the decision-making process. However, emotions can also be used in a positive way in implementing a decision. For instance in the case of independency a possible solution was to assign Library E and acquisition to Content and Development so they could proceed with the work they have been doing for years and Marketing could have focused on Library C and marketing. So to end on an encouraging note, emotions are not necessarily negative for the decision-making process. When acknowledging that they exist, we can employ the emotionally attached decision-makers in the field they are attached to and they will be intrinsically motivated to work harder to achieve their goals, which eventually will help the manager to achieve the organizations goals. After all, emotions are one of the most powerful drivers of human behavior in everyday life. Why would we expect it to be any different in organizational life?

## Acknowledgments

We would like to thank Bas Overbeek for assistance with data collection and an anonymous reviewer as well as participants at the SMS Mini-conference on Innovating Strategy Processes for their helpful feedback on earlier versions of this chapter.

## Notes

1. Some authors investigate the role of affect (which incorporates both moods and emotions, e.g. Isen and Baron, 1991), but we refer to emotions only.

## References

Abelson, R.P. 1988. Conviction. *American Psychologist*, **43**(4): 267–75.
Amason, A.C. 1996. Distinguishing the effects of functional and dysfunctional conflict on strategic decision making: Resolving a paradox for top management teams. *Academy of Management Journal*, **39**(1): 123–48.
Baron, R.A. 1998. Cognitive mechanisms in entrepreneurship: Why and when entrepreneurs think differently than other people. *Journal of Business Venturing*, **13**(4): 275–94.
Bowlby, J. 1969. *Attachment and Loss (Volume 1): Attachment*. London: Hogarth.
Burgelman, R.A. 1994. Fading memories – A process theory of strategic business exit in dynamic environments. *Administrative Science Quarterly*, **39**(1): 24–56.
Collis, D.J. 1991. A resource-based analysis of global competition – The case of the bearings industry. *Strategic Management Journal*, **12**: 49–68.
Dean, J.W. and Sharfman, M.P. 1996. Does decision process matter? A study of strategic decision-making effectiveness. *Academy of Management Journal*, **39**(2): 368–96.
Dooley, R.S., Fryxell, G.E., and Judge, W.Q. 2000. Belaboring the not so obvious: Consensus, commitment, and strategy implementation speed and success. *Journal of Management*, **26**(6): 1237–57.
Eisenhardt, K.M. 1989. Making fast strategic decisions in high-velocity environments. *Academy of Management Journal*, **32**(3): 543–76.

Eisenhardt, K.M. and Bourgeois, L.J. 1989. Politics of strategic decision-making in high-velocity environments – Toward a midrange theory. *Academy of Management Journal*, **31**(4): 737–70.

Eisenhardt, K.M. and Zbaracki, M.J. 1992. Strategic decision making. *Strategic Management Journal*, **13**: 17–37.

Fineman, S. (ed.). 1993. *Emotions in Organizations*. London: Sage.

Forgas, J.P. 1995. Mood and judgment – The affect infusion model (Aim). *Psychological Bulletin*, **117**(1): 39–66.

Forgas, J.P. and George, J.M. 2001. Affective influences on judgments and behavior in organizations: An information-processing perspective. *Organizational Behavior and Human Decision Processes*, **86**(1): 3–34.

Fredrickson, J.W. and Mitchell, T.R. 1984. Strategic decision processes: Comprehensiveness and performance in an industry with an unstable environment. *Academy of Management Journal*, **27**(2): 399–423.

Guth, W.D. and MacMillan, I.C. 1986. Strategy implementation versus middle management self-interest. *Strategic Management Journal*, **7**(4): 313–27.

Hochschild, A.R. 1983. *The Managed Heart: The Commercialization of Human Feeling*. Berkeley, CA: University of California Press.

Huy, Q.N. 2002. Emotional balancing of organizational continuity and radical change: The contribution of middle managers. *Administrative Science Quarterly*, **47**(1): 31–69.

Isen, A.M. and Baron, R.A. 1991. Positive affect as a factor in organizational behavior. *Research in Organizational Behavior*, **13**: 1–53.

Jehn, K.A. 1997. Qualitative analysis of conflict types and dimensions in organizational groups. *Administrative Science Quarterly*, **42**(3): 530–57.

Keil, M. 1995. Pulling the plug: Software project management and the problem of project escalation. *MIS Quarterly*, **19**(4): 421–47.

Kim, W.C. and Mauborgne, R.A. 1993. Procedural justice, attitudes, and subsidiary top management compliance with multinationals corporate strategic decisions. *Academy of Management Journal*, **36**(3): 502–26.

Kisfalvi, V. and Pitcher, P. 2003. Doing what feels right – The influence of CEO character and emotions on top management team dynamics. *Journal of Management Inquiry*, **12**(1): 42–66.

Knight, D., Pearce, C.L., Smith, K.G., Olian, J.D., Sims, H.P., Smith, K.A., and Flood, P. 1999. Top management team diversity, group process, and strategic consensus. *Strategic Management Journal*, **20**(5): 445–65.

Marris, P. 1986. *Loss and Change*. London: Routledge.

Schweiger, D.M., Sandberg, W.R., and Rechner, P.L. 1989. Experiential effects of dialectical inquiry, devils advocacy, and consensus approaches to strategic decision making. *Academy of Management Journal*, **32**(4): 745–72.

Sillince, J.A.A. 2000. Rhetorical power, accountability and conflict in committees: An argumentation approach. *Journal of Management Studies*, **37**(8): 1125–56.

Simons, T.L. and Peterson, R.S. 2000. Task conflict and relationship conflict in top management teams: The pivotal role of intragroup trust. *Journal of Applied Psychology*, **85**(1): 102–11.

Vince, R. and Broussine, M. 1996. Paradox, defense and attachment: Accessing and working with emotions and relations underlying organizational change. *Organization Studies*, **17**(1): 1–21.

Welcomer, S.A., Gioia, D.A., and Kilduff, M. 2000. Resisting the discourse of modernity: Rationality versus emotion in hazardous waste siting. *Human Relations*, **53**(9): 1175–205.

Yin, R.K. 1984. *Case Study Research: Design and Methods*. Beverly Hills, CA: Sage.

# CHAPTER TWENTY

# The Search Process and Dimensions of Long-Term Growth[1]

Gaurab Bhardwaj, John C. Camillus, David A. Hounshell

## Search for Long-Term Growth

Between 1902 and 1921, the DuPont Company either considered entering or entered many new businesses in its quest for long-term growth (Table 20.1). As revenues tripled from $27.7 million in 1905 to $84.6 million in 1925, and net income quintupled from $5.1 million in 1905 to $24.9 million in 1925, the company transformed itself from a major explosives manufacturer to a dominant chemicals company, setting the foundations for decades of continued growth. The bewildering array of choices considered or made (Table 20.1) was central to DuPont's growth and transformation. But how was this exploration, or search, for new businesses done? The phenomenon is not unique to the company and the era. Over long periods, most companies are likely to consider an assortment of new businesses and then enter some in their bid for long-term growth (Chesbrough, 2002; Dyer and Gross, 2001; Penrose, 1995; Steinbock, 2001).

Understanding the nature of the search process for avenues of long-term growth is important for both managers and researchers. The process is complex because a series of choices must be considered and made, the outcomes of which emerge gradually over many years. And managers must make such choices over long periods in circumstances characterized by high uncertainty and causal ambiguity. In such settings, decision possibilities and their consequences are not obvious and given. They must be searched, that is, created and discovered over time from innumerable possibilities that are mostly unknown (Simon, 1976). Because the many possible search paths can lead to varying outcomes, the search process specifics have a fundamental impact on growth eventually attained (Burgelman, 2002; Holbrook *et al.*, 2000; Hounshell and Smith, 1988; Noda and Bower, 1996). Thus, the search process is fundamental to seeking long-term growth. Although the literature offers various suggestions on how such searches *should* be conducted (e.g., Dixit and Pindyck, 1994), comparatively little is known about how they are *actually* conducted (e.g., Garud and Van de Ven,

**Table 20.1** Some businesses DuPont considered entering or did enter, 1902–21

| | | |
|---|---|---|
| Ammonia | Explosives plant construction | Pigments |
| Artificial leather | Fertilizers | Potassium |
| Artificial silk | Fireworks | Printing ink |
| Bags | Food flavorings and preservatives | Pulp |
| Banking | Fulminate of mercury | Pyrites |
| Blasting caps | Fusel oil | Quicksilver mining |
| Boat bottom paint | Fuses | Railroads in Chile |
| Camphor | Glycerin | Refining refuse salt |
| Cartons | Growing castor beans | Rifles |
| Cartridges | Inorganic chemicals | Rubber and synthetic rubber |
| Cattle feed | International markets | Saccharin |
| Celluloid | Investments | Saltpeter |
| Cement | Loaded ammunitions | Sawmill |
| Chlorine | Magazine publishing | Selling explosives machinery |
| Cinematographic films | Motor cars | Soap |
| Copper shells | Motor fuels | Sulfur |
| Copper wire | Muriate of potash | Tetraethyl lead |
| Cotton cloth | Nitrate of potash | Timber |
| Cotton hose lining | Nitrate of soda | Time fuses for shrapnel |
| Cotton purification | Nitrogen fixation | Tin boxes |
| Cottonseed hull fiber | Oilcloth | Toluene |
| Diphenylamine | Paints | Varnishes |
| Drugs | Paper | Vegetable oils and fats |
| Dyes and intermediates | Paraffin from waste paper | Water distillation |
| Electric air drills | Perfumes | Waterpower |
| Electric fuses | Photographic chemicals | Waterproofed material |
| Enameling fuse wire | Photographic films | |
| Ethyl alcohol | Picric acid | |

1992). Knowing the latter, however, is a necessary prior step in improving decision making for long-term growth and competitiveness. Hence, this chapter addresses the question: *What is the search process of decision makers in pursuit of their firm's long-term growth?*

The literature on search processes has grown in recent years but the most widely used concept is still that of local search. In local search, the alternatives considered are marginally different from current choice, and decision makers settle for a satisfactory rather than an optimal solution (Simon, 1976). If needed, aspirations are lowered until a local alternative becomes satisfactory (Cyert and March, 1963). Another treatment of search as random has proved useful for modeling purposes (Nelson and Winter, 1982), but cannot explain actual decision-making processes (Burgelman, 2002; Lovas and Ghoshal, 2000). Neither conceptualization of search is about the process of discovering and creating decision possibilities over long periods. Thus, both fall short in explaining the actual long-term growth possibilities DuPont considered in its search (Table 20.1). Recently, new conceptualizations of search have emerged from sophisticated analysis of links among patents (e.g., Fleming, 2001; Katila and Ahuja, 2002; Rosenkopf and Nerkar, 2001). Although capturing an important aspect of innovation – new scientific knowledge that was patentable – patents cannot capture all search considerations for long-term growth, especially business possibilities that were considered and not pursued, and scientific outcomes that were not patented. Moreover, because different kinds of decision-making settings or contexts are associated with different kinds of decision-making processes (Papadakis, Lioukas, and Chambers, 1998), search process models from different settings cannot be automatically presumed to explain how decision makers actually pursue a search for a firm's long-term growth. Instead comprehensive field data are required to identify and develop the actual search process.

## Research Methods

To develop search process-based explanations of long-term growth, we adopted the case research method, which is well suited for investigating processes and under-researched complex phenomena (Eisenhardt, 1989; Pettigrew, 1992). The method requires using rich case data to develop process theory, and not testing hypotheses based on a limited literature. Drawing on an extensive archival collection of the DuPont Company's internal documents, we wrote a comprehensive case history on search considerations and choices for long-term growth at DuPont from 1902 to 1921. We then generalized from a set of events in the case study to develop process explanations of search for long-term growth (Garud and Van de Ven, 1992).

The modern DuPont Company traces its origins to February 26, 1902 when an earlier family partnership was dissolved and the new entity incorporated (Chandler, 1962; Hounshell and Smith, 1988). An executive committee, comprising more than a dozen senior managers, a few of whom belonged to the du Pont family, was formed to lead the company. At the first meeting of the committee in February 1903, DuPont was only in the explosives business, as it had been for 100 years. In choosing 1902 as the starting point of the period under study, there is little risk of left-censoring data. Subsequent years saw a great deal of ferment and exploration as DuPont managers strived for long-term growth through scientific research and business diversification. To support this effort, by 1903, they had created the Experimental Station to pursue long-term scientific research, and the Development Department to conduct planning, technology screening, firm acquisition, and market studies. In the 20 years following incorporation, DuPont considered entering or did enter numerous new businesses and grew into a large chemicals company. During this time, the company endured all phases of the economic cycle and two external shocks – an antitrust lawsuit and the First World War. A vast collection of company documents, written for internal use and running into hundreds of linear feet of stacks, reveals the nature of decision making during the period of study. The documents we used were those dealing with the works of the Executive Committee, Experimental Station, and Development Department. They contained details on decision making from 1902 to 1921 by senior and middle managers, research managers, scientists, and others. The collection included memos, summaries of Executive Committee meetings, letters, and an extensive collection of detailed reports on the work conducted by the Development Department and Experimental Station, which were used in the Executive Committee's deliberations. The documents described conditions and considerations as they unfolded and often contained information on expectations regarding the future. Because they were written for internal use, they were a valid source of information on actual decision making, as well as on the perspectives of decision makers. In addition, multiple documents over time from the Executive Committee, Development Department, and the Experimental Station contained information on the same deliberation, providing triangulation. In collecting and analyzing data, we considered all deliberations and did not limit ourselves solely to the business-entry choices made. We included all possibilities considered; some that were later not pursued and those that were. In writing the case, to capture actual decision making, we took the perspective of decision makers based on facts and reasons spelled out in the documents as deliberations proceeded.[2] Drawing on this field study, we developed the "moving, anchored search" (MAS) process that depicted the search for long-term growth. The MAS process was also robust in explaining search in field studies of invention and entrepreneurship because all three phenomena involved distant returns – the temporal horizon was distant, and the likelihood that any particular outcome would emerge exactly as desired was also remote (Bhardwaj, 2000).

## Moving, Anchored Search Process for Long-Term Growth

Consistent with the theme of this book, the MAS process deals with innovation for growth and is itself a novel contribution to the literature and practice of strategy. MAS is located conceptually in between the polar extremes of local and global searches, which are mutually exclusive but not completely exhaustive concepts. MAS deals with both the "how" and the "where" of search, thereby melding process and content. It reveals that to deal with high uncertainty and ambiguity, decision makers begin by first selecting a broad domain for their search (Figure 20.1; Table 20.2). Then, within it they choose a search anchor. Neither choice is necessarily obvious; each precludes others that could have been made. Taking the domain as given, subsequent search is tethered to the chosen anchor (Figure 20.1). Multiple anchors may also be chosen (Table 20.3). Over time, an anchor can shift so that subsequent tethered search is far removed from earlier considerations. New search paths are thus created. Two kinds of search movements are evident: those around an anchor, and shifts of the anchors – hence, a "moving, anchored search". The MAS process encompasses routine work, imaginative leaps, serendipity, external shocks, new information, persistence, success, and failure. It includes not only the business entry choices made, but also those possibilities that were considered and discarded.

### Selecting search domains

Pursuing long-term growth often requires searching grounds that are untrodden for a company. The universe of specific possibilities can be vast, with some possibilities vaguely understood and others yet to be discovered. Owing to bounded rationality, decision makers define a subset in the universe of possibilities – a search domain – within which to discover and create specific possibilities. The domain choice, which is not necessarily obvious or a given for decision makers, draws a perimeter around the possibilities for subsequent consideration, because much of the search is yet to be

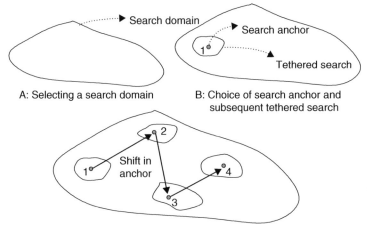

A: Selecting a search domain

B: Choice of search anchor and subsequent tethered search

C: Shifts in search anchors and further tethered search

**Figure 20.1**    The moving, anchored search (MAS) process

conducted. During the search, domains change infrequently, if at all. If, however, search results or other indicators strongly suggest that search is being conducted in the wrong space, or if interests and strategic context change, a domain may be abandoned. Between 1902 and 1921, in their quest for long-term growth, DuPont managers established nine new search domains, after having operated solely in the explosives domain for 100 years (Table 20.2). It should be noted that a search domain is not the same as a product or a market but is a broader concept. Domains typically precede the conception and creation of product-markets, as we see today in biotechnology and nanotechnology. Products and markets are narrower than search domains and are eventually a part of the latter.

Past research has mainly shown that search and risk taking increase with recent bad performance and dampen with recent good performance (e.g., Cyert and March, 1963), although a few have instead argued for the affects of expectations on search and risk taking (e.g., Bromiley, 1991). Although the nitrocellulose domain did follow bad performance, documents did not reveal a causal link. The domain was really established in response to the antitrust lawsuit and other actions taken by the government (Table 20.2). Similarly, DuPont's poor performances of 1913 and early 1914 and 1920–1 did not lead to new domains. The remaining domains followed good performance, but their creations were similarly not caused by the good performance, except partly in the case of motor cars. The considerations described in the documents show that domain choices were not due to recent good or bad performance, but due to *expectations of significant and lasting deviations in future performance.* DuPont did respond to recent bad performance, but by modifying business strategy and improving operational efficiency, not by establishing new search domains. Perhaps short-term decision making is related to recent performance as noted in the literature. But this study provides the complementary result that new domains are due to expectations of significant and lasting deviations, deleterious or beneficial, in future performance.

**Table 20.2**  Reasons for domain choices at DuPont, 1902–21

| Search domain | Reasons for domain choice |
|---|---|
| Explosives (1802–beyond 1921) | Profitable market opportunity discovered by founder in 1802 for better quality black powder; founder's research expertise in explosives |
| Biomanufacturing (1903–16) | Anticipated shortage of glycerin, an important explosives ingredient, available only as a byproduct of tallow candle manufacture, laundry soap production, and slaughterhouse waste. Novel synthetic production method needed. Wine and beer distillation known to yield minute amounts of glycerin as by-product. Use of fundamental research on bacteriological fermentation to raise yield of glycerin |
| Nitrogenous compounds (1904–beyond 1921) | Anticipated shortage of nitrate of soda used to make nitric acid for explosives manufacture; Chilean mines were sole global source; inventing an industrial nitrogen-fixation method would yield from the atmosphere an inexhaustible supply of nitrogen that could be used to make nitric acid and other nitrogenous compounds |
| Nitrocellulose (1908–beyond 1921) | U.S. government filed antitrust lawsuit in 1907. In 1908, the government canceled large orders of smokeless powder from DuPont, started construction of its own plants, and Congress passed a bill preventing Navy's explosive purchases from a monopoly. Utilize idle plant capacity by finding new uses for nitrocellulose, which was manufactured as an intermediate step in the production of smokeless powder |
| Synthetic organic chemicals (1915–beyond 1921) | Imports of organic chemicals from Germany ceased during First World War; severe shortages, sky-high prices; some organic chemicals used in explosives manufacture also used in other industries; potential for public and political backlash. Find uses for anticipated massive idle plant capacity after war; utilization of "organization"; avert post-war layoffs; new businesses that would pave entry into others later |
| Inorganic chemicals (1916–18) | Complement ongoing work on photographic and pharmaceutical organic chemicals, and paints and varnishes |
| Vegetable oils (1916–18) | Utilize anticipated post-war excess capacity; many uses of vegetable oils in other industries – "nucleus" industry as gateway to others later; "non-organized" in manufacturing and commercial terms, but high growth and profit potential |
| Varnishes and paints (1916–beyond 1921) | Utilize post-war excess capacity; skills and equipment required are simple in "general" paints and varnishes; processes, equipment, and raw materials similar to those of pyroxylin solutions already being produced; market complement to pyroxylin solutions |
| Paper (1916–19) | Utilize cotton purification plant used in explosives manufacture; war shortages of cotton rags in paper trade; DuPont could produce purified cotton fiber or cotton pulp that paper manufacturers could use as substitute for cotton rags |
| Motor cars (1917–beyond 1921) | Need to invest large war profits. DuPont's treasurer and Pierre S. DuPont, who had both been personally investing in GM, were instrumental in DuPont's buying shares in GM and Chevrolet. Young auto industry profitable and promised strong growth. DuPont artificial leather, paints and varnishes, celluloid plastic, and rubber-coated fabrics could be sold to GM. DuPont's large engineering department could construct auto plants for GM and others in the growing industry to avert post-war layoffs |

**Table 20.3**  DuPont's search domains, anchors, and diversification choices, 1902–21

| Search domains | Search anchors | Diversification choices |
|---|---|---|
| Explosives (1802–beyond 1921) | 1. Consolidation (1902) 2. Securing supplies (1903) 3. Related products (1903) 4. Foreign markets (1905) | *Enter*: fuses, blasting caps, fulminate of mercury, alcohol from sawdust, copper shells, timberlands, sawmill, Chilean nitrate of soda properties, cartridges, explosives in Canada, picric acid *Exit*: pulp kegs, shell loading, torpedoes *Not enter*: fireworks, rifles, cotton from seed hulls, sulfur, selling supplies and equipment to others, plant construction and explosives in foreign countries, pyrites, quicksilver, railroads in Chile |
| Biomanufacturing (1903–16) | 1. Bacteriological fermentation (1903) | *Enter*: no entry |
| Nitrogenous compounds (1904–beyond 1921) | 1. Nitrogen fixation (1904) 2. Other methods (1908) 3. Fertilizers (1910) | *Enter*: ammonia (1925) *Not enter*: fertilizers, waterpower |
| Nitrocellulose (1908–beyond 1921) | 1. Artificial fibers (1908) 2. Celluloid (1909) 3. Coating materials (1909) | *Enter*: artificial silk, artificial leather, rubber- coated fabrics, celluloid, camphor, cinematographic films (1924) *Not enter*: photographic film, boat bottom paint |
| Synthetic organic chemicals (1915–beyond 1921) | 1. Dyes and intermediates (1915) 2. Drugs (1915) 3. Rubber chemicals (1915) 4. Food preservatives (1916) 5. Perfumes and flavorings (1916) 6. Photographic chemicals (1916) | *Enter*: dyes and intermediates *Not enter*: drugs, rubber chemicals, food preservatives, perfumes and flavorings, photographic chemicals |
| Inorganic chemicals (1916–18) | 1. Water-soluble inorganic chemicals (1916) 2. Pigments (1916) | *Enter*: pigments *Not enter*: water-soluble inorganic chemicals, printing ink |
| Vegetable oils (1916–18) | 1. Oils and fats (1916) 2. Downstream businesses (1916) | *Not enter*: oils and fats, oilcloth, soap |
| Varnishes and paints (1916–beyond 1921) | 1. "General" varnishes and paints (1916) 2. "Mixed" varnishes and paints (1916) | *Enter*: general varnishes and paints *Not enter*: mixed varnishes and paints |
| Paper (1916–1919) | 1. Purified cotton pulp and fiber (1916) | *Not enter*: paper, cotton cloth, supply of cotton pulp/fiber to paper industry |
| Motor cars (1917–beyond 1921) | 1. Plant construction (1918) 2. Motor fuels (1919) | *Enter*: tetraethyl lead (1922) *Exit*: Plant construction |

Notes:
1. Years in the first column indicate domain duration, and in the second column show anchor establishment.
2. "Not enter" refers to a definite choice made to not enter a business. It is different from "Enter: No entry" which refers to circumstances in which search continued but did not yield results that could lead to entry.
3. In cases where entry was made soon after 1921 and was a consequence of the continuation of a 1902–21 search, the date of entry is provided.

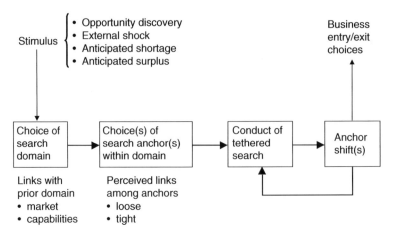

**Figure 20.2**    Moving, anchored search process for long-term growth

DuPont documents revealed four kinds of stimuli influencing the creation of new domains (Figure 20.2). The stimuli were: opportunity discovery, external shock, anticipated shortages, and anticipated surpluses. Whether anticipated or unforeseen, the stimuli imposed limits to growth from existing domains or opened growth opportunities from new domains. Besides the threats or opportunities they signaled, the stimuli lowered uncertainty about what the future might be, affecting the specific content of domain choices. The effect of stimuli on domain content was reflected in whether the link between the new domain and earlier ones dealt mainly with markets or capabilities (Figure 20.2).

Biomanufacturing and nitrogenous compounds domains were established soon after 1902 in anticipation of shortages of critical explosives inputs glycerin and nitrate of soda (Table 20.2). Because the supply of these inputs was limited by natural sources, DuPont created the two new domains to use fundamental research to develop synthetic means of producing these inputs and obviate the reliance on limited natural sources. DuPont intended to use these inputs for itself and had no plans of selling them to outsiders. The link between the new domains and the existing explosives domain was one of markets. DuPont lacked research and manufacturing capabilities that could have been leveraged from the old domain into the new. But part of the reason for the new domains was to search and create such capabilities, along with the needed products.

The antitrust lawsuit and threat of a big loss in revenues during 1907–8 brought an unanticipated external shock to DuPont managers who had to respond hurriedly. Using the company's infrastructure and capability in manufacturing the highly inflammable nitrocellulose in industrial quantities for its explosives business, DuPont managers established the search domain of nitrocellulose. Although this domain was far removed from existing ones in terms of markets, research, and much of manufacturing, given the need for a quick response, there was at least a partial manufacturing capabilities link between the nitrocellulose and explosives domains.

The advent of the First World War was another unanticipated external shock, but one that did not immediately require setting new domains. DuPont could barely keep up with demands for explosives that came from governments in Europe. However, a year after the start of the war and a many-fold leap in the company's production capacity, DuPont managers foresaw the massive idle capacity that would result following the end of the war. The company was highly profitable but it was clear that post-war explosives sales would plummet. The anticipated surplus, fear of a backlash, and other factors (Table 20.2) affected the specific content and timing of the five search domains established in the war years. Without worries caused by these stimuli, some of these five domains may arguably have never been established, whereas others may have been established much later and with less urgency. And fewer financial resources would have been made available. The establishment of the important synthetic organic chemistry domain was in the belief that there were significant infrastructure and manufacturing links between this domain and explosives. It later proved to be otherwise. DuPont managers also believed that the remaining four domains, although they saw far less intensive searches, were also linked in the same manner with explosives and with synthetic organic chemistry. Some of them were also viewed to have partial links with one another in terms of markets (Table 20.2).

The entry into the motor cars domain was due to a combination of surplus cash and the belief that the young industry immediately offered high growth and returns to investment. However, there was no link in terms of capabilities and markets with earlier domains. Entry into this final domain was thus quick – through stock purchases.

It should be noted that although search can be pursued without a formally established domain, such search is less likely to endure. Before the formal setting of the synthetic organic chemicals domain, suggestions by DuPont scientists to begin the manufacture of dyes had been turned down. Similarly, the company dismissed suggestions by the sales department for DuPont to conduct research on the use of kerosene as motor fuel. A few months later, following the establishment of the motor car domain, the company was aggressively pursuing the motor fuels search anchor. A formal domain increases the likelihood that decision makers will be engaged, and that search will receive the requisite resources and support. A formal domain is also a signal about which search outcomes are more likely to lead later to business entry. This does not, however, suggest that domain ideas emerge only by design. But it does mean that for the domain to endure and yield growth and competitiveness, the firm must, at some point, adopt it formally, whatever the original source of the idea (Table 20.2). Formal adoption is part of the search process because in taking a company into new areas, domains require investing considerable resources, developing new skills and capabilities, operating in a different competitive environment, and perhaps abandoning an older domain (Burgelman, 2002).

### Anchor choices, tethered search, and anchor shifts

Once established, a domain still contains innumerable specific possibilities that yet remain largely unknown. Hence, decision makers select one or a few simultaneous search anchors to determine *where* within a domain's content to pursue search (Figures 20.1, 20.2; Table 20.3). Subsequent deliberations are tethered to these conceptual anchors, or guides. The choice of an anchor is not necessarily obvious or a given to decision makers, owing to uncertainty and sketchy information inherent in long-term growth considerations, but may be based on a variety of reasons. At DuPont, market needs and growth potential played a role in selecting anchors, but so did the desire to simply explore. Anchors were established in support of existing businesses, to complement other searches, and to pursue a logically connected set of businesses. Anchors were created to leverage capabilities, but they were also created to utilize idle resources and avoid lay-offs. And in the pursuit of long-term growth, some search anchors were chosen and business entries were made despite not possessing the required capabilities. In fact, these choices were made explicitly to develop new capabilities and knowledge, most clearly evident in the case of dyes, which could aid future diversification. The state of technology and knowledge were also important in setting search anchors. Following anchor selection, tethered search proceeds (Figures 20.1, 20.2). Not every aspect of anchored search results from great deliberation and thought. Often, the marginal cost of anchored search is not high, making it worth a try.

An anchor may be retained in the absence of promising findings because there is still space left to explore or for lack of better options. Over time, a critical decision is made to shift to a new anchor, moving search to a significantly different area (Figures 20.1, 20.2; Table 20.3). This shift can follow the abandonment of an initial anchor, or it can be made while pursuing search around the initial anchor. The anchor shift can result from dissatisfaction with findings or a definite indicator of the futility of the current anchor, exhaustion of local possibilities around the current anchor, new technology and information, rapidly changing circumstances, or simply the decision to try something new. By moving the search area, anchor shifts create new search paths so that initial choices do not rigidly predetermine the entire subsequent search. Simultaneous, multiple anchors serve the same purpose as anchor shifts, and they may be pursued especially in situations of high uncertainty and urgency, such as at DuPont during the First World War. Over time, some anchors may be abandoned. And new information may entail returning to an old anchor. Search thus continues tethered to multiple and sequential anchors. Domains change relatively infrequently. Taking them as givens, most considerations deal with the search within (Table 20.3).

To illustrate the search process within a domain, we present the example of DuPont's search within the explosives domain (Figure 20.3; Table 20.3). Following the 1902 incorporation of DuPont and installation of new management, the first search anchor was established that year to "consolidate" DuPont's interests scattered across more than 100 explosives companies dealing with black powder, smokeless powder, and high explosives. Subsequent considerations were tethered to this anchor. From its initial internal focus, tethered search soon extended externally to consolidating the U.S. explosives industry by means of acquisitions. By 1908, search driven by this anchor had ceased as consolidation was achieved, the economy entered a recession, and the antitrust lawsuit was filed (Table 20.2). But for sporadic tethered search during the First World War, DuPont abandoned this anchor. Search also shifted to a different part of the explosives domain when a second search anchor to "secure supplies" was established in 1903 to meet DuPont's supply requirements that the market could not, ensure reliability in supplies, and obtain the best possible input prices. Tethered search included many explosives ingredients and components. Although the emphasis on various inputs varied over the years, search was intensive and persistent. This tethered search was, however, conducted solely to support the explosives business. DuPont did not view supply-related businesses as a new means of growth and specifically decided against selling supplies to others. Anchors fundamentally affect what is considered and precluded, and the outcomes reached. For instance, making explosives machinery for itself was seen as part of tethered search around the securing supplies anchor but selling it to others was not. That would have entailed a separate anchor that the company was unwilling to establish. The First World War also took DuPont in new directions when it began manufacturing the organic chemicals diphenylamine and toluene. Managers, however, initially viewed this as securing supplies rather than entering the new domain of synthetic organic chemicals (Table 20.2). That decision had yet to be made. On the other hand, the need for novel sources of glycerin and nitrogen was pressing enough that the company conducted additional searches in radically different domains (Table 20.2). DuPont pursued a third search anchor of related products occasionally and never intensively (Figure 20.3). This anchor could have been active and long lasting, but the company limited its interests to the long time and more profitable businesses of black powder, smokeless powder, and dynamite. With industry consolidation well under way, the foreign markets anchor was established in 1905 as another growth avenue. Starting with the geographically proximate Mexico and Canada, tethered search expanded, but remained occasional (Figure 20.3). Search increased briefly after the 1907 antitrust lawsuit. DuPont studied South American markets, but did not enter any. Doing so would have required high expenses and losses for a few years, and competing with well-entrenched European explosives companies. In the later years of the war, DuPont began discussions with the Nobel Company to jointly enter foreign markets after the war, but it made no moves. After the war, explosives search almost ceased as demand plummeted and the economy entered a recession. But by now the company was actively pursuing diversification search in other, more promising domains (Table 20.2). Search over 20 years within the explosives domain was thus conducted by means of anchors, tethered search, and anchor shifts.

Such searches were similarly evident within the remaining domains (Table 20.3). Case history details of these searches indicate the additional importance of links among anchors. Conceptually, there are many links possible among anchors in terms of search content and knowledge, value chain activities, markets, and resources and capabilities. And arguably, some links must exist among all anchors within a domain, by definition. But for decision makers, what seems to matter are their *perceptions* of the number and nature of links between anchors that span the spectrum from few and loose to many and tight (Figure 20.3). The perceptions may later prove inaccurate or inadequate but have a deep influence on search nonetheless. DuPont managers initially thought that the anchors they were considering for the post-war utilization of excess capacity were tightly linked in terms of raw materials and intermediates, manufacturing, distribution, and research. It proved to be otherwise. Consequently, DuPont abandoned some domains and ended up not entering the drugs business when it found that the tight links that had been perceived between the drugs business and the dye business, which it did enter, remained tenuous and elusive. Inaccuracy and incompleteness in perceiving links among anchors is inevitable partly because some

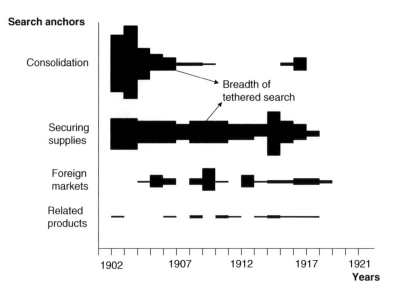

**Figure 20.3**   Conceptual illustration of moving, anchored search within the explosives search domain, 1902–21.
Note: Each of the four patterns represents tethered search driven by the corresponding conceptual search anchor. The varying width of each pattern illustrates the varying breadth of tethered search over time.

links can only be revealed through search. In assessing links there is also a tendency to focus on some kinds of links and not on others. For instance, anchors within the nitro-cellulose domain were unrelated in terms of manufacturing and marketing, despite their common use of nitrocellulose and the possibility of DuPont's leveraging its nitrocellulose-making capabilities across them. The links were few and loose but the company had to respond quickly to the antitrust lawsuit and the threat of losing much of its smokeless powder business. Links may be also misjudged when the required resources and capabilities are viewed in macro terms. Despite the assumed relatedness in research and manufacturing, at a macro level, among explosives, dyes, and drugs, the links proved tenuous or missing when considered in specific and micro terms.

## Conclusion

Drawing on extensive field data, we have developed a novel search process that depicts how decision makers search for long-term growth (Figure 20.2). It would be misleading to consider the applicability of the MAS process and framework as limited because the process was developed from data from a single company from a long-ago period. It should be noted that the 20-year period included innumerable decisions made by senior and mid-managers, scientists, research managers, and other employ-ees working at the Executive Committee, Development Department, Experimental

Station, and other parts of the organization; and dealt with a variety of choices in the pursuit of long-term growth. We argue that the MAS process and framework can be usefully applied to a variety of companies pursuing long-term growth in different periods (e.g., Chesbrough, 2002; Dyer and Gross, 2001; Steinbock, 2001). The MAS search process can also be useful in understanding other phenomena such as invention and entrepreneurship (Bhardwaj, 2000), and the emergence and evolution of new fields like biotechnology and nanotechnology. The validity of application, by both academics and practitioners, depends on the setting involving distant returns – high uncertainty and ambiguity in decision making, and sequences of choices and outcomes that span long periods (Bhardwaj, 2000). It should, however, be noted that the framework cannot assure success (no analytical framework can). Success is influenced not only by the decision-making process but also by the specifics of the content searched, the decision-maker's risk propensity, timing of choices, and a host of factors that cannot be predicted and controlled. The MAS process framework can, however, make decision making more effective by providing a language, structure, and useful analytical questions for the pursuit of distant returns endeavors like long-term growth.

## Notes

1. This chapter is based upon fieldwork supported by the National Science Foundation under grant SBR-9872070, and by a research grant from the Eleutherian Mills-Hagley Foundation. We thank Steve Floyd, Franz Kellermanns, Raghu Garud, Jennifer Bethel, presentation attendees at the SMS mini-conference on process research, conference reviewers, and editors of this volume for helpful suggestions.
2. The case history is available from the first author. Rich descriptions of DuPont during 1902–21 can also be found in Chandler (1962), Chandler and Salsbury (1971), and Hounshell and Smith (1988).

## References

Bhardwaj, G. 2000. *Search for Distant Returns: A Decision-Making Process Model from Choices at DuPont for Invention, Entrepreneurship, and Growth*. Unpublished PhD Dissertation, University of Pittsburgh.

Bromiley, P. 1991. Testing a causal model of corporate risk taking and performance. *Academy of Management Journal*, **34**: 37–59.

Burgelman, R.A. 2002. Strategy as vector and the inertia of coevolutionary lock-in. *Administrative Science Quarterly*, **47**: 325–57.

Chandler, A.D., Jr. 1962. *Strategy and Structure: Chapters in the History of the American Industrial Enterprise*. Cambridge, MA: MIT Press.

Chandler, A.D., Jr. and Salsbury, S. 1971. *Pierre S. du Pont and the Making of the Modern Corporation*. New York: Harper and Row.

Chesbrough, H. 2002. Graceful exits and missed opportunities: Xerox's management of its technology spin-off organizations. *Business History Review*, **76**: 803–37.

Cyert, R.M. and March, J.G. 1963. *A Behavioral Theory of the Firm*. Englewood Cliffs, NJ: Prentice-Hall.

Dixit, A.K. and Pindyck, R.S. 1994. *Investment Under Uncertainty*. Princeton, NJ: Princeton University Press.

Dyer, D. and Gross, D. 2001. *The Generations of Corning: The Life and Times of a Global Corporation*. New York: Oxford University Press.

Eisenhardt, K.M. 1989. Building theories from case study research. *Academy of Management Review*, **14**: 532–50.

Fleming, L. 2001. Recombinant uncertainty in technological search. *Management Science*, **47**: 117–32.

Garud, R. and Van de Ven, A.H. 1992. An empirical evaluation of the internal corporate venturing process. *Strategic Management Journal*, **13**: 93–109.

Holbrook, D., Cohen, W.M., Hounshell, D.A., and Klepper, S. 2000. The nature, sources, and consequences of firm differences in the early history of the semiconductor industry. *Strategic Management Journal*, **21**: 1017–41.

Hounshell, D.A. and Smith, J.K., Jr. 1988. *Science and Corporate Strategy: Du Pont R&D, 1902–1980*. New York: Cambridge University Press.

Katila, R. and Ahuja, G. 2002. Something old, something new: A longitudinal study of search behavior and new product introduction. *Academy of Management Journal*, **45**: 1183–94.

Lovas, B. and Ghoshal, S. 2000. Strategy as guided evolution. *Strategic Management Journal*, **21**: 875–96.

Nelson, R.R. and Winter, S.G. 1982. *An Evolutionary Theory of Economic Change*. Cambridge, MA: Harvard University Press.

Noda, T. and Bower, J.L. 1996. Strategy making as iterated processes of resource allocation. *Strategic Management Journal*, **17**(special summer issue): 159–92.

Papadakis, V.M., Lioukas, S., and Chambers, D. 1998. Strategic decision-making processes: The role of management and context. *Strategic Management Journal*, **19**: 115–47.

Penrose, E. 1995. *The Theory of the Growth of the Firm*, 3rd edn. New York: Oxford University Press.

Pettigrew, A.M. 1992. The character and significance of strategy process research. *Strategic Management Journal*, **13**: 5–16.

Rosenkopf, L. and Nerkar, A. 2001. Beyond local search: Boundary-spanning exploration, and impact in the optical disk industry. *Strategic Management Journal*, **22**: 287–306.

Simon, H.A. 1976. *Administrative Behavior: A Study of Decision-Making Processes in Administrative Organization*. 3rd edn. New York: The Free Press.

Steinbock, D. 2001. *The Nokia Revolution: The Story of an Extraordinary Company that Transformed an Industry*. New York: AMACOM.

# Integrating Theory and Practice

# CHAPTER TWENTY-ONE

# Strengthening our Practices as an Academic Field of Inquiry

Anne Sigismund Huff

Ongoing strategizing is particularly important to success in innovative settings. It might seem unnecessary to begin a commentary with that declaration, since almost everyone at the Connecticut conference and in this resulting volume has chosen to work on strategy process. But in my opinion, a shared view of strategy process – what it means and how further understanding can be accumulated – has declined over the last 20 years. I want to focus on why that might be, and what might be done about it, precisely because we have important work to do on innovation and other competitive issues.

## Barriers to Development

V.K. Naryanan, who shares my general concern, pointed out in conversation that the number of courses on strategy process has gone down dramatically in the last 20 years, pushed out as doctoral programs and doctoral curricula in many universities have decreased in size. Even in places that have not suffered an overall decline, the increasing number of required courses, including quantitative methods and background in economics, means that there is little room for training in the theory and methods of strategy process.

One important consequence is that insights of major theorists of the past (e.g., Chester Bernard, Mary Parker Follet, and Philip Selznick) that might contribute to organizing frameworks have been neglected. This seems almost inevitable as very few strategy students choose dissertation projects in the process area. Career advising has worked against process dissertations. They take a long time to carry out, the results are unlikely to be as "crisp" as results from a more quantitative study, and thus (the story goes) harder to publish.

This bias against process dissertations, by itself, is more disorienting than observers may realize. It means that only a small number of those entering the strategy field are doing their first work on strategy process. We therefore lose the links that new dissertations make between the past and the future. Furthermore, in a highly pressured world, where tenure decisions are increasingly rigorous, path dependency alone suggests that second and third topics of study by emerging scholars also are unlikely to be process oriented. The perceived limits of process research still apply. In addition, reputation, contacts, data, and competence have begun to accumulate in other areas of study.

This is a problem not only for research, but also for teaching and impact on practice. If there is a declining number of faculty committed to doing research on strategy process, the subject occupies a smaller portion of the undergraduate and MBA teaching curricula. That means that we graduate people who understand less about process issues; they are less likely to pay attention to problems or opportunities related to process; and they are less likely to reach out for further inputs on process as practitioners. For the important issue of increasing innovativeness in organizations alone, these are worrying trends.

## Strategy, and Strategy Process, as Young Fields of Study

Is it true that process is more difficult as a subject of study and practice than other strategy subjects? Doesn't everyone feel that the larger world should pay more attention to the subject they feel is most important? I am equivocal in answering both questions, but I do feel a frustrating lack of coherence in the process field today, and I believe it is symptomatic of an important underlying issue: Strategy is a young science. As a parent who until very recently had young people in the house, I can easily list some of the major pleasures and problems of being young.

One sign of our youth as a field would be that we are wildly enthusiastic about the topics that currently interest us, but that we also drop these ideas when distracted by attractive alternatives. That seems true of the strategy field as a whole, and process as a subfield. As a young science, we would be innovative in our approach to solving the problems that interest us, and likely to put together interesting resources for working on these issues; but we would tend to lose the "stuff" we have gathered together, relying instead on a process of ad hoc response to new issues. Though it sometimes works for teenagers, most of us would not recommend it to managers operating under competitive pressure.

And we are in a competitive world. Within business schools strategy competes for students and resources with marketing, accounting, finance, and other fields. In the larger university we compete with a broad range of contenders, from well-articulated science agendas to often compelling creative programs. While recognizing that all of these alternatives contribute to the essential richness of academic life, I want strategy and strategy process to do well in this environment.

The "young science" metaphor helps explain some of our difficulties as a field, and more particularly as a subfield. Many process consultants and academics embrace topics (like total quality management) for a short period of time and then quickly move on. We develop "new" methods (like cognitive mapping), let them languish, and then reinvent them. The particular subjects I have used as example do not matter; an important problem for the field is that before too much work is done on a topic of current interest, like innovating, we have our eyes on another opportunity.

This behavior means that our relatively small numbers are fragmented, and the work we do is less cumulative. It erodes our credibility not only in academic environments but also in relating to practice. Furthermore, because we have less collective experience, we are less confident about what we have to offer in either setting.

## A Preliminary Agenda

Since this is a short commentary, I will move directly to a possible agenda, developed through informal conversation with a number of people in the field.

1. *Establish and share academic coursework.* Formal coursework at the doctoral level provides an interesting and important ground for organizing a field of inquiry. I believe our maturity as a field would be enhanced if everyone interested in strategy process could reference courses on:
   - theoretic foundations (e.g., Barnard, institution theory)
   - current theories (e.g., social capital)
   - classic methodological alternatives (especially participant observation, grounded theory, action research – all three of which, in my opinion, tend to be misrepresented in current research)
   - newer methodologies (e.g., network analysis).
2. *Supplement university coursework with conference workshops on theory, methods, and practice.* Given the pressures on Ph.D. programs, and a world where education is more likely to be continuous, interest groups like the one sponsoring this volume have a job to do. The Managerial and Organizational Cognition roundtables at the Academy of Management provide one quite successful model. These largely self-organizing sessions bring together individuals with subject matter to share. A similar tradition in the strategy process field would provide an annual opportunity to take the pulse of the field, and advance it.
3. *Identify subject areas as a common task framework for research.* This volume offers a preliminary list of topics useful not only for work on innovation, but also other topics of competitive interest:
   - entrepreneurship (Dess and Lumpkin; Gedajlovic and Zahra; Regnér; Corbett; Koppius, Germans, and Vos)
   - ethics (Victor)
   - process over content issues (Hafsi and Thomas)
   - action (Canales and Vilà; Jacobs and Statler)
   - non- "cognitive" approaches (Fabian and ogilvie)
   - innovation (Lane)
   - complexity of processes (Lyles, Dhanaraj, and Steensma)
   - politics (Kellermanns and Floyd)
   - dilemmas (Chakravarthy)
   - our own subjectivity as researchers/narrators (Roos)
   I would like to see volunteers approach journal editors with these and other subjects in hand. The current promise of strategy process for innovation and other topics must continually be demonstrated in public settings.

4. *Commit to multiple levels and sites for analysis of strategy process.* Again, this volume offers a rather complete set of examples:
   – micro-strategy within the firm (Johnson, Whittington, and Melin; Volberda)
   – multi-business (Paroutis and Pettigrew), multinationals (Cuervo-Cazurra and Ramos) and corporations (Bhardwaj, Camillus, and Hounshell)
   – networks (Marx and Lechner)
   – institutions (Garud and Karnøe).
5. *Press for design commitments.* The increasing, and international, lean toward management as a social science, which is largely a result of the Carnegie Report in the 1950s in the United States, is a powerful and positive force in creating academic legitimacy. However, an interesting conversation developing in both the United States and Europe suggests that management might also look to models in other professions, like medicine and architecture, that are willing to be much more prescriptive (Boland Jr. and Collopy, 2004). The question is: What do we know about process with sufficient confidence that we will recommend it to practice as a design template?
6. *Share undergraduate and MBA curricula ideas.* Just as Ph.D. courses take the pulse of an area of inquiry, and display it for conversation and potential alteration, coursework at other levels also offers a way to examine, preserve, but also change current design recommendations. The job is made more difficult as process issues become part of courses with other titles (e.g., information management, economics), but these crossovers are particularly worth identifying and discussing.
7. *Develop a continuing infrastructure.*
   – Do we need a web site? This is something that volunteers(s) from within the interest group could do under the Strategic Management Society's umbrella. While many sites are developed but not used, there are interesting sites (Positive Organization Scholarship at the University of Michigan, Social Entrepreneurship at Oxford's Said Business School) that illustrate how a subject of interest can be given shape and coherence by collecting materials in one place.
   – Would established subcategories be helpful for international Strategic Management Society meetings? Agenda item 3, above, provides a starting place.
   – Are there important questions that could be answered by task forces (similar to the ones that the BPS division at the Academy of Management carried out on Ph.D. programs in the late 1980s and 1990s)? As a process interest group, we might also be interested in querying those who develop MBA courses, and corporate university curricula.
   – Can we be more effective in drawing younger scholars into the study of strategy process?
   – How can we link to other areas in SMS? It is important that strategy process is not marginalized, even though it is relatively small in size. Two natural links within the evolving SMS structure would appear to be:
     • resource base theory
     • entrepreneurship.
8. *Recognize and draw on international colleagues.* An enormous area of vitality in academic work today can be found in management research and teaching

outside of the United States. This work is growing exponentially. We miss an important part of the future of the field, as an SMS interest group and more broadly a group of scholars concerned about strategy practice, if we do not find ways of connecting scholarship from many national settings.

9. *Clarify theoretic roots in base disciplines.* Sociology, psychology, political science, and cognitive science would appear to be our closest sources, but the humanities and other professions are among other alternatives. This is a much broader base that the economic one that currently supports most "content" work, and part of our distraction, but also part of our strength.

## Overview

Every strategy has its risks and limitations, which have to be weighted against potential gains (as we tell our students in basic strategy courses).

### Promise

I have often felt, in attending and helping to organize events for this interest group, that we are wandering, unable to find a common framework or agenda for further work. Some people have a clear view of strategy process and their contributions to it. Bala Chakravarty, for example, provides an excellent example of someone who over time has developed an increasingly rich theoretic framework in the area and supported it with interesting empirical studies. This brief comment is motivated by the view that we would be able to make a more forceful contribution to an important subject like innovation, if there were more leaders like him, and a more consensual view of important subjects and process levers.

Lack of consensus is a sign of relative immaturity in an area of research and teaching. Greater maturity would serve our academic self-interests by increasing cohesion among reviewers, making evaluation by those in our own and other academic disciplines more likely to be positive. Increasing maturity would also make contributions to practice more probable. And, as we speak with a more unified voice from various locations on a rich but delimited set of subjects, our audience should increase and our recruiting capacity improve. I want that to happen, without losing the innovativeness and energy that characterizes much current work in the field.

### Risks

The agenda only outlined calls for increasing focus, which has at least two potential downfalls:

- Capture by the few, and consequent decreasing innovation, energy, and participation in the strategy process field by a broader group of participants.
- Emphasis on fewer subjects, like innovation, that no matter how important decreases the interface with practice, as well as other fields of inquiry.

I think the possibilities are worth the risk. We have not yet grown into our potential.

## Conclusion

The conference in Connecticut was preceded by one in Rotterdam that emphasized the inevitable, but enriching, contradictions of strategy. A summary of the above argument can easily be put into this form:

- Support and grow current leadership, while reinforcing leadership in the next generations.
- Develop a clearer, more compelling agenda, while remaining open to new topics.
- Be aware of time pressures, but take time to preserve and draw on past resources.
- Increase global perspective, but draw on insight from various locations.
- Provide structure, but do not let it squelch agency.

Why do these things? Because research on strategy process can make a difference. It is increasingly important as strategy is defined in more dynamic ways. We are contributing to organizations that are innovating, but we can do more.

## Reference

Bolard, R.J. Jr. and Collopy, F . (eds.) 2004. *Managing as Designing*. Stanford, CA: Stanford University Press.

# CHAPTER TWENTY-TWO

# On the Moral Necessity of Strategy Making

## Bart Victor

*The Emperor – so they say – has sent a message, directly from his deathbed, to you alone, his pathetic subject, a tiny shadow, which has taken refuge at the furthest distance from the imperial sun.*

So Franz Kafka (2003) begins a story about ancient China, telling of the emperor's efforts to communicate with his subjects. By the time the messenger winds his way through the Forbidden City, though, still so far away from the subject of his message, the emperor is dead: communication, in a larger sense, has been futile. Through this story Kafka is asking us if leadership of complex organizations is even possible.

To this day, the practical necessity of strategy making remains an open question. Even if we agree that a course must be set, can the leadership of an organization willfully and skillfully direct the complex organization? There are many good reasons to doubt the effectiveness of strategy making, ranging from the complexity theory's implications for the possibility for knowing, to the post-modernists' challenge to the possibility of understanding. Add to these doubts the difficulties of motivation, the unintended consequences of incentives, the resistance to change, the emergence of unanticipated events, turnover, and we can be understandably skeptical about the utility of strategy making.

Can we then justify minimizing or even eliminating the costly activity of strategy making? I believe not. My conclusion is based on my belief that the justification for strategy making does not lie alone, or even primarily, in its economic utility. I will argue, instead, that the cost and effort leadership devotes to strategy making is *morally required*. That is, leadership has a moral obligation to form its strategic intent with care. Failure to do so would be tantamount to reckless negligence.

Strategy making must embrace dual objectives:

1. to decide in advance, based on ethical considerations, what could be anticipated; and
2. to provide moral guidance for the inevitable choices that cannot be so pre-ordained.

Both the choices made in advance and the guidance given to those facing an unknown future are rich in explicit and implicit moral contentin – cluding the good for various stakeholders affected by the organization and the integrity of the actors directed by its leadership.

Early management practice did not necessarily envision the development of strategy as rich in moral content, i.e. it was science not practical wisdom that was seen as needed for organizational action. The early ideas on the emergence of bureaucracy were described as a quasi-natural evolution. To the extent it was called for, theorists explained the emergence of modern markets and industrial enterprises as "natural" and inexorable. Invisible hands, naturally selecting evolutionary processes, or some notion of a race toward or away from Eden caused the modernity that swept the West. In turn, the planning of organizational intent was modeled on natural science. Industrial engineers, economists, managers trained in their applied disciplines sought to anticipate, compare, and select the best actions. Their criteria were optimized, objective, and countable efficiencies.

Moral considerations have played an explicit role heretofore in strategy discussions, to a large extent in negative terms. Aristotle raised one of the most enduring indictments of the moral problem of capitalism. He was worried by the emergence of money, which, while he understood its practical purpose, seemed to him fraught with unintended and morally problematic consequences. Coinage, he saw, allowed for the easy accumulation of wealth both alienated from the source of its value and useless in its abstracted state. To the extent that capitalism is motivated by the acquisition of such wealth, it portends a collapse of the good under the weight of unbounded greed.

To this day, we grapple with the moral problem of the distribution of accumulating wealth. Morality has been called for as a constraint and/or a guide to the distribution of the consequences of the enterprise. Any number of propositions have been, and continue to be, offered to share the wealth among "stakeholders," invest in socially responsible activities, limit the greed of capitalists, and/or justify the inequality of the haves and have-nots.

Thus the distribution of accumulated wealth and costs as the surplus of organizational action continues to be a moral problem for every enterprise. The moral challenge for organizations though, goes beyond profit distribution to encompass the integrity of all those who participate in the work of the firm. With or without intent, capitalism's organizations are powerful sources of meaning. Much of the human experience in our organizations is built on an idea of the virtuous: cream rises to the top, potential, not blood selects members, and an unbiased rationality presides. In some accounts, capitalist community receives near utopian attributions: only merit derives power, belongingness creates joy, and work fulfils a longing for meaning. Unfortunately, along with these paeans to a capitalist lifestyle are heard cries of dehumanization, alienation, exploitation, and clattering against the bars of the "iron cage." While some theorists explained the emergence of modern markets and bureaucracies with historical and even quasi-natural mechanisms, this emergence has also elicited profound moral concerns. Even those theorists, who foresaw the modern capitalist industrial age as a necessary consequence of some extra-volitional force, did so with moral trepidation. Industrial and post-industrial enterprises are the largest, most pervasive autocratic institutions in the world. Unlike their autocratic political brethren, the powerful in enterprises do not even make rhetorical allusions to democratization. Barnard (1968) described the crating of this context for work as essentially moral creativity. Work is a primary source of meaning for members of the organization. When strategy making, leaders search for mission and vision to explicitly address the problem of the integrity for themselves and those to whom they would make the call to follow.

Thus, morality is an essential quality of both life in and of organizations. Strategy making is necessarily moral decision making. Thus, I argue, efforts to find the moral foundation for strategy making only in either the situational ethics in the distribution of wealth or from the way of being within the enterprise, ultimately fail. They fail because in and of themselves they are both morally and practically insufficient. Capitalism is, as a human experience, far more than the net measure of wealth generated and distributed, and life in capitalist institutions cannot be considered necessarily utopian.

In looking at strategy making in moral terms, I suggest a rejustification of strategy making. I argue that strategy making is best characterized in terms of the intentional and continuous transformation of human imagination and effort into profits. Following Amartya Sen (2000), I propose a moral foundation for strategy making in the dynamic between human capability and wealth – between capitalism as development and capitalism as freedom.

For strategy researchers, the implications of this analysis are twofold:

1. strategy research must more explicitly and more critically integrate the moral content of strategy both as content and as process; and
2. strategy research must explore the factors which more powerfully associate leaders' moral intent with the choices and actions of organizational members.

The first agenda would significantly expand the idea of strategy-making as a topic. It would challenge researchers to question and investigate how strategy is made (e.g., who participates, how participation is mediated, how strategy is reified) in terms of the consequent moral guidance. Such investigations may raise questions such as: Do more inclusive strategy-making processes engender more equitable distributions of wealth? Can, as Jack Welch once claimed (Slater, 1998), an autocratic strategic leadership lay the moral foundation for a more democratic organizational form?

The second question would challenge the question of execution on a much more morally attentive agenda. The slippage between the espoused mission and the emergence of both structure and action in the organization can be seen as questions of integrity and morality. Obligations for organization action under uncertainty can be tied to real leadership action. This research would bring the field of strategy making to questions already being created in the United States by such regulatory phenomenon the Sarbanes–Oxley rules and the new federal sentencing guidelines for corporate crimes. Most importantly though, strategy-making research could serve to enable leaders to better understand what they do when they make strategy and what they risk when they choose not to.

As difficult, frustrating, and often disappointing strategy making may seem, I believe it remains a fundamental moral necessity. Without it, leadership chooses amorality. Failing to make strategy, and do so with great care and effort, is simply to choose amorality and to do nothing to limit immorality. In contrast, strategy making that embraces the moral foundations of democratic capitalism and the good of its stakeholders can capture the moral imagination and resound loudly enough to reach even the most distant of its subjects. Kafka captured this need for the moral voice of leadership when, he imagined that even though we doubt that the moral voice of leadership will ever reach us, even still:

> . . . you sit at your window and dream of that message when evening comes.

## References

Barnard, C.I. 1968. *The Functions of the Executive.* Cambridge, MA: Harvard University Press (originally published 1938).

Kafka, F. 2003. *The Great Wall of China* translation, prepared by Ian Johnston of Malaspina University-College, Nanaimo, BC, Canada.

Sen, A. 2000. *Development as Freedom*, New York: Anchor.

Slater, R. 1998. *Jack Welch and The G.E. Way: Management Insights and Leadership Secrets of the Legendary CEO.* New York: McGraw-Hill.

# CHAPTER TWENTY-THREE

# Reflections on the Field of Strategy

Taieb Hafsi, Howard Thomas

## Introduction

Strategic management (Bowman, 1974) has three elements: its roots in practice; its methodology; and its theoretical underpinnings. While there has been an incredible surge of research in the last 20 years (paralleling the growth of the *Strategic Management Journal*), it is clear that practice and theory are not always well connected (Bettis, 1991) and that most research does not really address the field-defining issues. We believe that the ontology of the field is misunderstood, the epistemological issues are confounded within those of the more established social sciences, and the methodologies that dominate the field are not always appropriate.

We reflect on the growth of the field from the joint perspectives of a macro-organizational process-oriented researcher (Hafsi) and an eclectic, originally analytic-focused, but lately (perhaps reformed and enlightened) more pluralistic researcher and business school Dean (Thomas). Our argument starts with Thompson's (1967) search for science in strategic management, continues with our views on the field of strategy, provides a tentative framework for strategy researchers, and offers some concluding remarks.

## In Search of Science in Strategic Management

Thompson (1967) asserted forcefully that:

> No useful theory can rest on the assumption that everything is unique. It is probably inevitable that the early history of a scientific endeavor will be characterized by the opposite assumption, and by the search for universals ... the discovery of universal elements is

necessary, but alone it provides a static understanding. To get leverage on a topic, we must begin to see some of the universal elements as capable of variation . . . .

The economist, sociologist, political scientist, or social psychologist will each find that I have overlooked refinements and intricacies of concepts that he knows well. I have done so deliberately, in order to achieve generality across typical categories of organizations . . . My focus is on the behavior of organizations.

Thompson recognized that the questions with which, in situations of complexity, practitioners and researchers alike have to wrestle have neither the level of elegance nor the structure that the purists hope they would. Yet the researcher cannot be content with case analyses, always situational and hardly amenable to generalizations.

Thompson did not ignore the strategy problem. In the last chapter of his book (1967), widely considered one of his most significant contributions, he provides a striking expression of the nature of strategic management. In particular he emphasizes the need for co-alignment:

The basic function of administration appears to be co-alignment, not merely of people (in coalitions) but of institutionalized action – of technology and task environment into a viable domain, and of organizational design and structure appropriate to it. Administration, when it works well, keeps the organization at the nexus of the several necessary streams of action. Paradoxically, the administrative process must reduce uncertainty but at the same time search for flexibility.

Following in Thompson's steps, quantitative, more precise research, generally focused on interactions between a limited number of variables, dominates the field. There are exceptions as some conceptual developments were holistic in their approach (Chakravarthy and Doz, 1992). These could be clustered into four groups of research:

1. Chandler's (1962) study of U.S. firm growth and the related strategy–structure relationship, reinforced by such works of Mintzberg (1978) and Rumelt (1974).
2. Bower's (1970) study of the resource allocation process in large diversified firms, followed by many others of which Burgelman (1983) is an example.
3. Miles and Snow's (1978) study of organizational strategic adaptation.
4. Finally, the contributions related to Montreal's school of configurations (Miller, 1996).

Although more attuned to the realities of the nature of the co-alignment that Thompson (1967) talked about, they are increasingly pushed back to serve as an exotic background or reinterpreted to be used as frameworks for content-based quantitative research.

Reality is given by a look at the *Strategic Management Journal*'s index of topics for the 1990s. It shows more than a thousand different topics addressed by fewer than a thousand authors. Assuming that the topics as expressed by the authors are a reliable indication of what is being presented, such a variety suggests the Babel syndrome, that authors are barely talking to each other, and a closer look shows that the field is spread all over traditional disciplines or functional areas. More specifically, of all the articles examined in the 10 years, about 60 percent can be related to specific disciplines. Economics alone represents the bulk of all these articles.

Many academics – we mention Schendel (1994) and Prahalad and Hamel (1994), representative of many others – believe that this is acceptable, even a stimulus to research and creative practice. If that is the case, almost 25 years after the creation of the Strategic Management Society, we have no indication of its positive effects on the practice of strategic management. Prahalad and Hamel (1994: 5) recognized that "Even well-known consulting firms, such as McKinsey and Boston Consulting Group (BCG), who built their reputations on strategy consulting, started to de-emphasize their strategy focus ... Academic disillusionment with the value of strategy literature and schools of thought, while not as widespread, followed quickly."

## So What is the Field of Strategy?

First, let's say what the field is not. It cannot be reduced to specialized analytical research similar to those of the disciplines, for a simple commonsense reason. At best, what would then be the difference between the strategy researcher and his colleague of the disciplines? At the worst, wouldn't that be a route to sneak away from the more rigorous scrutiny of researchers in those disciplines? The specialized contributions should probably be considered contributions to the related disciplinary field.

The strategy field cannot be reduced either to the strategic approach of the practitioner. The latter is entitled to believe that academics are probably less qualified than he is to articulate such an approach, since they do not practice it, nor know well enough the reality to which it is applied. The search for knowledge in strategic management should therefore follow a different path. A meaningful approach should reconcile the findings of research in the disciplines with practical concerns. The meaning and relevance of academic disciplinary research for the improvement of practice are not obvious. First, disciplinary research results do not apply directly, but in combination with other findings. Second, applying them requires some familiarity with the phenomena concerned.

This is very similar to what happens in medicine. The medical researcher is faced with the same difficulty. In medicine, it is accepted that the researcher can belong to a discipline, while the practitioner, with the help of his association, is in charge of translating to improve his practice. And even there, in actual practice, the physician is often confused when faced with the multiplicity and sometimes-contradictory findings of research. For example, are some specific foods or drugs good or bad for health, for whom, and in what circumstances? These are daily questions to which no one has a clear answer. What is a scientific fact becomes slowly a bureaucratic decision made by professional associations under the scrutiny of government offices and other stakeholders.

We believe that, in strategic management, the variety of relevant phenomena is even greater, because the researcher is not only concerned about the individual's health, but also by the collective action of numerous individuals. In other terms, compared to medicine, we are still beginners, at the age of mystery, not unlike that of primitive tribes.

We cannot even fear to lose our credibility. We have none, even though, as gurus, sorcerers, or prophets, we may still impress the naive (Prahalad and Hamel, 1994).

The object of research in strategy does, however, exist. It can be practical, both heuristic and methodological. Its heuristic nature is double-faced:

1. Discovering, through the practice of managers, unusual regularities and patterns, specifying them and submitting them to analysis and debate. This systematic effort is scientific, because it helps describe and thus discover the varied nature of the phenomena to which managers are exposed. It can also help conduct an orderly discussion of the reasons that explain results.
2. Experimenting, modeling in an attempt to predict the behavior of organizations.

In both of these, it is possible to call on the findings of the disciplines in an organized search for meaning. The nature of this work is to be compared to what has been done for some of the natural sciences, for the understanding of complexity and the development of scientific approaches to deal with it (Waldrop, 1992). It is indeed a relevant example for us, because strategic management phenomena deal with unclear, non-linear, cause–effect relationships. As a consequence, the combination of research results to come to bear on reality can be neither direct nor linear, but creative in the scientific sense of the word.

Similarly, the methodological nature of the strategic management researcher contribution is fundamental. In strategy, we are not dealing with a traditional science but with a science of complexity. The approach that leads to propositions and conclusions is itself a stake and a result of research (complexity ...). Thus, confronted with small samples, but with rich data, informed with a multiplicity of partial disciplinary research results, the strategy researcher has to invent his approach and rationalize it, then build the needed heuristics, and constantly adjust both to reach convincing results.

The researcher in strategy is therefore a formidable intellectual. He must have the encyclopedic knowledge needed to comprehend the results of the normal science, and the familiarity, the intimacy with the phenomena, that stimulates creativity in search of explanations and heuristics. His problem is similar to that of a management practitioner with two differences: (i) the practitioner does not have to justify his decisions intellectually; but (ii) must survive the consequences of his decisions. However, like the practitioner, the academic muddles in the dark.

## A Framework for Researchers in Strategy

The development of a general framework to give meaning to specialized research and also to generate research specifically designed to deal with reality in all its complexity calls for researchers who are generalists, concerned with syntheses, such as those offered by Bower (1970), Miles and Snow (1978), Miller (1996), or Mintzberg (1978). Frameworks in strategy research should be a creation of the researcher. His goal is to represent reality by taking into account disciplinary research, but going beyond it in a search for convincing explanations of reality. At this point, we should be reminded of Henderson's (1970) recommendations about the utilitarian character of such a construction and its temporary nature.

Given the complexity of strategic management reality, it should be clear that the most appropriate frameworks are not those that emphasize content of strategy, because strategy is by definition necessarily situational and contingent. Rather, they must help reveal the mysterious mechanisms that lead to the formation of strategy and to its evolution over time. Patterns of strategic content can, however, be useful segments of a process-based conceptual framework.

To illustrate this idea of a strategic management framework, we could have taken the example of the traditional concept of strategy. Instead, we have decided to provide a different example to make its development transparent. In a search for meaning in strategy-related research, we started off with research up to 2000. In a comprehensive literature review, we developed a framework that tries to encompass the findings. The resulting model suggests that strategy research can be clustered into two basic groupings:

1. Intellectual aspects intended to conceive the mechanisms by which coordination and convergence of collective action is ensured.
2. Practical aspects designed to achieve the intended convergence.

The intellectual aspects have been grouped into five different sections:

(i) Strategy as a leader's statement
(ii) Strategy as a community's statement
(iii) Strategy as a guiding track
(iv) Strategy as the building of competitive advantage
(v) Strategy as a relationship to the environment

The intellectual aspects are of course intimately related to the practical aspects of individual and collective actions and their effect on how the organization functions. When many are to act together there is a need for ways to keep the action orderly, through goals, structure, and systems (planning, performance measurement and control, rewards and punishments, training, resource allocation, management information and communication).

Structure and systems give life to decision processes that are unique to each firm. As mentioned by Barnard (1938), managing these processes is a critical function of executives. It is through the combination, either rustic or savant, of management mechanisms that strategy is revealed and given life.

Ultimately, action is a series of decisions (Simon, 1945). How are decisions made? What motivates them? How are decisions integrated in specific situations? How are managerial mechanisms used to encourage or orient decisions? These are some of the questions that one can ask when using decision and planning models as integrating tools.

Finally, taking into account all these aspects, strategy can be seen as a revelation of voluntary, systematic, rational, objective, but also emotional, sentimental, affective, intuitive action. To represent strategy as a model or theory of action, one has to include in it all the aspects mentioned and associate them in such a way as to recognize how they combine to generate action. The representation proposed here is shown in Figure 23.1. The intellectual dimensions of strategy are represented as layers of reality, related to life through the mechanisms that lead to decision and action, which in turn feed back to affect the intellectual dimensions.

Figure 23.1 is a framework for policy dialogue. We believe, following Cummings and Wilson (2002) that:

> strategy frameworks, images, or maps help people to do their own mapping, thereby kick-starting an oscillating thinking/acting or strategizing process, which instils a momentum that brings other choices and possibilities to the fore. It may not get people "down the mountain" in a straight line but it gets things moving and, when things move, other things come into view. In short, the interaction between the general map and the mapping of a particular course of action orients and animates and no course is likely to be taken effectively without a measure of each of these things.

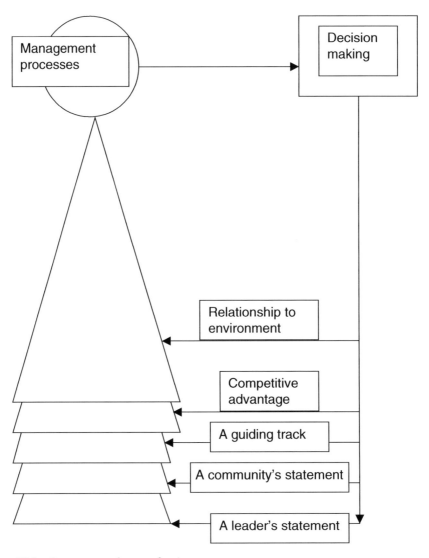

**Figure 23.1**    Strategy as a theory of action

## Concluding Remarks

The *raison d'être* of the field of strategy can be stated as being: helping through heuristics and creative methodologies to the understanding and transformation of reality. As research moves away from such a goal, strategic management practice is left alone and the field dies. Managers may start losing interest in theoretical developments, which help neither to explain reality nor to facilitate action designed to influence it.

Such a situation is the source of concern about the future of strategy as a field of academic teaching and learned research. From the traditional academic point of view it is much more legitimate to simply go back to the disciplinary research, since strategy research looks more and more like a pale reflection of these. It takes a deliberately deviant behavior to innovate and resist the dominant isomorphic pressures (Powell and DiMaggio, 1991). We should not only conceive our research better so that the understanding and transformation of reality is not relegated to the background, but becomes center stage. Also, we should work at developing more and better ways to integrate and reconcile research findings.

These ways to reconcile and integrate research cannot be completely different from those that help managers in their practice. The scientific field of strategic management of organizations should be devoted to the development of the conceptual frameworks needed to bring together research and practice. As vehicles for policy thinking and dialogue (Thomas, 1982) the model described in this chapter is but a simple example of the direction that research should take. The most powerful models should emphasize process, leaving the specialized works to deal with content.

The field of strategy has no future except close to reality. Its methods are those of complexity, often qualitative and when possible experimental, simulating reality to better represent its dynamics. Despite the fact that practice and theory are not well connected (Bettis, 1991) and that strategic management has not yet produced the volume of useful results expected by management, perhaps one day, these methods will be powerful enough to really help managers predict such dynamics.

## References

Barnard, C.I. 1938. *The Functions of Executives*. Cambridge, MA: Harvard University Press.

Bettis, R.A. 1991. Strategic management and the straitjacket: An editorial essay. *Organization Science*, 2(3): 315–19.

Bower, Joseph L. 1970. *Managing the Resource Allocation Process: A Study of Corporate Planning and Investment*. Boston, MA: Division of Research, Graduate School of Business Administration, Harvard University.

Bowman, E.H. 1974. Epistemology, corporate strategy, and academe. *Sloan Management Review*, 5(2): 35–50.

Burgelman, Robert A. 1983. A process model of internal corporate venturing in the diversified major firm. *Administrative Science Quarterly*, 28(2): 223–45.

Chakravarthy, B.S. and Doz, Y. 1992. Strategy process research: Focusing on corporate self-renewal. *Strategic Management Journal*, 13(1): 5–15.

Chandler, A.D. 1962. *Strategy and Structure: Studies in the History of American Enterprise*. Cambridge, MA: MIT Press.

Cummings, S. and Wilson, D. 2002. *Images of Strategy*. Oxford: Blackwell.

Henderson, L.J. 1970. *On the Social System: Selected Writings*. Edited by Bernard Barber. Chicago, IL: University of Chicago Press.

Miles, R.E. and Snow, C.C. 1978. *Organizational Strategy, Structure, and Process*. New York: McGraw-Hill.

Miller, D. 1996. Configurations revisited. *Strategic Management Journal*, 17(7): 505–13.

Mintzberg, H. 1978. *The Structuring of Organizations*. New York: Prentice-Hall.

Powell, W.W. and DiMaggio, P. 1991. *The New Institutionalism in Organizational Analysis*. Chicago, IL: University of Chicago Press.

Prahalad, C.K. and Hamel, G. 1994. Strategy as a field of study: Why search for a new paradigm? *Strategic Management Journal*, 15(1): 5–16.

Rumelt, R.P. 1974. *Strategy, Structure, and Economic Performance*. Boston, MA: Division of Research, Graduate School of Business Administration, Harvard University.

Schendel, D.E. 1994. Introduction to the summer 1994 special issue – Strategy: Search for new paradigms. *Strategic Management Journal*, 15(summer special issue): 1–4.

Simon, H. 1945. *Administrative Behavior*. New York: Macmillan.

Thomas, H. 1982. Screening policy options: An approach and a case study example. *Strategic Management Journal*, 3(3): 227–45.

Thompson, J.D. 1967. *Organizations in Action*. New York: McGraw-Hill.

Waldrop, W.J. 1992. *Complexity: The Emerging Science at the Edge of Order and Chaos*. New York: Simon and Schuster.

# CHAPTER TWENTY-FOUR

# Regaining Relevance Lost

## Bala Chakravarthy

A few years back, while selecting readings for a doctoral seminar, I surveyed both prominent practitioners and academics asking them to list the top 10 writings that had influenced their work the most. Surprisingly, there was zero overlap between the two lists, both in the authors and ideas that were represented. The work that we do in our field, studying how strategy processes can be effectively deployed and managed to enhance firm performance, is of paramount interest to managers. However, in conference after conference, the participating practitioners always lament the lack of good theories that can help them with their pressing challenges. They tell us that they find our research, with a few exceptions, obtuse and irrelevant. Yet, we march on, impervious to these criticisms. For an applied field like ours this is a risky approach.

Management schools are under increasing pressure, together with their sister professional schools in the university, to become financially independent. This calls for the forging of closer links with the business community. Regaining our lost relevance has to be an urgent concern for us in academia. I have written elsewhere on how our research can be fruitfully redirected (Chakravarthy et al., 2003; Chakravarthy and White, 2001; Chakravarthy and Doz, 1992). I will not repeat those recommendations here. Rather, I wish to reflect in this short piece on what I see as the crippling parochialism in our approach to research.

## The Need of Practice

Let me start with a few examples that set the stage for my reflections here. My recent work at the Institute for Management Development (IMD) has brought me close to the inner workings of several leading multinational companies around the world. I will illustrate the challenges facing these companies through three examples.

The first is a company called Dr. Reddy's Laboratories, a generics player from India listed on the New York Stock Exchange. It was recently recognized for its excellence in the *Forbes* magazine's list of 200 small global companies to watch. Instead of resting on its laurels, this $400 million firm is busy transforming itself into a discovery-led pharmaceuticals company ready to compete with the Goliaths of its industry. The second is a leading mid-sized Belgian company called Bekaert. It is the world's largest independent producer of steel cord for tires and a global leader in many steel wire based products. It faces all of the challenges that globalization can bring: low-cost competitors from Asia; commoditization pressures for its products; and the accelerating pace of innovation in its industry. Bekaert too is engaged in a metamorphosis that will restructure its manufacturing, migrate its presence up the value chain, and redouble its commitment to innovation. Or take the case of Best Buy, the leading retailer of consumer electronics products in North America. This industry giant is currently ripping up a very successful business model in order to build an even more successful one for defending its future.

These companies differ on many dimensions, size, industry focus, and geographic scope, to name just a few. And yet they all face a common challenge. The metaphors that their CEOs use to describe this challenge are: How do you change wheels on a fast-moving train? Or how do you erect a new mast on a boat sailing at full speed?

Investigating how a firm's strategy and its distinctive competencies mediate the effect of its business context on the firm's performance has been the domain of strategy content researchers, but strategy process researchers must complement this work in important ways by discerning how new competitive positions are innovated and realized, and how distinctive competencies are accumulated, protected, and leveraged. In the examples that I have noted above, Dr. Reddy's Laboratories, Bekaert, and Best Buy are each trying to retain the current equilibrium and the performance that it brings while simultaneously abandoning it in search of future opportunities. There is risk involved here. But staying the course also has its risks. Having enjoyed leadership in their industries, these firms are now seeking to successfully renew themselves in order to sustain their profitable growth well into the future. How can academia help these and countless other firms that are engaged in self-renewal? As I know from first-hand experience working with these companies, our current theories are not of much help to their leaders. Why?

## Dealing with Dilemmas

One of the most obvious reasons is our inability to focus on the right outcome variable in our research. A well-performing firm is expected to *grow profitably and on a sustained basis.* This will enhance its market value, if it is publicly listed or intends to be one. Yet, the bulk of our research looks only at profitability as the sole measure of firm performance. Very few studies consider growth. Even fewer use *sustained profitable growth* as the metric to measure firm success. We start with a handicap of our limited view of performance. Growth and profitability pull in opposite directions. Sustaining both over time is a difficult challenge. Underlying this performance dilemma are other recurring dilemmas:

1. How do you draw from the firm's legacy and yet not make it an obstacle for competing in the future?

2. How do you commit to specific strategies and resources, and yet retain the flexibility to walk away from them – should the competitive marketplace show these commitments to be ineffective?
3. How do you manage to be both externally and internally fitted?
4. How do you work toward innovation and still enhance productivity?
5. How do you provide empowerment without abdicating control?
6. How do you compete and cooperate with your partners, at the same time?

Balancing these and other related dilemmas requires new knowledge. The reductionism that has characterized our research to date will not help in the building of this new knowledge. It is frustrating in this context to witness the phony debates in academia on whether strategy is only planned or only emergent; whether the competitive analysis framework or resource-based view is paramount; whether any process can help nurture creativity and entrepreneurship or by its very nature process can only breed bureaucracy and control. I call them phony because any contact with the world of practice would quickly disabuse the researcher on the futility of these black and white caricatures in our field. The world of practice is a world of dilemmas.

It is true that the sheer genius of top management is not enough to set a firm's strategies. In any large diversified firm, the enormity of this task is bound to exceed the cognitive capacities of top management. Strategies are better realized through the collective efforts of multiple organizational actors operating at many levels in the organization: functions, business units, and corporate. On the other hand, free-spirited entrepreneurship of front-line managers is effective only when a shared vision and the visible hand of top management also guide it. Strategy is surely about exploiting the opportunities in a firm's competitive environment but it is not sustainable without a complementary investment in its distinctive competencies. Large firms need formal processes. I do not know of any that have forsaken these. But the better-managed firms have found a way of designing processes that not only help implement agreed-upon strategies, but also help formulate new strategies for the firm's continuous transformation.

The shaping, implementing, and changing of strategies requires the paradoxical blend of exploiting existing competencies while investing in new, both top-down and bottom-up efforts, planned and emergent actions, autonomy and collectivism in decision making and action taking. These are dilemmas, because they represent two equally useful but sometimes-opposed ideas. A parochial championing of one or the other pole of these dilemmas may be convenient and perhaps even encouraged by academia as it is currently structured. Journals publish opposing ideas without daring these to a debate. It is only when we venture out of this insular world to engage with practitioners that we realize the impracticality of our unipolar theories of strategy and management.

## Where Do We Go From Here?

With the ascendancy of positivism as the guiding approach to research we have lost our early roots of being relevant to managers. We now have to complement our

**Table 24.1**  A complementary approach to research

|  | Positivism | Participatory action research (PAR) |
|---|---|---|
| Research objective | Empirical truth | Creative adaptation of knowledge base to solve real problems |
| Role of researcher | Disciplinary expert | Facilitator for solving real problems |
| Research process | Hypothesis testing (mental motor on/off/on) | Validating and falsifying emerging heuristics. Reformulating existing explanations (mental motor always on) |
| Research context | Well-defined path | Unfamiliar pathways |
|  | Often a singular framework or conceptual anchor | Multiple disciplines (team) |
| Dealing with human behavior | Measure perceptions and attitudes | Study behaviors that drive these perceptions and attitudes |

Adapted from Argyris, Schön, and Whyte, in W.F. Whyte (1991).

devotion to positivism with a revival of what Whyte (1991) called participatory action research (PAR). Table 24.1 provides a quick comparison of the two approaches.

Positivism seeks empirical truth. But what is this truth? Metaphors involving flow-waves (Mintzberg and Lampel, 1999) and rivers (Pettigrew, 1990) have been productively employed to describe the strategy process. Positivism invites researchers to take repeat samples of the river in order to get a statistically valid result. But these samples can at best describe the water quality, clarity, or temperature of the river. They say very little about its dynamic quality, the flow of the river – where it has been and where it is destined; how the surrounding terrain affects and is affected by the river; the impact of exogenous factors like rainfall or drought. The dynamic aspects of a larger active process cannot be fully explored with static samples from that process. These can be better understood only by being part of the process.

The challenge for the action researcher is to go beyond the available knowledge base and adapt it to solve real problems like the ones experienced by Dr. Reddy's, Bekaert, or Best Buy. The emerging heuristics have to be constantly validated and refuted, and new guiding principles forged in real time. Undertaking participatory action research requires the knowledge base that good positivistic research can provide, but it calls on the researcher to abandon the parochialism of a single discipline, and to have the modesty to borrow from other disciplines with a single-minded focus on addressing real problems that confront managers.

The current reward structure of academia may not permit our brightest minds, the new entrants to the field, to engage in action research. I realize that. But I hope that at least a few established scholars would be willing to take the plunge, with all of its associated risks. Their perceived productivity may suffer, since they may not be able to maintain the same output in scholarly journal publications. Participatory action research is time consuming. While the journey can be exhilarating, the trophies from it are less tangible. The primary reward is a deeper understanding of the challenge of practice and the satisfaction of having helped address it. The output of good action research is a well-crafted story that embeds this deep knowledge.

Monographs may have to be the primary outlet in the short run for reporting the findings from participatory action research. However, the quality of this work should not be judged by the criteria of paradigmatic research. As Bruner (1986) advocates, we have to legitimize the narrative mode. While positivist arguments seek to convince one of their "truth", stories are best judged by their lifelikeness – verisimilitude. A good story needs two landscapes: action and consciousness (how the actors know, think or feel or don't). The latter is not the domain of positivist research. Action researchers may also not be able to fully capture the inner thoughts, fears, and hopes of the actors in their studies. But they can at least provide a description that "rings true". Identification is key. While the actual text is unchanged, in a good narrative the virtual text changes moment to moment in the act of reading. By engaging the readers in a description of a river, the researcher can help them navigate other rivers. The CEO of Dr. Reddy's must find insights on how to resolve his own challenge by reading the exploits of Bekaert or Best Buy! Making that happen is our challenge. Regaining the lost relevance of our field has to be our ambition.

## References

Bruner, J. 1986. *Actual Minds, Possible Worlds*. Cambridge, MA: Harvard University Press.

Chakravarthy, B. and Doz, Y. 1992. Strategy process research: Focusing on corporate self-renewal. *Strategic Management Journal*, **13**: 5–14.

Chakravarthy, B., Mueller-Stewens, G., Lorange, P., and Lechner, C. (eds.) 2003. *Strategy Process: Shaping the Contours of the Field*. Oxford, UK: Blackwell.

Chakravarthy, B. and White, R. 2001. Strategy process: Forming, implementing and changing strategies. In A. Pettigrew, H. Thomas, and R. Whittington (eds.), *Handbook of Strategy and Management*, pp. 182–205. London: Sage.

Mintzberg, H. and Lampel, J. 1999. Reflecting on the strategy process. *Sloan Management Review*, spring: 21–30.

Pettigrew, A.M. 1990. Longitudinal field research on change: Theory and practice. *Organization Science*, **1**(3): 267–92.

Whyte, W.F. (ed.) 1991. *Participatory Action Research*. Beverly Hills, CA: Sage.

# CHAPTER TWENTY-FIVE

# I Matter: Remaining the First Person in Strategy Research

## Johan Roos

### I Was There

"Welcome to our first strategy retreat together! I'd like us to get to know one another a bit more before we 'get down to business,' and I would like to start. Let me tell you about my private life ..." The new CEO, Mary, had gathered her entire leadership team for a first retreat to revisit and revise the company strategy. This was the kick-off presentation and as a consultant hired by Mary to help with both facilitation and content inputs, I remember how much I enjoyed this assignment. That evening Mary shared very personal stories from her professional and private life – successes and failures, hopes and aspirations – with the people whose trust she sought and needed, to do a good job. While her final anecdote was met with laughter, several participants later told me that it set the stage for the subsequent conversations and outputs. In one of her previous jobs she had asked her boss to share the company strategy with her. "I can't," he supposedly said, "it is in the safe." Mary was not only talking about herself, she was talking about what strategy meant to her and how she had been initiating and leading processes to develop and implement strategy in other companies. I tried to listen, observe the people gathered, and take as many notes as possible, while thoughts raced though my mind. It was difficult to know what to scribble down, and my already bad handwriting gradually became unreadable. I let go of the pen and made a conscious effort to sharpen my senses and memorize the experience instead.

The two days unfolded in a spirit of trust and people often cited each other's personal stories from the evening before. I was not the only one who seemed to be enjoying this retreat, and I had rarely seen people work so hard to share and respect one another's views about what they thought should be done.

My own feelings surprised me: I really liked, and, even admired this CEO. She was the best I had ever seen in eliciting what became two days of frank conversations about strategy. This retreat was so unlike the many others I had observed and facilitated. To this day I can recall the background smells and sounds when Mary kicked off the retreat in front of the sparkling fireplace in that chilly lodge on an island in the Stockholm archipelago. During this strategy retreat, I learnt about ways to create a context in which people feel appreciated and ready to open up, aspects of the role of the leader, and points relating to what can be done when managers practice strategy.

Conversely, my feelings toward the man I had been instructed to address as "Dr. Siebermann" at another client company were very different. It was not just his autocratic leadership style that disturbed me, but the way he talked about strategy with the people working for him, and his explicit assumptions about their role in it. This day Siebermann looked isolated, standing in front of 34 of his managers in the conference room, with a PowerPoint slide summarizing "his" strategy on the screen behind him. He was there to share the strategy as he and his top-management team had formulated it, and as he had put it to me, to "align" these 34 managers with the strategy.

In addition to making a presentation, which took twice the intended time, he was also there to answer any questions about the strategy. This explicit "openness" was part of the set-up for his intervention, which I had spent hours discussing with him. I was representing the faculty responsible for an in-company executive education program in his firm, focusing on "profitable growth." As a researcher interested specifically in how strategy is made, I took advantage of this program to learn more. During the previous year I had gradually come to learn about the company, its industry, strategic challenges, as well as the way senior managers behaved and acted, especially with respect to practices labeled "strategy." Yet, even after interviewing all of the senior management team I still did not understand what they had done when they had developed their strategy. I had tentatively concluded that strategy for these people meant the "plan," or the paper document, whereas related activities included rational analysis of facts gathered by others, jockeying for a position close to the CEO, while avoiding having a strong opinion. I also suspected that the strategy document was locked away in a safe. Siebermann found it difficult to understand and then agree with my suggestion of handing the managers a strategy summary before the session in which he sought to align the 34 managers. Eventually he arranged carefully numbered copies of a summary document that carried a red "CONFIDEN-TIAL" on the cover page. Each participant signed for and returned it at the end of the session.

I got the impression that Siebermann was lying when I saw him touch his forehead and then quickly cross his arms and look down before answering what he clearly thought was an impertinent question. The question came from an enthusiastic manager two levels lower in the hierarchy, and hidden in it was his disbelief of some facts on which the strategy rested. Earlier in the day this enthusiastic manager had been agitated and rallied his group around to discuss his doubts. However, when he asked the question, not only had this previously brave manager lost the forcefulness of his inquiry, but the question was now nowhere near its earlier clear and carefully formulated version. While the CEO elaborated his answer I deduced from the reactions in the room that Siebermann was possibly insulting half of those present, thus shutting down the Q&A session. When I asked the questioner immediately after the session why he had not pursued the issue, he answered: "I have a family to support." From this experience, I learnt how to intimidate people, how one allowed oneself to be intimidated, and how to prevent others from questioning "one's" strategy. Additionally, I learned that Dr. Siebermann had indeed been lying about fundamental matters – he was arrested three months later for leading an illegal cartel.

## Bringing Out the First Person

These are two reports of practices that have something to do with strategy in very different firms, involving different people and situations. These vignettes are also extremes: the warm and cozy retreat led by an honest, competent CEO versus the intimidating setting created by the leader of a criminal conspiracy. Though life is rarely so black or white, I have chosen these true stories to help me illustrate a point. Both narratives are written in the first person, and that person is me, the narrator.

Imagine re-reading these two narratives without me. Imagine I had used the conventional third-person voice. What would remain? Stories told by participants about a CEO at a strategy retreat, and another CEO doing a strategy Q&A session? Although incomplete, would this now be raw data about managerial dialogue or information dissemination about strategy, from which you might abstract context-free variables to explain and predict future states? If so, I would be perfectly in line with the current approach to strategic management research. From developing simple concepts of strategy, intended to give practical advice to managers, the field has moved to a rigorous search for explanatory and predictive power (Furrer *et al.*, 2002). The consequence is that the present, affective, and perceptive first person becomes the absent and de-humanized third person.

As compelling as the logic of this "scientific" approach may be, there is a problem: people practicing strategy do not seem to care about our explanatory and predictive concepts, models, and theories about strategy practices. As many strategy journal editors and conference organizers are painfully aware, despite our efforts to be taken seriously by the people we study, they rarely participate in our conferences (leaving aside the token keynote speaker). Could our "pure," third-person scientific understanding of strategy practice be simply too lifeless to be useful? At the risk of upsetting the reader, I suggest it is.

How did we get to this point in our research practice? By imitating our colleagues in the natural sciences, aspiring to explain and predict strategy practices as if they were like photosynthesis or interstellar radiation. More importantly, is that really what we *should*be doing? Research about strategy practice rests on the foundations of social sciences, which have as their object of study the irreducibly meaningful behavior of human beings (Flyvbjerg, 2001). *If strategy practice (so far) is about humans interacting how can we ever believe in observer-free knowledge about it?* It is as if we authors think we do not matter! Simply because we were there and since we tell the story, we matter a lot. I matter when I consciously or unconsciously select what I look at, sanitize my views about what I see, and decide what to tell you. As the third person, my views and ultimately my moral stance disappear into comfortable anonymity. As the first person I have to remain with my work and deliberate my stance. In the remainder of this essay I shall seek to clarify and argue that *narrators of strategy practice should remain in their narrative.*

## Struggling to Remain the First Person

Despite some hesitation over the years, I have tried to stay out of my work, and it has been a struggle. In my early work I focused, as I had been trained, on explanation and prediction. However, a decade or so ago, I was inspired by the Mintzbergian notion of "emergent" and "crafted" strategy. In response, I engaged in action research projects about strategy-making practices in the early and mid-1990s. My co-researchers and I worked in close collaboration with senior management, to help them improve their strategy-making practices. Unlike the "objective" knowledge that resulted from my earlier analysis of context-free variables, I learnt from these projects how managers manipulated information and one another during strategy conversations, playing Wittgensteinian "language games" with key terms like "strategy."[1] I began to see that who I studied mattered, but I personally was still not inside the narrative.

Even as I stuck to the rules of ethno-methodology, I never reconciled with the practice of separating out my own views, hopes, and fears and reporting these data as if I were an anonymous voice from the outside. Experience told me that what is not being said was as important, if not more important than what was actually said. When I tried to write "confessional" tales (rather than realist ones[2]), about my research practices, my co-researchers, and myself, I still checked myself at the door. Who was I to question what made these people's decisions and actions worthy of their selection? Sharing my views implied selective attention determined by my own interests, emotions, and prejudices, which seemed to me to conflict with the dominant paradigm of third-person research on strategic management. Instead I left such affective matters to deliberations with colleagues during coffee breaks and with my wife during long dinner conversations. I pretended that my observations and outputs were free of me. Werner Heisenberg's principle of indeterminism prefaced the closest I came to acknowledging that I really mattered for what I produced: During more than a year my co-researcher and I engaged in a process of "matching" our language and theoretical concepts with that of a practicing manager, assuming that all of these are equally legitimate (see von Krogh, Roos, and Slocum, 1994). Yet, when we converted our "matched" understanding into text, we conformed to most of the conventions of publishing in scientific management journals. After all, that was what everyone I knew or read was doing.

Over the last few years I have reflected over my own awareness of this paradigm and the limits associated with it. Remaining the first person is much more difficult than slipping into the anonymous third-person mode, simply because I have to take a stance, reflect over it, and be prepared to take the consequences. From the minute I first met Siebermann and his colleagues I experienced an awkward conflict, which was dramatically accentuated after the CEO's arrest. On the one hand, my instinct told me I did not want to have anything to do with this firm or its leaders. However, I had a professional obligation to continue to service them. My mixed feelings were always in the background as I informally and formally interacted with the managers in this firm. This background of feelings influenced my choices about what to include in my descriptions of them. As part of my own research agenda, I interviewed a handful of the people reporting to Siebermann after his arrest, suspecting that they were all part of the criminal scheme, or at least well aware of it. Most of them gave evasive answers as I asked for their reactions in relation to what had happened. One of them, strengthened by many years with the firm, stated bluntly: "The only thing that was wrong was that we were caught" and that Dr. Siebermann would eventually (after serving a prison term) "be rewarded for being our scapegoat." My growing aversion toward the leaders of this organization culminated at this moment, and I decided to end my involvement with them.

In the first situation described above, I struggled as well, but in a different way. The way Mary acted as leader and the meaning she gave to strategy work by her actions were very close to my own beliefs about these matters. Throughout these days I kept reminding myself that I was there to question and challenge their practices, including those of Mary. I ought not be just agreeing with and even admiring what I observed.

Most strategy research seems to rest on the assumption that there is a domain of understanding shared by observers, and that the individual observer's view does not matter. Because of the inherent human dimension of strategy practices, and my own personal, embodied knowledge and feelings as a researcher, I have grown to think that only a very limited part of what I report, if anything, consists of facts or value-free knowledge. If this is so, any description of strategy practice must always include the role of the observer. Just as I tried to do in the two vignettes about Mary and Dr. Siebermann, consequently, I need to be open about my views and about who I am rather than hide as an anonymous third person.

Not only, though, is there an epistemological problem with remaining in the third person, it may also simultaneously undermine the value of my work. Paradoxically, in my experience, practicing strategists seem to value executive education sessions taught by the same faculty whose research work they ignore. When I teach I regularly share my own strong views, as well as personal testimonies from their well-known peers, and articles riddled with first-person anecdotes from marquee firms. Why does executive education work while our research fails? On one level, perhaps such anecdotal knowledge sharing has the proximity to reality that is called for? Perhaps it better accomplishes what early strategic management research intended to do: to give practical advice to managers? The number and type of subscribers of more "popular" business media may be evidence for this. On another level, perhaps such knowledge is significant to the people we study because the narratives are told by someone in particular? Maybe Maturana and Varela (1987) were right when they claimed that "everything said is said by somebody?" If so, we have to take this somebody into consideration. The stories I allude to above are indeed told by someone who typically was and remained "participant," either as manager, consultant, or researcher. Unless we are talking about facts or value-free knowledge, perhaps practicing managers need the overt first-person body to gain significant insights from our research?

What are the practices that might enable us as researchers to become a vital part of the narratives generated in our field? The epistemological stance I argue for builds on Polanyi (1958), who rejected the idea of the objective observer in any inquiry and instead argued for joining facts and values in a participatory mode of understanding. It also benefits from the emergent, evolutionary, and educational ways of knowing (including the important role of the "self") in "participatory" inquiry (Heron and Reason, 1997) and worldview (Reason and Bradbury, 2000). Based on re-reading the literature on positivism, postpositivism, critical theory, and constructionism, Lincoln and Guba (2000) concluded that values (at least, ethical and aesthetical) should be embedded in, rather than be "defined out" of social science inquiry. What I suggest is to take another step in this line of reasoning: The values of the people observed are indeed intrinsic to my study, but so are mine.

From my own research experience I have concluded that any inquiry that aspires to be participatory, must consider the values of the observer-narrator. After all, who is selecting and collecting data, identifying and recognizing patterns, making inferences to existing literature, and drawing conclusions? Only by pretending to be an anonymous third person can I attempt to bracket my own affective intuition, reflective consciousness, "blind spots" and "hunches." Unfortunately, it is this anonymous voice that has become the norm for scholarly discourse, not only in the strategy field. The inherent limit of our subjectivity as observers-narrators shapes rather than distorts our research, and this is perfectly fine as long as it is transparent. As illustrated by the narratives about Mary and Dr. Siebermann, what I think and feel influences what I tell you about them and their particular situation. What I call for resembles the autobiographical genre of writing called "autoethnography" (Hayano, 1979), where the idea is to, typically in first-person narratives, feature action, dialogue, emotion, embodiment, thought, language, spirituality, and self-consciousness.[3]

Under what conditions can we strategy scholars embrace rather than avoid our inherent, human subjectivity? When would I not feel obliged to check my value-laden "first-person voice" at the door? How can my personal narratives matter? When can I legitimately write more directly, from the source of my own experience, without hiding my hopes and fears? In what types of research practice would the two subjective stories I began with be both legitimate and credible as research data? My answer lies in an old Aristotelian ideal of pragmatic, participatory, and very personal inquiry.

## Not Just the Good Eye: Phronesis

Unless I seek the "pure" scientific, value-free knowledge that Aristotle called *epistême*, my research resembles a habit he called *phronesis*, or "practical wisdom."[4] In this habit I apply my (personal) knowledge, which is always mediated by my (personal) values, toward the achievement of what I believe is the common good. This is a very high standard of self-knowledge, and without claiming that I have reached it, it is an ideal that I strive toward in my current research. Thus, not only do I need a scholarly good eye in judging what to study, I also need to be aware of and be overt about my idea of what is the good. The current paradigm of scientific management (with its ideal of context-free and value-free *epistême*), sadly, may so far have excluded this habit altogether.[5]

Like many of my colleagues a major motivation in my own research is to improve management practice and ultimately society at large. As a pragmatically optimistic scholar I want to help managers do the "right" thing, and I believe that what I learn and share with them might help (I have already stated that I am an optimist). What "phronetic" science requires is for me to be authentic, to remain the first person I really am. Others will have to judge if I exhibit phronesis, but the point is that my values (indicated in the two opening vignettes) matter, just as do those of the people I study, like Mary and Siebermann.

What would phronetic research practice in our field entail? In short, it would entail more authentic versions of what we do today, and narratives told in the first-person voice. We would not refrain from normative judgments even as we describe what we understand to be going on. Imagine that I expanded the short narratives about Mary and Siebermann into much more context-rich descriptions, in which I paid much more and careful attention to their (and other's) judgment, attitude, tact, character, emotions, opinion, moral, common sense, narratives, intuition, and imagination. That contextual data, very much in line with the strategy-as-practice literature,[6] would certainly help me better understand what is going on. Add to this yet another layer of description and corresponding self-reflection concerning what I perceived and thought about what I observed and took part in. In addition to clarifying my ontology and epistemology this way, I would have to clarify and share my perceptions and emotions, to the extent that I can articulate them. The result would be an overt and authentic description of what is going on, *according to me*, and with all my limitations.

Building on the descriptive, the next natural step is to seek to develop *normative* frameworks that address why certain things are worthy of orienting actions in certain situations: simply stated, how *should* the people I study act? Specifically, what are their objectives, obligations, and worries in light of one another? What is required, allowed, and prohibited in the particular situation at hand? How ought Mary and Dr. Siebermann respond to and shape the various issues of strategy practices they faced? How should they strike the balance between the inter-personal and intra-personal? How should they balance the tensions between the long term and short term? Between the individual interests and those of the organization? These are just examples of puzzles that scholars in adjacent fields[7] have begun to integrate into research agendas, inspired by phronesis and its consequence, namely, ethics. Thus, what I tried to do in the opening vignettes I would do more carefully, consciously, and deliberately, and in much more detail overtly include more self-reflection.

## So What?

Being in the early phase of my own attempt to engage in phronetic research about strategy practice I can only self-reference and speculate about what my suggestion would imply for how we research strategy practices.

Firstly, *phronetic strategy research may enhance our self-awareness as scholars.* Through my studies of Mary, Siebermann, and many others I have learnt more about myself as a scholar. Instead of suppressing a large part of what makes me human at work, I no longer hesitate to express and reflect over my personal views about the object of my studies. Phronetic strategy research requires me to explicitly understand my own values, perspectives, and attitude of self and others. As the subject of my studies, I am intrinsically motivated by my aspiration to both know more about, and to improve the way practices of strategy are performed in companies. To this end, in my research I seek to embrace human subjectivity and imagination and recognize the importance of embodied knowledge.

Secondly, *phronetic strategy research may help us understand more about what is going on*. With this enhanced self-understanding I think I have understood more of the activities that make up strategy – what is actually done when strategy is practiced. In turn, this has helped me clarify what I think is going on and thus narrow the gap between what is present to me as the observer and what is available to the people I study and with whom I interact (Weick, 1999). Mary and Dr. Siebermann are just two of many people practicing strategy, from whom, upon the deep reflection and self-reflection that phronesis requires, I have leant much about what to do and not to do when practicing strategy.

Thirdly, *phronetic research may force us to take a moral stance*. With the benefit of hindsight, many colleagues are openly musing about how individual strategy gurus, consultancies, and business schools were all intertwined in creating the Enron scandal, and how this made us co-responsible for the questionable actions of its leadership (Whittington *et al.*, 2003). As I write this text, I am reminded of my own uncritical stance toward some of the people and firms I have reported on in my previous research. An executive I met during a teaching case development has recently been arrested (NB: this was not Dr. Siebermann), accused of using his practical intelligence to reap vast and illegal financial benefits from the company for himself and his family – at about the time of my interviews. Because the knowledge I generate with phronetic research can be framed normatively in addition to descriptively, I am now free, and required, to take the stance I previously hid away with third-person accounts of what was going on. With phronetic research my aspirations will shift away from a need to explain and predict strategy practices in terms of de-humanized variables, toward contextually bound and morally grounded knowledge about strategy practices. It is a call for ethical conduct in strategy research.[8]

Fourthly, *phronetic strategy research may call for additional experiments with methodologies*. As Thomas Kuhn (1962) pointed out, paradigms are characterized as much by routinized methodologies and data-gathering practices as they are by tacit interpretative frameworks. Hence, any new paradigm in strategy practice research will entail both new methods and new forms of knowledge. Balogun, Huff, and Johnson (2003: 220) assert that more contextually bound knowledge about strategy-as-practice asks "much more of ourselves and our colleagues in organizations." Adding morally grounded knowledge from phronetic research asks much more than paying attention to the particular, regardless of research methodology. As the first person, I must indeed integrate myself into and remain with the knowledge I generate. Playing with the words, on a more practical level, rather than "confessing" some kind of guilt for the limits of my *epistême*, maybe I should provide an authentic self-description, in which I identify myself (values, aspirations, etc.) to the reader?

Fifthly, *phronetic strategy research may change the discourse in our field*. Because it would be perfectly legitimate to be normative as well as descriptive, and to write in the first person in addition to the third person, phronetic research practice may change the process and content of academic discourse in our field. In addition to arguing about statistical significance, predictive power, and construct validity, our debates might include and eventually migrate toward what each of us considers to be "right" and "good" in the situations we study. In turn, this research practice would call for a similar evolution among journal editors, reviewers, and conference chairs devoted to the advancement of strategy practice.

Sixthly, *phronetic strategy research may be more significant to practicing managers.* Remember that the "original" purpose of strategic management was to provide practical advice to managers. Just like I do when I teach and consult, with phronetic research the reader can perceive, feel and ultimately morally judge what I say. Thus, for the practicing strategists, my open first-person stance about what I think is going on might have far more perceived value than a covert, anonymous third-person account.

In sum, in this chapter I have argued that because our field is about humans and humans interacting, strategy researchers should try to remain the cognizing, prescriptive, and affective first-person narrator they are rather than escaping into the convention of third-person anonymity. By enhancing our self-awareness as strategy scholars this way we may also understand more about what is actually going on in and around our object of study. By taking a moral stance and by experimenting with methodology we may develop the discourse of our field and even enhance the perceived value of what we do for the people we ultimately serve, practicing managers.

## Acknowledgments

I gratefully acknowledge many helpful comments and suggestion from my colleagues at Imagination Lab Foundation (www.imagilab.org) and Bart Victor.

## Notes

1. Reported in von Krogh and Roos (1996), and Roos and von Krogh (1996).
2. See Van Maanen (1988) for a discussion of these forms of writing ethnography.
3. See Ellis and Bochner (2001) for an excellent summary, illustration, and critique of this category of ethnography.
4. Aristotle (translation 1962) defined *phronesis*as the virtuous habit of making decisions and taking actions that serve the good of the polis and his point was that neither scientific knowledge (*epistême*) nor cunning intelligence (*metis*) was appropriate for the complex human social world, where decisions and actions must be judged on moral grounds.
5. Yet, the concept of practical wisdom has been taken up with renewed vigor in recent years by researchers in the fields of law (e.g., Kronman, 1995), political science (e.g., Smith, 1999), philosophy (Gadamer, 2002), education (e.g., Noel, 1999), medicine (e.g., Hoffman, 2002), sociology (e.g., Bourdieu, 1998), organizational theory (e.g., Eikeland, 2001; Calori, 2002), and in management studies (Statler, Roos, and Victor., 2003). See Flyvbjerg (2001) for an argument about practical wisdom in the social sciences in general.
6. See Johnson, Melin, and Whittington (2003), Regnér (2003), Samra-Fredericks (2003), Whittington (2002) and (1996).

7. I have adapted these questions from Margolis and Walsh (2003) and Sternberg (1998).
8. For a discussion about this topic in management research see Kakabadse, Kakabadse, and Kouzmin (2002).

# References

Balogun, J., Huff, A.S., and Johnson, P. 2003. Three responses to the methodological challenges of studying strategizing. *Journal of Management Studies*, **40**(1): 197–224.
Bourdieu, P. 1998. *Practical Reason*. Stanford, CA: Stanford University Press.
Calori, R. 2002. Real time/real space research: Connecting action and reflection in organizational studies. *Organization Studies*, **23**(6): 877–83.
Eikeland, O. 2001. Action research as the hidden curriculum of the western tradition. In P. Reason and H. Bradbury (eds.), *Handbook of Action Research: Participative Inquiry and Practice*, London: Sage.
Ellis, C. and Bochner, A.P. 2000. Autoethnography, personal narrative, reflexivity. In N. Denzin and Y. Lincoln (eds.), *Handbook of Qualitative Research*, 2nd edn., pp. 733–68. Thousand Oaks, CA: Sage.
Flyvbjerg, B. 2001. *Making Social Science Matter*. Cambridge, UK: Cambridge University Press.
Furrer, O., Thomas, H., Goussevskaia, A., and D. Schendel. May 2002. Working Paper. Warwick Business School, UK.
Gadamer, H.G. 2002 (1960). *Truth and Method*. New York: Continuum.
Hayano, D.M. 1979. Auto-ethnography: Paradigms, problems, and prospects. *Human Organization*, **38**: 113–20.
Heron, J. and Reason, P. 1997. A participatory inquiry paradigm. *Qualitative Inquiry*, **3**: 274–94.
Hoffman, B. 2002. Medicine as practical wisdom (phronesis). *Poesis Prax*, **1**: 135–49.
Johnson, G., Melin, L., and Whittington, R. 2003. Guest editors' introduction: Micro strategy and strategizing: Towards an activity-based view. *Journal of Management Studies*, **40**(1): 3–22.
Kakabadse, N.K., Kakabadse, A., and Kouzmin, A. 2002. Ethical considerations in management research: A "truth" seeker's guide. *International Journal of Value*, **15**(2): 105–38.
Kronman, A. 1995. *The Lost Lawyer*. Cambridge, MA: Harvard University Press.
Kuhn, T. 1962. *The Structure of Scientific Revolutions*. Chicago, IL: University of Chicago Press.
Lincoln, Y. and Guba, E.G. 2000. Paradigmatic controversies, contradictions, and emerging confluences. In N. Denzin and Y. Lincoln (eds.), *Handbook of Qualitative Research*, 2nd edn., pp. 163–88. Thousand Oaks, CA: Sage.
Margolis, J.D. and Walsh, J. 2003. Misery loves companies: Rethinking social initiatives by business. *Administrative Science Quarterly*, **48**: 268–305.
Maturana, H. and Varela, F. 1987. *The Tree of Knowledge*. Boston, MA: Shambala Press.
Noel, J. 1999. Phronesis and phantasia: Teaching with wisdom and imagination. *Journal of Philosophy of Education*, **33**(2): 277–87.
Polanyi, M. 1958. *Personal Knowledge*. Chicago, IL: University of Chicago Press.
Reason, P. and Bradbury, H. 2001. Inquiry and participation in search of a world worthy of human aspiration. In P. Reason and H. Bradbury (eds.), *Handbook of Action Research: Participative Inquiry, and Practice*. London: Sage.
Regnér, P. 2003. Strategy creation in the periphery: Inductive versus deductive strategy making. *Journal of Management Studies*, **40**(1): 57–82.

Roos, J. and von Krogh, G. 1996. *Managing Strategy Processes in Emergent Industries: The Case of Media Firms*. Basingstoke, UK: Macmillan.

Samra-Fredericks, D. 2003. Strategizing as lived experience and strategists' everyday efforts to shape strategic direction. *Journal of Management Studies*, **40**(1): 141–74.

Smith, T. 1999. Aristotle on the conditions for and limits of the common good. *American Political Science Review*, **93**(3): 625–37.

Statler, M., Roos, J., and Victor, B. 2003. Illustrating the need for practical wisdom. Working Paper 2003:9, Imagination Lab Foundation, Switzerland (www.imagilab.org).

Sternberg, R. 1998. A balance theory of wisdom. *Review of General Psychology*, **2**(4): 347–65.

Van Maanen, J. 1988. *Tales of the Field*. Chicago, IL: University of Chicago Press.

von Krogh, G., Roos, J., and Slocum, K. 1994. An essay on corporate epistemology. *Strategic Management Journal*, **15**: 53–71.

von Krogh, G. and Roos, J. (eds.) 1996. *Managing Knowledge: Perspectives on Cooperation and Competition*. London: Sage.

Weick, K. 1999. That's moving: Theories that matters. *Journal of Management Inquiry*, **8**(2): 134–42.

Whittington, R. 1996. Strategy as practice. *Long Range Planning*. **29**(5): 731–5.

Whittington, R. 2002. The work of strategizing and organizing: For a practice perspective. *Strategic Organization*, **I**(1): 119–27.

Whittington, R., Jarzabkowski, P., Mayer, M., Mounoud, E., Nahapiet, J., and Rouleau, L. 2003. Taking strategy seriously: Responsibility and reform for an important social practice. *Journal of Management Inquiry*, **12**(4): 396–409.

# Index

Printed and bound in the UK by
CPI Antony Rowe, Eastbourne

Printed and bound by CPI Group (UK) Ltd, Croydon, CR0 4YY

24/04/2025

14661400-0001